DILEMMAS OF TRANSITION

DILEMMAS OF TRANSITION

The Hungarian Experience

edited by
AUREL BRAUN
and
ZOLTAN BARANY

ROWMAN & LITTLEFIELD PUBLISHERS, INC.
Lanham • Boulder • New York • Oxford

ROWMAN & LITTLEFIELD PUBLISHERS, INC.

Published in the United States of America
by Rowman & Littlefield Publishers, Inc.
4720 Boston Way, Lanham, Maryland 20706

12 Hid's Copse Road
Cumnor Hill, Oxford OX2 9JJ, England

British Library Cataloguing in Publication Information Available

Library of Congress Cataloging-in-Publication Data

Dilemmas of transition : the Hungarian experience / edited by Aurel
    Braun and Zoltan Barany.
        p.   cm.
    Includes bibliographical references (p.   ) and index.
    ISBN 0-8476-9004-0 (alk. paper). — ISBN 0-8476-9005-9 (alk.
    paper)
        1. Hungary—Social conditions—1989–   2. Post-communism—Hungary.
    3. Hungary—Economic conditions—1989–   4. Hungary—Politics and
    government—1989–   I. Braun, Aurel.   II. Barany, Zoltan D.
    HN420.5.A8D55   1999
    306′.09439—dc21   98-36859
                                                                   CIP

Printed in the United States of America

∞ ™ The paper used in this publication meets the minimum requirements of
American National Standard for Information Sciences—Permanence of Paper
for Printed Library Materials, ANSI Z39.48–1992.

To Julianna, Daniel
and David Braun; and to
Zsuzsi and Valentine Lovekin

Contents

Acknowledgments

This book was inspired by a desire to produce a work that would contribute to a better understanding of the issues and prospects for post-communist transitions. Though aware of the pitfalls and excesses of "transitology," and the shortcomings and quagmire of the "post-communist breakdown" literature, we decided that there were seminal dilemmas that were worth addressing. First, we sought to identify the most important questions regarding transition. Second, in using Hungary as a case study of successful transition we hoped to suggest certain explanations and lessons. We have tried to combine the benefits of comparative and area studies to address the issues and sought to enhance the analysis by also using concepts drawn from international relations theory and security studies. We concluded that a collective work, bringing together some of the leading specialists in the field could be made much stronger through an international conference where the draft chapter contributions could be discussed by key scholars in the field. We were most fortunate that we had a very generous response to our conference invitation. The participants at the conference, at the University of Toronto, included John Mueller, University of Rochester; Richard Gunther, Ohio State University; Janos Kornai, Harvard University; Andrew Janos, U.C. Berkeley; Gale Stokes, Rice University; Stephen Holmes, Princeton University; Scott Eddie, University of Toronto; Barry Ickes, Penn State University; Walter Connor, Boston University; Ronald Linden, University of Pittsburgh; Sarah Terry, Tufts University; Donald Horowitz, Duke University; and Wendy Dobson, University of Toronto. All these individuals were immensely helpful in their comments on the chapters of the contributors and in the general discussions on the dilemmas of transition. We are most grateful for their important input.

We wish to thank the primary funders and supporters of this project, the Hungarian Research Institute of Canada, and its chair, Dr. Laslo

Simon, for their financial help. We would also like to thank the Centre for Russian and East European Studies at the University of Toronto and its chair, Professor Robert Johnson, for additional financial support. The organization of the conference owed much to the efficiency and hard work of Karen Leppik, Adam Fallenbuchl and Gabriella Nagy who worked tirelessly to ensure its success. We wish to thank Valentine Lovekin for his expert and generous advice that greatly helped to keep this project on track. We would also like to thank the senior editor of Rowman and Littlefield Publishers, Susan McEachern for her help and encouragement in bringing this project to fruition. And we express our appreciation to Karen Johnson, Matt Hammon, and Scott Horst at Rowman and Littlefield for their editorial and production work. Of course, we assume responsibility for all errors and omissions.

Aurel Braun
University of Toronto

Zoltan Barany
University of Texas, Austin

Chapter 1

Introduction: The Continuing Dilemmas of Transition

Aurel Braun

Patience is a scarce commodity in the West. And the academe in the West is hardly an exception. Not only do we have proclamations about the end of history, however facetious these may have been, but there are signs of increasing impatience with the relatively new field of transitology, particularly as it is applied to the post-communist states. Transitology, perhaps more of an approach to analyzing transformation than a subdiscipline, is relatively recent and has been applied to change not only in the case of the former communist states but also to transformations of political systems in Latin America and Southern Europe. In the case of the former communist states, the twenty-seven sovereign states that emerged following the collapse of Marxist-Leninist rule, transition has eventually involved *fundamental* change. Even those communist states where the leadership had been willing to tolerate or encourage limited transformation, such as Mikhail Gorbachev's Soviet Union or Janos Kadar's Hungary, reforms were transmogrified into revolution. Consequently, transition, not only in much of Western analysis but in the declared goals of those who have led it, has shape, purpose, and an apparent teleology. All this is not always clearly articulated, but this seems to be the general trend.

To some, transition really refers to the past, because in their opinion it has already taken place.[1] This is debatable. Although it is correct that, at least in part, transition and indeed "post-communism" refer to the past, both are at the same time, we suggest, forward-looking and thus involve the past, the present, *and* the future. It is not the contention here that the past is prophetic or that the present predetermines the future, but rather that influences and interplay among the three may

1

help explain the problems, prospects, and choices. It is assumed in this collective work that the post-communist states in general and our case study, Hungary, in particular faced, are facing, and will confront dilemmas of transition that have not been adequately understood and that, consequently, more scholarship can and should be done to better understand these dilemmas.

Thus, it is the overall assumption in this work that transitology remains relevant. Further, this is so not because the contributors have developed a grand theory or believe that they can formulate a general paradigm, but rather because there is much to be learned from what has and is occurring in the post-communist states and more needs to be understood about future development. And precisely due to the uncertainties, and the absence of a clear road map, there are important opportunities to gain a better understanding of post-communist transition.

In arguing for the continuing relevance of transitology and while recognizing the seminal contributions of numerous scholars, this work, however, is hardly uncritical of several of the approaches and methodologies. As with any probative analysis, it critiques these approaches and methodologies, whether examining the general issues of transitology or the particular dilemmas confronting a specific state. There is a concern about the epistemological contradictions and tensions between the macro and micro levels of analysis, about the anti-neoliberal attitudes, or at least the discomfort with neoliberalism in some of the works on post-communist transitology, as well as with the exaggerated expectations and at times the overly pessimistic interpretations of the prospects for democracy in the post-communist states. There is apprehension about transferring that which has been learned from transitions in Southern Europe and South America holus-bolus to post-communist Europe. There is an awareness of the continuing and yet largely needless tension between comparative politics and area studies. And there is a recognition of the need to add to the examination of post-communist transitions the dimension of strategic/security studies.

There is moreover a need for conceptual clarification, a larger vision of transitions of post-communist states (even in the absence of a general theory of transitions) while retaining the ability to focus on specific states and particular issues. In such a work the contributors inevitably find themselves looking at such matters as the movement from civil society to political society, the difficulty of developing a rule of law, the building and sustaining of institutions that allow for stable governments, and the development of what some have called an economic society.[2]

To synthesize the various approaches and to reconcile and combine comparative politics, area studies, and security and strategic studies are onerous tasks that we concluded were best tackled by a group of scholars and a multidisciplinary approach. We brought together specialists in political science, economics, sociology, history, and international relations to examine the general problems and specific issues of transition. At the general level Guy Hermet, John Higley, and Anders Åslund cover the first of four parts of the book and bring a wide-ranging assessment of the issues of transitology and, more specifically, the problems of post-communist transitions.

In selecting Hungary as a case study, we intended to benefit from the case study methodology and speak inductively to the most crucial issues of transition. These have to include both comparative and regional conundra. The selection of Hungary should be helpful in achieving this task especially given our assumption that post-communism and transition refer to the past, the present, and the future. Hungary is a state that *seemed* better positioned and appears to be more successful than most post-communist states at transition. Further, in light of the stable transfers of power in a number of elections and its progress towards integrating itself into the community of pluralistic democratic states after several years of transition, the time seems to be propitious to examine Hungarian transition as part of a regional, comparative, and general theoretical assessment of transition.

In the four-part division of this work, there is then a movement from the general issues of transition to the problems of post-communist democratization, the issues of marketization and social change in Hungary to the dilemmas of Hungary's international relations and security. Zoltan Barany's chapter provides a crucial bridge between the general and the country specific. Overall, in moving from the general issues to the specific there is a common thread in the examination and assessment of motor forces for change, the emphasis on conceptual clarification, the formulation of the criteria for assessing success, and the continuing interplay of domestic and external variables.

To merely suggest, however, that there are dilemmas of transition risks the danger of lapsing into description. Probative questions need to be formulated. Without a road map for transition, moreover, how questions are formulated and what specific questions are asked are pivotal to making them relevant and probative. This collective work revolves around seven principal questions with numerous subsidiary ones. First, what is the role and significance of preconditions? Second, how significant is the role of elites and particularly that of elite persistence in transition? Third, what is the function of civil society? Fourth, how important is the interplay of economic and political variables and are there causal linkages? Fifth, is it possible to discern some motor forces that drive change during the transition period? Sixth, how does the interaction of domestic and external variables affect the issues and the resolution of dilemmas of transition and promote or undermine long-term stability? And seventh, how is success assessed and what are some of the early warning signs of failure?

Preconditions

It is not merely a matter of learning from history. It is crucial to learn the right lessons. In studying post-communist transition, the communist past is to be examined not merely for historic interest but also to ascertain whether it performs, at least in part, a predictive function. The English writer G. K. Chesterton spoke of the recent past as the prophetic past. Given the fundamental political, economic, and social changes taking place in the post-communist states, particularly in East Central Europe, it is unlikely however that the communist past can in whole predict the non-communist future. Some analysts of post-communist transitions, such as Guy Hermet, in fact move in the opposite direction. Hermet, in highlighting the epistemological contradictions and tensions between the macro and micro levels of analysis (among other difficulties of analyzing transition), posits forcefully the unpredictability of the future of young democracies. Yet Hermet does not take the approach that there can be no predictability whatsoever or that the communist past does not in any way influence the post-communist present and future.

But clearly, there are intrinsic dangers in assuming that the best indicator of the future is the past. And it may be entirely correct that notions of teleological development making the twenty-seven post-communist states similar to the West are unsustainable and inaccurate. Nevertheless, the post-communist governments have embraced enthusiastically, in their public pronouncements at least, the idea of constructing political democracy and establishing market economies. Legacies do matter, because they have to build on what they have. It is in the scholarly examination of the past, moreover, that we at times see some of the greatest differences. Too much or too little may be read into historic developments, institutions, processes, and attitudes, or differing interpretations of the same issues may lead to contrasting pessimistic and optimistic assessments.

To some, their reading of preconditions give them cause for considerable pessimism. Charles Gati, for instance, has expressed considerable concern for the future of democratic governments because of the uncommonly difficult economic and political legacies of the communist past.[3] Philippe Schmitter and Adam Przeworski have also expressed considerable trepidation about democratic progress because of difficulty of the past legacies.[4] These concerns may indeed be well founded and at least some of the pessimistic projections may prove to be correct, particularly in the case of the post-Soviet states.

Nevertheless, it is important to treat the past cautiously, contextually, and even skeptically. The past is rich and, as Stephen Holmes has argued, it is possible to find foreshadowing of just about anything that comes to pass.[5] Further, Holmes rightly warns against confusing *analogy* with *causality*.[6] Yet, despite his just warning against the notion that cultural legacies, for instance, can and would obstruct the successful creation and function of democratic and market institutions, Holmes has argued that certain legacies or preconditions do have an affect. That is, he appears to accept that there can be a casual relationship between the past, present and future. Specifically, Holmes has contended that constitutional precommitment "enfranchises future generations" while deciding certain fundamental questions ranging from freedom of speech to property rights.[7] It is therefore not merely a matter of legacies but what legacies and further how these legacies are to be weighed in terms of their impact on the overall success or failure of transition.

Anna Seleny, in her chapter, perhaps gives us the most positive assessment of some legacies, though she emphasizes that these may relate only to Hungary. In the process of providing conceptual clarification of legacies, identities, and political discourse, which of course includes the role of political culture, she concludes that Hungary is in a better position to consolidate democracy than other post-communist states. This despite the fact that Hungary's politics are corporatist and coalitional at the elite level (as she readily acknowledges). But she argues that Hungary's relatively consensual party politics gives it an advantage over the oppositional and divisive politics in other post-communist states.

Most importantly, she asserts that Hungary is the one state which inherited from the state-socialist period an important positive legacy of reform whose *result* is analogous to the benefits of constitutional precommitment, and this is so even though the *process* by which such a precommitment was entrenched was neither fundamentally liberal nor always formally codified. There was a process, she contends, which continued to broaden the rights of Hungarian citizens as was manifested, for example, in the reform of property rights. Further, she cites the current activism of the Hungarian Constitutional Court in favor of social protection as evidence that there is causality to be found in the preconditions that existed in the socialist past, such as the incremental process of socioeconomic compromise between the party-state and society.

The latter contention though also illustrates the problem of interpretation. Even if causality is accepted, the results are not necessarily seen in the same positive light. Andras Sajo, without rejecting (or confirming) the premise of causality has contended that the Hungarian Constitutional Court's activism in the post-communist period has in fact killed essential welfare reform and thus helped preserve an old system that was neither just nor efficient and that favored the well-to-do and the middle class.[8]

In his chapter Andrew Arato comes closest to Seleny. He suggests not only that the concept of civil society has played a major role in recent transformations to democracy, but that of the countries that lead in the post-communist transition, the civil society strategy was the historical precondition for the successful turn to political society and for the successful achievement of radical regime change through political negotiations. In both Poland and Hungary, he contends it was the prehistory of civil society based politics that made pacts and roundtables possible in the transition.

Others in this volume are considerably less sanguine about the legacies of the communist state. Focusing on Hungary, Rudolf Tokes cites Janos Kornai's assessment of a "premature welfare state" in Hungary. Kornai himself speaks of the difficult economic (and political) legacy and the negative impact of "Goulash communism" in Hungary.[9] Tokes assesses how heavy the burden is and how much of a prejudicial impact it has on current and future political and economic developments in Hungary. He asserts that the mismatch between the Kadarist institutional legacy and the new political architecture and between the past economic misdevelopment and the imperatives of the market is not likely to be reconciled soon, a view considerably at variance with Seleny's hope for a post-communist political and economic synthesis.

Still, other contributors to this volume, in their examination of preconditions, have concluded that it was at best a mixed picture. Though Hungary was not badly positioned for transition in comparison to other communist states, its past was also some cause for concern. Zoltan Barany, in his chapter, points out that by the late 1970s the Hungarian economy and society were suffering from the most pervasive case of malaise in the region. The regime's eroding legitimacy, he points out, was not reversed by reforms, which resulted in piecemeal changes to the political system, nor could the regime break the old pattern of economic development. Further, Barany reiterates Samuel Huntington's[10] assessment that Hungary did not possess the top ranking in the region in such important criteria pertaining to democratization as previous experience with democracy; levels of social and economic development; and the extent, depth, and strength of independent and social political organizations.

Paul Marer also paints a mixed picture in his chapter. Though he acknowledges the importance of the movement in Hungary between the mid-1960s and the late 1980s towards a market economy, and the significance of the goodwill that the country enjoyed in the West, he also points to the dangers posed by the politically motivated cumulative excess consumption under communist rule. The legacies of the latter negatively impact on current and future economic and political developments. Marer argues that excess consumption resulted not only in a massive foreign debt but also in other kinds of debt—the decline in investment as a percentage of the GDP and several expensive and not fully funded legislative commitments to guaranteed pensions, family allowances, maternity benefits, sick pay, and other welfare transfers. Further, Marer contends that this excess consumption, in masking the monumental economic and political problems granted a kind of semilegitimacy to the communist regime that diminished the eagerness of the population to rid itself of the system and, importantly, made the population much more reluctant than some of the other postcommunist states to accept the necessary economic sacrifices during transition. Thus, ironically, foreign loans and generosity may have had a deleterious effect as did Kadarist palliatives by confusing the population about the need for urgent and fundamental political, economic, and social change.

Lastly, Anders Åslund, in his chapter, which deals with the general issue of transition, acknowledges the significance of preconditions, notably culture and history, either as causal or correlative answers, but contends that these can be transcended. His emphasis is on the primacy of economic policy. This suggests at least a correlation between the nature of reform and the political regime. Liberal democratic regimes, according to Åslund, would choose radical reform (that is, fundamental change), would avoid what he calls "rent-seeking" (revenues extracted thanks to the government and state privileges, either through subsidies or monopolies), and thus could overcome negative cultural, historical, or economic preconditions. Whatever the assessment of the role of the past, however, there is more of a consensus about who leads the transition. The relevant decisions, it seems, are mainly made by the elites, and consequently there is a need to assess the specific role of elites in transition.

Elites and Transition

Several leading analysts of transition including Guillermo O'Donnell, Philippe Schmitter, and Terry Karl have argued that elites and their interactions are central to transitions.[11] Others such as Adam Przeworski worried about the authoritarian temptations of frustrated *reform-elites* during transition.[12] John Higley, who has produced some of the most seminal works on elites, addresses in this volume the pivotal issue of elite persistence in transitions. In his chapter he argues persuasively for the need to pay more attention to elite persistence in studying regime transitions. He points out that most transitions have involved little change in the composition and the relations of elites and produced mainly cosmetic changes in political institutions and processes— amounting to what Juan Linz and Alfred Stepan have called new "within-private" regimes.[13] Higley suggests therefore that the twentieth century's vaunted waves of democratization have not been as cumulative as is often thought, for under nominal democratic institutions entrenched elites have continued to engage in irreconcilable struggles for power. Belarus, and until the defeat of the Ion Iliescu regime in the fall of 1996, Romania, as well as several other post-communist states starkly illustrate the problem of elite persistence as posited by Higley.

Are there, however, some variations on the modal revolutionary, settlement, and imposition patterns of change suggested by Higley? Some of the contributors do suggest different perspectives which at least raise certain additional questions. Guy Hermet goes beyond Higley's notion of elite settlements which, in the case of post-communist states, only occurred in Hungary and Poland. Though Hermet declares unequivocally that there is no general law which suggests that in a transition the old authoritarian elites are best suited to bring about democracy, he contends that there is a "paradox of Friends and Foes" where indeed the former authoritarian or totalitarian "enemies" of democracy, at least those who were the opportunists or the "flexible pretenders," are well or best suited to alleviate the disillusionment of the population during transition and enhance confidence.

The examples of Spain and Argentina that Hermet cites, however, may be applicable only with some difficulty to Eastern Europe; but given the return to power of ex-communists in Hungary and Poland (until their electoral defeats in 1998 and 1997, respectively), Hermet's "paradox" bears examination. Much depends on the attitudes and the perceptions of the elites. In her chapter, Anna Seleny suggests that under Gyula Horn in Hungary the coalition of former enemies, of whom by far the largest partner were the ex-communists, there was not merely opportunism but, in the case of the socialists, many of the same elites emerged with fundamentally changed indentities and important political lessons. This would also go beyond the settlement pattern suggested by Higley where there is not much change in the composition of elites, but they transform their relations in order to become more united.

Here, unlike the Bourbons, the ex-communist elites have forgotten much and learned a great deal that is useful, if not everything that there is to know. Seleny indeed refers to identity-transformation. This is a *sine qua non* for the functioning of political processes that facilitate the creation and maintenance of elite consensus and political moderation, as posited by such scholars of transition as Richard Gunther, John Higley, and Adam Przeworski.[14]

Lastly, Andrew Arato puts an interesting twist on the role of elites in his chapter assessing the impact of civil society on transition. He argues that pressure for change in Hungary came both from above and below. He posits that the process of transition in Hungary was negotiated at the mezzo level of political society, where political parties emerging from both civil society and from the party-state played the central role. Elites in such a scenario then are at the very least bracketed as movement is made through the mezzo level of political society (since civil society has been or is being institutionalized). Thus, the role of elites as well as the overall nature of transition may indeed be better understood by more closely examining the function of civil society in the transition to democracy.

Fitting in Civil Society

Juan Linz and Alfred Stepan define civil society as the arena "where self-organizing groups, movements and individuals, relatively autonomous from the state attempt to articulate values, create associations and solidarities and advance their interests."[15] To them the existence of a lively civil society is one of the five interacting arenas whose interplay determines the road that a society is likely to take. A second such arena, they argue, is a relatively autonomous political society. Andrew Arato, in his chapter, brings the two arenas together.

Much of the literature on transitions ignores the relevance of the concept of civil society in assessing the negotiations leading to transition pacts. And much of the literature also implies that with a turn to "political society" the corresponding demobilization of the civil sphere means that the politics of civil society have little to do with the consolidation of democracy. Is it then that civil society, in the case of East European states, meant merely liberalization rather than democratization in the sense that democratic institutions and culture are being built? Is there a kind of demobilization of the civil sphere? Linz and Stepan[16] show that civil society is linked to political society and quite rightly point out that the two are not identical. Political society, in their view, refers to the institutionalization of the arena of competition for power, the arena where questions about the existence, scope, strength, and diffusion of local parties arise. Further, it is here that not only questions but also the rules about electoral laws and the power of legislators are determined. Ultimately, political society involves the creation of a set of mechanisms that enable a polity to control the government and the state apparatus and to ensure that the rules of the game will not be changed arbitrarily by the powers engaged in the exercise.[17]

Andrew Arato, who only partly agrees with the demobilization thesis, links civil society, transition, *and* the consolidation of democracy. This is important, first, at the initial level of transition and, second, at the level of consolidation. Arato first contends that in the transition-leading countries of Poland and Hungary the civil society strategy was, at the very least, the historical precondition for the successful turn to political society. Here, he argues, radical regime change was achieved through political negotiations. He contends, moreover, that civil society had an impact even in places like Russia, where *glasnost* had the effect (if not the intent) to stimulate the reconstruction of the public sphere and of civil actors. The case for Russia is more difficult to make, one would think, but in the cases of Poland and Hungary, Arato raises several important questions regarding the role of civil society. Arato's argument is that civil society based movements were necessary conditions for genuine, negotiated transitions. This is very different from contending that they were sufficient conditions. As Rudolf Tokes shows in his chapter, even in Hungary, where the transition agreements created what appeared to be well-crafted provisions for institutional transition from a one-party communist system to parliamentary democracy, several volatile matters, such as social consensus on post-communist policy, local justice, and some weighty issues on privatization, were left in abeyance. And how would one compare the transition in Poland and Hungary, on the one hand, with that of Czechoslovakia on the other? We find that there were further differences in civil society strategy and in negotiations.

Second, Arato argues that some or even significant demobilization of the civil sphere does not mean that civil society becomes irrelevant for the consolidation of democracy. He contends that, on the contrary, there is mutual interdependence between the institutionalization of civil society and the consolidation of democracy. Now "consolidational democracy" must be treated carefully, for I and others would argue it is not some final stage or some immutable plateau. Zoltan Barany rightfully refers to the Jeffersonian axiom that democracy is a process which needs perennial improvement. In his definition of democracy, Arato does not deny the notion of democracy as a process and in fact describes the consolidation of democracy as a process by which "democracy becomes the only game in town."

Just as significantly, he rejects the notion that the consolidation of democracy is simply the creation of an equilibrium resting on a desirable combination of interested spheres. Rather, he links it to the idea of legitimacy. The latter ties in neatly with Seleny's concerns in her chapter with the role that reform socialism played as a legitimating framework for Hungarian politics. But as transition progresses the notion of legitimacy must confront the present and look to the future. The legitimacy of a government of course may be understood in political, sociological, and legal terms. But, ultimately, it is central to the survival of democracy as a political system and the ability to govern effectively.

From Habermas to Weber the sources of political legitimacy are understood differently in the various traditions of political philosophy.[18] Some political theorists define a government as legitimate if it upholds the rule of law, governs in a procedurally correct manner, and ensures the personal rights of citizens; others link legitimacy with a substantive notion of the "good life," defined with reference either to traditional values or to a consensually determined social purpose. In both these views, I would contend, a legitimate political order is one that in the minds of citizens *ought* to go on. Arato comes close to this definition of legitimacy when he declares that, in addition to a favorable interest constellation, there is a need for a sufficiently large number of actors to accept a given system as legitimate.

Contained within this notion that for legitimacy citizens need to believe that the political order ought to go on is the vital element of the rule of law. Leonard Schapiro, who perhaps understood socialist totalitarianism better than anyone, wrote that a free society can only exist and grow organically if it possesses a well-rooted legal system and a strong and independent judiciary to safeguard it.[19]

Linz and Stepan also emphasize the rule of law by making it one of their five criteria for successful transition.[20] In their approach to the rule of law, there is a need for a structure in which all significant actors, including the government, respect and uphold the accepted normative order, the hierarchy of laws, and the relative independence of the judiciary and the judicial system. Surely "relative," though, could not mean any level of independence, but it is likely to entail a rather high one.

Problems of transition in this area quickly become evident even in states such as Hungary. The effective rule of law presupposes favorable circumstances. It is not just a matter of the existence of courts and the promulgation of laws. There is a need for competent and honest courts and public bureaucracies. There is a need for a positive public perception of the rule of law. And, ultimately, the efficacy of the rule of law needs to be judged in terms of the effectiveness of implementing laws, regulations, and procedures. The problems faced by the post-communist states in this area are enormous, even in the case of those that are at the cutting edge of transition. Given the kind of requirements cited above, legal scholars such as Andras Sajo are thus justified in speaking about the underdevelopment of the rule of law in the post-communist states.[21]

It would seem that to ensure the consolidation of democracy, to preserve or enhance legitimacy, and to maximize the positive benefits from a well-functioning civil society, there is a need for movement on several fronts. Political, economic, and socio-legal conditions all need to improve in the post-communist states. They are all intertwined, and Marer, in his chapter closely links political conditions and attitudes with economic change.

Economic-Political Linkages

What are the possible links? Is there causation, correlation, or even inverse correlation? Do economics and politics operate independently? There are sharply differing views on these issues. It is worth reiterating that the governments of the post-communist states at least profess their goals to be the construction of political democracy *and* the establishment of a market economy. It would appear that these governments presume a linkage. But are they right?

Hermet, in his chapter, expresses skepticism about the linkages, or at least the way in which such linkages are understood. He criticizes Przeworski's assessment of the interaction of the positive and negative economic effects of market-oriented reform and political reform. At the very least Hermet suggests that excessive economic demands, exaggerated expectations, and inordinate economic pain can damage political stability. Consequently, he rejects the arguments of those like Hayek who assert that there is an irrefutable functional linkage between the representative and even the social versions of democratic institutions and the free market. And he warns of the dangers of trying to carry out economic reforms without some demonstrably positive results in the daily lives of the people. He fears that in such conditions the very legitimacy of the new democratic regimes could be endangered.

Linz and Stepan challenge the prevailing assumption of linkages, at least in terms of some sort of causal relationship between democracy and markets. An economic society is one of their five criteria for successful transition, but they stress that this is not identical with a market economy. They contend further that the supposed connection between consolidated democracy and the pure market economy is an ideological myth.[22]

It is hardly my intent here to launch into a defense of Milton Friedman, Hayek, or Thatcherism. But it is my contention that Linz and Stepan (among others) trot out something of a straw man. Free market economies and "pure free market economies" are not identical. Linz and Stepan are right in suggesting that Adam Smith, the great proponent of *laissez-faire*, was not speaking of a pure market economy in *The Wealth of Nations*. There always is a government, and it is a primary duty of government to provide a degree of protection for society; there must be rules and norms. Certainly there can be different kinds of market economies. There is however an enormous ideological difference between command economies on the one hand and market economies on the other. It is not merely one of degree as to the amount of regulation, but one of philosophy. In market economies, the preponderant economic decisions are made by the market responding to supply and demand.

Of course, markets never operate in a political vacuum.[23] Jeffrey Sachs, who is so closely associated with the notion of "shock therapy," viewed the market as a revolutionary break with the past but one that was premised on political will and consensus.[24] Even economic positivists, such as Milton Friedman, who speak of the relevance of the work of the market to social issues, seemingly assign the central role to the market and assume that there is a prior public consensus on market values. That consensus is reached *politically*, and in a transition period it is particularly difficult to do so. Yet this is pivotal. By its very nature, a market cannot be mechanically transferred from the West nor imposed by *diktat*. It can only take root and become efficient if the people are willing to commit themselves to it and thereby express this commitment through support of a political order which, in turn, decides the rules for economic and social interchange. Now, true, in the transition period, there is a kind of Schumpeterian "creative destruction," which is painful, but this can also be helpful. To be helpful, though, there has to be that political consensus, which is ultimately manifested in a commitment to a political order—that is, political legitimacy.

In his chapter, Anders Åslund using the term *capitalism* rather than *market economy*, asserts that the former is more compatible with democracy than other economic constructs.[25] More significantly, Åslund also argues that authoritarian rule has proven to be a disadvantage in post-communist transition. Åslund asserts that those pushing for fundamental reform need to explain their policies to the population, for poor popular understanding of their own interests creates political difficulties. But he contends that the real threat to the construction of what he calls the "normal capitalist system" does not come from the population or the workers, but from the old recalcitrant elite.

It is not Åslund's argument that for successful transition the states should wither away, but rather that transition has to urgently address the far-reaching politicization of the economy that was a central feature of communist rule. Consequently, in his view, the primary task of post-communist economic transition is to depoliticize the economy. This of course presupposes fundamental political change.

In advocating the depoliticization of the economy Åslund makes an argument that is similar in terms of political linkages to that of Robert Skidelsky, the great Keynesian scholar. The state has to let go, Skidelsky has argued, for contrary to much elite expectation, the modern state's claim to superior knowledge (compared to the market) has proven to be invalid. Moreover, it has proven to be impossible to centralize knowledge concerning public good or the community's preferences and thus define ambitious collective goals.[26] But in order to reduce the size of the state, there must be political will. Skidelsky argues that it is an act of political will that is needed to break structural conditions which, for instance, would significantly alter the inflationary pressure and heavy unemployment that plague most of the post-communist states.[27]

To reduce the state, to build a capitalist or market economy, to depoliticize the economy as Åslund suggests, certain steps must be taken. One of the most important, according to Åslund, is the depoliticization of ownership which is to be achieved through privatization. This is the focus of Keith Crane's chapter. He assesses privatization both in relation to the goals of the privatizers (in Hungary) and in comparison with Poland and the Czech Republic. In all these states, particularly in the case of the Czech Republic, privatization has strong political goals. He points out that in Hungary privatization goals have been remarkably constant despite the change from the Antall–Boross government to that of the socialist one under Gyula Horn. But political consensus has come up against the problem of the government explaining policy to the population, the inability or difficulty of instituting reasonably corrupt-free programs, and of the will of the population to bring about fundamental change. The latter, which, as Paul Marer points out, can be affected by popular misconception of the gravity of the situation, can stifle the political will necessary to bring about the needed changes. Crane, in his criticism of delays in privatization, comes back to the idea of political will and the ability of governments to get the job done.

Are there conclusive answers here or are we still left with questions regarding the nature of possible linkages between political and economic goals and policies? Are politics then the primary force in transition? Will success ultimately depend on delivering prosperity? We might be helped in this quest by that fact that in examining transition one can discern, at least at one time or another, goals, purpose, and intent. There is a need for movement in transition, and this is why it should be useful to ascertain whether there are some discernible motor forces of society that can give us a better understanding of the character of transition and its prospects for success.

Motor Forces

That societies change is obvious. What makes them change is where the debate starts. During a period of transition, such as in the case of the post-communist states where change ranges from the cosmetic to the most fundamental alteration of political, economic, and social relations, there are multiple factors at work. What are, however, the primary factors driving change? Is it, for instance, economic crisis? Is it a search for political legitimacy? Or is it a particular combination or interaction of forces? In all the chapters there is a sense that, in the post-communist states in general, and in Hungary in particular, there is continuing movement. Some developments give cause for optimism, others for pessimism, and there is an element of ever-present uncertainty. But some of the chapters focus more on what may be viewed, not unreasonably, as at least possible motor forces driving the transition.

Rudolf Tokes suggests the existence of a motor force that moves transition. The main hypothesis that he puts forth in his chapter posits a dialectic—the manifest conflict between, on the one hand, the requisites of democratization, marketization, and the rule of law and, on the other, the imperatives of societal priorities and inherently unattainable social expectations for public goods. This dialectic shapes the character of the transition and Tokes suggests that as a result, instead of a picture-perfect democracy, a smoothly working market economy, and a contented citizenry, even Hungary will have to make do for some time with second-best solutions. The transition is incomplete and is likely to remain so for awhile. This dialectic, in the process of shaping the transition, affects and will affect its pace and direction. And it is not inconceivable, one would think, that the attempt to resolve existing contradictions could in time result in new and difficult ones.

Hermet also speaks of contradictions and paradoxes. These occur not only in the conflicts between the desire for theory-building and empirical requisites but are also manifest, he argues, in the conflict between political and economic goals and the expectations and tolerance for pain of the populations of the post-communist states. Because it is this type of dialectic that drives development in the transition, Hermet contends, first, that it may be that in young democracies certain types of populism provide a basic source of legitimacy; second, that emerging democracies are likely to look different from established ones; and third, that there is considerable uncertainty and therefore unpredictability in terms of outcome.

In some respects, it may also be argued that, at least in addition to the post-communist states trying to deal with the aforementioned contradictions, there is a concomitant struggle to maintain legitimacy. This struggle for maintaining legitimacy may prove to be a far more important motor force for change than economic crisis. Arato shows that, without consultation and consensus, the legitimacy of governments, at least in the sociological sense, can be eroded. With a severe drop in sociological legitimacy (and I would argue that this also involves a drop in political legitimacy), a government can become immobilized in the sense that it can lose pace and direction. This happened to the Antall government, Arato suggests, in the wake of the October 1990 strikes. Therefore, there is a need on the part of the governments to explain, to consult, and to take into account interest groups, according to Arato. Furthermore, he suggests that there could be pressures from the other side as well, that is, in instances where the politics of civil society can become fundamentalist or antipolitical. Therefore, it is important to develop a culture and discourse of self-limitation.

If these are indeed the primary domestic motor forces during transition then they do imply certain solutions that would ensure, or at least facilitate, the attainment of the declared goals of post-communist governments. There is a need for greatly increased political confidence-building measures, which in turn would involve far more open and effective communication by the elites with the public and much greater commitment to the honesty and integrity of political and economic processes. Further, it would involve a lowering of popular expectations since, as Janos Kornai has suggested, the transformational recession is bound to be deep and long.[28] Consensus building would also be essential, and this would involve self-limitation both on the part of the governing elites and the population. The above three suggestions would also mean that there would need to be a far better and more productive link between civil society and political society, and this would be particularly contingent upon a fuller exercise of both the *rights* and the *responsibilities* of citizenship.

Despite the focus so far on domestic factors, it should be recognized that these do not determine the character of the transition in the post-communist state independent of external forces. None of the post-communist states are autarkic or autochthonous. Just as the collapse of communism was in part induced by external factors (among these Western containment and *Ostpolitic*), so transition is likely to reflect an interplay between domestic and foreign variables. This interplay of variables has been reinforced by the professed desire of the post-communist states to join important Western organizations, such as the European Union (EU) or NATO, and to resolve bilateral issues with their neighbors. These considerations are particularly important to the East European states. Paul Marer points out in his chapter that becoming a member of these organizations requires a commitment to align the country's political and economic institutions and practices with those of the democratic and developed West. Such commitments (as well as those for resolving bilateral issues with neighboring states) at the very least reinforce the direction of movement towards political pluralism and marketization, and expectations of membership likely influence the pace of the transition.

The External Factors

Three chapters by Bennett Kovrig, Aurel Braun, and Daniel Nelson explore the external influences on the post-communist states, and the interplay of domestic and foreign variables, with a particular focus on Hungary. If the degree of interest in joining the community of Western democratic states varied among the former Soviet states, in the wake of the collapse of Soviet imperial power the East European countries have all looked to the West for aid and inspiration, convinced of the desirability of regional integration. Especially in the case of Hungary, Poland, and the Czech Republic, together with transition, there has been an attempt to effect a simultaneous process of integration. As noted, such integration would be achieved primarily through membership in the European Union and NATO. External factors therefore are likely to have domestic reverberations, but it remains uncertain whether they would function as moderating, enabling, motivating, stabilizing, or legitimating influences.

Though the Council of Europe is the oldest and the primary agency dedicated to the principles of democracy and human rights in Europe, the requirements for membership are relatively lax as illustrated by that organization's cozy relations with countries such as Romania, under the rule of Ion Iliescu. The EU, resting on twin pillars, one a requirement for political pluralism, and the other the attainment of a certain level of economic achievement, would have a far greater potential for positively influencing domestic developments in the post-communist states, especially in the cases of those closest to gaining membership. Membership could help moderate political extremism, enable more rapid economic progress, motivate governments to be more sensitive to minority rights, strive for more neighborly relations, and undertake bolder economic programs that would bring greater long-term economic and political stability. Ultimately, membership in the EU could also help legitimate the new political order by demonstrating the benefits of belonging to this large and spectacularly successful group of nations.

Kovrig's chapter shows that Budapest has been determined to satisfy the criteria for accession to the EU. Such determination and Hungary's good reputation in the West should help that country gain membership. Specific steps taken by Hungary should also impress the EU. Hungary has dramatically reduced its current-account deficit, devalued its currency by introducing an effective "crawling peg" devaluation system, cut social programs, and brought down real wages by 15 percent.[29] And the new Fidesz-led government, despite earlier concerns, promised not to change the system, at least not before 1998.[30]

Yet, as Kovrig shows, despite Hungary's determination to satisfy the criteria for accession, the prospects for early membership are dim. The EU, states Kovrig, is an experiment in comprehensive economic, social, and political integration that makes enlargement a very difficult task. The EU is confronting enormous difficulties and does not wish to take on new commitments. There is no consensus on the future course of integration, and old rivalries, particularly between Germany and France, have not died out.

Consequently, East European states in general and Hungary in particular may be deluding themselves about early membership and may possess exaggerated expectations of the immediate benefits. Kovrig demonstrates that the political and economic vagaries of the process of EU enlargement mean that the process itself is fraught with uncertainty. And he warns that if European integration is delayed too long, and if the benefits seem too skimpy, there is a danger of a negative domestic development—specifically, that the response may be the rise of dangerous neonationalism.

Some would take a more cynical view of Western Europe's policies. Michael Mandelbaum, for instance, suggests that Western Europe is trying to divert East European attention away from the West's unwillingness to admit new members. Mandelbaum has contended that, at least in part, membership in NATO is being offered to countries such as Hungary as a diversion or at best a compensation, because the West European governments do not want the Eastern European countries in the EU and have no desire to deal with the concomitant economic problems of enlarging the union.[31]

My own chapter analyzes the role of NATO in the context of examining the Russian factor and Hungarian security concerns. It is not merely my contention that this continually important relationship is increasingly filtered through the prism of NATO enlargement, but rather that this is all part of the process of transition in which strategic/security studies must be synthesized with area studies and comparative analysis. Moreover, there is a need for rethinking and restructuring security both in Hungary and the states in the region. The concept of security has to be linked to domestic changes. And the process of democratization throughout the post-communist states needs to form an important component of the reconceptualization of security. Ignoring the debate as to whether democracies go to war with each other, I do at least support the proposition that democracies have less of a propensity to engage in armed conflict with each other.

NATO membership can help democratization. There are visible benefits in NATO membership for the East European states. Membership brings prestige, the promise of extended protection, at least some external legitimization of political order and, with NATO's insistence of political control over the armed forces, greater democratic stability. Thus, there is a potential for a fruitful interplay of the external and domestic variables. Enlargement, however, also raises several concerns that can negatively affect transition and I will focus on three of them.

First, despite signing the Founding Act and the creation of the NATO–Russia Permanent Joint Council on May 27, 1997, Russia will be kept out of NATO[32] (that is, it will not become a full member). Whatever the political spin, once Hungary and other East European states are in NATO, the process of inclusion will foster a correlative process of exclusion. In Russia, despite the major steps toward democratization and marketization that occurred with the appointment of Anatoly Chubais and Boris Nemtsov as first deputy prime ministers, and the reshuffle that brought in Sergei Kiriyenko as prime minister, in the spring of 1998, democracy remains fragile. There is a risk that not only will Moscow feel alienated from the post-Cold War settlement in Europe but that such alienation, by fueling ultranationalism, may help to imperil the prospects for democracy. Should that scenario occur, what would be the impact on Hungarian security? Would a hostile and non-

20

democratic Russia also help to foster ultranationalist forces in Hungary and elsewhere in Eastern Europe?

Second, NATO criteria for entry also stipulate that new members cannot simply enjoy security—they must contribute to it as well.[33] Making a positive contribution to security would likely entail increased military expenditures. Hungary expects that joining the alliance will increase its military spending by about 35 percent and Poland projects a 20 percent rise.[34] This has raised concern not only in the International Monetary Fund (IMF) but has important domestic implications as well.[35] Given the difficult task of reducing social spending in the post-communist states, how will the population cope with increases in military spending? A United States Information Agency (USIA) survey in Poland, for instance, found that three-quarters of the people favored spending more money on health and education rather than weapons.[36] In Hungary public enthusiasm about NATO is already low.[37] (This is so despite the positive results of the November 16, 1997, referendum on NATO.) Will increased spending on the military, as a result of NATO membership, help to undermine what Arato referred to as "sociological legitimacy"in the East European states?

Third, enhancing security means that new members also have to resolve regional or bilateral conflicts. This is a potentially positive requirement. But eagerness to join, as I have indicated in my chapter, may lead states such as Hungary to enter into bilateral agreements with neighboring states without fully resolving the issues. Premature or poorly thought-out bilateral settlements can create future problems, both domestic and external. Would the Hungarian–Romanian basic treaty, for instance, help or hinder the resolution of the problem of the treatment of the large Hungarian minority in Romania? This is a significant issue with multiple implications and is dealt with at great length in Daniel Nelson's chapter.

Nelson clearly links Hungary's security concerns to relations with its immediate neighbors. He focuses specifically on the issues of the treatment and status of the Hungarian minorities in neighboring states. He argues persuasively that the link between ethnic minorities and Hungary's security concerns is far deeper than implied by inferences drawn from demographic data or the historical record. Moreover, there is an interplay he suggests among the concepts of state, nation, ethnicity, self-determination, sovereignty, and individual versus collective rights. Neighbors are an important factor in determining security in general, but in the case of Hungary in particular, the treatment and status of the Hungarian minorities in the neighboring states is a vital component of its (perceived) security. Nelson further contends that the ethnic Hungarians in Romania, Slovakia, and Serbia constitute a "minority issue" of enormous importance because their numbers compare favorably to a declining population in Hungary itself. He also points out that Hungarians in general continue to see regional history and, in particular the post-World War I and II settlements as unjust. Therefore, the nationalities issue, according to Nelson, constitutes fertile ground for demagogic appeals.

Yet, Nelson is relatively sanguine about the current situation. Extremist politicians have not generated sufficient support to gain power and some, such as Istvan Csurka, have been pushed into the political wilderness, at least temporarily. (This has not, however, been the case for Torgyan and his Smallholders' Party.) The post-communist governments, particularly that of Gyula Horn, have managed to steer a relatively moderate course on nationalism, though even Horn, Nelson admits, raised some concerns among neighboring states.

But has nationalism, in its manifestation as a force that endangers democracy by exclusion and discrimination, died out completely in any of the East European states? Nationalism, as Elie Kedourie wrote years ago, is in many respects ideologically based.[38] Rogers Brubaker, more recently, has contended that few if any of the post-communist states will render ethnicity legally and politically irrelevant.[39] Thus, the seeds of a major problem remain even in the case of Hungary.

Regarding specific bilateral relations, Nelson contends that in general there is satisfaction in Hungary with the Hungarian–Romanian basic treaty. Yet that treaty, which enumerates human rights for minorities in both countries, does not make the Council of Europe's Recommendation 1201 binding and does not guarantee *collective rights*. In light of the fact that throughout Eastern Europe there is still an emphasis on ethnicity rather than citizenship, how confident can one be that the absence of agreement on the protection of collective minority rights will not in the future endanger bilateral relations and security, or that, by possibly encouraging ultranationalism in Hungary, it will not negatively affect democracy itself?

Judging Success: Identifying Dangers

The process of identifying and assessing the success of post-communist transition presents a most difficult conceptual task. Yet this is an essential task both for the policy-makers and the peoples of the post-communist states as well as for Western governments and analysts. Judging success and failure is a prerequisite for policy-makers in the post-communist states if they are to take the appropriate corrective or preventive measures. It is also pivotal for the West in assessing the prospects of these states, calibrating aid, and deciding on enlarging Western institutions. In making such assessments, balance and context are important. It would be a mistake to underestimate the achievements of the post-communist states yet, at the same time, it would be foolish to deny failures or remain blind to dangers.

Assessing success brings us into a debate involving democratic theory and economic philosophy. Zoltan Barany goes beyond John Mueller's minimalist definition of democracy in assessing the success of Hungary's transition and, as noted, points to the Jeffersonian notions of democracy as a process. He also anchors his assessment in an empirical comparative regional evaluation, stressing foremost a comparison of Hungary's progress with that of the Czech Republic, Poland, and Slovakia.

In his chapter, Guy Hermet argues forcefully that the post-communist states should not be judged by the standards of established democracies. It is not that he is uncritical of the abuse of human rights or of the excesses of majority rule, but rather he is concerned with the sustainability of the process of transition. Consequently, he argues that a successful type of democratization is one that can be sustained under prevailing conditions. The argument for sustainability is a powerful one, but does it not run the risk of selling short the post-communist states in general and the East European ones in particular? Let us not forget that these governments have professed their goals to be the construction of political democracy and the establishment of a market economy as quickly as possible. Russia's former finance minister, Boris Fedorov, a committed democrat, warned Western policy-makers and scholars, "Don't pretend that democracy is one thing in the West and something else in Russia."[40]

Anders Åslund begins with the notion of intent when he poses the question, "What is the purpose of post-communist transition?" But even if we could reach a consensus on "intent," the post-communist states must decide more specifically on direction and sustaining the process. It is perhaps in the specifics that we may more easily discern both the success of transition and the warning signs of danger. Åslund looks to international standards in setting qualitative targets (which can nevertheless be quantified). These are financial stabilization, liberalization, and private-sector development. Marer, for his part, takes as a standard the average or the median performance of democratic governments around the world. Further, in judging success he differentiates between strategies and economic policies (or tactics). Keith Crane, focusing on privatization, assesses success in terms of overarching goals laid out by the governments themselves and in terms of a regional comparison with post-communist states at a similar level of development.

Judging direction and momentum is difficult in many areas. This is quickly evident in the economic realm. Both Åslund and Crane suggest that the more radical the reform, the more rapid the pace, and the greater the likelihood of successful economic transition. Yet, as Marer shows, the debate over "shock therapy" versus gradualism may oversimplify the process of economic transition. Shock therapy, he argues, can be both broadly and narrowly defined. He contends that Hungary did not need the narrowly defined version of shock therapy and that in terms of broadly defined shock therapy, its overall pace of transformation was not slower than that of Poland and the Czech Republic. Yet both Marer and Crane suggest that in many specific areas Hungary's transformation was slower than it should have been, and this is where one may indeed detect possible dangers to economic progress and successful transformation.

If we could formulate efficacious standards for judging economic success, then these may also suggest the potential dangers to transition. Åslund speaks of the failure of state building, persistent financial instability, inadequate privatization and, perhaps more significantly, the entitlement trap. Åslund also suggests that the West European economic model that the East Europeans are emulating is a poor choice in terms of growth potential. Åslund and Jeffrey Sachs[41] contend that the post-communist states would be better off opting for a liberal model closer to that of the United States.

But how do we continue to ensure that we ask the relevant questions about political success and failure? Valerie Bunce has justly warned us about asking the right questions when she pointed out that, for instance, in comparing the transitions in Russia and in Hungary, it may be far more important to investigate the problems of transition in each state rather than to ask whether Hungary was made more secure because it opted for a parliamentary system.[42] This kind of problem is evident in trying to formulate questions about political effectiveness. Linz and Stepan posit a "usable state and state machinery" as one of the five interacting arenas that are needed to achieve successful transition.[43] Stephen Holmes has argued that the central problem in the post-communist states is that, in contrast to the communist era, the state is too weak to enforce the rules.[44] But Linz and Stepan, in speaking of a usable state, take a Weberian approach and make the essential point that the very existence and attributes of the state—whether it's the boundaries of its citizenship, its unifying symbols, or its historical anchoring in the consciousness of the majority of its people—depend upon whether it is accepted as legitimate. In light of this, should the primary political question be, "Is the state too weak?" or would we be better off asking, "Does it have sufficient legitimacy?"

If it is primarily an issue of legitimacy (and Seleny and Arato, as noted, speak to this), that would elicit another question. How is legitimacy best enhanced or preserved during the transition period? Does our case study, Hungary, at least show a significant level of correlation between levels of legitimacy and the functioning of a "usable state"? There are at least three major factors evident in this volume that could significantly affect legitimacy and in turn inhibit the effective functioning of a government. These include corruption, a lack of self-limitation, and the rise of ultranationalism.

First, the problems of corruption are examined at least in part by Åslund, Marer, and others in this volume. The deligitimizing effects of corruption, moreover, are well illustrated by developments in the Czech Republic in the spring of 1997. It turns out that the vaunted economic progress under Prime Minister Vaclav Klaus masked severe structural and policy problems. Klaus sought to develop a German style of capitalism with close links between banks and industry but, failing to establish clear and fair rules for the stock market, he created a system with a policy vacuum that was an invitation for insider trading and widespread corruption.[45] This has resulted not only in a loss of foreign confidence but, more importantly, in a diminution of domestic political legitimacy.

It should not be forgotten that the post-communist states have emerged from decades of a political culture in which the popular mind equated wealth with theft. The rather sharp erosion of legitimacy in the Czech Republic has not only created an immediate political crisis, but it appears to be impairing the ability of the government to continue on a generally successful path of transition. In Hungary, too, corruption can easily lead people to equate democracy with grossly unfair deprivation. Hungary already suffers from a widening gap between rich and poor and 20–30 percent of the nation lives below the poverty line.[46] Corruption, cynicism, and envy could easily play into the hands of demagogues like Torgyan. His Independent Smallholders' Party won 48 seats in the 1998 election and could give Fidesz' Hungarian Civic Party (148 seats) a center-right majority.[47] In return, Torgyan would get several ministries and, unless he moderates his extremist views,[48] he and his party could have a significant negative effect on the development of democracy, the status of minorities (especially the Roma), and relations with neighboring states.

Second, what are the dangers of fundamentalist or antipolitical versions of the politics of civil society? Arato suggests that these would pose a major problem to the proper functioning of political society. Is there a real possibility of societies in the post-communist state abjuring self-limitation? One such possibility could come from the development of a new kind of victimology. A "victimized majority" is hardly likely to engage in the kind of self-limitation that Arato thinks necessary. A victimized majority would tend to absolve itself from the need for normal political intercourse and compromise. It would likely block political introspection or any objective reexamination of the past.[49] Further, such majorities are not likely to be sensitive to the needs of minorities.

Third, ultranationalism, which often goes hand in hand with the notion of the majority as victim, affects domestic stability as well as minority rights. How significant is this danger? As Barany suggests, Hungary has been rather successful in keeping extremism and ultranationalism in check. Yet, given the general virulence of ultranationalism,[50] even in Hungary the danger has not disappeared entirely. Kovrig and Nelson touch on some of the risks. But if dangers from ultranationalism exist even in Hungary, which has achieved a high degree of political and economic success and is relatively ethnically homogeneous then what are the risks in the cases of those states which lag in the transition?

Conclusion

What then is the balance of assessment? How do we achieve sufficient conceptual clarification? How sanguine can we be about the prospects for transition? Are Hungary, Poland, and the Czech Republic good indicators of the overall prospects for post-communist transition, or are they more likely to prove exceptions?

Post-communist states clearly face a number of often interlocking dilemmas. There is much to be encouraged about. There are unique opportunities for political and economic progress in the post-communist states, for integration, and for the creation of a new security architecture that would bring reassurance from Vancouver to Vladivostock. Yet can we ignore the dangers? Throughout much of the post-communist world there is the risk that inconclusive struggles, between the forces of democracy and marketization, on the one hand, and their opponents of the left and the right, on the other, will create a political system that would resemble democracy in form but not in substance. There is a danger that these states might descend into a kind of Third World morass, a region of underachievers enmeshed in fruitless debates over the possibility of creating some hybrid combining authoritarian traditions with elements of the American and West European models. Instead of real democracy we would have "democratoids." Would it make sense in such cases to pretend to see democracy where in fact it does not exist?

Notes

1. John Mueller, "Democracy, Capitalism, and the End of Transition" in Michael Mandelbaum, ed., *Post-Communism: Four Perspectives* (New York: Council on Foreign Relations, 1996), 102–67.

2. See also Juan J. Linz and Alfred Stepan, *Problems of Democratic Transformation and Consolidation—Southern Europe, South America, Post-Communist Europe* (Baltimore: The Johns Hopkins Press, 1996).

3. Charles Gati, "If Not Democracy, What? Leaders, Laggards and Losers in the Post-Communist World" in Mandelbaum, *Four Perspectives*, 168–97.

4. Philippe C. Schmitter, "Dangers and Dilemmas of Democracy," *Journal of Democracy*, Vol. 5, No. 2 (April 1994): 57–74; Adam Przeworski, *Democracy and the Market* (Cambridge: Cambridge University Press, 1991).

5. Stephen Holmes, "Cultural Legacies or State Collapse? Probing the Post-Communist Dilemma" in Mandelbaum, *Four Perspectives*, 27.

6. *Ibid.*

7. Stephen Holmes and Cass R. Sunstein, "The Politics of Constitutional Revision in Eastern Europe" in Sandford Levinson, *Responding to Imperfection: The Theory and the Practice of Constitutional Amendment* (Princeton: Princeton University Press, 1995).

8. Andras Sajo, "How the Rule of Law Killed Hungarian Welfare Reform," *East-European Constitutional Review (EECR)*, Vol. 5, No. 1 (Winter 1996); "Universal Rights, Missionaries, Converts, and 'Local Savages,' " *EECR*, Vol. 6, No. 1 (Winter 1997): 44–49.

9. Janos Kornai, *The Socialist System: The Political Economy of Communism* (Princeton: Princeton University Press, 1992); "Paying the Bill for Goulash Communism: Hungarian Development and Macro-Stabilization in a Political Economy Perspective," Discussion Paper 1748, Harvard Institute for Economic Research, Harvard University, Cambridge, Mass., 1996.

10. Samuel P. Huntington, "Democratization and Security in Eastern Europe" in Peter Volten, ed., *Uncertain Futures: Eastern Europe and Democracy* (New York: Institute for East-West Security Studies, 1990), 42–43.

11. Guillermo O'Donnell, "On the State, Democratization and Some Conceptual Problems," *World Development*, 21, 1993, 1355–69; Philippe C. Schmitter, "Dangers and Dilemmas of Democracy," *Journal of Democracy*, Vol. 5, No. 2 (April 1994): 57–74; Philippe C. Schmitter and Terry Karl, "The Conceptual Travels of Transitologists and Consolidologists: How Far to the East Should They Attempt to Go?" *Slavic Review*, Vol. 53, No. 1 (Spring 1994): 173–85.

12. Przeworski, *Democracy* , 189–90.

13. Linz and Stepan, *Problems of Democratic Transformation*.

14. John Higley and Richard Gunther, eds., *Elites and Democratic Consolidation in Latin America and Southern Europe* (New York: Cambridge University

Press, 1992); Adam Przeworski, "Economic Reforms, Public Opinion and Economic Institutions: Poland in the East European Perspective" in Luiz Carlos Bresser Pereira, Jose Maria Maravall, and Adam Przeworski, eds., *Economic Reforms in the New Democracies: A Social Democratic Approach* (New York: Cambridge University Press, 1993).

15. Linz and Stepan, *Problems*, 7.
16. *Ibid.*
17. *Ibid.*
18. Aurel Braun and Richard B. Day, "Gorbachevian Contradictions," *Problems of Communism* (May–June 1990), 36–38.
19. Leonard Schapiro, *Russian Studies* (New York: Penguin Books, 1987), 24.
20. Linz and Stepan, *Problems of Democratic Transformation.*
21. Sajo, "How the Rule of Law Killed Hungarian Welfare Reform," 44–49.
22. Linz and Stepan, *Problems of Democratic Transformation*, 11–12.
23. Aurel Braun, "Political Developments in Central and Eastern Europe" in *U.S. Relations with Central and Eastern Europe*, Aspen Institute Congressional Program, Vol. 9, No. 4, 1994, 9–10.
24. Jeffrey Sachs and Andrew Warner, "Economic Reform and the Process of Global Integration," *Brookings Papers on Economic Activity* (Washington: Brookings Institution), Vol. 25, No. 1, 1995.
25. Åslund goes into far greater detail to show the important linkages and how capitalism is essential for the creation of a stable pluralist society. See in particular Anders Åslund, Peter Boone and Simon Johnston, "How to Stabilize: Lessons from Post-Communist Countries," *Brookings Papers on Economic Activity* (Washington: Brookings Institution), Vol. 26, No. 1, 1996, 217–313.
26. Robert Skidelsky, "The State and Economy: Reflections on the Transition from Communism to Capitalism in Russia," in Mandelbaum, *Four Perspectives*, 85.
27. *Ibid.*, 99–100.
28. Janos Kornai, "Transzformacio Visszaeses," *Kozgazdasagi Szemle* (Budapest), No. 7–8, 1993.
29. *The Economist*, May 31, 1997, 65.
30. http://www.centraleurope.com/ceo/news, June 1, 1998, 2.
31. See article by Thomas L. Friedman, "NATO or Tomato?" *New York Times*, January 22, 1997.
32. Aurel Braun, "The Risks of Rushing to Enlarge NATO" *The Globe and Mail* (Toronto), May 27, 1997.
33. Frits Bolkestein, "NATO: Deepening and Broadening?" *NATO Review*, No. 4 (July 1996): 21–24.
34. Jeff Gerth and Tim Weiner, "Arms Makers Seek Bonanza by Selling NATO Expansion," *New York Times*, June 29, 1997.
35. *Ibid.*
36. *Ibid.*
37. The *Economist*, July 29, 1996, 31, citing United States Information Agency surveys and the European commission survey in *Nepszabadsag*, March 16, 1996.
38. Eli Kedourie, *Nationalism* (London: Hutchinson, 1960), 72.

39. Rogers Brubaker, *Nationalism Refrained: Nationhood and the National Question in the New Europe* (New York: Cambridge University Press, 1996).

40. Boris Federov interview with the author, Berlin, August 26, 1994, Aspen Institute Congressional Program Conference, Berlin, Germany, August 1994.

41. Jeffrey Sachs and Andrew Warner, "Economic Reform and the Process of Global Integration," *Brookings Papers on Economic Activity* (Washington: Brookings Institution), Vol. 25, No. 1, 1995, 1–118; Jeffrey Sachs, "Nature, Nurture and Growth: The Limits of Convergence," *The Economist*, June 14, 1997, 19–22.

42. Valerie Bunce, "Should Transitologists Be Grounded?" *Slavic Review*, Vol. 53, No. 1 (Spring 1995): 122–123.

43. Linz and Stepan, *Problems*, 16–37, 366–401.

44. Stephen Holmes, "Cultural Legacies or State Collapse? Probing the Post-Communist Dilemma" in Mandelbaum, *Four Perspectives*, 22–76.

45. *The Economist*, May 31, 1997, 18, 65–67.

46. *Transition*, The Newsletter about Reforming Economies, Washington, Vol. 8, No. 2 (April 1997): 25.

47. http://www.centraleurope.com/ceo/news, June 1, 1998.

48. Aurel Braun and Stephen Scheinberg, eds., *The Extreme Right: Freedom and Security at Risk* (Boulder, Colo. and Oxford, U.K.: Westview Press, 1997), 212–13.

49. Braun and Scheinberg, *The Extreme Right*, see particularly chapters 7–10.

50. Donald L. Horowitz, "Ethnic and Nationalist Conflict" in Michael T. Klare and Daniel C. Thomas, eds., *World Security: Challenges for a New Century*, 2nd ed. (New York: St. Martin's Press, 1994), 175–78.

Part One

Transition

Chapter 2

Rethinking Transitology

Guy Hermet

Embarrassing Contradictions

Years ago, Philippe Schmitter published an article titled "Still the Century of Corporatism?"[1] Though he could claim paternity for the word, it is ironic to imagine that he should now write another investigative paper called "Still the Century of Transitology?" What is the reason for this? Primarily it is because the most crucial concern affecting our small world of observers and theorists of transitions probably does not stem from our disappointment in the processes of democratization which destroyed existing political communities in Central Europe and the former Soviet Union, and it is not even induced by the genocide of the minority ethnic group by the majority as in the Republic of Rwanda. The most crucial concern stems more from the intrinsically logical difficulty induced by two epistemological contradictions. The first derives from the growing divergence that separates the abstract concept of transition from the empirical ambition called "transitology." That is to say, the two have ceased to be on good terms. As for the second contradiction, this stems from the short history of transitology, shaped as it has been by the peculiarities of the political changes in Latin countries in the 1980s, and then too haphazardly applied to another period of time and very different East-European, Asian, and African contexts.

We must recognize that "democratic transition" has been the common expression at the beginning of the story. Suggested by the exemplary peaceful and unrevengeful changeover of power in post-Franco Spain, with this hopeful combination of words it was almost taken for granted that the fall of a dictatorship had no other "goal" than to give

31

way more or less rapidly to democracy. Better still, this optimistic view did not prevail only in the aftermath of the collapsed military regimes of Mediterranean Europe and Latin America. It extended to the former communist states, since it appeared between 1989 and 1991 that the "Kirkpatrick doctrine"[2] had been refuted. Believed so far to be all-embracing and irreversible, the Soviet power and its communist subsidiaries then unexpectedly revealed that they were, in fact, erodible and fragile. In these conditions, the henceforth unchallenged wave of democratization, the biggest world event since decolonization, seemed to become, all of a sudden, a promise for the whole of humanity, or nearly so. And from now on, the transitions which were supposed to produce no other outcome than democratic regimes also were seen to be in no other need than of two types of generous support: the first, economic/financial and political, to be supplied by the Western governments with the cooperation of corporate investors; and the second, to be provided by the unparalleled skills of political experts. In this particular case, what was deemed to count most concerned less the immediate occurrence of liberal regimes, which was beyond doubt, than the enlightened development of their governability in societies that had to prove their capability to make use of their new-found freedom. Transitology would provide them with the necessary instructions.

This triumphalism of the "winners" concealed the gap which differentiates the substantial uncertainty of transitions in progress from the assumption of certainty involved by the project of a technological device offered by would-be professionals in transitology. Even then, in 1984, Adam Przeworski had already advised the political scientists about the fact that the primary distinctive feature of democracy as a set of institutions and procedures was the unpredictable nature of its outcome. In his opinion, political transitions were, consequently, even more uncertain, starting from one authoritarian point without any assurance of reaching democracy as their final point.[3] He stressed an unamusing parallel between transitions and the pin-ball machine in which "once the ball has been sent spinning up to the top, it may come inexorably spinning down again."[4]

Unhappily, Przeworski has proven to be prescient. It was only after the bloodshed of Tienanmen Square in China, and the more recent failure of democratization in the Arab world and the main part of Africa, that our professional community as well as the public in general began to question the linear concept of democratic transitions. We first had to rethink the democratic process, to accept it as it is—quite unpredictable, as John Higley and Anders Åslund demonstrate in later chapters of this book. And at the same time, we had to reduce it to a process in time and reject the idea that this process could designate a precise political mechanism. On the contrary, the Hungarian example, considered here by Barany, Tokes, Seleny, Marer, Crane, Arato, Kovrig, and Braun, illuminates the fact that each transition displays a specific character. Now, it is widely understood that transitions correspond only with the extremely varied and unpredictable period of time that elapses between the fall of a regime and the moment when the wheels of power come under the complete control of the political order replacing it—in the best circumstances, democracy. Obviously, the innumerable forms (and accidents) of transition, which respond to multiple instincts rather than strictly political ones, make it impossible to continue to believe that a single methodology or theory, even the most sophisticated and/or fortunate one, can provide the tools for a prescriptive approach to democratization. Therefore the current studies of transitions do not point to any "grand theory." On the contrary, they must be described as a return to the more traditional fragmentation of political objectives and of research goals in place.

The second contradiction to be considered deals with the self-delusion of some scholars who specialized in exotic comparative politics at the end of the 1980s and the start of the 1990s. At that time, a number of researchers indeed virtually abused their own prejudices. Some of them, long familiar with the vagaries of politics in Southern Europe, Latin America, or, less so, Eastern Asia, were as much surprised as anybody by the formidable earthquake that disrupted Central Europe after the fall of the Berlin Wall.

Nevertheless, they had an advantage as the "patented" Sovietologists who had clung to the "scientific truth" that the communist powers were indestructible, and had been unwilling to entertain an alternative future. Room remained for non-Sovietologists, brave enough to confront the immense complexity of the political rebirth taking place in the eastern part of Europe. The more theoretically prepared among the specialists of the Latin transitions accepted this challenge. They had just formalized the nascent paradigm of transitology. And though it referred basically to the political changes observed during the mid-1970s and the 1980s in Mediterranean Europe and South America, they thought that it would be expedient to test their invention in a fundamentally different environment. For sure, the new experts in transitology did not pretend for one second that the process of change they used to explore was exactly reproducible outside its original historical and cultural milieu. And they were convinced as well that democratic institutions were always to be hybridized or adapted to each of those milieus. But except for Juan Linz and a few other widely informed persons, these adventurous scholars remained ill-balanced even when they protested, in writing, of the purely tentative nature of their offerings. Their expertise was restricted to political or, at most, to sociocultural phenomena which were overtaken by the terrific flood of "nonconventional" factors intervening in Eastern Europe and later in Africa. Moreover, as Javier Santiso notes, for instance, their skills have been challenged or upset by a considerable, worldwide regression in politics as well as in political science itself.[5] The world was already getting less interested in the formal extension of democracy and increasingly obsessed with the mere reconstruction of authority in the states worthy of this name whence they had disappeared.

This assessment does not suggest the absence of any rethinking of transitology. It is only that for those who consider the immense range of variables to be taken into account for such a purpose in terms of structural, cultural, political, spatial, and temporal factors, there is no doubt that the construction of an all-encompassing practical theory of the ways and means of "good democratization" exceeds the capacities of the academic community. Now, this does not prevent opportunities from being realized provided that two challenges are overcome.

One of them concerns the very definition of what is currently deemed desirable or acceptable democracy. It has been assumed rather simplistically that the young democratic regimes must resemble a pluralistic and representative Western model based on its supposedly tight relationship with a vigorous and secularized civil society. Conversely, it seems ever clearer that some democracies in the making should be entitled to contemplate other arrangements when this celebrated "civil society" does not shape their environment in the way democratic theorists conceived it would. The second challenge to overcome involves the acceptance of less ambitious frameworks of analysis, which refer to specific objectives such as the return to power of neocommunists in Eastern Europe or the political effects of economic reform, as they are illustrated in this book by Seleny and Åslund.[6]

A Subjective State of the Art

In this second perspective, a considerable number of works have already provided penetrating insights or case studies covering in detail the whole of the recent democratization processes in the south of Europe and South America and, in part, of the current process in Central and Eastern Europe, Africa south of the Sahara, or Eastern Asia. In a sense, Linz and Stepan inaugurated some of these fundamental analytical changes by tackling the problem through a reversed analysis by starting with democratic breakdown. They edited the *Breakdown of Democratic Regimes*, which embraced a wide historical perspective and covered a large variety of countries.[7] This was followed by a series of books edited by Guillermo O'Donnell, Philippe Schmitter and Lawrence Whitehead[8] and by Enrique Baylora.[9] James Malloy and M.A. Seligson's[10] work appeared in 1987, still totally or primarily devoted to the transitions in South America. A few years later, works edited again by Linz, Larry Diamond, and Seymour M. Lipset included studies on African or Asian countries like Malaysia.[11] Recently, Linz and Stepan have published an important book of theoretical reflection based on a thorough survey of democratic transitions and consolidations not only in Southern Europe and South America but also in post-communist countries.[12]

However, even when these works deal with the consolidation of young democratic regimes (after considering the previous stage of their transition from some kind of dictatorships), their overall examination amounts only to a preliminary step. There now remains no doubt about the uncertain course of transitions characterized by the inherent risk of reversion to authoritarianism in the case of failure, or of democratization being halted in an unfinished state, as has occurred in so many cases in the former Soviet Union and Yugoslavia as well as Romania. On the other hand, regarding democratic consolidation, it is increasingly and generally admitted that the institutionalization of the new regime in no way means that the democratic institutions involved in this process have taken root. Sometimes the institutions serve merely as a screen and as a superficial source of legitimization in conditions where substantive political dealings take place outside them, backstage, or in the drawing rooms of some ruling class or refurbished nomenklatura.

Leonardo Morlino highlights the elusive nature of consolidation and the attendant conceptual problems when he restricts his analysis to a kind of unimpeded process without defining it in a very strict sense. For Morlino, democratic consolidation entails the inculcation of standards of behavior shared by all the political protagonists, the practical interpretation and effective implantation of institutions, the real acceptance of democracy by the governed and the elite, as well as the erection of a new political machinery that structures interests and ensures mediation between society and the state or among the various sectors of society.[13] The definition seems complete but is mainly subjective, and with good reason. In a word, consolidation for Morlino spells the end of the period of learning about the workings of democracy. The relationship of distrust which had prevailed between the various political or social sectors during the period of transition is over. Consolidation thus becomes self-confirming when the various societal sectors convince themselves that they need to and will respect the rules of the

democratic game for whatever reason: either because they are motivated by a strong normative commitment, or simply because they
reckon that this respect ensures the most viable means of retaining
some influence in a country that no longer tolerates political violence.
But what can the political or social scientist do when confronting this?
Most reasonably, abandon theoretical macrodesigns or all-encompassing comprehensive field studies in favor of studying the initial stage of
democratization, and resort to the microdesigns of much more strictly
focused investigations.

This is the road that Przeworski has taken by analyzing the whole
network of internal and external interactions which have influenced
the interconnected "games" of the economic and political reforms inherent in the turmoil of the birth of the young democracies.[14] A similar
approach is taken here by Paul Marer and Keith Crane in respect to
Hungary. Although Przeworski's approach has been stimulating
(though criticized in the past few years),[15] it has become entirely obso-
lete in light of certain recent conditions where the crucial problem
deals less with democratization than with a "primitive accumulation
of capital" ensured by a predatory privatization of the former state
property to benefit ex-nomenklaturists, now converts to a very aggressive version of the market economy. The "invisible hand" is theirs and,
for now at least, they don't care to see this process disturbed by the
operation of a democratic rule of law.

A second option stems from the return of political research to the
long-neglected institutional aspects of politics in general as well as of
democratic transitions and consolidations in particular. But, it does not
suffice for such research to proclaim, as politicians often do, that (supposedly) free multiparty elections and representative, responsible governments will bring happiness to all the peoples on earth. There is a
real need to ascertain and probe which institutional systems would
prove to be the most desirable or, at least, the least counterproductive
in the new democracies. This should be done not *in abstracto* but after
a careful examination of each practical national example in its specific
cultural and historical context.

Observed first in the mid-1980s, on the occasion of the fierce Brazil-
ian constitutional debate, the most important issue in this respect has
so far concerned the choice that the Latin American states (just emerging from military authoritarianism), had to make between their traditional presidential regimes patterned on the U.S. model and the alternative, European-styled parliamentarian regimes. Linz and Arturo
Valenzuela again threw themselves into this enterprise, with the cooperation of eminent scholars like Giovanni Sartori, Arend Lijphart, and

Ezra Suleiman, who did not belong for once to the usual circle of transitology. As suggested by the title of their collective book, *The Failure of Presidential Democracy*, their conclusion was rather pro-parliamentarian.[16] Moreover, Linz subsequently edited, with Yossi Shain, a series of studies devoted to another practical problem: the role of interim governments mixing the former authoritarian rulers and the democratic leaders.[17] In this case, the geographical and chronological scope was extended much more than in the previous volumes on presidential versus parliamentarian regimes. Oddly enough, it included none of the Latin American countries except Argentina, but embraced by contrast a substantial number of ex-communist states, including Afghanistan and Cambodia as well as the unusual examples of Iran, Portugal, and even post-World War II France. This book as well as another one edited by Douglas Greenberg, among other works,[18] show that the former Latin American provincialism of the incipient transitology is being transcended.

This is even better illustrated by the wide variety of topics selected besides those we just singled out. The theme of this book further evidences this development. Transitions, political consolidations, or regime changes are no longer neglected by mainstream social scientists. The subjects considered at present here and elsewhere include almost the whole array of political scientific query: the classical analysis of elections and parties;[19] the fields of public policies and privatization as related to the globalization process[20] (which are here considered in detail by Marer and Crane); the cruel revision of the welfare state; the revived interest in citizenship, nationality and nationalism; political identities; public opinion[21] as well as civil society (as illustrated in this book by Andrew Arato); the problem of individualistic values versus community values, or again the revisitation of democracy in the light of its changing link with the dimension of the time and of the future; and in addition not forgetting those topics no less thoroughly modified by the transformation of the space of international relations in a global sphere, as they are observed here by Braun in respect to security concerns in Hungary.

The list could be infinite, but that in itself reflects the fact that our "transitional job" has already gathered momentum. It has come of age, and this fact seems well proven by the interest that political scientists from other fields of research, such as Arend Lijphart or Michel Dobry,[22] are now showing in "transitology." Yet this job faces one serious risk, namely, forgetting the immensity of what is still left unexplored in the innumerable facets of democratization processes, and the associated danger of diluting the focus on that specific area.

Transitions From Democracy to Contradictory Desires

There is still much to be done, especially by virtue of a paradox. On the one hand, the very consideration of the remarkably successful Hungarian democratic consolidation suggests without any doubt that we have no reason to become so pessimistic about the development of "decent" democratic regimes as to abandon this field of study. Yet it reminds us, on the other hand, that the simultaneous confusion of sentiments among certain analysts who take democracy for what it is not also constitutes an inexhaustible object for research. Democracy cannot be a miraculous transformation able to redeem injustice once and for all in tropical or ex-communist countries plagued by misery and the humiliation of confronting arrogant industrialized societies. But it is precisely this mistaking of one thing for another which should probably be considered first in the analysis of democratization.

The failure of so many attempts at democratization, now complicated by the eruption of religious, ethnic, or nationalist fundamentalism, is unfortunately tending to overshadow the democratic changes achieved or under way in the Southern Hemisphere or in Central Europe. The example of India has illustrated for many years that democracy is not the privilege of affluent, Christian, and individualistic societies, while another example, Japan, demonstrates that those who thought with Karel van Wolferen that "Japanese power" perverted the true concept of democracy have been contradicted by new realities in recent years.[23]

But this does not obviate the problems of sustainability and adaptation of new and unfamiliar democratic powers. There is no reason for establishing such governments only to see them, sooner or later, collapse both because of their own mistakes and because of the disillusionment of a population which not only demands the "impossible" but does not appreciate the possibility that democracy may be nothing but a trite procedural "system of processing conflicts."[24] Disillusionment is of course not the only threat to the stability of democracies which have been freshly established in the most disastrous economic conditions accompanied by the most appalling examples of unequality. The most basic threat in fact is produced by a primordial misunderstanding of the limited nature of democracy which in turn demands a new mapping of topics.

Traditionally, an all-embracing topic dealt with the governance, understood in the broadest sense, of societies belonging first to what we used to call the Third World, and more recently to the former communist sphere. It had been assessed for many decades that democracy constituted a privilege for the rich nations, and that helping and transforming the poor ones required more assertive or even more authoritarian governments in order to resist what Albert Hirschman has called the "tunnel effect," that is, the counterproductive turmoil generated by impatient and premature demands of needy populations who want to allocate for immediate consumption the early and precarious benefits of economic growth. Instead, these benefits should be devoted to the pursuit of long-term development. Certainly this was the contention, for instance, of Samuel Huntington and Gunnar Myrdal in the 1960s and 1970s.[25]

More recently, however, the bankruptcy of state-run collectivist economies of all types signaled (at least) the temporary death knell of such stern assessments. For one, the notion of the "third wave" of democratization of the 1990s[26] impelled some optimistic refurbishing of the merits of democracy in terms of its capacity for good developmental governance. The argument (or motto) wielded in defense of the democratic way of decision making contrasted its transparency with the unpredictable arbitrariness of brutal authoritarian rule. Democracy it was argued provided for thorough discussion and consultation on economic policies, whereas dictatorships, it was contended, were simply masquerading as systems providing strategic steadiness and tactical flexibility. And since political stability conditions development, it was further argued that democratic governments could ensure overall stability based on possible popular consensus for immediate sacrifices made for the sake of the long-term well-being of society. Democratic systems could do this much better than others who could achieve this only by force. And there was an additional argument, namely, that there exists irrefutable functional linkage between the representative and even the social version of our democratic institutions and the free market economy. Hayek as well as Karl Marx or Jürgen Habermas would have been reconciled to this latter point.

Unfortunately, this comforting evaluation did not last long. It is indeed being challenged by a return of development directed from above by iron-handed though not overtly dictatorial governments. It was during the wave of rapid, brilliant, and record-breaking economic successes by the New Industrial Countries (NICs) or "small dragons" of East Asia, that ex-president Lee Kuan Yew of Singapore asserted this compromising recommendation when he stated: "I would say that democracy is not conducive to rapid growth when you are in an agricultural society. . . . Without military rule or dictatorship or authoritarian government in Korea and Taiwan, I doubt whether they could have transformed themselves so quickly." He even added, "During their own rise to wealth, most of them [the European countries] were just as authoritarian as Asia is today."[27]

This declaration was nothing but personal opinion (and its relevance seems now severely contradicted by the financial and monetary crisis in Southeast Asia). But this does not prevent it from being given much academic and political weight when the Oxford University Press published, two years later, a World Bank-commissioned report entitled *The East Asian Miracle*.[28] In examining what should be the appropriate role of public policies in economic development, this report stressed more diplomatically the crucial importance of the intervention of a strongly centralized state. Thus, we are back to some of the basics in the sense that the scope of politics becomes again reduced to a question of who can run the economy best.

Do strong states provide automatically the requisites of political stability, control of social unrest, and the economic continuity required for a steady process of development? While general Pinochet's dictatorship in Chile seemed to confirm this assumption, did the poor performance of the military regime in Argentina contradict it? Is a strong state necessarily undemocratic and authoritarian, or is democracy the unavoidable condition for the legitimation of real political authority? These are questions worth raising.

Another seminal question concerns the notion of majority rule in emerging democracies in various parts of the world. A still substantial number of political scientists openly or subtly continue to push for a democracy greatly resembling a Western model. In contrast to the popularity in Western democracies of the doctrine of multiculturalism, they keep endorsing, mainly as a product for export, Rousseau's idea of the general will. They still think in principle that this will has to be expressed through the mechanism of an all-purpose and reversible majority rule, based in turn on the assumption that social interests are at the same time legitimately diverse, and, when in conflict, bound for democratic conciliation.

Though Bernard Manin for instance has already argued that majority rule is nothing but a contingency or opportunistic device serving uniquely the procedural necessities of democracy,[29] the point here is not that this rule is often mistakenly equated with a definition of democracy. The real difficulty is that those who share this interpretation overlook its logical consequences of majority rule. They wax indignant at the consequences in social contexts where the legitimacy of a plurality of interests is rejected as a destructive Western concept or considered as a mere protection given to small permanent minorities. But they ignore the fact that what disturbs them is caused less by the evil nature of these communities than by the quite predictable negative effects of the export of our principle of majority rule. It is this ignorance which drives the prejudice against the different rationality of the Iranian revolution in particular and of the Islamic concept of democracy in general. And it is curtailing to what is a justified castigation of the slaughters perpetrated in Africa. For these bloodbaths are indeed an appalling consequence of an inevitable primordial ethnic interpretation or manipulation of the majority rule. As David Miller reminds us, the concept of citizenship is based on a principle of reciprocity or a cooperative scheme.[30] Unfortunately, this sentiment of reciprocity hardly exits between the different African ethnic groups. This is the reason why the advocates of majoritarianism in these states are prone to converting democracy into a form of criminal tyranny.

The point here, of course, is not to justify bloodshed or ill-disguised tyrannies in the name of some inhumane cultural pluralism, but this discussion hopefully makes the case for discarding two misconceptions: one which claims that young democracies have to unquestioningly emulate the older ones (classic representative pluralist regime), and the other symmetrical one which assumes the absolute impossibility and illegitimacy of any kind of original democratic invention in the young democracies. Neither of these simplistic positions is defensible.

We in the West need to restrain our pride in our own democracy in order to confront the evidence of the terrible miscarriage of majority power among ethnic groups not only in other regions but in Europe as well. As unpalatable as it may seem, this deplorable development is indirectly related to the overriding idea of territorial democracy which is now called into question even in Europe and North America. (It deserves particular criticism in the rest of the world.) In Western industrialized societies, democratic citizenship and nationality have been intentionally mingled in such a way that they incorporate a specific form of political allegiance combining the possession of civic rights with its compulsory attachment to the territory of a national state. Yet, as Michel Foucault believed, it is obvious that our current, smug Western democratic governments employ what amounts to a technique of coercive national control that is inconsistent with the libertarian dimension of pure democracy.

This is precisely the reason why it makes no sense to argue dogmatically that the genuine, democratic citizen must inevitably belong to a body politic that is confined within specific territorial boundaries. Territorial attachment may be a fact that this is a result of historical development and not a logical derivation of democratic theory. And though it may be unsettling for us, we may need to dissociate democracy from the territorial nation. Then it would become possible at last to create room for a new body politic, amalgamating citizenship with some reasonable ethnic component instead of forcing it into some desperately inaccessible ideological allegiance.

In considering communities which reject the values of individualistic democracy, more evidence emerges of the problems of transition. We need however to view this broadly instead of restricting it to its most extreme form—what could be called the Iranian–Islamic syndrome. And we need to be more receptive to this key point: the whole fabric of democracy must comprise two interdependent elements, represented on the one hand by its institutional and contributory instruments, and on the other by something which is nothing more than its populist appeal. In our societies, the daily routine of politics has superseded the communitarian dream of popular unanimity by the political amusement—one produced by the continuous and theatrical show biz of political marketing. But as at the time of the fall of the Bastille, populism which is deplored here in the West as the worst demagogic civic profanity remains the most fundamental pillar of political legitimation at the outset of young democracies where the prestige of constitutionalism cannot quench the thirst for dignity of the newly proclaimed People's Power. As in the Republic of the Philippines in 1986, Haiti, Brazil, or Russia and Iran, these peoples desire passionately charismatic leaders able to confirm their desire for a unanimous "omnicratic" communion, totally alien to our concept of conflicting plural interests. (Years ago, David Riesman could have labeled these peoples as "communion-oriented" in the face of supposedly "pluralist-oriented" Western citizens.)

The only additional remark to be made about this inclination is a word of caution against the oversimplification of such a holistic view. The dwellers in the young democracies do not consider us in the West as individualistic extraterrestrials deprived of faith and of any sense of communitarian solidarity. They are rather of two minds, prompted to discard the mean mechanisms of Western democracy under the pressure of their political, religious, or social masters, but equally imbued with individualistic personal desires. This confusion of sentiments is what complicates matters and makes the unpredictability of the future of democracy even greater. In the young democracies, the populist appeal on the one hand can be acceptable as a basic source of legitimacy whenever it contributes to the creation of what Miller calls a "commonality"—a shared sentiment of open citizenship.[31] On the other hand, it turns out to be thoroughly antidemocratic when it promotes or reinforces the idea of a "community" based exclusively on nonpolitical links such as ethnicity, religion, or language.

There is yet an apparently more pressing and immediate issue. It arises out of the return to power of ex-communists, now rebaptized socialists, in Central or Eastern Europe and especially in Hungary (until their defeat in May 1998). Does such a return threaten the progress of democratization in this region? Or could it provide, by contrast, the fresh political resources capable of restoring the lost confidence of the populations of these states? This is at once a practical and a theoretical dilemma. In *Democracy and the Market*, Adam Przeworski was not in a position to confront this problem, as he wrote his book before the "return of the left" and focused the study on the initial reciprocal agendas of economic and political reforms. But what is to occur once these reforms, mired in difficulties, have been carried out without yielding any demonstrably positive result in the daily life of the people and, consequently, without confirming the legitimacy of the new democratic regime? Since they have already spoiled all their credibility, it would be pointless to imagine that discredited real or ersatz democratic leaders could resume their positions and policies just by revising their strategies. There is thus no other choice than to appreciate that the only probative research must aim at ascertaining in each particular case the expected effects of what we could name as the "paradox of the Friends and Foes."

This paradox does not concern the designation of an external enemy which serves to strengthen the internal cohesion of a state as was defined by Carl Schmitt. It deals instead with the political role that the former authoritarian or totalitarian "enemies" of democracy can play after prevailing in competitive elections through which they gained new legitimacy via the ballots (as is or has been the case in Hungary, Bulgaria, Poland, and other countries or as they failed by a small margin to do in Russia). Quite different cases have to be distinguished in this respect. Some of these returnees clearly just simulate their conversion to political freedom and to a market society. But a great many did not come from the higher nomenklatura; they were just opportunist communists, alien to the official ideology living in societies where being a member of the communist party was pivotal to upwards social mobility. When it appears, by chance, that these "flexible pretenders" are the only ones among the current politicians able to alleviate the disillusionment of the governed and enhance confidence, then this becomes more than a matter for mere observation. There is a need for the serious assessment of this paradox.

And it is worth adding to what has been done already[32] more detailed empirical research, comparing the performance of the genuine democratic leaders who came to power at the beginning of the transition, with that of their transformed adversaries in the subsequent stage of at least possible consolidation. Twenty years ago, leaders such as King Juan Carlos and his Prime Minister Adolfo Suarez of Spain provided persuasive evidence that men trained in Franco's authoritarian seraglio were also experts in its demolition. And more recently, President Menem of Argentina demonstrated that a Peronist was able to consolidate a democracy which had been disintegrating under the guidance of a more presentable democrat such as Raul Alfonsin. Of course, there is no general law mandating that democracies in the making are best served by those who know perfectly well what nondemocracy is. But why not admit that it is a possibility, even in some postcommunist or African countries.

An Opportunity to Revisit Democracy

There is, of course, much more to be said about the ways and means of past and present democratic transitions and consolidations. At present, it goes without saying that the people who rose up and continue to rise up in revolt in Africa and Asia do so, or will do so, not so much *for* the sake of democracy *as against* their former leaders. At the same time, everybody realizes that the greatest danger for Eastern Europe is that the fragile and very imperfect democratic governments established there are becoming the target of populist movements. When hopes have been set too high, failure militates in turn against those who were cherished only the day before but who are now seen as corrupt, incompetent, or disappointing. Yet the most agonizing fact is that the very unpredictability of political processes (which are never predetermined to succeed) is presenting even more dangers than before by virtue of the connection established between democracy and a free market economy. But this very uncertainty in transitology is, at the same time, what gives us a chance to revisit, more globally, the universe of democratization in order to gain a better understanding of what it means for us.

This goal perhaps could be expressed in Hans-Georg Gadamer's terms, though not in his conservative spirit; that is, as a "fusion of horizons" interpreted as an effort of rapprochement between the world we are used to and from which we cannot hope to detach ourselves, and other quite different worlds that we are painfully trying to understand.[33] In so doing, we could, perhaps, overcome the prejudice that leads us to be surprised to find mixed popular feelings in the postcommunist states (though such mixed feelings also exist closer to home). And this rediscovery should also confirm that no general paradigm can explain any political phenomenon much less transition to democracy or ephemeral democracies. If one certainty remains, it is that a democratic government in its initial stage cannot be analyzed or judged in the same terms as an advanced democratic regime. In terms of the former, our guiding principle should be: Insofar as a democracy is new, what level and type of democratization can it attain under current conditions?

Notes

1. Philippe C. Schmitter, "Still the Century of Corporatism?" *The Review of Politics* 36 (1), 1974.

2. Jean Kirkpatrick, "Dictatorship and Double Standard," *Commentary* 68 (5), 1979.

3. Adam Przeworski, "Ama a incerteza e seras democratico," *Novos estudos* (CEBRAP) (9), 1984.

4. Adam Przeworski, et al., *Dilemas da consolidacao da democracia*, Sao Paulo, Paz e Terra, 1989, 19.

5. Javier Santiso, "De la condition historique des transitologues en Amerique latine et en Europe Centrale and Orientale," *Revue internationale de politique comparee* 3 (1), 1996.

6. See also Anders Åslund, P. Boone, and Johnson, "How to Stabilize: Lessons from Post-Communist Countries," Washington: Brookings Institution, *Brookings Papers on Economic Activity* 26 (1), 1996; J.R. Kluegel, D.S. Mason, and B. Wegener, eds., *Social Justice and Political Change: Public Opinion in Capitalist and Post-Communist States*, (New York: Aldine de Gruyter, 1995).

7. Juan Linz, and Alfred Stepan, eds., *The Breakdown of Democratic Regimes*, 4 volumes (Baltimore: The Johns Hopkins Press, 1978).

8. Guillermo O'Donnell, Phillipe Schmitter, and Lawrence Whitehead, eds., *Transitions from Authoritarian Rule* (Baltimore: The Johns Hopkins Press, 4 volumes, 1986).

9. Enrique Baylora, ed., *Comparing New Democracies: Transition and Consolidation in Mediterranean Europe and the Southern Cone* (Boulder: Westview Press, 1987).

10. James Malloy and M.A. Seligson, eds., *Authoritarians and Democrats: The Politics of Regime Transition in Latin America* (Pittsburgh: University of Pittsburgh Press, 1987).

11. Larry Diamond, Juan Linz, and Seymour Martin Lipset, eds., *Democracy in Developing Countries* (Boulder: Lynne Rienner Publisher, 1991).

12. Juan Linz, and Alfred Stepan, eds., *Problems of Democratic Transition and Consolidation* (Baltimore: The Johns Hopkins Press, 1996).

13. L. Morlino, "Consolidacion, democratica: definicion, modelos, hipotesis," *Revista espanola de investigaciones sociologicas* 39, 1986.

14. Adam Przeworski, *Democracy and the Market* (Cambridge: Cambridge University Press, 1991).

15. J. Elster, "The Necessity and Impossibility of Simultaneous Economic and Political Reforms" in D. Greenberg, et al., eds., *Constitutionalism and Democracy: Transitions in the Comtemporary World*, (Oxford: Oxford University Press, 1993).

16. Juan Linz, and A. Valenzuela, eds., *The Failure of Presidential Democracy* (Baltimore: The Johns Hopkins Press, 1994).

17. Juan Linz, and Y. Shain, eds., *Between States: Interim Governments and Democratic Transitions* (Cambridge: Cambridge University Press, 1995).

18. D. Greenberg, et al., eds., *Constitutionalism and Democracy: Transitions in the Comtemporary World* (Oxford: Oxford University Press, 1993).

19. I. Crew, "Voters, Parties, and Leaders Thirty Years On: Western Electoral Studies and the New Democracies of Eastern Europe" in I. Budge and D. McKay, eds., *Developing Democracy* (London: Sage, 1994); G. Wightman, ed., *Party Formation in East-Central Europe* (Aldershot, Hants: Edward Elgar, 1994).

20. J. Sachs, and A. Warner, "Economic Reform and the Process of Global Integration," Washington: Brookings Institution, *Brookings Papers on Economic Activity* 25 (1), 1995.

21. J.R. Kluegel, D.S. Mason, and B. Wegener, eds., *Social Justice and Political Change: Public Opinion in Capitalist and Post-Communist States* (New York: Aldine de Gruyter, 1995).

22. B. Crawford, and A. Lijphart, "Explaining Political Change and Economic Change in Post-Communist Eastern Europe: Old legacies, New Institutions, Hegemonic Norms and International Pressure," *Comparative Political Studies* 28, 1995; M. Dobry, "Les processus de transition a la democratie," *Cultures et conflicts* 17, 1995.

23. Karel van Wolferen, *The Enigma of Japanese Power* (London: Macmillan, 1989).

24. Adam Przeworski, *Democracy and the Market* (Cambridge: Cambridge University Press, 1991), 12.

25. Samuel P. Huntington, *Political Order in Changing Societies* (New Haven: Yale University Press, 1968); G. Myrdal, *Le drame de l'Asie* (Paris: Seuil, 1976).

26. Samuel P. Huntington, *The Third Wave* (Norman: University of Oklahoma Press, 1991).

27. Lee Kuan Yew, "A Map Here, in the Mind", *The Economist* 320 (7713), 1991, 18–20.

28. World Bank, *The East Asian Miracle* (Oxford: Oxford University Press, 1993).

29. B. Manin, "On Legitimacy and Political Deliberation," *Political Theory* (15), 1987.

30. D. Miller, *On Nationality* (Oxford: The Clarendon Press, 1995), 71.

31. *Ibid.*, 140.

32. M. Waller, "Adaptation of the Former Communist Party of East-Central Europe: A Case of Social Democratization?" *Party Politics*, October 1995.

33. H.G. Gadamer, *Truth and Method* (London: Sheed and Ward, 1975).

Chapter 3

Transitions and Elites

John Higley

Gaetano Mosca, Vilfredo Pareto, and Robert Michels, the fathers of elite theory, tell us that second only to the inevitability of elites is their persistence, and this in two respects. First, through the control of major organizations, as well as through wealth, family connections, and privileged educations, the grip of elites on power and influence is so strong that they are dislodged only in the most extreme circumstances. Although individuals move into and out of elite positions, mainly in step with the life cycle, a large circulation of elites is rare. Second, the political relations between elite groups and the norms regulating them—what Pareto thought of as the order or system of elites—are entrenched. Relations of distrust and enmity, or of accommodation and cooperation, are reproduced across generations. Pareto thought that over the long haul elites do degenerate, becoming less capable of combining force and persuasion to sustain their dominance and more at odds with mass sentiments. There must eventually be a "sudden and violent disturbance," analogous to a river overflowing its banks, in which existing elites are swept away and replaced by new elites more capable of ruling and more in tune with the masses.[1] But short of such revolutionary upheavals, elite formations are highly persistent.

The study of regime transitions needs to pay more attention to this axiom about elite persistence. Transitions that involve significant change in elite composition and elite relations differ importantly in their processes and outcomes from those in which elites remain largely unchanged. The former transitions alter the character of politics and produce what Juan Linz and Alfred Stepan call "out-of-type" or fundamentally different regimes; the latter transitions involve minor, relatively superficial changes in political institutions and patterns amounting to new "within-type" regimes.[2] The extent of elite persistence during regime transitions is, thus, critically important. Four broad patterns are worth investigating:

1. Modal: There is not much change in the composition or relations of elites. A few top political leaders are knocked off their perches, but they are quickly replaced by people around or behind them. Most elite groups, their codes of behavior, and the conflicts and rivalries between them, persist. Although the proximity of some cliques and persons to government executive power is altered, the transition is primarily a game of elite musical chairs.

2. Revolutionary: There is wholesale change in both the composition and relations of elites. Not only political but also most state administrative, economic, military, media, and professional elites are displaced by a doctrinaire counterelite that wins a revolutionary struggle or that is imposed by an external power through military conquest. The newly ascendant counterelite builds a sharply centralized and coercive regime aimed at transforming society to accord with its doctrinal precepts.

3. Settlement: There is not much change in the composition of elites, but established leaders of warring elite camps negotiate a sudden, deliberate, and relatively comprehensive "settlement" involving compromises of core disputes. The result is a much more integrated set of elites whose competitions are more restrained and whose relations are more mutually accommodating. This lays the basis for a stable democratic regime.

4. Implosion: Coincident with the sudden decompression or grave weakening of state apparata, there is an abrupt but usually nonviolent exodus of top political leaders, much movement of elite persons between positions and sectors, and a fragmenting of elite relations. The transition involves reconstituting the state, possibly with new territorial boundaries. The regime that emerges reflects the fluid composition and fragmented relations of elites, and its trajectory is, therefore, quite uncertain.

I want to show how these four patterns improve our understanding of regime transitions and the politics they portend. I begin with some general observations about elite circulations, elite relations, and regime transitions.

Transitions and Elite Circulations

Elites are the several thousand persons who hold top positions in large or otherwise powerful organizations and movements and who participate in or directly influence political decision making.[3] The extent of elite circulation and the character of elite relations vary between countries and within some countries over time. These variations are critical determinants of political regimes, defined as basic patterns in the organization, exercise, and transfer of government executive power. There are, of course, multiple determinants of regimes.[4] Nevertheless, the circulation and relations of elites are often decisive for the basic character of new regimes, and they are not simply manifestations or products of other regime determinants.

Many types of political regimes have been distinguished, but I adopt the most central and familiar typology: democratic, authoritarian, and totalitarian regimes. In this, I follow the well-known distinctions that Juan Linz, often in association with Alfred Stepan, has drawn between these types, including a "sultanistic" variant of authoritarian regimes and a "post-totalitarian" variant of totalitarian regimes.[5] I make, however, a distinction between stable and unstable regimes. Although there are no agreed-upon definitions of regime stability and instability, most comparativists would accept that a key element is the occurrence or perceived likelihood of irregular, forcible seizures of government executive power through coups and uprisings. Where such seizures have recently occurred or been attempted, or where political practitioners and informed observers think they are likely events, a regime is unstable. Conversely, where there has been no recent resort to power seizures and there is no wide expectation of them, a regime can be considered stable.

Regime transitions always involve increased elite circulation. The key questions are its scope and mode. The scope of circulation has two dimensions: range and depth. It is important to ask if the circulation associated with a transition is narrow or wide—whether only the most prominent and politically exposed position holders are replaced, or incumbents of elite positions across the board are changed. It is also important to ask if circulation is shallow or deep—whether new elites are drawn from second-echelon positions within existing political and social hierarchies and, thus, represent the established elite social type, or they come from far down political and social hierarchies or even from outside them (i.e., from exile, prison, or an illegal underground movement). The dimensions of range and depth tend to co-vary: wide circulations typically bring many persons to power and influence who were previously distant from elite positions. The other key question about elite circulation is its mode. What is the speed and manner in which it occurs? Circulations may be sudden and coerced, as in violent revolutionary overthrows, or gradual and negotiated, with elites being replaced incrementally through voluntary resignations, retirements, and transfers.

The scope and mode of elite circulation are of obvious importance. Yet, we know relatively little about how they influence regime transitions. One problem is that our imagery of circulation, which is colored by Pareto's theory of revolution, leads us to expect more circulation than usually occurs. A related problem is our tendency to see existing elites as preventing desired ends such as democracy and freedom, and this leads us to assume, too readily in my view, that the more circulation there is during transitions, the better the outcomes will be. The possibility that large amounts of elite circulation often produce quite undesirable outcomes receives too little attention.

As an empirical matter, in most regime transitions the scope of circulation is narrow and shallow. Only the top political leaders—chief executives and cabinet ministers, some party leaders and parliamentarians—are affected. Second-echelon political elites, especially those in regional centers and units beyond the national capital, remain in place or move to newly vacant positions in the capital. Changes in the makeup of state administrative, economic, military, media, and professional elites, who stand at some distance from the apex of government power, are usually quite limited. Empirically, elite circulation in most transitions mainly involves reshuffles of position holding. Circulations of such limited scope are characteristic of transitions to within-type regimes (for example, between the several military regimes in Nigeria during recent decades). Circulations that are similarly limited in scope, but whose mode is sudden and coerced, characterize transitions from sultanistic to authoritarian regimes (for example, forced retirements or overthrows of the charismatic but despotic leaders who founded or soon took over many postcolonial regimes in Africa).

The scope of elite circulations is wider and deeper, and their mode is more frequently sudden and coerced, in transitions to out-of-type regimes. In revolutionary transitions to totalitarian regimes, there is wholesale liquidation and replacement of existing elites by a previously excluded or peripheral counterelite (as in Russia after 1917 and the Soviet Union after 1922, China after 1949, Cuba after 1960, Iran after 1979). In nonrevolutionary transitions from democratic to authoritarian regimes via military coups or takeovers by strong plebiscitary movements, there is usually a thorough replacement of political, media, and trade union elites (as in the fascist takeovers in Italy and Germany, General Francisco Franco's victory in Spain, General Augusto Pinochet's coup in Chile), but with administrative, business, military, and professional elites left largely untouched. In reverse transitions from authoritarian to democratic regimes, the scope and mode of circulation are more situationally contingent. Where a democratic transition results from defeat in warfare, a thorough replacement of political, media, and military elites, but a quite limited replacement of administrative, business, and professional elites, typically occurs (as in Germany and Japan after defeat in World War II).[6] However, where an authoritarian regime gives way through negotiations with its opponents, there is little elite circulation and, instead, much reshuffling of position holding within the political elite and between it and other elites, especially after the first democratic elections are held. This pattern, which has unfolded in a number of countries during the third wave of democratization (for example, Brazil, Chile, Peru, South Korea, Spain, Taiwan, Uruguay), characterized the democratic transitions in Hungary and Poland during 1989–90, which I will discuss below.

I merely want to suggest at this point that elite circulations that are limited in their scope and negotiated in their mode appear to be propitious for transitions to stable democracies. Where circulation is wide, deep, sudden, and coerced, new elites are so politically inexperienced, so concerned with consolidating power and on pursuing rigid agendas that the restrained competitions and policy trade-offs necessary for stable democracy are unlikely to result. On the other hand, if a democratic transition entails virtually no circulation, new democratic institutions and processes may amount to little more than tools with which entrenched elites fend off challengers by rigging elections and resorting to demagogic and plebiscitary stratagems against challengers. Too much or too little elite circulation is likely, in short, to prevent or undermine democratic transitions.

Transitions and Elite Relations

How elite circulation affects regime transitions is only half the story. Equally important are continuities and changes in elite relations. There is no hard and fast connection between amounts of elite circulation and changes in elite relations.[7] In transitions that involve little circulation, elites may nevertheless achieve basic accommodations, learn from past mistakes, undergo ideological conversions, or begin to emulate patterns they discern in other countries. Alternatively, transitions in which no large circulations occur may merely perpetuate elite distrusts and resentments. By itself, the extent of circulation does not reliably indicate the resulting character of elite politics; attention must be paid to how elite relations persist or change, independent of circulation.

For this purpose, I suggest that we draw a basic distinction between united and disunited elites. United elites are characterized by joint, concerted, and continuing political actions, and, therefore, by common political purposes; they are "united" in the sense that they are closely linked to each other in one or more distinctive ways. The persons and groups making up disunited elites, by contrast, are divided and isolated from each other; they lack strong bonds and the common purposes on which bonds would rest. Let me briefly elaborate this distinction by considering three fairly obvious patterns.

Elites in stable democracies are affiliated with competing and conflicting parties, movements, policy programs, and beliefs. They subscribe, however, to norms about the desirability and proprieties of restrained political competitions, and they are linked through overlapping and interlocking networks that amount to vast "webworks" of elite power and influence.[8] As Pareto saw, the most important elite groups in stable democracies constitute what are in effect cartels, the members of which essentially scratch each other's backs.[9] They form what may be called a "consensually united" national elite because shared understandings and uncoerced but inclusive interaction networks enable diverse and competing groups to coexist in relative harmony. The complex structure and behavior of consensually united elites involve many ambiguities that generate scholarly and popular debates about the "true" character of such elites.[10] When viewed comparatively or historically, however, it becomes apparent that such elites are more internally accommodating and restrained in their political behaviors and relations than are elites in most other countries or historical periods. Consider, for example, the pacific competitions among British elites and the internecine struggles among French elites throughout the eighteenth, nineteenth, and first two-thirds of the twentieth centuries; or, again, consider the restrained competitions and accommodative relations among Spanish elites during the past twenty years and their deeply conflicted relations during any previous period in Spain's modern history.

There is another, radically different kind of united elite. In it, all or most persons and groups belong to a single party or movement, and they uniformly profess its distinctive ideology, religious doctrine, or ethnonationalist creed. This is an "ideocratically united" elite because of the importance of an official belief system for elite action and organization.[11] In such an elite, there is necessarily much coercion: some group has gotten the upper hand, imposed its beliefs on all other groups, and closely monitors the profession of those beliefs in order to weed out troublemakers. There is a semiformal hierarchy that runs through the single party or movement so that persons are in effect licensed for elite positions according to their ideocratic fidelity and their party or movement connections. Although economic development may promote functional specialization within the elite, the semiformal hierarchy and the requirement to affirm official shibboleths loosen very slowly. Until the late 1980s, elites in the Soviet Union and its satellite countries in Eastern Europe (except Poland, as discussed below) were good examples of ideocratically united elites.

In most countries and times, however, elites are neither consensually nor ideocratically united. They are, instead, basically disunited. Persons and groups adhere to conflicting beliefs and norms of political behavior, dispute the worth of existing institutions, view politics in winner-take-all terms, and engage in unrestrained struggles for dominance. Typically, two or three elite camps face each other in fairly open warfare. There is a climate of fear and insecurity. One camp is ascendant, controlling the government and backed up by military and police forces, though it perceives itself to be threatened mortally by its opponents. The struggle between opposing camps consequently has a no-holds-barred character. Although there may be long periods during which the ascendant camp clings to government power, intrigues within it, as well as uprisings, riots, and terrorist actions fomented by opposing camps, generate deep and repeated political crises.

These distinctions between disunited and two kinds of united elites are, of course, simplifications. In reality, most groups have nothing to gain in a war of all against all, so no set of elites is completely disunited (though recent chaotic and savage struggles among elites in Liberia, Sierra Leone, and Somalia have come close to this extreme condition). Conversely, elites in all countries and times compete for advantage, so no national elite is ever fully united. Elite professions of ideocratic unanimity always conceal doctrinal disputes and much jockeying for power, while elite expressions of unbridgeable oppositions in countries like Britain or the United States conceal an underlying consensus and many more or less unacknowledged policy compromises. The extent to which elites are disunited or united is, in short, a matter of degree, fluctuating with changing circumstances, and the ambiguities of elite behavior make its assessment difficult. I nevertheless believe that the modalities of elite relations, especially when they are viewed comparatively or historically, can be seen to differ in these disunited or united respects between countries or within some countries over time. Once they are created, moreover, they tend to be highly persistent.

In Western Europe during the nineteenth century and earlier, disunited elites operating unstable authoritarian regimes were the rule. Two exceptions were Britain and Sweden, where the main opposing elite camps became consensually united through crisis-induced settlements—in England's Glorious Revolution of 1688–89, and in Sweden's constitutional revolution of 1809.[12] A consensual fusion of Dutch provincial elites following the collapse of French military occupation in 1813, and an accommodation achieved by Swiss elites after a brief civil war in 1848 made the Netherlands and Switzerland two further exceptions to the general European pattern. After their settlements, fusion, or accommodation, competing party elites in all four countries made restrained appeals for support by conservative or liberal segments of sharply limited electorates, and on that basis they took peaceful turns operating representative, protodemocratic regimes that have lasted, albeit in greatly evolved democratic form, to this day. During the nineteenth century, however, all other national elites in Western Europe were disunited. This was true of Belgium after national independence in 1830, Denmark down to the confrontation between monarch and Parliament in 1901, France despite a handful of regime transitions during the sixty years between Napoleon's downfall and defeat in the Franco-Prussian War, Italy after unification in the 1860s, and Portugal and Spain amid much political warfare and many regime upsets. During the last quarter of the nineteenth century, to be sure, all of these countries had regimes featuring popularly elected parliaments, but the parliaments were less than sovereign, electoral participations, and processes were subject to many limitations and distortions, political crises were frequent and deep, and prospects for continued representative government were highly uncertain.

In Central and Eastern Europe during the nineteenth century, aristocratic landed elites operated powerful monarchical–military states through which they repressed elites at the head of bourgeois and tiny working-class forces. Assassinations, attempted coups, and uprisings testified to the disunited elite configuration in the Austro–Hungarian, Ottoman, and Russian empires throughout the century. After Germany's unification in 1871, Prussian aristocratic and military elites kept liberal bourgeois and revolutionary socialist elites from serious power. Outside Europe, socially exclusive but disunited elites operating unstable, almost always authoritarian regimes persisted in Latin America, Japan, China, and Thailand. Virtually all other political entities were in the grip of European colonial rule. Consensually united elites and stable, protodemocratic regimes were, thus, limited to the four West European countries mentioned above, plus British-settled countries that had achieved or were moving toward independence from British colonial rule (the United States from the 1780s, the Australian and New Zealand home-rule colonies from about 1850, and Canada from 1867).

Transitions to democratic regimes have comprised one of the twentieth century's most prominent trends. But wars and revolutions, together with the crumbling of European colonial empires, have generated an equally prominent countertrend toward authoritarian and totalitarian regimes. I want to take brief stock of twentieth-century regime transitions, especially those that have occurred recently in Central and Eastern Europe, by viewing them in terms of the four patterns of elite persistence and change that I sketched at the outset.

The Modal Pattern: Unchanged Elites and Unstable Regimes

Regime transitions involving little change in the composition and relations of elites have been the twentieth century's modal pattern. In Latin America, with a handful of exceptions noted below, struggles between entrenched but disunited elites produced numerous oscillations between authoritarian and putatively democratic regimes. During the century's second half, struggles between less entrenched but even more disunited elites produced similar oscillations in most newly independent countries of sub-Saharan Africa. This was also the case in countries such as Bangladesh, Pakistan, Thailand, and Turkey. In the Middle East and North Africa after about 1950 (apart from Israel, for a while Lebanon, and eventually Iran), elites associated with mainly sultanistic regimes held sway, often brutally, over democratizing opponents and fundamentalist exponents of Islam. The most common pattern in non-communist East and Southeast Asian countries was also that of elites based in militaries or hegemonic parties operating strong authoritarian regimes.

This modal pattern has had three broad origins, which were not mutually exclusive. One was the forced integration of elites located in quasi-independent territories and regions into territorially and administratively centralized national states. Integration involved the repression of state-resisting elites by state-building ones, with lasting hostilities being the usual result.[13] A second origin was the face-off in preindustrial societies between elites at the head of entrenched aristocratic and landed strata and elites leading emerging business, professional, and other modernizing organizations and strata.[14] A third origin was the dismantling of colonial empires (including, between 1989–1991, the Soviet empire) and the birth of many postcolonial states with elites that had little previous opportunity to practice restrained and representative politics and that found support principally by mobilizing ethnic, religious, and linguistic communities against each other.[15]

In the modal pattern, political crises trigger regime transitions in which dominant elites often acquiesce in new democratic institutions and processes rather than risk wider struggles they might lose. During the last quarter of the twentieth century, acquiescence in such democratic transitions has been a prominent feature of politics in Latin America, sub-Saharan Africa, and non-communist East and Southeast Asia. This was in part because affluent Western countries and international lending agencies made economic support contingent on such democratic transitions, and in part because overtly authoritarian and totalitarian alternatives lost credibility. It is possible that these late twentieth-century transitions signify the modal pattern's attenuation, i.e., most of the democratic transitions that took place will not be reversed and the frail democratic regimes to which they led will acquire stability and substance through electoral competitions that gradually induce elite accommodation and restraint.[16] Many comparativists are not optimistic on this score, however.[17] The absence of much elite circulation and changed elite relations from the disunited to the consensually united condition implies that many, perhaps most, of these democratic transitions were further iterations of the modal pattern.

Do the recent transitions to post-communist democratic regimes in Central and Eastern Europe conform to this pattern? The Bulgarian, Romanian, and Slovakian transitions appeared, at least initially, to do so. In Bulgaria and Romania, the persistence of former communist elites was marked, and no basic accommodation with weak and fragmented opposition elites occurred. Zhelyu Zhelev, Bulgaria's president from 1990 until 1996, observed that in his country persons and groups associated with the old communist regime retained the upper hand through an "over-weaning state," a "malign type of corporatism," and a rhetoric that "harks back to Kafka's Castle and the corridors of communist power."[18] In the midst of a profound economic crisis in early 1997, however, opposition elites won the Bulgarian presidency and a majority of parliamentary seats. Their victory produced significant circulation within the political elite, though there was no indication that a basic elite accommodation occurred. It is doubtful that, by itself, the elite circulation that occurred in 1997 set Bulgaria on the road to a stable democratic regime.

In Romania, the Communist Party and army leaders who toppled Nicolae Ceausescu at Christmas 1989 continued to control the country through a coalition of "communostalgic" and ultranationalist parties, dominated by President Ion Iliescu's Party of Social Democracy. Although this ruling coalition was finally defeated in elections during November 1996, the opposition coalition that replaced it consisted of more than a dozen small and politically inexperienced groups, Iliescu's party remained the largest in Parliament, and business, state administrative, judicial, and media elites continued to be laced with persons who held high positions in the communist regime.[19] After making a promising start at democratic and economic reforms during 1997, the multiparty coalition that took power in late 1996 began to fragment, and political deadlock was apparent by early 1998. As with Bulgaria, there is no compelling reason to judge Romania as securely on the road to a stable democratic regime.

As a consequence of how the Czechoslovak communist regime collapsed in late 1989 (see below) and of how Czechoslovakia then divided at the end of 1992, elite circulation in Slovakia was greater during the early 1990s than in Bulgaria or Romania.[20] But after 1992, Vladimir Meciar, the former communist and strongly populist prime minister, and his associates purged opponents from elite positions and stifled political discourse through control of the state-owned media. Meciar engaged in ugly moves to dislodge President Michal Kovac from office, install himself in the presidency, and make the office more powerful by altering the constitution. By having his parliamentary forces refuse to vote for a new president when Kovac's term ended in March 1998, thus leaving the presidency empty, Meciar arrogated most presidential powers to his prime ministerial position. A series of peremptory moves by Meciar to further consolidate power followed and showed disdain for accommodative democratic processes. It would, therefore, be a rash observer who sees Slovakia as moving toward stable democracy.

In sum, although there has been some amount of circulation within the political elites of Bulgaria, Romania, and Slovakia, it has been narrow in scope and shallow in depth, mostly occurred well after formal transitions to democracy took place, and has not been accompanied by any basic reduction in intra-elite hostility and distrust. To date, all three countries exemplify the modal pattern, with their democratic regimes veiling the continuation of disunited elites and, in Slovakia, of authoritarian rule.

The Revolutionary Pattern: New Elites and Totalitarian Regimes

The victory of a doctrinaire counterelite in a revolutionary upheaval, its displacement of most existing elites, and the required profession of its beliefs by all who subsequently hold or aspire to elite positions constitute this pattern. A totalitarian regime operated by an ideocratically united elite is its result. I have already mentioned the major instances: Russia and the Soviet Union, Yugoslavia, China, Cuba, and Iran. To them must be added the countries on which ideocratic elites and totalitarian regimes were imposed through conquest in warfare: East Central Europe and North Korea after World War II, South Vietnam in

1975. More ambiguous instances are the brief but brutal dominance of Cambodia by the Khmer Rouge between 1975–78, the Dergue's revolutionary rule in Ethiopia between 1974–77, and the dominance of a fundamentalist Islamist elite in Sudan after 1989.

Where they have stemmed from indigenous revolution, rather than foreign imposition, totalitarian regimes have been long lasting. Formally speaking at least, the Soviet regime lasted seventy years, the Chinese regime has reached the half-century mark, the regime in Yugoslavia lasted nearly as long, and the Cuban regime has lasted almost four decades. Defeats in warfare are one way in which totalitarian regimes are terminated (the Khmer Rouge regime by Vietnam's invasion in 1978, the several European fascist regimes in World War II, if one chooses to regard them as essentially totalitarian). Transitions to post-totalitarian regimes following the demise of charismatic leaders and the institution of political reforms aimed at achieving greater elite security are a second way. As Linz and Stepan outline these transitions, there is a gradual increase in nonpolitical pluralism, rigid adherence to ideological precepts gives way to an insistence on programmatic consensus, mass mobilization slackens and becomes pro forma, while the actions of top leaders become more subject to party and institutional checks.[21]

Regimes that have moved beyond the strict totalitarian configuration appear to be exceptionally vulnerable to drastic economic declines and to regionally based ethnonationalist revolts. They risk imploding at an early point (the Soviet Union and Yugoslavia in 1990–91, potentially China and Cuba). However, where they have been imposed by outside force, as in East Central Europe, ideocratically united elites and totalitarian regimes appear to last only so long as that force is able to shore them up. A key reason is that, short of absorption by the outside power, the elite circulation that occurs with the imposition of such regimes is necessarily somewhat limited. This is because there is no escaping reliance on the administrative, managerial, military, and cultural skills of preexisting elites, and from the start many of these persons and groups regard the imposed elite and regime formation as illegitimate. They quickly begin to undermine or circumvent it; and, as in Hungary during 1956, they may even try to destroy it.

The revolutionary pattern has moved into partial eclipse during the last decade or so. There is ground for saying that the elites and regimes it produces linger on in the formerly communist but now ultranationalist elites and authoritarian regimes of Serbia–Montenegro and Croatia. But, on the whole, the post-communist European countries have passed beyond the pattern and are therefore probably inoculated against its recurrence. Outside Europe, moreover, the communist version of the revolutionary pattern has been so thoroughly discredited that it is unlikely to enjoy a recrudescence. If the pattern regains prominence, it is likely to take theocratic and ethnonationalist forms. The spread of religious fundamentalist movements and tendencies toward ethnocracies in much of today's world make this a distinct possibility.

The Settlement Pattern: Consensually United Elites and Stable Democracies

Although they produce little change in the composition of elites, some transitions involve circumstances and incentives that propel sudden and deliberate settlements of core disputes by key leaders of opposing elite camps. This is a possibility where there is a background of costly but inconclusive elite conflict, where a new crisis threatens intensified but probably still inconclusive conflict, and where the main elite camps are led by persons with sufficient political authority, experience, and skill to impose basic compromises on their respective colleagues and followers. Settlements typically involve secret collusions among key leaders of opposing camps to topple a "sultan" or an authoritarian ruling group, compromise the issues that most divide their camps, and thereafter share and take turns exercising government power through restrained, electorally centered competitions. The paradigmatic cases, as noted, were the conspiracy among Tory and Whig elites to unseat James II in the crisis that triggered England's Glorious Revolution of 1688–89, and the altogether similar conspiracy among "Hat" and "Cap" elites, facing foreign invasion and economic collapse, to rid themselves of Gustav IV Adolph in Sweden's constitutional revolution of 1809. The outcome in each case was a consensually united elite. Initially, this approximated a cartel or liberal oligarchy whose factions respected each other's interests while engaging in restrained competitions for government office on the basis of appeals for the support of sharply truncated electorates. However, with elite competitions tamed and stabilized along broadly representative lines, the settlements unleashed democratizing dynamics that gradually dispersed the cartels or oligarchies and created modern polyarchal democracies.

Elite settlements are, like revolutions, rare events. Amounting to fundamental reorganizations of elite relations, they go beyond issue-specific elite pacts. There were probably no more than a dozen instances of successful settlements during the twentieth century. In Latin America, settlements aimed at removing an oppressive regime or preventing a slide back into unchecked elite warfare occurred during crises in Mexico in 1928–29, Costa Rica in 1948, Colombia and Venezuela in 1957–58, and Uruguay in 1984.[22] In Europe, settlements appear to have been reached by leaders of Austria's "black" and "red" political camps who negotiated a durable grand-coalition government and an elaborate power-sharing (*proporz*) arrangement as the seminal steps toward post-war construction in 1945, and by leaders of all the main elite groups (except the Basques) in post-Franco Spain during 1977–78.[23] Two instances of settlements in Asia were the elite negotiations that propelled the transition from an authoritarian to a democratic regime in South Korea during 1987, and the extensive negotiations that occurred in Taiwan, first in 1990 at the time of Taiwan's democratic transition, and again in 1996 amid a confrontation with mainland China.[24] The only instance of a settlement in Africa was the extensive 1993–94 negotiations, principally between leaders of the National Party government and its African National Congress (ANC) rivals, that transformed South Africa's exclusionary democratic regime into an inclusionary one.[25] In the South Korean, Taiwan, and South African cases, however, changes in the global arena and strong foreign pressures for democratization played crucial, perhaps determining roles in forcing settlements, and the odds against the inclusionary democratic regime in South Africa achieving stability are sizable.

In East Central Europe, only two of the transitions to post-communist regimes during and after 1989 involved elite settlements: Hungary and Poland. In the framework of Linz and Stepan, Hungary was by 1989 the only "mature" post-totalitarian regime in the region, while Poland was a unique "communist authoritarian regime." During the 1980s, both countries had well-organized communist and anti-communist elite camps that were essentially at loggerheads, and in this respect key conditions for settlements existed. The Hungarian settlement had its roots in the significant reshuffling of elite position holding that occurred under the Kadar regime after the late 1960s. As technocratic personnel became more numerous and prominent in the cabinet and state bureaucracy, various reformist and quietly dissident policy factions, which were careful to maintain personal ties with leaders and cliques in the Socialist Workers Party, emerged. When the threat of Soviet intervention, à la 1956, receded under Gorbachev's nascent post-totalitarian regime in Moscow, factions cum parties quickly came into the open in Budapest. Freely competitive elections were agreed upon during the elaborate, two-stage roundtable negotiations that took place between March and September 1989, and the transition to a democratic regime was completed in spring 1990. To an important degree, however, the Hungarian settlement was icing on a cake that elites had already baked because it capped two decades of circulation that had been fairly wide in scope yet gradual and negotiated in mode, owing much to the shared elite fear of repeating the crisis of 1956.[26]

In Poland, by contrast, there was never more than an armed truce between communist elites on one side and embittered intellectual, church, and eventually trade union elites on the other. The outward forms of an ideocratically united elite and a totalitarian regime were maintained by exclusion and intimidation, but the communist elite's hegemony was always quite limited. During 1980–81, church leaders and prominent intellectuals aided and abetted the organization of discontented workers in Solidarity. Facing the prospect of Soviet intervention if they failed to reassert themselves, the ascendant communist elite, led by General Wojciech Jarulzelski, imposed martial law—in effect, a party-military dictatorship that clearly indicated a disunited national elite. Protracted, largely secret negotiations between communist leaders and their Solidarity-led opponents during 1988–89 amounted to a settlement. A "historic compromise" was reached that involved relegalizing Solidarity, recognizing the need for pluralism and constitutional reform, and agreeing to hold contested but controlled elections. The communists were guaranteed a majority of Sejm seats, but it was also agreed that a freely elected Senate would be created and that the Senate would elect a president with ambiguous but potentially large powers. When Solidarity won all but one of the contested seats in both the Sejm and the Senate in the June 1989 elections, while thirty-three of the thirty-five leading communist candidates who had been guaranteed Sejm seats failed to gain popular election, a further compromise was struck. Solidarity leaders acquiesced in the Senate's election of General Jarulzelski as president by one vote and accepted communist domination of the Sejm, despite the election results, in return for promises that Jarulzelski would not move against Solidarity and that a host of liberalizing laws would be enacted.[27]

The first fully free elections in Hungary and Poland, in 1990, produced thorough circulations of the top political elites.[28] This, combined with the accommodations reached during the preceding year, enabled consensually united elites to form in both countries. Elite cooperation and restraint survived the electoral comebacks of former communists during 1993 in Poland and in Hungary during 1994. In the winter of 1995–96, Polish elites managed to defuse a serious crisis when, following former communist Aleksandr Kwasniewski's electoral defeat of Lech Walesa for the presidency, Jozef Oleksy, the prime minister allied with Kwasniewski, was forced to resign over allegations that he shared state secrets with Russian spies. Although, as other chapters in this volume discuss, there continue to be sharp political conflicts in Hungary and Poland, all significant elites, including former communists, appear committed to democratic game rules, they are widely agreed about entering the European Union and NATO, and the main lines of further economic reform are not in much dispute. Despite often heated rhetoric to the contrary, the behavior of elites in both countries suggests a strong disposition to pull punches in order to keep politics tame and democratic.

The Implosion Pattern: Fragmented Elites and Uncertain Regimes

Implosions involve the sudden decompression or grave weakening of state apparata, especially military and police forces, leading rapidly to regime collapse. Unlike most transitions, implosions do not stem from violent confrontations between ruling and challenging elites, from deliberate mobilizations of discontented masses, or from collisions with hostile foreign powers. They are not, in a word, regime overthrows. Instead, implosions result from accumulating economic inefficiencies, spreading elite corruption, and, sometimes, rising ethnonational discontents. Implosions are political upheavals rather than violent social cataclysms (though, as in the former Yugoslavia, they may be followed by organized warfare). Although the societies in which implosions occur suffer great distress, most elites and institutions manage to survive, and there is no chaotic interregnum when power is "in the streets." There is, however, much elite disarray. Unless they can cloak themselves in a new and sturdy mantle (sewed, typically, with ethnonationalist thread), leaders of imploding regimes are discredited. Their lieutenants are left to repackage themselves politically and set about reconstituting the weakened state. Reflecting the traumas of implosions and the positional scrambles they entail, elites fragment. Their relations and political game rules become uncertain, and conflicts among them proliferate.

Implosions have occurred in less than a handful of countries, they have done so quite recently, and one cannot, therefore, be confident that implosions constitute a distinct and recurring pattern. Linz and Stepan believe that implosions (or regime "collapses" as they term them) are peculiar to "near-totalitarian" or "frozen post-totalitarian" regimes, in which ruling elites have become rigid, ossified, and incapable of anticipating and heading off implosive circumstances and crises. In such regimes, there are no well-organized opposition elites able to capture the weakening state or negotiate a transition from it, and this makes an implosion all the more likely.[29]

Linz and Stepan treat the Czechoslovak communist regime's collapse, in the space of ten days during November 1989, as the paradigmatic case, with the nearly as rapid collapse of the German Democratic Republic (GDR), during several weeks in the preceding autumn of 1989, a second case. For at least three reasons, however, the Czechoslovak and GDR transitions were less than pristine implosions. First, they occurred only after developments in Hungary and Poland made it clear that the Soviet Union would not rescue any of the satellite regimes whose longevity had always depended heavily upon Moscow's support. Second, the Czechoslovak and East German transitions were strongly influenced, even impelled, by the Hungarian and Polish transitions. Third, the fully democratic outcomes in what, after 1992, became the Czech Republic and what, after 1991, became the eastern states of a reunified Germany were "over-determined" by their geographic proximity to, previous immersion in, and rapid resumption of West European democratic practices.

The disintegration of the Soviet regime during 1991, as well as the Yugoslav regime's complex disintegration during 1990–91, were less influenced by external circumstances or prior democratic experience, and to this extent they were purer cases of implosions. However, the Soviet and Yugoslav events resulted most directly from ethnonational power competitions among elites in the context of decentralized federal political systems (formally in the USSR and actually in the 1980s in Yugoslavia) and from the stringencies of marketizing reforms that were not preceded by political reform and stabilization.[30] These distinctive aspects of the Soviet and Yugoslav implosions may make them sui generis.

The Soviet and Yugoslav implosions have been dealt with by many specialists, and I will rehearse them here.[31] I want only to highlight the combination of elite persistence and disarray that characterized both cases. First, no large elite circulations occurred in either country. Jacek Wasilewski has calculated that between 1988 and 1993 in the Russian Federation, the overall ratio of national-level elites who retained elite status to those who lost that status was 90:10.[32] Elite circulation was even more limited at the level of Russia's republics and autonomous regions.[33] There was, on the other hand, considerable turnover among holders of ministerial positions in the government of Russia immediately before and after the Soviet regime imploded. Of the roughly 145 ministers appointed by Boris Yeltsin between June 1991 and October 1993, about half were "new men" recruited primarily from academic and research institutions, who previously held no significant government or party position.[34] Comparable measures of elite circulation, or its absence, during the Yugoslav implosion are harder to find. In Serbia–Montenegro, the communist elites led by Slobodan Milosevic clearly retained their dominant positions, despite the emergence of significant opposition elites. Milosevic and his lieutenants in the renamed Socialist Party won resounding victories during elections in 1990 and 1992, and they eventually forced their principal opponent, Milan Panic, from the prime ministership. In Croatia, political elite circulation was apparently greater because ultranationalist leaders of the Croatian Democratic Union, led by former communist General Franco Tjudman, dislodged many communists from power.

Elite relations fragmented badly during the Soviet and Yugoslav implosions. As the communist party-states weakened, many elites clung to power by seeking support in regionally based ethnic discontents and identities. This abandonment of the political center in Moscow and Belgrade became a stampede when competitive elections were held at the level of constituent republics instead of the national level. What remained of ideocratic uniformity evaporated. Comparing responses in interviews, conducted in 1993, with 116 Soviet political leaders who held top posts under Gorbachev between 1985–91 with the responses of 100 holders of equivalent positions in Yeltsin's Russia during 1992–93, interviewed in 1994, David Lane studied the deep elite conflicts that opened up. He found that well before the Soviet Union's final disintegration at the end of 1991, the Gorbachev elites were split in half over the "fundamentally sound" or "basically unsound" nature of the Soviet system. Among the Yeltsin elite in 1994, there was little agreement about the extent of democratic control in post-Soviet Russia, about the roles of its executive, legislature, and government generally, about the desired balance between private and state property, and about the amount of inequality that would be acceptable.[35] Although Russian elites managed to hold peaceful, more or less freely competitive elections for the State Duma in 1993 and 1995, and also for the presidency in 1996, the abiding fears and desperate gambits that pervaded those contests testified to elite fragmentation. Reconstituting the Russian state has been perilously close to a zero-sum power struggle among elites, and the regime's democratic prospects are quite uncertain. In the former Yugoslav republics, states and regimes have been reconstituted more rapidly. But this has been due largely to the exigencies of organized warfare and to the disciplined ultranationalist movements that have grabbed power. Except perhaps in Slovenia, the former Yugoslav regimes all have sharply authoritarian characters.

Conclusion

The study of regime transitions must pay more attention to elite persistence. Most transitions involve little change in the composition and relations of elites, and this makes the consequences of many transitions more apparent than real. One implication is that the twentieth century's vaunted waves of democratization have not been as cumulative or substantively profound as is often assumed. Under nominally democratic institutions in many countries, entrenched elites continue to wage implacable struggles for power. Most often, there has been no decrease in regime instability. Many of today's new democracies are thus likely to break down in various new crises where they do not, as in Croatia and Serbia during the past few years, display steadily more authoritarian complexions.[36] Without early and presumably stabilizing admission into the European Union, which appears unlikely, such outcomes are quite conceivable in Bulgaria, Romania, and Slovakia.

We need, therefore, to distinguish and study more intensively regime transitions that do involve substantial elite circulation and changed elite relations. Communist and fascist transitions to totalitarian regimes through sweeping elite circulations and the ascendancy of a doctrinaire counterelite are understood well enough. However, the extent of elite change and its consequences in transitions to theocratic regimes like the Iranian remain hazy, and the possibility that the incidence of such transitions may increase makes their study urgent. Transitions that involve relatively little change in elite composition but a fundamental reorganization of elite relations through settlements are increasingly noticed, and the Spanish and Hungarian cases have been studied quite thoroughly in this respect. Still, scholarly agreement about other transitions via settlements is not great. For example, whether the Polish transition entailed a settlement from which a consensually united elite and a stable democractic regime have emerged is disputed. Finally, it will be apparent from their treatment here that we are only beginning to comprehend what happens to elites during and after regime implosions. The Soviet and Yugoslav cases are very recent, they had many idiosyncratic features, and, especially in Russia, outcomes are as yet unclear. Depending upon developments in China, Cuba, Vietnam, North Korea, and perhaps even Iran, we may eventually conclude that the Soviet and Yugoslav transitions were too situationally specific to exemplify a pattern. What does seem clear, at any rate, is that they have been particularly graphic illustrations of this chapter's contention that elite persistence is a marked feature of most regime transitions.

Notes

I want to thank David Lane for useful comments on an earlier version of this chapter.

1. Vilfredo Pareto, *The Mind and Society* (New York: Dover, 1935), par. 2056.
2. Juan J. Linz and Alfred Stepan, *Problems of Democratic Transition and Consolidation* (Baltimore: Johns Hopkins University Press, 1996).

3. See Michael G. Burton and John Higley, "Invitation to Elite Theory: The Basic Contentions Reconsidered" in *Power Elites and Organizations*, G. William Domhoff and Thomas R. Dye, eds. (Newbury Park, Calif.: Sage, 1987), 219–38.

4. Huntington lists twenty-seven variables that are used to explain the emergence of democratic regimes, though he observes that the beliefs and actions of elites are the "most immediate and significant explanatory variable." Samuel P. Huntington, *The Third Wave: Democratization in the Late Twentieth Century* (Norman: University of Oklahoma Press, 1991), 36–8. Diamond, Linz, and Lipset canvass a dozen broad determinants of democratic regimes, though they likewise tend to assign greatest importance to what political leaders and elites do. Larry Diamond, Juan J. Linz, and Seymour Martin Lipset, "Introduction: What Makes for Democracy?" in *Politics in Developing Countries: Comparing Experiences with Democracy*, 2nd ed. (Boulder, Colo.: Lynne Rienner, 1995).

5. A sultanistic regime is characterized by a despotic, idiosyncratic ruler who is unencumbered by rational-legal or ideological constraints. A post-totalitarian regime is characterized by some restraints on the maximum leader, some tolerance of regime critics, a nascent pluralism, and an increasingly senescent official ideology. See Linz and Stepan, *Problems*, 38–54.

6. For summaries of research on elite circulation in Germany and Japan after World War II, and also during the turbulent decades that preceded the war, see Ursula Hoffmann-Lange, "Germany: Twentieth-Century Turning Points" and Hiromitsu Kataoka, "Japan: Crises and Elite Transformations" in *Elites, Crises, and the Origins of Regimes*, Mattei Dogan and John Higley, eds. (Boulder, Colo.: Rowman & Littlefield, 1998).

7. This is a point made by David Lane, "Transition Under 'Eltsin: The Nomenklatura and Political Elite Circulation," *Political Studies* 45 (April 1997): 1–19.

8. John Higley, Ursula Hoffmann-Lange, Charles Kadushin, and Gwen Moore, "Elite Integration in Stable Democracies: A Reconsideration," *European Sociological Review* 7 (May 1991): 35–53.

9. Samuel E. Finer, "Pareto and Pluto-Democracy: The Retreat to the Galapagos," *American Political Science Review* 62 (July 1968): 440–50.

10. I have in mind the long controversy about the pluralist power elite, or ruling class character of American elites, well summarized by G. William Domhoff, *Who Rules America? Power and Politics in the Year 2000* (Mountain View, Calif.: Mayfield Publishing Co., 1998).

11. Jaroslaw Piekalkiewicz and Alfred Wayne Penn, *Politics of Ideocracy* (Albany, NY: State University of New York Press, 1995).

12. John Higley and Michael Burton, "Elite Settlements and the Taming of Politics," *Government and Opposition* 33 (Winter 1998): 98–115.

13. On this origin of disunited elites in Latin America, see Oscar Oszlak, "The Historical Formation of the Nation-State in Latin America: Some Theoretical and Methodological Guidelines for Its Study," *Latin American Research Review* 16 (April 1981): 3–32.

14. Gerhard Lenski, *Power and Privilege* (New York: McGraw-Hill, 1966), 231–42.

15. Myron Weiner, "Empirical Democratic Theory" in *Competitive Elections in Developing Countries*, M. Weiner and E. Ozbundun, eds. (Washington: American Enterprise Institute, 1987), 3–36.

16. John Higley and Richard Gunther, eds., *Elites and Democratic Consolidation in Latin America and Southern Europe* (New York: Cambridge University Press, 1992).

17. See, inter alia, Guillermo O'Donnell, "Delegative Democracy," *Journal of Democracy* 5 (January 1994): 55–69; Larry Diamond, "Is The Third Wave Over?" *Journal of Democracy* 7 (July 1996): 20–37.

18. Zhelyu Zhelev, "Is Communism Returning?" *Journal of Democracy* 7 (July 1996): 6.

19. Linz and Stepan, *Problems*, observe that Bulgaria and Romania were the only countries in East Central Europe in which repackaged communist parties won the first free elections in 1990, and that down to 1996 in Romania "no leaders have gained power who did not have a career in the Communist Party apparatus" (p. 365).

20. Lubomir Brokl and Zdenka Mansfeldova, "Czech and Slovak Political and Parliamentary Elites" in *Postcommunist Elites and Democracy in Eastern Europe*, John Higley, Jan Pakulski, and Wlodzimierz Wesolowski, eds. (London: Macmillan, 1998).

21. Linz and Stepan, *Problems*, 42–51.

22. These settlements are examined in Higley and Gunther, *Elites and Democratic Consolidation*.

23. The Austrian case has yet to be treated explicitly by scholars as an elite settlement. The Spanish settlement has been examined extensively. See, inter alia, Richard Gunther, "Spain: The Very Model of a Modern Elite Settlement" in Higley and Gunther, *Elites and Democratic Consolidation*, 38–80; Linz and Stepan, *Problems*, 87–115.

24. Michael G. Burton and Jai P. Ryu, "South Korea's Elite Settlement and Democratic Consolidation" in *Classes and Elites in Democratization and Democracy*, Eva Etzioni-Halevy, ed. (New York: Garland Press, 1996), 194–204; and John Higley, Tong-yi Huan, and Tse-min Lin, "Elite Settlement and Democratic Consolidation in Taiwan," *Journal of Democracy* 9 (April 1998).

25. Hennie Kotze, "South Africa: From Apartheid to Democracy" in Dogan and Higley, eds., *Elites, Crises, and the Origins of Regimes*.

26. In a large literature on the Hungarian transition, the most comprehensive treatment, and one that deals in detail with the features encapsulated here, is Rudolf L. Tokes, *Hungary's Negotiated Revolution: Economic Reform, Social Change, and Political Succession* (New York: Cambridge University Press, 1996).

27. For citations of a large literature, see the chapter on Poland in Linz and Stepan, *Problems*.

28. On the basis of extensive survey data covering the turnover of Hungarian and Polish political, economic, and cultural elites between 1988 and 1993, Jacek Wasilewski calculates that for every two persons who retained elite status, there was by 1993 one person who was new to that status. See Jacek Wasilewski, "Hungary, Poland, and Russia: The Fate of the Nomenklatura Elites" in Dogan and Higley, eds., *Elites, Crises, and the Origins of Regimes*.

29. Linz and Stepan, *Problems*, 322.

30. I encapsulate the thrusts of two analyses, that of Russia by Linz and Stepan, *Problems*, 366–400, and that of Yugoslavia by Susan L. Woodward, *Balkan Tragedy: Chaos and Dissolution after the Cold War* (Washington: Brookings Institution, 1995).

31. Jerry Hough, *Democratization and Revolution in the U.S.S.R. 1985–1991* (Washington: Brookings Institution, 1997); David Kotz with Fred Weir, *Revolution from Above: The Demise of the Soviet System* (London: Routledge, 1997). For Yugoslavia, see, inter alia, Susan L. Woodward, *Balkan Tragedy*.

32. Jacek Wasilewski, "Hungary, Poland, and Russia: The Fate of the Nomenklatura Elites" in Dogan and Higley, eds., *Elites, Crises, and the Origins of Regimes*.

33. Stephen White and Olga Kryshtanovskaya, "Russia: Elite Continuity and Change" in Dogan and Higley, eds., *Elites, Crises, and the Origins of Regimes*.

34. David Lane and Cameron Ross, "The Changing Composition and Structure of the Political Elites" in David Lane, ed., *Russia in Transition* (London: Longman, 1995), 52–75.

35. David Lane, "The Gorbachev Revolution: The Role of the Political Elite in Regime Disintegration," *Political Studies* 44 (April 1996): 4–23. See also David Lane, "Transition under 'Eltsin."

36. Larry Diamond in "Is the Third Wave Over?" marshals evidence that this trend is already under way.

Chapter 4

Post-Communist Economic Transformation

Anders Åslund

There are no less than 22 formerly Soviet-type, post-communist countries in East Central Europe and the former Soviet Union, leaving aside
the former Yugoslavia but including Albania. As they all abandoned
communism in a brief spell from 1989 to 1991, we have a unique opportunity to compare their experiences of alternative economic policies.
After almost seven years of transition from communism to democracy
and capitalism, we can say quite a lot about which factors are more
or less important and what policies do or do not work. A substantial
comparative literature has appeared.[1]

Although all these countries faced similar problems, they have
ended up in rather different situations. The fall in output has been dramatic, but the variations have been even more striking. The accumulated decline in official output at the nadir varies from 18 percent of
GDP in Poland and 86 percent in Georgia.[2] The recorded drop in production is exaggerated. In reality, output might have plummeted by
about 5 percent in Poland and one-half in Georgia. These numbers reflect considerable social suffering, but they further emphasize the differences. No less than 13 countries in the region have experienced hyperinflation,[3] almost as many hyperinflations as have previously been
recorded in world history. Only Czechoslovakia and Hungary escaped
high inflation.

Depending on expectations, values, focus, and evaluation, assessments of the outcome vary from the truly dark to the relatively optimistic. The key to any evaluation is to determine the essence of post-
communist transformation. The purpose of this paper is to concentrate
on these basic questions, and the paper is structured accordingly. We

must first ask, what was the purpose of post-communist transition? Second, what are the success criteria? By what objective standards can we judge whether the transition has been successful or not? Third, why have certain countries been more successful than others? Fourth, what are the worst dangers and traps during the transition? Finally, what economic model may result?

The Purpose of Post-Communist Economic Transition

Why did communism collapse? The answers vary, but one important component is that the economic system was not dynamic enough. The growth rate was too low, because the socialist economies were slow to innovate and to absorb new technologies, and they utilized inputs inefficiently. A broadly held conviction has taken hold: capitalism is a more efficient economic system than socialism. This belief is corroborated theoretically by the new institutional economic history[4] and empirically by multiple recent econometric studies.[5]

The shortest explanation of the aim of post-communist economic transformation is to establish capitalism in order to accomplish sustained economic growth. This is a long-term aim, and it does not mean that capitalism is necessarily superior to socialism in terms of growth in a limited period in one particular country. The task was not quantitative—to maximize economic growth in the short or medium term, but qualitative—to build a solid capitalist system. Therefore, the short-term evaluation of the systemic transformation should be based on how well the pillars of capitalism were built.

Other economic considerations are stability, that is, inflation and unemployment, and equity, or income distribution and social safety. Their relation to economic growth will be discussed below. Capitalism seems to be more compatible with democracy and provide a base for a pluralist society, but that theme falls outside the scope of this paper.[6]

We have thus transformed our question about the purpose of post-communist economic transition to; What is the essence of capitalism? One way of answering that query is to negate the peculiarities of communism. Janos Kornai[7] has provided the authoritative assessment of the kernel of communism. The most fundamental feature of the socialist economy was the far-reaching politicization of the economy. Everything was politicized: ownership, allocation, and prices. It was politicized in a very peculiar fashion, being subject to the "undivided power of the Marxist-Leninist party." From this perspective, the primary task of post-communist economic transition was to depoliticize the economy. This was a destructive task, namely, to eliminate the control by the Communist Party over the economy. Ownership would be depoliti-cized through privatization, allocation through liberalization of trade, price-setting through price deregulation. Obviously, all this would be much more easy to achieve under a pluralist regime than under a dic-tatorship. Moreover, for a lingering communist dictatorship, all the re-quired steps would be concessions. For a liberal democracy, they would be ends in themselves.

Other tasks were constructive: to replace communist mechanisms with capitalist tools. The vertical links of the authoritarian state had to be replaced with horizontal links, that is, contracts on the market were to substitute for commands from the State Planning Committee and branch ministries. Similarly money would become active and replace commands, because a well-functioning market requires limited trans-action costs, and monetary exchange is cheaper than barter trade. However, monetization is only efficient if the value of money is stable, that is, that financial stability is maintained. In short, the formation of a market required manifold deregulation, financial stabilization, and the evolution of the legal system. The essence of marketization was the legitimization and facilitation of the conclusion and execution of con-tracts.

The other prerequisite was that enterprises got real owners who could impose their interests in the enterprise. Privatization should be seen as depoliticization of ownership.[8] It is disputed who was the real owner of state enterprises under socialism, if anybody at all. It is not enough to appoint anybody as an owner. The owner should be en-dowed with actual control over the enterprise, effective or corporate governance. These two processes—the nominal privatization of enter-prises and the introduction of effective control by owners—have been remarkably separated in several countries. Also the reinforcement of property rights requires a considerable development of the legal system.

Thus, in order to prepare for sustained economic growth, capitalism had to be built. Capitalism implies depoliticization of the economy through the creation of markets (liberalization and financial stabiliza-tion) and privatization (the creation of real owners).

What Are the Success Criteria of the Transformation?

When has capitalism been built? A few countries already appear to have entered a period of sustained economic growth. In 1997, four transition countries had reached growth rates of 7 percent or more, namely, Poland, Estonia, Georgia, and Kyrgyzstan.[9] Poland in particular has recorded several years of considerable growth. All four of these countries stand out as the most radical reformers in their respective subregions. However, in most countries years have gone by without significant growth. What other criteria can we look for?

We have settled for a qualitative target—capitalism, and it should be measured by qualities. Three obvious standards are financial stabilization, liberalization, and private sector development. Each of these criteria can be quantified, and the question is where to put the hurdle when a market economy and a point of no return have been reached.

The most obvious success indicator is low inflation. The limitation of inflation and the return to economic growth are closely related. No post-communist country has returned to growth with inflation over 40 percent per annum, while all countries that have got inflation under control so far have returned to growth within a year or so.[10] The correlation is strong between inflation and decline in output.[11] In 1995, as many as 13 countries had still not complied with this criterion, although virtually all inflation rates were lower than in the preceding year. In 1997, most countries had got inflation below 40 percent per annum, with only two exceptions in Central Europe (Bulgaria and Romania) and three in the former Soviet Union (Belarus, Tajikistan, and Turkmenistan).

In some cases, inflation has fallen temporarily to a low level and then swung up again, for instance, in Russia and Ukraine in the summer of 1994, and in Bulgaria and Romania in 1996. The key problem was that these temporary stabilizations were based primarily on monetary policy—very high real interest rates, while budget deficits remained excessive. A successful and sustained stabilization needs to be based on fiscal adjustment—a sufficient reduction of the budget deficit. Only when the budget deficit has been reduced so far that the remaining budget deficit can be financed by noninflationary means has inflation been brought under permanent control.[12]

The scary border case is Bulgaria. Its reforms were gradual with little liberalization and privatization. In 1993, its inflation had decreased to 64 percent, but it doubled the next year, to 122 percent. Inflation was brought down to 33 percent a year in 1995, but the budget deficit stayed at almost 7 percent of GDP, and the foreign debt service was only barely managed[13]. However, the government continued bailing out failing large state enterprises, and finally the confidence in the Bulgarian leva collapsed in 1996. People withdrew their leva from the failing banks and exchanged them for dollars, and 14 banks went into bankruptcy. The exchange rate collapsed, falling 98 percent between February 1996 and February 1997. As a consequence, inflation surged to 300 percent in 1996 and 600 percent in 1997, prompting a fall in real òutput of 10 percent. The government lost all popularity and was unable to deal with the severe crisis, whose eruption was completely unnecessary. The Bulgarian experience shows the danger in trying not to do more than what is necessary. Fortunately, democracy held in Bulgaria, and the gradualist communist government was replaced by a radical reform government through parliamentary elections in April 1997.

The countries most successful in controlling inflation have not even calculated how large a deficit they can finance. Instead, they have made a balanced budget their standard, but inflation still stays relatively high. Croatia had a budget surplus of 0.7 percent of GDP and a deflation of 3 percent in 1994; the Czech Republic has a steady budget surplus of 0–1 percent of GDP, and its inflation was 8 percent in 1995; Slovenia has balanced its budgets almost perfectly, but inflation was still 9 percent in 1995; Estonia maintains a budget surplus of 0.5–1 percent of GDP, but it recorded an inflation of 29 percent in 1995.[14] With the exception of Croatia, not one single post-communist country has managed to get what would be considered low inflation by Western standards. This shows how difficult it is to combat inflation. Part of the explanation is the existence of hidden semifiscal deficits, often in the form of debts taken over by the government. Another reason is that these countries started with extremely devalued currencies, and the necessary real revaluation often takes the form of inflation. Substantial relative price adjustments are a third reason for lingering inflation. In hindsight, common complaints that too much effort was devoted to combat inflation appear misplaced.[15]

Another important criterion of success of transition is deregulation. In theory, stabilization can take place without liberalization, but in the post-communist reality it has proved impossible, because price regulation is usually connected with substantial subsidies that have to be reduced if financial stabilization is to succeed. Today, there are a number of competing liberalization indices.[16] In spite of all deregulation, most post-communist countries rank low internationally on the rather varied liberalization indices. The EBRD and the World Bank do not compare the transition countries with countries in other parts of the world, and the EBRD has not even elaborated a composite index. The Heritage Foundation index, that endeavors to reflect 1996, includes 140 countries. It ranks the Czech Republic as number 12, and Estonia as number 26, but the next transition country on the list is Hungary that figures as number 57. Bulgaria and Russia are number 100. The Fraser Institute ranks 103 countries for 1993–95. The earlier date puts the transition countries at a disadvantage, and the highest ranking transition country is the Czech Republic as number 51. Hungary is number 85 out of 103, while none of the post-Soviet states is included.

Yet a reasonable threshold for the minimal liberalization to qualify as a market economy appears to be 0.5 on the World Bank's liberalization index. By that standard, all the post-communist countries had passed the mark in 1994, with the exception of Belarus, Ukraine, Georgia, Armenia, Azerbaijan, Kazakhstan, Uzbekistan, Turkmenistan, and Tajikistan.[17] Since then, Ukraine, Kazakhstan, Georgia, and Armenia have undertaken substantial liberalization, so that they probably have surpassed that level in 1996, and Uzbekistan was close to the hurdle in 1994. The remaining delinquents are Belarus, Turkmenistan, Tajikistan, and Uzbekistan. We could also use the standard of an open economy by the criteria set by Jeffrey D. Sachs and Andrew Warner,[18] which they identify as the threshold to economic growth. The result would be that approximately the same four countries would be excluded.

After a significant liberalization, few backlashes have been recorded, notably Ukraine in 1993, and again in 1995–96, but that was a country that had not liberalized much. With the exception of the four outlayers, we dare suggest that a point of no return has been passed, but this is only a tentative empirical conclusion. Much remains to be deregulated, but a market economy has been introduced. Also, with regard to liberalization, it is clear that the danger is not to go too far but to stop short of a market economy.

The third natural standard of transition to capitalism is the expansion of the private sector, whether through privatization or private enterprise development. Privatization and private enterprise development are often presented as alternatives, but both tend to go together, and private sector development is generally greater in countries with more liberalization and stabilization.[19]

To expand the private sector takes longer time than to liberalize or undertake financial stabilization, and statistics on ownership tend to be particularly bad. EBRD[20] offers the most complete picture, but it contains only estimates which tend to be conservative. No Western country has larger public employment or public output than some 35 percent of GDP. Thus, a reasonable standard for a point of no return might be that the private sector produces 65 percent of GDP. By 1996, all of Central Europe, apart from Bulgaria and Romania, appear to have reached that level, while only the three Baltic states, Russia, and Kazakhstan had gone that far in the former Soviet Union.

Summing up these three criteria, there is a remarkable correlation between them. Ten countries have complied with all of them: Poland, the Czech Republic, Slovakia, Hungary, Albania, Estonia, Latvia, Lithuania, Russia, and Kazakhstan, while six countries have not passed the hurdle in privatization: Moldova, Ukraine, Armenia, Azerbaijan, Georgia, and the Kyrgyz Republic. Reforms and privatization have caught up in most of the six countries, and almost all seem likely to make it at long last (with the possible exception of Ukraine). Bulgaria and Romania are swiftly recovering after serious macroeconomic destabilization caused by not only too large budget deficits, but also too little deregulation and privatization. The problematic countries are Belarus, Tajikistan, Turkmenistan, and Uzbekistan, which do not comply with any of the capitalist criteria, save Uzbekistan who has inflation under control. To date, we are left with these four failures, while eighteen countries seem to be making the transition to capitalism.

This strictly qualitative perspective draws more attention to the achievements than the ordinary review of decline of production. Yet, the transition from communism to capitalism has been marked by substantial social hardship, though the social costs have varied considerably. Initially, the anticipation of high social costs because of a sharp fall in output, leading to a drastically falling standard of living and massive unemployment, were widely used as arguments against a swift transition. Today, we have the record and it is remarkably clear.

In general, there is a clear correlation: the more radical the reform—in terms of deregulation, financial stabilization, and private sector expansion—the smaller the decline in output.[21] Statistics for income differentiation exist only for a few countries, but there appears to be a stark divide between Central Europe with more radical reforms and the former Soviet Union with less radical reforms, and the least radical reformer in Central Europe, Bulgaria, displays the greatest income differentiation in Central Europe.[22] Unemployment is confusing, because there does not appear to be any correlation between unemployment and the fall in output or between unemployment and the nature of reform. On the whole, unemployment is greater in Central Europe than in the former Soviet Union, but within Central Europe, the Czech Republic, with its radical reforms, maintains very low unemployment.[23]

A frequent argument has been that the population will only accept a certain amount of social costs and that those absolute limits must not be reached. A large number of possible disasters have been invoked, including starvation, social unrest due to excessive poverty, price rises and income differentials, as well as labor unrest because of low wages and mass unemployment. Although social suffering has been great, it is remarkable that these widely expected problems did not blow up. Yet, as we have seen, the assumption that radical reform would aggravate the suffering was wrong, so this was not an argument against radical reform.

Serious social unrest has erupted in Albania and Bulgaria because of

the demise of democracy in Albania and socialist economic mismanagement in Bulgaria, but nowhere have radical economic reforms
caused significant social unrest. Today few remember that the EU sent
food aid to Poland in the winter of 1989–90 because of fears of starvation. In Russia, in the winter of 1991–92, the fear of starvation was even
stronger, but it did not happen there. For a long time, communist governments had reckoned that they could not raise consumer prices because that would ignite social disturbances. When the Soviet government raised meat prices in 1962, it faced bloody riots, notably in
Novorossiisk. The Polish government fell because of strikes when it
tried to raise food prices in December 1970 and suffered serious unrest
again in 1976. However, none of the post-communist governments has
had any serious problems with popular unrest because of price liberalization. One explanation is that a price rise is perceived as a redistributive measure directed against some social group. A price liberalization,
however great the ensuing redistribution, represents primarily a
change of paradigm, and it is not obvious who will gain or lose. Therefore, it is more easily accepted.

Labor unrest was another concern. Many of the new post-communist governments have been greatly worried about strikes over wages,
but, on the contrary, the region has been characterized by few strikes
and wage pressure has been limited. Nor has unemployment skyrock-
eted, although forecasts were that unemployment would rise to half
the labor force in a year or two. Unemployment has risen, but on average it has remained less in East and Central Europe than in Western
Europe. Instead, real wages have fallen sharply, and labor has turned
out to be very weak in post-communist society. To date, both the population at large and the workers have shown a surprising patience during the transition to capitalism.

Why Have Some Countries Been More
Successful than Others?

Whatever measurement we use, the differences in success between various post-communist countries are substantial. In Central Europe, Poland stands out as an astounding success with great dynamism, while
Bulgaria remained a basket case until 1997. A fundamental question is
why certain countries have been more successful than others. A prolonged discussion has taken place about whether preconditions, notably culture and history, or economic policy are most important. Even
if the causality is disputed, there is a clear correlation between certain
factors and the success of economic reform.

The first overall conclusion is clear from the prior section. Economic policy has proved decisive, and virtually all aspects of radical reform are positively related to successful economic transformation. This was predicted by a large mainstream Western literature on policy prescription.[24] Other preconditions are important as far as they influence the ability of the new government to pursue a good economic policy. Radical financial stabilization brings down inflation faster and leads to a smaller decline in output than a less decisive approach. Fast stabilization and liberalization appear to stimulate faster privatization and development of new private enterprises. These observations are not only impressionistic or based on a few examples but founded on regressions with all relevant countries and variables.[25] Yet, a sharp rift remains between the former Soviet Union and Central Europe. This could be explained with the ruble zone that destabilized all the former Soviet economies from 1991 to 1993.[26]

The second general conclusion is a correlation between the nature of reform and political regime. Liberal, democratic regimes tended to choose radical reform, while all socialist regimes opted for gradual reform. Table 4.1 shows a very clear scheme. We can identify five initial radical reform countries (Poland, Czechoslovakia, Albania, Estonia, and Latvia) based on their actual stabilization and liberalization. All started off with democracy and liberal governments. Five countries began democratic non-socialist governments, but they opted for, or ended up with, gradual reform. The governments of Hungary and Lithuania were primarily nationalist and favored gradual reform, while the Russian and Bulgarian governments tried to launch radical reform, but they soon fell because of weak political bases. In the Kyr-

Table 4.1: Correlation Between Political Regime and Type of Reform (Initial Choice after the Democratic Breakthrough)

Type of Government	Radical Reform	Gradual or No Reform
Non-socialist	Czechoslovakia, Poland, Albania, Estonia, Latvia	Hungary, Bulgaria, Lithuania, Russia, Kyrgyz Republic
Post-communist with democratization		Romania, Moldova, Belarus, Ukraine
Post-communist without democratization		Kazakhstan, Uzbekistan, Turkmenistan
War-torn countries		Georgia, Armenia, Azerbaijan, Tajikistan

gyz Republic, reform strategy was simply missing to begin with so that radical reforms were delayed. All governments dominated by post-communists chose gradual reforms, regardless of whether they were democratic or not.

A third major conclusion is that the main hazard of the transition policy is not structural adjustment costs but rent-seeking.[27] Although we cannot easily distinguish how large each effect is, it is evident that the biggest losses in output, welfare, and equity have occurred where rent-seeking has been blatant. Rents imply revenues extracted thanks to the government and state privilege, either through subsidies or monopoly rents, generated by state regulation, while profits are earned on competitive markets. The two most important forms of rents in the post-communist world were subsidized credits and implicit export rents. In 1992, Turkmenistan topped the list, issuing net credits amounting to 63 percent of GDP. Interest rates were heavily subsidized, and interest stopped below one-tenth of this sum. Export rents rose because domestic prices of export commodities were regulated by the state below the world market level, and exports were therefore controlled. In the spring of 1992, the Russian oil price was only one percent of the world market price, generating huge rents. Export rents were greatest in Russia, as its raw material exports were large and the price distortions palpable.[28]

This seems the main explanation why radical policies have proved so much more effective than gradual or late reforms. The dominant problem was not structural adjustment costs, which were the focus of many articles advocating gradual reform, but rent-seeking. Four measures were needed to end the inordinate rent-seeking: the introduction of positive real interest rates; the unification of the exchange rate; the liberalization of raw material prices; and the deregulation of exports. All these measures were part of the radical reform agenda and of a standard IMF standby agreement, but they were resisted by proponents of gradual reforms, who knowingly or unknowingly catered to the interests of the privileged rent-seekers. They ignored rent-seeking, which was the larger problem, and it was of a political nature. Inflation persisted for so long because some people benefited from inflation, primarily those privileged with access to subsidized credits.

The prevalence of rent-seeking also explains why only some non-socialist regimes carried out radical economic reforms. Governments controlled by members of the old communist elite, notably state enterprise managers, initially pursued inflationary policies and maintained price distortions, which facilitated transfers of large resources to their supporters. Over time, however, most of these governments have tilted towards a more ordinary market economy for several reasons. After the privileged had made large fortunes, many wanted to safeguard them. Another reason was that rents declined over time. Inflationary revenues dropped, as the velocity of money increased; export rents fell as initially highly undervalued exchange rates went through substantial real revaluations, as some stabilization occurred. The real revaluation led to smaller differences between domestic and world market prices. Moreover, the public swiftly adopted market economic norms, and it became intellectually impossible to defend heavily subsidized interest rates or export rents. In the end, a country with a policy of little or no reform has usually ended up in such a severe economic crisis that its only way out has been an agreement with the IMF, which would impose sound overall economic policies as a condition for financial support.

Finally, the prevalence of rent-seeking can also explain the sharp difference between Central Europe and the former Soviet Union. For many reasons, the former Soviet Union started with greater opportunities for rent-seeking. The initial financial collapse was greater in the former Soviet Union than in Central Europe, where some countries—notably Czechoslovakia and Hungary—faced no financial disaster. In the former USSR, financial instability was maintained for about two years by the ruble zone that rendered a sound economic policy impossible. Price distortions were far greater in the former Soviet Union than in Central Europe, the valuation of the ruble was initially extremely low, and raw material exports were larger. Therefore, export rents were greater in the former USSR. On the whole, the former Soviet Union had many more regulations and distortions than Central Europe and fewer market influences. Market economic norms were widely accepted in Central Europe when many of them were still unknown in the former Soviet Union. In addition, political institutions and civil society were much weaker in the former Soviet Union, which meant there were few forces that could balance the old communist elite when it opted for massive rent-seeking. Ironically, although Poland's Solidarity trade unions, workers' councils, Catholic Church, and conservative private peasants were all against radical economic reform, they actually rendered radical reform successful, as they provided a strong civil society that limited rent-seeking by communist directors.

Thus, the main economic task of the government during the post-communist transition was to build the pillars of a market economy and thereby eliminate the main mechanisms of rent-seeking. As much of the rent-seeking is connected with inflation, it is a good indicator of the degree of rent-seeking. To rein in the rent-seeking of the old communist elite can also be seen as the chief political task of the post-communist transition. The ways are many. The easiest option would be if the communists really lose power and no compromise with them is needed, and the new regime understands that radical reform is the best policy, as was the case in Czechoslovakia, Albania, and Estonia. A reform government with a weak political base can launch radical reform policies as a preemptive strike, as did the government of Yegor Gaidar. If a compromise has to be struck with the communists, it is better to give them finite resources and transform their interest resources than to make them dependent on continuous state largesse. In effect, it is better to give the powerful remnants of the old regime property rather than subsidies, and maximal transparency should be maintained to turn the population against the enrichment of managers. The best example of this is Russian mass privatization. In the spring of 1996, the total market value of 17,000 large- and medium-sized Russian enterprises privatized through voucher auctions and inside privatization was merely one-tenth of GDP, while the flow of rents in 1992 alone amounted to 80 percent of GDP in gross terms.[29]

Here is the explanation of why authoritarian rule has proved to be a disadvantage in post-communist transition. The threat to the construction of a normal capitalist system does not come from the population or the workers but from the old elite. In order to salvage the state from their machinations, democracy is the best tool, as democratic institutions can represent the population at large and check the power of the old elite.[30] The success of democracy depends on whether the population understands that they will benefit from radical reform, and on whether the reformers are sufficiently perceptive, honest, and firm in their actions, so that they succeed in building the pillars of capitalism. Hungary and Lithuania stand out as examples of a poor popular understanding of their own interests in the first democratic elections. In Bulgaria, the main problem was squabbles within the ranks of the democrats. The Russian reformers had too weak a political base and faced too strong a resistance from the old elite from the beginning. The Kyrgyz Republic initially lacked perceptive cadres.

Initial conditions and path dependence are likely to be important for the success of post-communist transformation,[31] but it is not obvious how. Path dependence is often invoked in favor of gradual reform, but gradual reform implies that state and society remain dysfunctional, and inequitable rent-seeking proceeds for longer than necessary. A prolonged breakdown of state institutions is likely to have lasting negative social consequences. Hence, path dependence appears an additional argument for radical reform. It is another matter that weaker civil societies—most of the former Soviet Union—are likely to do worse than Central Europe. Yet, economic policy matters, as the utter failure of Bulgaria and Romania and the current apparent success of Georgia and the Kyrgyz Republic show.

A somewhat surprising conclusion is that radical reform is actually more popular than gradual reform. Until 1996, the widely accepted view was that radical reformers lose all elections, but that is not true. Thirteen countries have held at least two competitive democratic elections.[32] In the five radical reform countries, which all started off with liberal governments, communists dominate the government only in Poland, while non-socialists dominate the governments in the Czech Republic, Estonia, Latvia, and Slovakia. Moreover, the Polish post-communist party received only 20 percent of the votes cast in the fall elections of 1993, but got 35 percent of the seats in parliament, because no less than 35 percent of the votes for center-right parties resulted in no seats because of party fragmentation on the right. Furthermore, the Polish Social Democratic Alliance is probably the most liberal post-communist party.

Of four countries that started off with non-socialist governments but launched gradual reforms—or failed to follow through with attempted radical reform—three (Bulgaria, Hungary, and Lithuania) were replaced by post-communists in democratic elections, and the old-style Russian communists have almost a majority in the Russian parliament. Hungary and Lithuania saw the biggest swings to the post-communist parties, no less than 22 percent in Hungary from 1990 to 1994. For these countries, the conclusion is that the non-socialists lost because they failed to carry out radical reform and thus lost credibility. In 1996, the post-communists have lost parliamentary elections in Lithuania and presidential elections in Bulgaria, as the popular dissatifaction with gradual reform now turns against the post-communists. For a non-socialist government it is sheer suicide to opt for gradual reforms.

Four countries with initial post-communist governments have held reasonably democratic elections: Romania, Moldova, Ukraine, and Belarus. In the presidential elections in Ukraine and Belarus in July 1994, the post-communist candidates lost out, although the elections were not very fair. The absence of serious reforms in Belarus was undoubtedly a major cause of the demise of democracy there in 1996. In Romania, the popularity of the post-communists has fallen sharply, and they finally lost both parliamentary and presidential elections in 1996. Moldova is the only country where the post-communist parties have won with great majority, no less than 65 percent of the votes cast in February 1994, but the government turned around after the elections and launched reasonable economic reforms. The electoral record is clear: gradual reform is extremely unpopular.

In a third round of elections, post-communist governments have

Table 4.2: Public Opinion about Direction of the Country, 1990–94 (net
percentage positive)

Country	1990	1991	1992	1993	1994
		Radical Reformers			
Albania		41	60	56	29
Czech Republic	37	17	24	28	25
Estonia		30	7	23	17
Latvia		47	-17	7	-9
Poland	13	-41	-29	-4	-30
		Gradual Non-socialist Reformers			
Hungary		-19	-47	-47	-34
Bulgaria	4	38	2	-37	-39
Lithuania		28	-39	-47	-49
Russia		-12	-24	-16	-51
		Gradual Post-communist Reformers			
Romania		26	-7	-6	-6
Belarus					-32
Kazakhstan					-33
Ukraine					-55

Source: European Commission, *Central and Eastern Eurobarometer: Public Opinion and
the European Union* (18-country survey), no. 5 (March 1995).

been routed both where they have pursued rather radical reforms
(Lithuania and Mongolia) and where they have stuck to gradual reforms (Romania and Bulgaria). The post-communists have done comparatively well in three kinds of cases. First, in Poland and Hungary
the former communist parties have become firm free marketeers and
right-wing social democratic parties. Second, in Moldova, Ukraine, and
Russia, reform has still not brought about significant growth, and the
communists obtain 25–30 percent of the vote, but they are far from a
majority. Finally, in Albania the former Communist Party won a majority in parliamentary elections in 1997, because it seemed to represent
the democratic option.

Admittedly, governments in the transition period lose elections
more often than not, and the non-socialists suffer badly from political
fragmentation in most countries. Issues besides economic policy matter, but given the impact of economic transformation after the demise
of communism, economic policy tends to dominate elections. The ver-
dict is clear: the electoral chances for non-socialists are far better after

Table 4.3: Are Your Country's Economic Reforms Too Fast or Too Slow? (percentage in 1994)

Country	Too Slow or no reforms	Too Fast	Difference
Radical Reformers			
Czech Republic	28	26	2
Albania	39	18	21
Estonia	48	9	39
Poland	51	15	36
Latvia	62	11	51
Slovakia	64	13	51
Gradual Non-socialist Reformers			
Lithuania	52	19	33
Hungary	48	13	35
Russia	59	18	41
Bulgaria	67	7	60
Gradual Post-communist Reformers			
Romania	58	15	43
Kazakhstan	59	14	45
Ukraine	65	12	53
Belarus	67	8	59

Source: European Commission, *Central and Eastern Eurobarometer: Public Opinion and the European Union* (18-country survey), no. 5 (March 1995).

radical than gradual reforms, while post-communists can thrive on gradual reforms of a non-socialist government.

These conclusions are supported by opinion poll data. The EU Eurobarometer has posed the same questions for years in 17 of these countries.[33] In 1993, there were only four countries in which a majority of the population thought their country was "going in the right direction" (see table 4.2). They were all radical reform countries: Albania, the Czech Republic, Estonia, and Latvia, while all countries with gradual reform showed massive popular disappointment. Similarly, when people were asked whether "economic reforms are going too fast, too slow, or about the right speed," a substantial majority answered "too slow" in 16 out of 17 countries, though this included only a small majority in the radically reforming Czech Republic (see table 4.3). The perception that radical reforms are not popular can be discarded as false.

Thus we can conclude, first, that economic policy seems decisive for the outcome of the transition. Second, early radical reforms have only been launched by some non-socialist governments. Third, the large variations of social costs in the transition are primarily connected with rent-seeking, which should be the focus of economic policy. Finally, contrary to the general perceptions, both the electoral record and opinion poll data bear out that radical reforms are more popular than gradual or delayed reforms.

Which Are the Worst Dangers during the Transition?

What dangers are the post-communist countries likely to encounter in the future? Four dangers are apparent. First, the very state-building may fail. Second, a country may not complete the elementary transition but end up with lasting financial instability. A third danger is that a country does not liberalize and privatize enough or that privatization leads to excessive concentration, so that the country gets stuck in a corrupt, cronyism form of capitalism. A fourth risk is encapsulation in the entitlement trap, with excessive taxes and social transfers.

The worst case is that the newly independent state fails in its nation-building, not even establishing basic law and order and elementary state institutions. The obvious example is Tajikistan, which has collapsed in every sense. Georgia appeared close to such a fate, but it seems to have been salvaged.

A few countries have so far failed in their transition because of irresponsible policies, leading to little liberalization and privatization and sometimes continued high inflation. The failures today are primarily Belarus and Turkmenistan. Belarus is run by a truly populist and authoritarian president who does not care about economic laws, and his entourage is considered to make money on illicit deals facilitated by economic chaos. Similarly, Turkmenistan is run by the most totalitarian leader in any former communist state, who could not be bothered by economics. Naturally, a long period of economic mismanagement is bound to undermine the legitimacy of the regimes, and none of these countries is democratic.

After four years of transition in the former Soviet Union, it is encouraging to see that many countries have eventually straightened up their economic policies. Yet, all over the former communist world, pervasive corruption reigns, as the government retains control over large resources—enterprises and real estate—and a large number of formal or informal state permissions are still required. A real danger exists that several countries will get stuck for a long time in "crony capitalism," implying that even the big capitalists remain heavily dependent on the state. Until the early 1990s, several Latin American countries and India were examples of such states, and they have not been very dynamic. Far too much property remains in public ownership, and much of the privatization is being directed to protégés of the regime. In some cases, private monopolies evolve with a cozy relationship with a regulative state. Slovakia has opted for a peculiar favoritism in its privatization, although it has carried out a successful stabilization and liberalization. Such a concentration of economic power could endanger democracy as well. With the exception of Slovakia, all the countries that might end up in either of these first three groups pursued gradual economic reform.

Even the successful leaders of the transition may end up in trouble. The apparent threat is the entitlement trap.[34] The four Visegrad countries have public expenditures around 50 percent of GDP. In particular, Hungary had public expenditures of as much as 62 percent of GDP in 1992 and 1993.[35] In the whole world, only Sweden and Denmark exceed this level. The problems are multiple. High public expenditures mean that taxes must be high, and still a big budget deficit easily results, which in turn leads to an excessive debt burden, as is in Hungary. Not only high taxes but also large social transfers—23 percent of GDP in Hungary in 1993—dissuade many from working. The combined effect is that people work less than in a more liberal economy, and thus produce less. No country with the high public expenditures that Hungary maintains has been especially dynamic. By comparison, the economic tigers in East Asia only spend a few percent of GDP on social transfers.[36]

Countries in the former Soviet Union are not likely to fall into the entitlement trap, because they cannot collect much taxes. Average state revenues as a share of GDP had plummeted to 29 percent in 1993, and the share is continuing to decline.[37] Hence, the former Soviet republics may opt for a much more liberal model than has Central Europe. So far, Estonia stands out as the country that has consciously done so.

What Economic Models May Result?

At the outset of the post-communist transition, a large number of possible economic models were discussed. Today, the number of feasible options has dwindled.

The Central Europeans are adopting much of the West European model. While preparing to enter the European Union, they promulgate large amounts of EU legislation. However, as a result they are facing the danger of limited economic growth and the entitlement trap most clearly developed in Sweden.[38] Poland is frequently compared with post-war Italy—corrupt and messy but in spite of everything highly dynamic.

Countries that have not reached equally far are in danger of getting stuck in worse corruption, amounting to crony capitalism, which appears to be like the old protectionist and interventionist Latin American model. Most of the former Soviet republics are in this state, notably Russia and Ukraine.

The way out for these countries would be to opt for a very liberal model more reminiscent of the United States, as Chile and Argentina have done. Estonia, Georgia, and the Kyrgyz Republic have adopted such a policy, but more countries are likely to follow, as they are being compelled to control their economic and social problems.

Finally, those few that fail to undertake their transition might end up in a terrible economic situation reminiscent of much of Africa without a functioning state or economy. At present, only Tajikistan is facing such a fate, adjusting to neighboring Afghanistan.

As time passes, the differences in the outcomes are becoming more striking than the similarities, and it is obvious that these great varieties were not predetermined. The quality of economic policy-making during the few years immediately following communism appears to have been of fundamental importance for all these countries for decades to come.

Notes

I would like to thank Simon Johnson and Peter Boone for collaboration on related themes, Aurel Braun for making me write this paper, and the participants in the Toronto conference for useful comments. In particular, I want to express my gratitude to Janos Kornai for his wise suggestions.

1. The main international organizations involved have produced impressive recent overviews that provide us with a solid factual base and sound analysis: World Bank (1996), EBRD (1994, 1995, 1996), and the IMF (Banarjee, et al, 1995; Citrin and Lahiri, 1995). I have contributed to two overview articles (Åslund, et al., 1996; Åslund, 1994), and I draw heavily on the latest of them in this paper.

2. Anders Åslund, Peter Boone, and Simon Johnson, "How to Stabilize: Lessons from Post-Communist Countries," *Brookings Papers on Economic Activity* (Washington: Brookings Institution) 26, 1: 217–313, 1996, 231.

3. Yugoslavia and Poland in 1989; Yugoslavia, Belarus, Ukraine, Moldova, Georgia, Armenia, Azerbaijan, Kazakstan, Uzbekistan, Turkmenistan, and Tajikistan in 1993.

4. Douglass C. North, *Structure and Change in Economic History* (Norton: New York, 1981).

5. See Jeffrey Sachs and Andrew Warner, "Economic Reform and the Process of Global Integration," *Brookings Papers on Economic Activity* (Washington: Brookings Institution) 25, 1: 1–118, 1995.

6. We have discussed it in Åslund, et al., 1996.

7. Janos Kornai, *The Socialist System: The Political Economy of Communism* (Princeton: Princeton University Press, 1992), 360–65.

8. Maxim Boycko, Andrei Shleifer, and Robert Vishny, *Privatizing Russia* (Cambridge: MIT Press, 1995).

9. Statistics from the UN Economic Commission for Europe. Belarus claimed a growth of 10 percent in 1997, but this was done by reviving the old command economy that produced what few demanded, and the statistics are subject to doubt.

10. Stanley Fisher, Ratna Sahay, and Carlos A. Vegh, "Stabilization and Growth in Transition Economies: The Early Experience," IMF Working Paper, mimeo, March 1996.

11. Åslund, et al., "How to Stabilize," 236–7.

12. Fischer, et al., "Stabilization and Growth in Transition Economies."

13. Stockholm Institute of East European Economies, *Key Economic Indicators*, vol. 4, no. 2, July 17, 1996, 1.

14. *Ibid.*

15. Domenico Mario Nuti, "How to Contain Economic Inertia in the Transitional Economies," *Transition* (World Bank), 3, 11: 1–3, 1992; Domenico Mario Nuti, and Richard Portes, "Central Europe: The Way Forward" in Portes, Richard, ed., *Economic Transformation in Central Europe: A Progress Report*, 1–20 (London: Centre for Economic Policy Research, 1993); Richard Portes, "From Central Planning to a Market Economy" in Islam, Shafiqul, and Michael Mandelbaum, eds., *Making Markets*, 16–52 (New York: Council on Foreign Relations, 1993).

16. The World Bank (1996, p. 14); the EBRD (1995); Heritage Foundation (Johnson and Sheehy, 1996); and Fraser Institute (Gwartney, et al., 1996).

17. Martha de Melo, Cevdet Denizer, and Alan Gelb, "From Plan to Market: Patterns of Transition," Policy Research Working Paper No. 1564 (Washington: World Bank, 1996).

18. Jeffrey Sachs and Andrew Warner, "Economic Reform and the Process of Global Integration," *Brookings Papers on Economic Activity*, (Washington: Brookings Institution) 25, 1: 1–118, 1995.

19. Åslund, et al., "How to Stabilize," 245–8.

20. European Bank for Reconstruction and Development (EBRD), *Transition Report 1995*, 1995.

21. Åslund, et al., "How to Stabilize."

22. World Bank, *World Development Report 1996: From Plan to Market* (Oxford University Press, 1996), 68–69.

23. Åslund, et al., "How to Stabilize," 237–43.

24. Lipton and Sachs, 1990; Kornai, 1990; Blanchard, et al., 1991; Fischer and Gelb, 1991; Åslund, 1992.

25. Åslund, et al., "How to Stabilize;" de Melo, et al., *From Plan to Market*.

26. Åslund, et al., "How to Stabilize."

27. Anders Åslund, "Reform vs. 'Rent-Seeking' in Russia's Economic Transformation," *Transition* (OMRI), January 26, 1996, 12–16.

28. Åslund, et al., "How to Stabilize," 256–61.

29. *Russian Economic Trends*, 1996; Åslund, "How to Stabilize."

30. Larry Diamond, "Democracy and Economic Reform: Tensions, Compati-bilities, and Strategies for Reconciliation" in Edward P. Lazear, ed., *Economic Transition in Eastern Europe and Russia* (Stanford, Calif.: Hoover Institution Press, 1995), 107–58; Jose Maria Maravall, "The Myth of Authoritarian Advantage," *Journal of Democracy* 5, 4:17–31, October 1994.

31. Robert D. Putnam, *Making Democracy Work* (Princeton: Princeton University Press, 1993), 177–83.

32. Åslund, et al., "How to Stabilize," 264–73.

33. Åslund, et al., "How to Stabilize," 271–72.

34. Jeffrey Sachs, "Postcommunist Parties and the Politics of Entitlements," *Transition* (Washington: World Bank) 6, 3:1–4 March 1995.

35. Biswajit Banarjee, Vincent Koen, Thomas Krueger, Mark S. Lutz, Michael Marrese, and Tapio O. Saavalainen, *Road Maps of the Transition: The Baltics, the Czech Republic, Hungary, and Russia*, IMF, Occasional Paper No. 127, Washington, 1995, 5.

36. Sachs, "Postcommunist Parties and the Politics of Entitlements."

37. Daniel A. Citrin and Ashok K. Lahiri, eds., *Policy Experiences and Issues in the Baltics, Russia, and Other Countries of the Former Soviet Union*, IMF, Occasional Paper No. 133, Washington, 1995, 78.

38. Sachs, "Postcommunist Parties and the Politics of Entitlements."

Part Two

Hungary's Post-Communist Transition

Chapter 5

The Regional Perspective

Zoltan Barany

Introduction

The preceding essays addressed three integral areas of systemic transitions in general terms. Before moving on to a specific examination of the various aspects of Hungary's democratic transition and consolidation, it would seem expedient to sketch out the comparative environment of our case study. Cross-regional disparities (between Eastern and Southern Europe and Latin America) in socioeconomic and industrial development, ethnic complexity, civil society, the international environment, and other factors present the East European states as the most logical base of comparison for Hungary.[1] In this chapter the focus is on the former members of the non-Soviet Warsaw Pact with the exception of the former German Democratic Republic whose reunification with the Federal Republic rendered its post-communist transition in many respects far too different to be included in the same group.[2] Moreover, although Bulgaria and Romania are included in the forthcoming analysis, I will emphasize developments in the East Central European states (the Czech Republic, Poland, and Slovakia), which have in many ways shared similar developmental patterns that set them apart from the Balkans.

What are the commonalities and disparities in the democratization processes of the East European systems? Where was Hungary situated in 1989 and, again, in 1998 in the spectrum of East European states in terms of its political and socioeconomic development? Has its comparative situation changed and, if so, how and why? This essay is predicated on the premise that the answers to these questions reveal much about not only the Hungarian but also about the East European transitions to democracy. The purpose of this chapter, then, is not to provide an exhaustive analysis of Hungarian developments but to build a bridge between the general and the specific in order to place Hungary's experience with post-communist transition and consolidation in a comparative regional perspective. Rather than looking at Hungary itself, I intend to look at the region of which Hungary is only a part. I make three arguments. First, the widely shared view in 1989 that Hungary was the "most likely to succeed" case in Eastern Europe was somewhat flawed because it neglected to factor into this assumption some important political, social, and economic considerations. Second, in the first five years after 1989 Hungary had fallen behind the Czech Republic and Poland in some respects of political and especially economic transition, although since 1995 it has managed to close the gap. Third, despite the numerous problems of the past eight years, Hungary—along with the Czech Republic and Poland—has been a leader of the transition process and has already largely succeeded in creating and consolidating a democratic political system.

Eastern Europe in 1989: Hungary as Ostensible Front-Runner

Throughout the late-communist period (1980s) and at the time of state socialism's demise, Hungary was widely expected to make the transition to democracy and the market with the least amount of difficulty.[3] While on the surface this seemed to be a reasonable assumption, I argue that some factors already put Hungary's apparent front-runner status in question in 1989. Using the regional context, first I will identify some of the most important reasons why giving Hungary top ranking seemed sensible at the time and then proceed to point out some factors that mitigated this interpretation.

Soviet-style communism imposed parallel political and socioeconomic structures on the region, but it could not, of course, eradicate the long-standing and profound differences between these countries. Historic disparities in political traditions, social attitudes, levels of economic development, and the like also had their effects felt in the communist era and, no doubt, will continue to do so in the future. The death of Stalin in 1953 coincided with gradually increasing diversity within the Soviet bloc, beginning in earnest with the emergence of Wladyslaw Gomulka's "national communism" in Poland in 1956. Hungary's ill-fated revolution of the same year was followed by a few years of quasi-mandatory political and social repression. Yet, by the early 1960s it was clear that the new leadership was moving away from the Stalinist paradigm. In the second half of the decade, a novel political and socioeconomic model took shape characterized by tolerance, pragmatism, and—critically important in the Soviet view—stability. Hungary became the "merriest barrack in the bloc" fundamentally as a result of two tacit agreements forged by Janos Kadar's regime (1956–1988) with Hungarian society and the Moscow leaders. In the former, the political elites took upon themselves to improve living conditions in return for the population's political acquiescence. In the latter, the Kremlin agreed to permit a measure of domestic liberalization and reform as long as the Budapest leaders could guarantee political stability and continued adherence to Soviet foreign and security policy imperatives. The outcome of these implicit bargains was overwhelmingly positive, especially given built-in systemic limitations. For the rest of the communist period, Hungarians enjoyed one of the highest living standards in the region, a plentiful supply of basic consumer goods, travel to the West, a lively cultural milieu, and, in Elemer Hankiss' words, a state-embracing ideological decompression and social demobilization: a singular combination in the region.[4] Until the mid-1970s few observers noted, however, that some of the meat in goulash communism was bought on credit which would have to be repaid.

In sum, Budapest gained little from Mikhail Gorbachev's *perestroika* and *glasnost*, save for the obvious benefit of a more favorable Soviet political climate that emboldened the reformist faction in the Hungarian Socialist Workers' Party. "To describe the Hungarian economic reforms as *perestroika* is also close to an insult. The Hungarians have been working at it for more than 20 years; they have gone farther in deeds than the Russians have in words; they now face problems of which the Soviets can only dream," wrote Timothy Garton Ash in 1987.[5] While Hungary remained a loyal bloc member, in the mid-1970s—roughly coinciding with the Soviet-imposed retrenchment of the economic reform process that was to have extremely detrimental long-term consequences—Budapest began to actively court the West. This new foreign policy yielded tangible benefits, such as membership in the IMF, GATT, and other international organizations; an expanding trade with the West; and a growing recognition as Eastern Europe's most reform-friendly regime.[6] It culminated in Miklos Nemeth's government's decision to dismantle the "iron curtain" on Hungary's border with Austria and its subsequent refusal to return East German refugees to their homeland in the summer of 1989.

These positive characteristics of Hungarian communism are even more noteworthy when contrasted with developments in the region. In terms of political liberalization, only Poland came close to replicating Hungary's record, but that country remained unstable, crisis-prone, and its elites—although not averse to the introduction of limited political and economic reforms—could not solidify their rule after crushing the independent trade union, Solidarity, in 1981. Following the suppression of the Prague Spring in 1968, the Czechoslovak leadership swiftly erased the reform movement's achievements (with the notable exception of Slovakia's expanded autonomy) and established one of the most orthodox regimes in Eastern Europe, eschewing social and economic, let alone political reforms. At the same time, Czechoslovakia's economic performance remained respectable by the humble standards of centrally planned economies.

The populations of the Balkan states fared worse. Bulgarian leaders steadfastly maintained their conservative and oppressive rule, allowing only cosmetic economic reforms impelled by the coming crisis. Soon after Nicolae Ceausescu's rise to power in 1965, Romania became the most repressive state in the region. Perturbed neither by the desperate poverty of the population nor the regime's increasing international isolation beginning in the mid-1980s, Romania's elites had continued "to apply the classical Stalinist framework of military mobilization" with dogged determination, until December 1989.[7] Moreover, both states' treatment of ethnic minorities received widespread and well-deserved international criticism.

What factors account for such apparent variety among the East European regimes that seemed, superficially at least, so much alike?[8] Although there are numerous explanatory variables, the two critical ones in my view are the political orientations of the East European regimes themselves and Soviet policy toward them. After the mid-1950s, Moscow's loosening control increased the authority of domestic elites. Thus, more reform-friendly regimes were willing to probe the patience of the Kremlin by introducing less restrictive, more liberal policies with more or less success (more with Hungary and, periodically, Poland, and less with Czechoslovakia in 1967–68,) while conservative elites chose to strengthen their control over state and society (Bulgaria, Czechoslovakia, and Romania).

The other crucial variable is the Kremlin's East European policy.[9] The USSR allowed Hungarian elites more domestic freedom owing to the bloody and, from Moscow's perspective, embarrassing and potentially destabilizing 1956 revolution; its confidence in the local leadership's ability to control the population; and because Hungary was strategically less vital than the states of the Warsaw Pact northern tier (East Germany, Poland, and Czechoslovakia). In a like vein, one might argue that Romania and Bulgaria—both of relatively minor economic and military-strategic significance as indicated by the absence (in Romania after 1958) of Soviet occupation troops—could have enjoyed a liberalization trend similar to Hungary's had their elites been favorably disposed to it. In contrast, the northern tier states were strategically (and economically) far too important for Moscow to jeopardize its control over them by letting them experiment with Hungarian-type liberal policies. The reasons why Poland had undergone some relatively liberal periods (e.g., most of the 1970s under the leadership of Edward Gierek) were the inability of its elites to prevent domestic crises (1956, 1970, 1976, 1980–81) and their unwillingness to repress entire social strata, and Soviet calculation that a heavy-handed repression of Poland à la Hungary in 1956 might well result in serious armed conflict.

For a number of reasons, then, those who expected Hungary to do the best among its East European neighbors in the post-communist age were not unrealistic. Still, several important factors should have tempered their optimism. In the late 1970s, the Hungarian economy and society entered a period which was aptly described as the "most pervasive case of malaise in the region."[10] Although the reform-minded communist political leadership that replaced Kadar in May 1988 tried to implement some political and economic reforms, it was unable to reverse the spread of systemic exhaustion and breakdown that had its effect felt in practically every area of political, economic, and social affairs.[11] By the mid-1980s, the regime's eroding legitimacy was signaled by growing ideological decay within and declining membership of the ruling party whose leaders were unable to find cures to Hungary's multiplying and deepening social and economic ailments. Reforms intended to "improve socialist democracy" resulted in piecemeal changes in the political system (multislate elections were held in 1985) that neither satisfied the population let alone the increasingly vocal democratic opposition, nor halted the progress of systemic decay.

The proverbial red flag that should have cautioned those underestimating Hungary's post-communist troubles was the state of the economy. As Ivan T. Berend commented at the time, the underlying problem was that—notwithstanding twenty years of reforms—the political elites could not completely break with the policy of economic development adopted in the late 1940s and early 1950s.[12] While certainly providing a measure of preparation for the economic transition, some of the economic reforms might, in fact, have taught the wrong lessons, for their implementation continued to depend on internal state subsidies, Council for Mutual Economic Assistance (CMEA) markets, and foreign loans rather than on hard budget constraints. Aside from some relatively bright spots, such as the performance of the agricultural sector and Hungary's increasing openness to foreign business, the economy had deteriorated to the point that by the late 1980s negative growth rates were registered. One of the most portentous long-term problems was the country's rapidly increasing external debt (nearly $20 billion

in 1989) coupled with growing budget deficits. Only rapid improvement in economic performance could be hoped to alleviate the multiplying social and economic problems, but such recovery was unreason-
able to expect, particularly given the short- and medium-term
economic dislocations that marketization was certain to entail.

Another cluster of concerns also suggested that, in some respects,
Hungary's post-communist transition might be more trying than those
of some of its neighbors. As Samuel Huntington noted in 1990, Hungary did not possess top ranking in the region according to several important criteria pertaining to democratization; for instance, in terms of
previous experience with democracy (Czechoslovakia), levels of social
and economic development (East Germany and Czechoslovakia), and
the extent, depth, and strength of independent social and political organizations (Poland).[13] In the period of transition and consolidation,
these were some of the factors that were to have profound implications
for Hungary's and Eastern Europe's political and socioeconomic development.

Political Transition and Consolidation in Eastern Europe: Patterns of Development

For the first time in its history, Eastern Europe gained the opportunity
to build democracies after World War I, following the collapse of the
Austro–Hungarian monarchy and the Paris peace treaties. In spite of
some auspicious beginnings, authoritarian states were established
everywhere within a decade, with the exception of Czechoslovakia's
partial success in constructing a democratic system.[14] The breakdown
of the Soviet empire offered another chance for democratization and,
eight years into this process, the overwhelming impression is that the
region's states have been fundamentally successful. Although Soviet
control had mostly negative consequences for the region, it—like the
domination of the Austro–Hungarian monarchy—did have some re-
deeming qualities. For instance, it precluded hostilities between and
within the bloc's member states and provided a steady market for uncompetitive East European products. (It is another side of the coin that
these products were uncompetitive in large part due to the economies'
systemic constraints.) Both of these benefits were noted after 1989
when, just as in the wake of World War I, interstate and intrastate conflicts arose, and the traditional markets within the empire collapsed.

Taking minimalist definitions as guideposts, as John Mueller does, it
is clear that in most of Eastern Europe democracy and capitalism have
already been established. There is much room for improvement in both

respects, yet it is undeniable that since 1989 free elections have been held on schedule, governments have not been forcibly overthrown, and people have been allowed to freely pursue their economic interests.[15] But what kind of democracy and capitalism and at what price? The argument of this section is that there have been significant differences in the political and socioeconomic developments between the East Central European and the Balkan states, on the one hand, and within these subregions on the other. Although we are not observing a horse race, it is important to note that East European leaders are keenly aware of each others' accomplishments and failures. Politicians and experts abroad—whether their primary interests are human rights or privatization—view these countries comparatively, implicitly, and explicitly and rank them according to various criteria, and their assessments impact upon such key issues as credit and loan extension and future membership in Western international organizations.

East Central Europe

The transition to and consolidation of democracy has progressed farthest in East Central Europe of all the former communist lands. Still, there have been important disparities between the four countries that make up this region. Until 1996, the Czech Republic was considered by most analysts as the most successful in terms of democratization and market reforms, closely followed by Poland and Hungary. Slovakia's political trajectory thus far leaves some profound doubts about the attainment of democratic consolidation there. Since 1996, Poland and Hungary, in several important political and economic developments, appear to have overtaken the Czech Republic.[16]

Notwithstanding the differences among them, in most fundamental areas of democratization all East Central European states (Czech Republic, Hungary, and Poland) states have already succeeded. Stable multiparty systems are in place, a new institutional structure has been erected, several regularly scheduled free and unfettered local and national elections have been held, the results of which have been accepted as fair by politicians and the electorate. Czechoslovakia, the only federal state of this region, did break up into its constituent parts but, in contrast with Yugoslavia and the Soviet Union, it did so peacefully and with remarkable civility.

Until 1997, political life had been relatively stable in the Czech Republic. The dominant political force through most of the post-communist period had been the Civic Democratic Party (CDP) and the coalition it formed with smaller partners after the elections in mid-1992. Vaclav Klaus, the charismatic Czech prime minister (and the CDP's leader), until his resignation as a result of a campaign finance scandal in November 1997, had been perhaps the most decisive East European politician who had shepherded his country through the transition process with uncommon pragmatism. The government had a clear vision of what it wanted to accomplish and shrewdly sidestepped some of the issues that proved so divisive elsewhere in the region. Until 1995, when the Social Democrats emerged as a strong opposition, the CDP benefited from the weakness of its rivals. The Czech Republic has been unique in the region to the extent that its population has viewed the previous system very negatively, and the former Communist Party has been politically marginalized.

The CDP was unusually effective in organizing a network of local chapters and, in large part owing to the government's economic policies, in maintaining the highest level of popular support in the region.[17] It should not be overlooked that the Klaus government—while masquerading in Thatcherite garb—had succeeded in preserving social peace by appeasing trade unions, spending billions of crowns in government subsidies to keep unprofitable enterprises afloat, and creating tens of thousands of nonessential government positions.[18] Although the CDP lost little support in the May 1996 elections compared to its showing four years before, the Social Democrats more than doubled their support. As a result, the CDP was unable to gain a majority, and Klaus and his advisers had to prove themselves in the art of compromise, a skill that they had not been compelled to perfect earlier. A conspicuous shortcoming of the Czech Republic's democratization process has been its treatment of national minorities, particularly the Roma, for which it has received a great deal of international criticism.

In the spring and summer of 1997, the Czech economy weathered several shocks which put its reputation as the region's most robust on the line. As it turned out, underneath the shiny facade supported by balanced budgets, low inflation, and unemployment, trouble areas continued to fester. The financial industry has been ravaged by corruption and attendant scandals.[19] Even more distressing has been the fact that unprofitable enterprises have been allowed to continue operating in the red. As The Economist noted, while "bankruptcies in Hungary have killed off more than 30,000 companies . . . in the Czech Republic there has not been a single major bankruptcy since communism collapsed."[20] The usually self-assured Klaus was forced to publicly admit the errors in his economic policy and that his country was heading for recession. As a result of a protracted political scandal rooted in improper campaign contributions and preferential privatization deals, Klaus and his government were forced to tender their resignations. Until new elections in mid-1998, the caretaker government is headed

by the highly respected, former Central Bank's governor, Josef To-
sovsky.

Perhaps the most important similarity between Poland and Hungary
is that in both states the voters returned the former communists to
power in 1993 and 1994, respectively. For a number of reasons this was
not—or, at any rate, should not have been—entirely unexpected.[21] As
a result of a relatively liberal and reform-friendly rule during the late-
communist period, in both countries popular memories of the recent
past were far less negative than in the Czech Republic. Communist parties in Poland and Hungary were also characterized by a measure of
internal diversity that eased their conversion and rendered them more
adaptable and more likely to succeed under the new (i.e., democratic)
rules of the political game. Although some economic reforms did take
place before 1989, both countries were burdened by heavy foreign
debts (unlike Czechoslovakia) that limited the economic elbow room
of the new governments.

The problem of the "first generation" of post-communist governments in these states was not that they were not making progress in
transforming their economies; it was their inability to improve the economic situation of most ordinary Poles and Hungarians. It appears that
the people found no solace in their country's (especially Poland's) macroeconomic successes but became increasingly nostalgic toward those
attributes of the communist system—guaranteed employment, social
security, and income largely independent of the quality of work—that
afforded them virtually assured albeit modest standards of living. An
impressive array of opinion poll data has shown that individuals adopt
political attitudes that offer maximum utility or benefit and define self-
interest "in relatively short-term calculations which figure directly on a
person's material well-being."[22] Prior to the 1993 Polish elections, only
about 10 percent of those polled admitted that their lives had become
better since 1989 in contrast to 60 percent who expressed the contrary
view.[23]

In the post-communist era Polish politics has been remarkably volatile. Between 1989 and 1993 the country had four prime ministers and
a number of governmental shake-ups, partly due to the pre-1992 electoral law that did not set a minimum threshold necessary for parliamentary representation. As Adam Michnik suggested, by returning
communist era leaders to power, Poles voted for a return to the only
normalcy, stabilization, and peace some of them had ever known.[24] The
"Solidarity" governments also took the wrong side (from the voters'
perspective) on a number of sensitive issues, perhaps most prominently by allowing the Catholic Church to acquire a great deal of political clout, as illustrated by its success in pushing a widely unpopular

and extremely restrictive abortion law through the legislature. After four years the voters returned another coalition of trade unionists, nationalists, and free marketeers (dominated by the Solidarity Electoral Action) to government in the September 1997 elections.

Although Hungary's first post-communist government served out its four-year term, economic matters constituted only one of its several shortcomings. The government could not convince the voters that it had clarity of political vision, an acceptable ranking of priorities, and the competence necessary for its tasks. Throughout its tenure, the governing Hungarian Democratic Forum (HDF) was rent with internal dissension and faced charges of corruption and nepotism. The HDF's inept handling of the media (which, to be sure, remained a bulwark of communist era holdovers), and its inability to distance itself quickly and unambiguously from extremist elements antagonized many of its former supporters. Some HDF leaders apparently failed to realize that the interwar era—especially the mannerisms and some of the personalities (particularly Admiral Miklos Horthy) of whom they seemed intent on emulating and/or celebrating—was not a source of pleasant memories for the majority of Hungarians. Furthermore, a tangible delusional factor was also at play. The public personae of many Hungarian politicians radiated smugness and superiority based on the exaggerated notion of what was achieved coupled with a reluctance to make sacrifices and adapt to the new socioeconomic conditions.

The socialist-dominated governments that took over in Poland in 1993 and in Hungary in 1994 did not change the fundamental direction of their predecessors' policies. Actually, in both cases the new masters of the economy pursued even more consistent market reforms. Their economic elbow room turned out to be just as limited as their predecessors' and their supporters—particularly the trade unions, the working class, and the pensioners—expected economic goods, such as increased spending on social welfare and more job security, which the new governments were ill-positioned to proffer. In fact, 1994 might be considered the high point of the Left's popularity, "the last moment when the electorate imagined that it is possible to have capitalism's strong currency and full shelves and socialism's job security" and social safety net.[25]

A further important difference between Poland and Hungary is that, while in the fall of 1997 a center-right government did return to power in Poland, at least following the first round of the national elections, the Hungarian Socialist Party (HSP) appeared on track to form another government. Still, the center-right parties had substantially improved their electoral performance, especially the Young Democrats who received 28.2 percent of the vote, just four percent shy of the HSP's showing.[26] (The Young Democrats ultimately prevailed and formed a coalition government.) No matter which of the two parties is going to dominate Hungarian politics at the turn of the millennium, the consolidation of democracy and the market economy are not at all in danger.

Notwithstanding the shortcomings of the East Central European states' political transitions, I agree with the broadly held view that these are the three states where democracy has developed the most substantial roots. To better appreciate their progress we need to look at the problems of the Balkan states.

The Balkans

I include Slovakia under the "Balkans" subheading because insofar as its post-communist political (though not economic) trajectory is concerned, it has approximated those of Romania and Bulgaria more closely than those of its East Central European neighbors. It deserves mention that these lands have been historically less developed both politically and economically than the states of East Central Europe. Some attributes of the Balkans' communist regimes had reinforced this comparative backwardness. One significant difference between the two subregions is that neither in the two Balkan states nor in Slovakia developed any notable democratic opposition to communist rule; therefore, in 1989, the communists—for want of another alternative—were replaced by reform-communist elites.[27]

Slovak leftist parties have managed to hold on to power in the post-communist period, and there is no indication of change in this state of affairs. When Vladimir Meciar's nationalist Movement for Democratic Slovakia (MDS)—itself composed in large measure of former communists—came to power in July 1992, it enjoyed the support of the Party of the Democratic Left (PDL) (the new name of the old Communist Party). The PDL soon became displeased with and increasingly critical of Prime Minister Meciar's authoritarian policies and went into opposition.[28] Following the March 1994 ouster of Meciar, the PDL formed a coalition government only to be defeated by Meciar and the MDS-Peasant Party coalition in the October 1994 national elections.

Meciar, who in J. F. Brown's words, "was (and remains) an impulsive, provincial, primitive politician—no matter how intelligent and successful,"[29] has dominated Slovak politics, supported primarily by nationalist heavy industrial workers. The governing coalition is widely considered to be intolerant and chauvinistic, and its political machinations have tempered whatever goodwill existed in the West toward Bratislava. Meciar has tried to twist the constitution in order to squeeze an opposition party out of Parliament, propose laws that would make "defamation of the country" an offense to be punished by a maximum five-year prison sentence, and ease the imposition of martial law.[30] By the standards of East Central Europe, Slovakia's democratic institutions remain unstable. Although the relationship between presidents and prime ministers is nowhere placid in Eastern Europe, the seemingly incessant feud between Meciar and former President Michal Kovac had a particularly disruptive impact on Slovak politics. As in Romania, the government's approach to ethnic minority rights has also been a cause for strong Western criticism. As one expert lamented, "Slovaks tend to equate democracy with economic prosperity."[31]

Using Mueller's minimalist definition, Romania, notwithstanding its ominous start in 1989–1990, has become a democracy in the past eight years. At the same time the Romanian case also demonstrates the problems with so loose a definition. Romanian political life has been stable precisely because—despite relatively free elections—it has not been democratic, and many key politicians have been holdovers from one of the region's most repressive dictatorships. In contrast with strong presidential licenses, the legislature is relatively feeble along with a very fluid party system. Unlike in Slovakia, in Romania a presidential system has developed with, until 1996, Ion Iliescu of the Democratic National Salvation Front at the helm. Similar to Slovakia, nationalism has been one of the most prominent ideological influences on the Romanian regime, which has at times exploited the antiminority (especially anti-Hungarian and anti-Roma) sentiments of some political parties and certain segments of society.

Romania has had the least stable party system in Eastern Europe where splits in the political landscape have continued to proliferate. After 1990 the country's leaders allied themselves with the segments of the working class least interested in radical reform and made an effort "to discredit the very notion of privatization or foreign investments by brandishing the horrors of capitalism and sounding the alarm that the country was about to be sold out to foreigners."[32] Since then, the political institutional system has become more stable, the ruling coalition has distanced itself from some of the most extremist political forces, and some—although often ignored—improvements have taken place in state-ethnic minority relations.[33]

In the June 1996 local elections opposition parties scored a number of impressive victories followed by the triumph of the Democratic Convention and its presidential candidate, Emil Constantinescu, in the November 1996 national and presidential elections. These new developments in Romanian politics are widely expected to signal the advent of a positive shift towards more democratic (if less stable) politics.[34] In a short time the president and Victor Ciorbea's new government made a number of painful but necessary economic decisions and embarked upon a policy of reconciliation with the Hungarian minority. The favorable reception of the new Romanian political and economic direction was also reflected by the country's improved international prestige.[35]

Ciorbea and his government were unable to control the coalition plagued by incessant squabbles, however, and encountered trouble in attempting to consolidate the early achievements of their reform program. During his short tenure, inflation had increased dramatically and corruption did not subside. Following his resignation in March 1998 Radu Vasile, Ciorbea's colleague in the Christian Democratic National Peasants' Party, formed a new government. His program includes lowering income taxes, courting foreign investment, subsidizing farmers, and streamlining the government.

Of the three states mentioned here, Bulgaria has been the most successful in its democratization efforts. Although its governments have been relatively unstable (the country has had seven governments and many more—usually unsuccessful—votes of no confidence in them), Bulgaria's party system has been one of the most steady in the region with the same three parties determining political outcomes since 1989. Bulgaria has not experienced the authoritarian tendencies often displayed by Slovak and Romanian politicians. In political crises neither soldiers (as in Serbia) nor miners (as in Romania) were called in to prop up the regime, the authorities have not interfered with peaceful demonstrations, and the constitution has been generally respected by all political players.[36] Moreover, the appalling treatment the country's main ethnic minority, the Turks, were subjected to during the communist period has stopped; their party has become one of the most important ethnically based political organizations in Europe. Bulgaria's fundamental problem has been its disastrous economic performance rooted in the reluctance of its leaders to ally themselves with unpopular but necessary economic policies.

In spite of the evident problems of democratization in the Balkans, I disagree with John Hall who, referring to Romania and Bulgaria (and Russia), suggested that "it is hard not to be more and more pessimistic . . . the further toward the East that one looks."[37] Clearly, these three states have had more difficult political transitions than the Czech Republic, Hungary, or Poland, but they have also had less favorable conditions before and during communism. Perhaps most importantly, Bulgarians, Romanians, and Slovaks have been able to express their political preferences in several free elections in the past six years.

Reflections on Eastern Europe's New Democracies

As impressed with the achievements and as optimistic concerning the future of East European democracies as I am, it seems prudent to note some of the more troublesome political issues that have shaped the region's new democracies. In this section I briefly elaborate on three such themes: political communication, political institutions, and extremism and nationalism.

Political Communication

In East European states where genuine elite change occurred following the fall of communism, many leadership positions were taken over by the intelligentsia. This was not unexpected considering that nearly all active members of the small and largely informal opposition groups were intellectuals. (The most conspicuous has been the ascension of writers, poets, and playwrights.) An important shortcoming of these new elites (especially in Poland and Hungary) was their marked inability to develop proper communications with the masses.[38] Confronted by a large gap between popular expectations and limited possibilities, many sophisticated intellectuals who found themselves in cabinet positions simply could not explain in plain language to ordinary citizens what realistic economic prospects were, what they needed to do, and why sacrifices were necessary.

A good case in point is the government of Tadeusz Mazowiecki (August 1989–December 1990) in Poland. This may well have been the "nearest to a government of philosopher-kings that Europe has witnessed" since World War II, but only its minister of labor, Jacek Kuron, himself an intellectual and long-time opposition activist, could effectively explain his own and his government's policies to the public.[39] This weakness had profound implications for the political fortunes of the first post-communist Polish and Hungarian governments in particular, who were quite incapable of selling their programs to the people. As Adam Przeworski noted, "The architects of reform were persuaded that their blueprint was sound—no, more: the only one possible. They viewed all doubts as a lack of understanding, even a lack of responsibility."[40] The heavy-handed treatment of the media by the governments of several states (especially in Hungary, Romania, and Slovakia) may be considered as a reflection of their deficient communications skills.

Partly as a result of this lack of communication skills, by the mid-1990s this "brief, spectacular, carnivalesque honeymoon between the intelligentsia and the 'people' " was over.[41] In contrast to the new politicians—most of whom were, by definition, amateurs who never held political office before—the former communists who remained or returned to power were seasoned politicians. They benefited from their "fifty-year head start," that is, from decades of virtual monopoly of the political system which allowed them to accumulate plenty of practical experience.

Political Institutions

In the wake of communism's demise, new institutional structures were developed in Eastern Europe. Some institutions that existed under communism had to be reshaped (e.g., the presidency, legislatures) or new modus operandi had to be agreed upon, while others that were indispensable for a democratic state, and not included by the communist coterie of organizations (e.g., constitutional courts), had to be created anew. These tasks were completed relatively quickly, but fundamental problems remain. Many political institutions in the new democracies (from parties to the police force) are weak, their procedural regulations often remain to be clarified, and the boundaries of their authority are demarcated vaguely.

A case in point is the presidency. I am not referring to the ongoing debate on whether presidential or parliamentary systems are more stable and more conducive to democratic consolidation.[42] Both Poland and Romania, the two states of the region that may be said to have developed presidential or quasi-presidential systems, have encountered authoritarian presidential behavior, although admittedly Poland has been far more successful in its political transition than Romania. Yet in the Czech Republic, Hungary, and Slovakia, states that Alfred Stepan and Cindy Skach classified as "pure-parliamentary" systems,[43] presidents have also overstepped the lines of their authority. The point is that in neither type of system has presidential authority been clearly defined. This deficiency, in turn, allowed a number of potentially serious problems to unfold, ranging from Polish President Lech Walesa's overt meddling in military affairs to Hungarian President Arpad Goncz's refusal to appoint heads of media agencies.

An important reason for these ambiguities (as well as a number of other defects in institutional design) has been the exceptionally rapid pace of legislative work, the notion of rushing through the transition. In Hungary, for instance (and Hungary, indeed, is just one example), in the first fifteen months after the formation of the new parliament in 1990, "one hundred and eleven laws were passed, and most dealt with such central issues as the structure of the ministerial system, the legal position of the deputies, the creation of a system of local justice," etc.[44]

Though failure of the Hungarian and Polish legislatures to ratify new constitutions has been blamed on legislative gridlock and procrastination, one might actually consider it to be a rare sign of political maturity and the recognition of the matter's importance. As Stephen Holmes has argued, the longer they "wait to create a 'definitive' constitution, the more likely they are to supplement negative with positive constitutionalism" and to create documents and, more generally, "a set of institutions that have a chance to endure."[45]

Extremism and Nationalism

After the fall of communism, nationalism and right-wing extremism returned to Eastern Europe or, more precisely, they once again rose to the surface. This should not have been surprising given the ideological vacuum created by the demise of Marxism–Leninism, new laws permitting free speech and association, the liberalization of the media, and the end of Soviet control. A large number of books and articles soon lamented the region's descent into the nationalist-extremist abyss.[46] I do not, of course, intend to trivialize the distressing presence and activities of anti-Semitic, anti-Roma, and xenophobic political and social forces. They exist in virtually all democratic states from Austria to the United States, and now they have also emerged in Eastern Europe. My point is that their political import has been overstated by many observers. Following their disturbingly "promising" start, by the mid-1990s extremist forces have been relegated to the political margins in Eastern Europe (and, one might argue, in Russia) as in democracies elsewhere.[47] The reason is that while voters in the region might have enjoyed the momentary political spectacle of outrageous speeches, articles, and demonstrations, with few exceptions they have been far too mature to bestow political power to left- or right-wing extremist forces.

This is not to say that in some states, particularly Slovakia and Romania, nationalist sentiments have not been exploited by central and local governments in order to obfuscate other troublesome issues. It is scarcely a coincidence, however, that both of these countries are hosts to large Hungarian (as well as politically weak Romanian) minorities. Political statements originating from Budapest, especially during the tenure of the Antall government, have not always served to put Bratislava's and Bucharest's fears to rest, however irrational they might have seemed to the outside observer.

Hungary has not been immune to the ephemeral attraction of nationalist forces. The best-known representative of this political line has been the noted writer, Istvan Csurka, a onetime vice president of the HDF.[48] Undoubtedly, the Antall government made a serious political mistake by not distancing itself from Csurka and his supporters in the HDF until June 1993, a mistake that was not forgotten by the voters in the 1994 national elections. More importantly, however, since his excommunication from the HDF, Csurka and his new party, the Hungarian Justice and Health Party (HJHP), have been marginalized in Hungarian politics, and in 1994 attracted less than two percent of the vote, far short of the five percent needed for parliamentary participation. To many observers' surprise, the HJHP did far better in 1998, garnering about 5.5 percent of the vote in the first round of the election. Another illustration of the same phenomenon is the case of Jozsef Torgyan, leader of the opposition Independent Smallholders' Party, whose popularity plummeted following his incendiary speech in March 1996.

Of the East Central European states (again, excluding Slovakia), the extreme right appears to be strongest in the Czech Republic. The Republican Party—favored by eight percent of the voters in the 1996 elections, which translated into eighteen deputies in the new legislature—entered Parliament on an anti-Roma and anti-Semitic agenda. The party's leader, Miroslav Sladek, likes to talk about the "final solution to the Roma problem," and in his nationally televised opening parliamentary speech, he argued that Roma children should be automatically considered criminals by having committed the villainous act of being born."[49]

Conclusion

The East European states under consideration in this chapter have succeeded in establishing democratic political systems, certainly by the minimalist criteria mentioned above. As Harry Eckstein suggested three decades ago, stable democracies were immensely difficult to achieve and were usually the result of "calamitously improbable combinations of circumstances."[50] What we currently have in Eastern Europe are imperfect, flawed, and in some places (e.g., Albania, Romania, Slovakia) fragile but, most importantly, *functioning, working, democratic polities.*

Many Western critics of the post-communist polities fell victim to the short-lived euphoria that swept through the region in the wake of communism's fall by way of exaggerated expectations. They overlooked the Jeffersonian axiom that democracy is not a state or condition but a process which needs perennial improvement. As Gale Stokes suggested, many of the disputes and political battles being fought in contemporary Eastern Europe are part of a healthy political life.[51] Surely, there are a number of profound problems in the region, but to avoid becoming unduly disheartened, we should put things in perspective. By considering the well-entrenched democracies, with their Jean-Marie LePens, Franz Schonhubers, and David Dukes; recurrent governmental crises in Italy and Japan; and the acceptance of corruption as a permanent feature of French politics, we can view Eastern Europe in a better light. East European democratization is eight years old; some of the above-mentioned democracies have worked at it for centuries.

Before turning our attention to a specific, in-depth examination of Hungary, it bears repeating that since the Middle Ages Eastern Europe has been the more backward, less developed part of the continent. Moreover, it has always been a region characterized by diversity. Some of the historical disparities that communism had temporarily muted have become more prominent since 1989. Just as the East Central European states have been more developed than their neighbors in the Balkans, it is fair to say that their prospects continue to be more promising.

Notes

I am grateful to Andrew C. Janos and Rudolf L. Tokes for their comments on an earlier version of this paper.

1. On this issue, see Sarah Meiklejohn Terry, "Thinking about Post-Communist Transitions: How Comparable Are They?" *Slavic Review* 52:2 (Summer 1993): 333–37; Valerie Bunce, "Should Transitologists Be Grounded?" *Slavic Review* 54:1 (Spring 1995): 111–27 and "Comparing East and South," *Journal of Democracy* 6:1 (July 1995): 87–100.

2. Although a founding member of the Warsaw Pact, Albania withdrew from the organization after the invasion of Czechoslovakia in 1968.

3. See, for instance, J.F. Brown, *Hopes and Shadows: Eastern Europe after Communism* (Durham: Duke University Press, 1994), 84. On the prospects of change in East European states, see *idem., Surge to Freedom: The End of Communist Rule in Eastern Europe* (Durham: Duke University Press, 1991), 247–69.

4. For comprehensive studies, see Bennett Kovrig, *Communism in Hungary: From Kun to Kadar* (Stanford: Hoover Institution Press, 1979); and Rudolf L. Tokes, *Hungary's Negotiated Revolution: Economic Reform, Social Change, and Political Succession* (New York: Cambridge University Press, 1996).

5. Timothy Garton Ash, "Blinded by *Glasnost*" in *The Independent*, 22 December 1987.

6. See, for instance, Matyas Szuros, "Hungary, Europe, and the World," *The New Hungarian Quarterly* 28, no. 107 (Autumn 1987); and *Mr. Kadar* (Budapest: Hirlapkiado, 1989).

7. Andrew C. Janos, "Social Science, Communism, and the Dynamics of

Political Change" in Nancy Bermeo, ed., *Liberalization and Democratization in the Soviet Union and Eastern Europe* (Baltimore: Johns Hopkins University Press, 1992), 102.

8. This discussion draws on Zoltan Barany, "Democratic Consolidation and the Military: The East European Experience," *Comparative Politics* 30:1 (October 1997): 25.

9. For analyses of Soviet-East European relations, see Zbigniew Brzezinski, *The Soviet Bloc: Unity and Conflict* (Cambridge: Harvard University Press, 1967); Sarah Meiklejohn Terry, ed., *Soviet Policy in Eastern Europe* (New Haven: Yale University Press, 1984); and Glenn R. Chafetz, *Gorbachev, Reform, and the Brezhnev Doctrine* (Westport, Conn.: Praeger, 1993).

10. Vojtech Mastny, "Eastern Europe and the West in the Perspective of Time" in William E. Griffith, ed., *Central and Eastern Europe: The Opening Curtain?* (Boulder, Colo.: Westview Press, 1989), 31.

11. For a summary statement, see Zoltan Barany, "The Bankruptcy of Hungarian Socialism," *Sudost-Europa* 38, no. 4 (April 1989): 191–212.

12. *Magyar Nemzet*, 16 July 1988.

13. See Samuel P. Huntington, "Democratization and Security in Eastern Europe" in Peter Volten, ed., *Uncertain Futures: Eastern Europe and Democracy* (New York: Institute for East-West Security Studies, 1990), 42–43.

14. See Hugh Seton-Watson, *Eastern Europe Between the Wars* (Hamden, Conn.: Archon Books, 1962); and Joseph Rothschild, *East-Central Europe Between the Two World Wars* (Seattle: University of Washington Press, 1974).

15. See John Mueller, "Democracy, Capitalism, and the End of Transition" in Michael Mandelbaum, ed., *Post-Communism: Four Perspectives* (New York: Council on Foreign Relations, 1996), 102–67.

16. For a sensible ranking of East European states from the perspective of European Union membership, see Anna Seleny, "EU Enlargement," paper presented at the conference on the European Union: Austria and the Future of Central Europe, Woodrow Wilson School of International Affairs, Princeton University, April 30–May 2, 1998.

17. Richard Rose and Christian Haerpfer, "Mass Response to Transformation in Post-Communist Societies," *Europe-Asia Studies* 46:1 (1994): 15.

18. *Washington Post*, 24 May 1994; and *New York Times*, 22 June 1994. See also Vaclav Klaus, *Renaissance: The Rebirth of Liberty in the Heart of Europe* (Washington: Cato Institute, 1997).

19. See *The Economist*, 3 May 1997, 67.

20. *The Economist*, 31 May 1997, 65.; see also *The Economist*, 17 January 1998, 70.

21. See Zoltan Barany, "The Return of the Left in East-Central Europe," *Problems of Post-Communism* 42:1 (January–February 1995): 41–45.

22. Mary E. McIntosh, Martha Abele MacIver, Daniel G. Abele, and Dina Smeltz, "Publics Meet Market Democracy in Central and East Europe," *Slavic Review* 53:2 (Summer 1994): 488–89.

23. Marcin Krol, "Poland's Longing for Paternalism," *Journal of Democracy* 5:1 (January 1994): 91. On this issue, see also Piotr Sztompka, "The Intangibles

and Imponderables of the Transition to Democracy," *Studies in Comparative Communism* 24:3 (September 1991): 306.

24. Adam Michnik, "The Velvet Restoration," *Transition* 2:6 (22 March 1996): 13–16. See also Hubert Tworzecki, *Parties and Politics in Post-1989 Poland* (Boulder, Colo.: Westview Press, 1996).

25. *Wall Street Journal,* 22 September 1993. See also Norman Stone, "The Hungarians: History Makes a Comeback," *The National Interest,* no. 36 (Summer 1994): 64.

26. *Magyar Hirlap,* 11 May 1998.

27. "New Masks, Old Faces," the title of an article by Vladimir Tismaneanu, succinctly summarized the superficiality of the elite change immediately following the Romanian revolution. *The New Republic,* 5 February 1990, 17–21.

28. See Martin Butora and Zora Butorova, "Slovakia after the Split," *Journal of Democracy* 4:2 (April 1993): 71–83.

29. J.F. Brown, *Hopes and Shadows,* 62. See also *New York Times,* 12 October 1997, 3.

30. *The Economist,* 9 March 1996, 55–56.

31. Martin Butora, "Slovakia: A New State One Year Later," *East European Studies Newsletter* (Washington: Woodrow Wilson Center), no. 93 (May–June 1994), 3.

32. Nestor Ratesh, "Romania: Slamming on the Brakes," *Current History* 92:577 (November 1993): 391.

33. See Tom Gallagher, *Romania after Ceausescu: The Politics of Intolerance* (Edinburgh: University of Edinburgh Press, 1995); and Lavinia Stan, ed., *Romania in Transition* (Brookfield, VT: Dartmouth, 1997).

34. See Michael Shafir, "Romania's Road to Normalcy," *Journal of Democracy* 8:2 (January 1997): 144–59.

35. *The Economist,* 3 May 1997.

36. See Jacques Coenen-Huther, ed., *Bulgaria at the Crossroads* (Commack, NY: Nova, 1996); and Iliana Zloch-Christy, *Bulgaria in a Time of Change: Economic and Political Dimensions* (Brookfield, VT: Avebury, 1996).

37. John A. Hall, "After the Vacuum: Post-Communism in the Light of Tocqueville" in Beverly Crawford, ed., *Markets, States, and Democracy: The Political Economy of Post-Communist Transformation* (Boulder, Colo.: Westview, 1995), 96. In fact, it is now clear that Hall overestimated the impact of Vladimir Zhirinovsky's electoral success on Russian politics.

38. See Zoltan Barany, "Mass-Elite Relations and the Resurgence of Nationalism in Eastern Europe," *European Security* 3:2 (March 1994): 161–79.

39. Brown, *Hopes and Shadows,* 69.

40. Adam Przeworski, "Economic Reforms, Public Opinion, and Political Institutions: Poland in the Eastern European Perspective" in Luiz Carlos Bresser Pereira, Jose Maria Maravall, and Adam Przeworski, *Economic Reforms in New Democracies: A Social Democratic Approach* (New York: Cambridge University Press, 1993): 183.

41. Zygmunt Bauman, "After the Patronage State: A Model in Search of Class Interests" in Bryant and Mokrzycki, eds., *The New Great Transformation?* 24.

42. See, for instance, Matthew Soberg Shugart and John Carey, *Presidents and Assemblies* (Cambridge: Cambridge University Press, 1992); Scott Mainwaring, "Presidentialism, Multipartism, and Democracy," *Comparative Political Studies* 26:2 (1993): 198–228; and Juan J. Linz and Arturo Valenzuela, eds., *The Failure of Presidential Democracy, Volume 1: Comparative Perspectives* (Baltimore: Johns Hopkins University Press, 1994). For an excellent recent contribution pertaining specifically to Eastern Europe, see Thomas A. Baylis, "Presidents versus Prime Ministers: Shaping Executive Authority in Eastern Europe," *World Politics* 48:3 (April 1996): 297–323.

43. Alfred Stepan and Cindy Skach, "Constitutional Frameworks and Democratic Consolidation: Parliamentarism versus Presidentialism," *World Politics* 46:1 (October 1993): 4.

44. Valerie Bunce and Maria Csanadi, "Uncertainty in the Transition: Post-Communism in Hungary," *East European Politics and Societies* 7:2 (Spring 1993): 268.

45. Stephen Holmes, "Conceptions of Democracy in the Draft Constitutions of Post-Communist Countries" in Crawford, ed., *Markets, States, and Democracy,* 81.

46. See, for instance, Joseph Held, ed., *Democracy and Right-Wing Politics in Eastern Europe in the 1990s* (Boulder, Colo.: East European Monographs, 1993); Paul Hockenos, *Free to Hate: The Rise of the Right in Post-Communist Eastern Europe* (New York: Routledge, 1993); Paul Latawski, ed., *Contemporary Nationalism in Eastern Europe* (New York: St. Martin's Press, 1995); and Aleksandar Pavkovic, Halyna Koscharsky, and Adam Czarnota, eds., *Nationalism and Postcommunism* (Brookfield, VT: Dartmouth, 1995).

47. A recent Hungarian article (*Nepszabadsag,* 28 June 1997), for instance, reports on the drastic diminution in the number of active skinheads and skinhead attacks between 1990 and 1997.

48. See Barany, "Mass-Elite Relations," 173–76.

49. Author's interview with Jonathan Stein of the European Studies Center of the Institute for East-West Studies (Prague, 14 August 1996).

50. Cited in Ken Jowitt, "Dizzy with Democracy," *Problems of Post-Communism* 43:1 (January–February 1996): 6.

51. See Gale Stokes, "Is It Possible to Be Optimistic about Eastern Europe?" *Social Research* 60:4 (Winter 1993): 685–704.

Chapter 6

Political Transition and
Social Transformation

Rudolf L. Tokes

Introduction

The dynamics of Hungarian society and politics in the mid-1990s are shaped by the interaction of two forces. These are long-term processes of socioeconomic, spatial, and cognitive transformation of human actors and their physical environment, and rapid short-term changes in political institutions and public policies that the label "transition" denotes. The task at hand is to determine the salience of each to Hungary's chances of implementing the region's new post-communist agenda of democratization, marketization, and the rule of law.

Pretransition pacts and understandings between the outgoing and the incoming political elites yielded ambiguous political and socioeconomic outcomes.[1] Whereas these initial agreements made well-crafted provisions for Hungary's institutional transition from a one-party communist system to a parliamentary democracy, such volatile matters as political justice and societal consensus on post-communist policy, especially resource allocation priorities, were left in abeyance. At issue is the way in which the new institutional architecture and key political actors—the government, the Parliament, the political parties, the president of the Republic, and the Constitutional Court—have responded to public expectations for employment, stable living standards, and the state's delivery of social-welfare services.

Hungary's institutional transition was essentially completed in 1994 with the election of its second-round post-communist government. However, the country's socioeconomic transformation is still in progress. From this, I propose as the main hypothesis of this paper an open-

113

ended scenario of manifest conflicts between the requisites, on the one hand, of democratization, marketization, and the rule of law, and the imperatives of societal priorities and inherently unattainable social expectations for public goods, on the other. The task of reconciliation of requisites with imperatives is central to the new Hungarian democracy's policy agenda.

In what follows I shall endeavor to identify and briefly discuss both transformative and transitive elements of Hungary's recent past. In doing so, I shall combine the "functionalist" and the "geneticist" approach to the matter at hand. The former takes its departure from "long-term development of the socioeconomic kind with emphasis on structural and environmental determinants of political change." The latter focuses on "political choice and strategy by actors during the actual transition process."[2] The aim is to set a framework for an argument concerning socioeconomic continuity and political stalemate in the mid-1990s. Accordingly, this discussion will address (1) Hungary's Kadarist socioeconomic and institutional legacy, (2) elite-brokered institutional change—opportunities and internal contradictions, and (3) post-communist socioeconomic trends, institutional performance, and public perceptions.

The Kadarist Legacy: A Viable Precedent?

Four decades of communist rule left a lasting imprint on every facet of life in Hungary. The coercive imposition of the Soviet model created political institutions, set patterns of resource allocations, shaped social interactions, and helped embed new and reinforce traditional values and cognitive orientations. The results are still with us today. To a remarkable extent, they are still defining characteristics of politics, the economy, the society, and public beliefs in the sixth year of "existing democracy" in Hungary. Much of this is true for the post-communist states and societies of East Central Europe.

Despite or because of the proliferation of unhelpful labels, such as "goulash communism," "Frigidaire socialism," and the like, Hungary's uniqueness in relation to the rest of the communist bloc remains a somewhat elusive proposition. My own investigation of the postwar record yielded six factors that, to a greater or lesser extent, set the country, its political regime, developmental strategies, and elite behavior apart from its similarly communist-ruled neighbors. These are (a) the exceptional harshness and the sheer dimensions of Stalinist political, economic, and social mobilization between 1948–1953, (b) the revolution of 1956, (c) Janos Kadar's coercive-terroristic, and subsequently consensus-seeking political leadership, (d) the regime's sustained commitment to legitimacy-building through economic reforms, (e) mutually self-limiting instrumental interaction between the regime and its internal opposition, and (f) the outgoing and the incoming political elites' pragmatic cooperation that spawned the National Roundtable Agreement (NRT) of September 1989.[3] The basic provisions and the implicit understandings associated with this agreement still constitute the de facto charter for the modus operandi of *all* key political institutions today.

It is axiomatic that the combination of the generic Soviet-Leninist and the arguably unique aspects of Hungary's experience under the Stalinist Matyas Rakosi, the reform communist-patriot Imre Nagy, and the quisling-turned-"good king" Janos Kadar constitute an ambiguous and in many ways contradictory legacy.

Modernization and Political Steering

The 1970s brought to Hungary a convergence and politically manipulated payoffs of long-term trends in economic development, social restratification, cultural modernization, and cognitive transformation. Specifically,

- Prewar programs and the communist regime's strategies of forced industrialization, albeit vexed by cyclical patterns of resource misallocation, hence unbalanced growth, laid the foundations for a semimodern industrial economy with the capacity either for continued misdevelopment or for "midcourse correction" by way of economic reforms.
- Regime-sponsored policies of social mobilization—including the initially aggressive promotion of low-status groups by class criteria—combined with major efforts to upgrade the public's technical skills and educational qualifications and the regime's subsequent abandonment of educational discrimination against members of the old middle class yielded a new social context and, with it, the potential for the rise of a new post-totalitarian society in Hungary.
- In the mid-1960s the regime's hitherto strident ideological stance gave way to cultural policies that were "socialist in form, national in content." As an unintended consequence, such policies created new space for the revival of indigenous cultural traditions and also sowed the seeds of a new kind of national identity. The latter contained elements of low-key nationalism, but it was mixed with a sense of consumerist contentment, bordering on smug pride, over well-stocked food stores, gratitude for the regime's unde-

manding ideological expectations, and unspoken endorsement of the self-effacing *national* leader's "anti-cult of personality."

The regime's repressive tolerance helped foster a new context of social interaction. It gave relatively free reign, in the Hungarian sociologists' terminology, to the realization of "personal interests" in the nonpolitical realm. As the result, a survival of the fittest (or best-connected) bargain culture was born in Hungary.

The upshot of this culture was the rise of an ameliorated sense of civic identity, political infantilism, and the widespread revival of pathologies of amoral familism. These predemocratic values and deviant behaviors engulfed both the official "first" and the private "second" societies of Hungary.[4] Corruption and misuse of power at the top and widespread societal disregard of laws and administrative rules became two facets of a symbiotic whole of moral decay and diminished civic competence. These have become modal behaviors that have remained largely unaffected by legal-institutional changes in the post-communist period.

Reforms: Intended and Unintended Outcomes

The New Economic Mechanism (NEM) began as a reform program with limited, mainly economic, objectives. For a variety of reasons, which I have discussed elsewhere, the NEM became a kind of Archimedean lever with which the regime, quite unwittingly, reshaped Hungarian politics, the economy, and society.[5] The reform experiment liberated a multitude of hitherto latent political, economic, and social forces that eventually led to the demise of the political regime in the late 1980s.

From the interaction of long-term processes of economic development, cultural modernization, social restratification, and cognitive transformation and the political regime's adaptive political strategies, there evolved a peculiar kind of stalemate between the rulers and the ruled of Hungary. Power realignment at the top was made possible by the NEM-induced transformation of many wage earners into semisovereign consumers and semiautonomous, second-economy entrepreneurs. The NEM was the midwife to the birth of a new Hungarian middle class with an agenda of its own. As may be inferred from opinion surveys, the central themes were personal autonomy, job security, social incomes, law and order, and fear of political instability.[6] These were modest aspirations that, with the judicious use of sticks and carrots, a younger leader and a less intimidated ruling oligarchy could have accommodated. However, this was not to be.

Stagnant, then declining, living standards alarmed the survivalist elites and brought to the surface the regime's illegitimate origins. At issue was the incumbents' political responsibility for the impending collapse, in Janos Kornai's phrase, of the "premature welfare state" in Hungary. The elites and the *homo Kadaricus* for whom they spoke had a vested interest in preserving the modest achievements—"little freedoms," little cars, and well-stocked food stores—that Kadar had bestowed upon them since 1968. Each cohort in its own way comprised insecure, egalitarian, viscerally antimarket, frustrated petty bourgeois consumers. They all yearned for stability, strong leadership, and a predictable future—but not necessarily of a liberal democratic kind.

Negotiated Revolution: Issues, Participants, and Outcomes

The historic NRT negotiations of June–September 1989 between the outgoing reform-communist incumbents and the Opposition Roundtable (ORT)-affiliated intellectuals had two principal objectives. The first was to reach consensus on the modalities of Hungary's peaceful institutional transition from one political system to another. The second pertained to the empowerment of citizens to become competent participants, mainly as voters, in the post-communist political arena. Peaceful transition called for a combination of drastic institutional change, such as the withering away of the ruling party and the enactment of a revised constitution; procedural guarantees for party formation and free elections; and mutual restraint to prevent the nonelites from taking to the streets to promote their, possibly radical, agenda.

The regime's NRT negotiators were "experts," that is, experienced political managers and their lawyers from the Ministry of Justice. On the other side of the table were enthusiastic political novices, yet also "experts" as professionals and academic intellectuals. Their shared objective was the salvaging, retrofitting, and modernizing of the socialist state's institutional architecture by bringing it into compliance with dimly understood democratic and European norms. No revolutionary changes were intended by either outgoing or incoming elite negotiators.

Hungary's post-communist institutions were built on unexamined foundations. In the 1980s the old regime's core legitimacy problems had been socioeconomic rather than political or ideological. The disintegration and subsequent exit of the ruling party cleared the political arena of redundant institutional actors. Whereas new and revamped political institutions could be created with the stroke of a pen—as they were—neither the stagnant economy nor the pathologies of the ailing society were amenable to elite quick fixes.

The NRT negotiators' deliberate failure to address economic and social issues was good politics but poor statesmanship. Moreover, the regime's and the opposition's flat rejection of the so-called third side's bread-and-butter agenda left the post-communist government's future social partners alone to fend the best they could for the nonelites whom they asserted they represented. Thus, the new institutional edifice of Hungarian democracy was erected if not on quicksand, then, with the exclusion of the intended beneficiaries from the planning process, on potentially unstable foundations.

The foregoing critique of the NRT Agreement is not an exercise in "what if?" theories of recent history but represents an opportunity to estimate the extent of mismatch between the Kadarist socioeconomic "base" and the newly crafted political "superstructure." At issue are the long-term evolution and, at the end, total hegemony of the socialist state and its relationship to the universe of socioeconomic actors under the old regime. Although Hungary's much-amended constitution provided for a reasonable clone of the Soviet model, the old regime's governing praxis and the nature of growing instrumental interaction among the state; the policy lobbies; and the agricultural, industrial, and cultural managerial elites were, in all but name, pluralistic. Insofar as these *institutional* socioeconomic actors had sectorial interests to promote, their increasingly assertive bargaining posture vis-à-vis the government could have been best accommodated by the emergence of a post-communist, "national salvation front"-led, de facto one-party, corporatist state rather than by a multiparty, let alone market-oriented, parliamentary democracy.

Hungary's old and new political elites had much in common. Both came from the top layer of the new middle class, both had inherited or acquired status, privileges, and distance from the nonelites to protect and preserve. In terms of group interests and political priorities, the negotiators represented but a partial spectrum—skewed heavily in favor of intellectuals and midlevel professionals—of the old regime, which by the mid-1980s constituted mainly meritocratic, nomenklatura elites. Their institutional blueprint for the new house of democracy made no provisions for the care and feeding of its inhabitants.

Post-Communist Hungary: Socioeconomic Trends, Institutional Performance, and Public Perceptions

Hungary's freedom was won not at the barricades but at the Malta summit and at the NRT negotiations. Regardless of the venue, the outcome offered a historic opportunity for the fulfillment of the nation's perennial quest for sovereignty and the public's aspirations for political freedom, economic security, and improved quality of life in parliamentary democracy. The outcome also raised hopes for the restoration of Hungary's place in the community of European nations. The realization of these hopes and aspirations hinged on the dynamic interaction of long-term socioeconomic and short-term political forces, as well as on intangibles, such as leadership, ideologies, and public opinion.

The Economy and Society

Let us begin with the economy. The object here is to call attention to such changes in existential conditions—work environment, income, and employment—that had measurable influence on public attitudes toward democracy, market, and government policies.

Central planning, budgetary allocations by ideological criteria, state ownership of means of production, chronic shortages, and in Hungary's case high external indebtedness, were the main characteristics of socialist economies.[7] In 1980 the public sector's share in the "official" GDP (which did not factor in what the World Bank calls the "unofficial economy") was 90 percent, versus 10 percent domestic private and zero percent foreign owned. The shares of these sectors in the GDP changed dramatically in the next fourteen years. The respective percentages and years were 76, 23, and 1 (1990); 70, 27, and 3 (1991); 56, 36, and 8 (1992); 42, 45, and 13 (1993). However, with the inclusion of the unofficial economy, the actual public-private-foreign ratios were 83, 17, and 0 (1980); and 37, 50, and 13 (1993).[8] According to a World Bank study, the share of the private (domestic and foreign-owned) sector in the GDP was 70 percent in 1990.[9]

Major corollaries of economic restructuring were declining output (in Hungary's case about 20 percent of the GDP between 1989 and 1994), declining incomes (about 8 to 10 percent in real terms between 1990 and 1994), and pronounced shifts in the occupational structure. Of the last, the most notable was the rapid growth in persons employed in the service sector of the economy.

The ratio of employment in the public and private sectors was 49.8 and 50.2 percent in 1993 (and probably lower in the state and higher in the public sector in 1996).[10] The labor force thus divided has been confronted with three state budget-driven and market-driven working environments. The first provided greater job security, better fringe benefits, and lower pay. The private sector offered less job security, fewer fringe benefits, longer hours, and 24 to 30 percent higher pay.[11] The third working environment was the unofficial economy in which people from both sectors traded marketable skills for unreported incomes.

The unemployed and the unemployable represented a novel facet of the macroeconomic equation. The first, about 11 to 13 percent of the labor force, and the second, for which no reliable data is available, are the inevitable victims of a state budget and market-energized triage of downsizing because of obsolescent skills and/or of poor physical health. The combination of the redundant labor force, demographic changes, and the exceptionally high ratio of pensioners placed crushing burdens on the active wage earners. The ratio of economically inactive young and old household dependents to 100 active wage earners was 117:100 in 1987 and 167:100 in 1993.[12]

Hungary's comparative economic performance in a post-communist, "from Turkmenistan to the Czech Republic" context of twenty-eight states earned high marks (0.84 versus 0.19 and 0.90, respectively).[13] However, neither such high marks nor Hungary's designation as an "upper-middle-income" country in the World Bank's (IBRD) *World Development Report 1996* can account for the social impact of rapid economic change there.[14]

The Kadar regime's economic strategies and policies of social engineering generated new patterns of social mobility and social stratification. Upon the change of the political regime and the revival of the private economy, new patterns of social mobility and stratification surfaced after 1992.[15] The key trends in the distribution of wage earners by occupational category between 1980 and 1993 were increases (a) in the shares of "executive/intellectual" and "white collar" categories from 30.3 to 39 percent, that of "entrepreneurs" from 1.5 to 7.2 percent, and of "independent farmers" from 0.6 to 3.3 percent; and (b) the decline in the shares of semiskilled and unskilled workers from 28.5 to 17.8 percent, and of agricultural laborers from 15.8 to 5.6 percent.[16]

Changes in the occupational structure may also be viewed as indicators of the economic winners and losers in Hungary's post-communist economic transition. According to one estimate, about one million people, or about 20 percent of the active labor force, were "winners," and the rest were victims of stagnant or rapidly declining incomes and deteriorated living standards.[17] The principal winners were those with higher education (8.1 and 14.5 percent of the labor force in 1980 and 1993, respectively), those with market-convertible skills, specific elite groups with discretionary access to market- and "unofficial economy"-generated incomes, and the recipients of preferential resource allocations by government agencies.

Longitudinal (1972–1993) trends in the distribution of incomes indicate a gradually widening gap between the lowest and the highest 20 percent of recipients. Whereas in 1972 the lowest fifth received 9.9 percent of incomes, its share remained the same in 1992, then declined to 9.5 percent in the following year. The share of the highest fifth was 33.7, 35.7, and 36.6 percent in 1972, 1992, and 1993, respectively.[18] This data, when put in a national context as measured by the Gini index, attests to a similar trend: 23.3 (1972), 21.1 (1977), 20.6 (1982), 23.5 (1989), 26.0 (1992), and 27.0 (1993).[19] Thus, income inequality did not begin but only gained momentum with the onset of economic transformation in Hungary.

From the public's viewpoint the problem has not been the market's high valuation of and rewards for technical and managerial skills and entrepreneurial talents. Rather, it is the lifestyle and conspicuous consumption of the upper one percent that is seen to be unjustifiable by market criteria, as well as morally reprehensible by the public's quasi-egalitarian standards. Groups and individuals who have become vulnerable on this score are the new partly managerial, partly "wild East"-type, entrepreneurial business elites and the new kleptocracy of politically well-connected senior executives of industry, banking, and commerce.[20] The "original accumulation" of these elites' "capital"— nomenklatura position, party membership, and political access—when converted into even higher positions, splendid homes, and luxury cars helped catalyze public skepticism about social justice in a parliamentary democracy.[21]

Both, particularly the first, post-communist governments have gone to extraordinary lengths to cushion the impact of economic transformation on the public. However, the disbursement of approximately 26–28 percent of the budget, arguably the highest percentage in Europe, for social welfare purposes has failed to slow down the exponential growth of those living at or below the "existential minimum."[22] The numbers were one million (1980s), 1.5 million (1991), 2 million (1992), 2.5 million (1993), and 3 to 3.5 million (1994).[23] Though this trend is alarming, the actual dimensions of the problem have yet to be determined by realistic criteria. On the other hand, it is essential to call attention to the post-communist "winners"—particularly the overwhelmingly redistributionist, and on the whole well-off, intelligentsia's unceasing efforts to keep the political incumbents on the defensive.[24] The object has been to make use of the poverty issue to forestall, as long as possible, the full implementation of economic restructuring and, with it, the inevitable decline of public welfare, disguised as state patronage of culture, disbursed to intellectuals.

Political Institutions

Hungary's political transition was eased, yet vexed, by what the economist Eva Voszka called "the unbearable lightness of non-cathartic transition.''[25] The incumbents' deft avoidance of revolutionary showdowns, correct management of critical transition issues, and businesslike transfer of power to the freely elected new government reassured the public, and thus helped legitimate the new institutional status quo.

The change of the political system offered a onetime opportunity to effect needed institutional changes, as well as to implement the administrative elites' long-incubating plans for more effective governance.[26] The outcome may be called "changing things so everything would remain the same," but such critical assessments overlook the incumbents' professionalism and openness to change, and underestimate the new political elites' determination to install democratic institutions and to restore popular sovereignty.

Due to space limitations, detailed analysis of the specifics of Hungary's post-communist institutional architecture will not be provided in this essay.[27] Instead, a brief commentary on the underlying premises and inner contradictions of the institution-building process might suffice.

The country's new political system rested on the interaction of five—one old, and four new or restructured—institutions. Their structure and intended functions were to be responsive to the old, the new, and the holdover elites' vested interests; to public expectations for enhanced citizen efficacy and systemic stability; and to Western pressures for legal-administrative measures for the implementation of democratization, marketization, and the rule of law in Hungary.

The state is the principal institutional survivor of the old regime. As the winner of a two-decades-long power struggle for resource allocation authority with the Communist Party, the state became central to the workings of the new and restructured institutions. It was the direct employer of 25 percent of the working population and, within it, of 63,000 (in 1969) and 108,000 (in 1990) people working in public administration.[28] Thus, by virtue of its size, the state was "strong" but, in terms of its statutory responsibilities, it was woefully overextended and therefore weak for efficient governance.

The elite pact-makers' commitment to governability yielded, more or less on the German model, a "strong" prime minister with limited accountability to the Parliament. This arrangement conferred broad powers on the chief executive, including those of the initiation of legislative action and of governance by administrative decrees by ministries and other government agencies. Since 1990, 95 percent of bills have originated with the government, and the ratio of laws enacted by Parliament to government decrees with the force of law was 374:1,660 between 1990 and 1993.[29] Although the revised constitution reserved jurisdiction over a number of subjects, such as "fundamental civil rights," to qualified majority vote by the Parliament, the prime minister had ample leeway to govern as he saw fit.

The translation of the post-communist governments' political will into administrative action has been aided and thwarted by several factors. On the plus side, there was the, generally cooperative state bureaucracy and the new "superministry," that is, the Office of the Prime Minister, with the statutory powers to make many things happen—with or without explicit legislative authorization.[30] On the minus side, there was the new regime's triple mandate—democratization, marketization, and the creation of a *Rechtsstaat*—that brought into being an inherently unmanageable legislative-administrative agenda for the executive branch of the government.

The large-scale exodus of experienced senior bureaucrats from several key ministries to the private sector and their replacement by political appointees contributed to decision overload, administrative improvisation, and interminable delays in rule making and rule implementation. However, the results to date have fallen short of public expectations. To overcome perceptions of underperformance, prime ministers Jozsef Antall and Gyula Horn sought to cover up for the government's unsatisfactory record. The means were the carrot of growing social expenditures and the stick of blaming historic and external scapegoats (Antall blaming the old regime, Horn blaming the IMF) for Hungary's economic woes.

In sum, notwithstanding the government's broad discretionary powers to effect, if need be by administrative fiat, proposed changes, these have been constrained by bureaucratic inertia, parliamentary opposition, the president of the Republic, the Constitutional Court, and the media. A combination of these impediments and of a multitude of self-inflicted political injuries led to the Antall government's resounding electoral defeat in May 1994. Similarly, as economic conditions did not improve sufficiently by 1998, Horn and the Hungarian Socialist Party were replaced by a center-right coalition in the May 1998 parliamentary elections.

The political intent of the NRT Agreement and subsequent elite pacts was formalized in the revised (amended several times since 1989) constitution, as well as in laws, parliamentary resolutions, government decrees, and opinions of the Constitutional Court.[31] Unlike the written provisions delineating spheres of legal competence, which need not be discussed here, the actual modus operandi of key institutions rests on implicit understandings and informal rules among the political elites. These may be characterized as a kind of floating, yet publicly never fully articulated, elite consensus in which themes of "self-limitation," "understeering, yet governability," "institutional self-perpetuation," "constricted public participation," and informal political bargaining are the operative components.

Over the years the manifest and latent elements of priority setting, decision making, and interest adjudication coalesced into typical pathologies of post-communist "transitional politics": a mixture of dedicated professional and amateurish legislative work; thoughtful and reckless party rhetoric; principled and petty conflicts between top public officials; and disorientation, shared by all actors, as to the proper means and ends of the political game in a working democracy. These were growing pains of an emerging political class. Its members, as cabinet ministers and state secretaries, legislators, behind-the-scenes power brokers in parliamentary committees, party officials, and justices of the Constitutional Court, were searching for their proper roles and institutional personae in the new constellation of post-communist politics. As will be shown below, the new public officials' efforts to define their roles by discharging their respective responsibilities have met at best with skepticism and at worst with outright rejection by the Hungarian public.

Public Opinion: Patterns of Contingent Consent

Since 1989, hundreds of polls have been taken to gauge public sentiment about issues of institutional change and socioeconomic transformation in Hungary.[32] This data may be assessed either in a regional post-communist or in a national context. The two are complementary and tend to support my earlier propositions about the generic and unique characteristics of Hungary's transition and transformation.

Comparative surveys depict Hungarians as being the "most pessimistic" about their life prospects, "most skeptical" about the possible benefits of the market economy, "most committed" to values of socialism (yet "most attached" to their homeland), and "highest" on Inglehart's M-PM scale.[33] One could produce another list in which Hungarians are shown as being regionally the "least supportive" of many institutional and policy attributes of the transition period. These findings have left both foreign and Hungarian analysts somewhat nonplussed. Whereas the former tend to mystify the matter by citing the Hungarians' "traditionally pessimistic outlook," the latter obfuscate the issue by focusing on the uniqueness of the country's Kadarist legacy as key to public perceptions. Unless longitudinal survey data for 1972–1996, as cognitive and effective components of the country's economic modernization and social restratification since the mid-1960s, are factored in, both explanations will fall short of adequately accounting for the way the Hungarian public thinks and feels about democracy, market, and law in the 1990s.

Let us briefly consider some recent survey data on politics, political institutions, economic policies, social conflicts, and public expectations of the government.

In 1995 one-third of the respondents could not correctly identify parties of the government coalition and the parliamentary opposition. This need not be surprising, because those with a "great deal," "middling," and "none whatsoever" interest in politics were 12, 34, and 25 percent of respondents, respectively.[34] However, of those who were "very much" interested in politics, 84.4 percent were prepared to vote in elections.[35]

Whereas in the early 1990s 80 to 85 percent of the national sample approved of, or at least accepted, the multiparty system, 78.7 percent were either "totally" or "overwhelmingly" critical of the political parties.[36] According to a late 1995 poll, such attitudes were also manifest in the public's ranking, on a scale of 1 (total distrust) to 100 (complete trust), of political institutions. The president of the Republic (the nation's well-liked grandfather figure) and the Constitutional Court (which had invalidated the government's austerity measures as unconstitutional earlier in the year) were at the top with an average rating of 64 each. The political parties were at the very bottom with a rating of 22. The Horn government and the Parliament, with ratings of 27 and 28, respectively, were only a notch above the parties.[37]

Evidence of the public's gradual radicalization may be gleaned from the growing numbers of those who explicitly identify with one or another kind of political ideology: 68 percent in 1989, 85 percent in 1995.[38] Although correlations between growing politicization and trends in public perceptions of social conflicts are unavailable, those who believed that conflicts were "very serious" between dichotomous sets of social actors grew significantly between 1990 and 1993. The pairs in these years were "rich and poor" 36 and 56 percent; "law-abiding citizens and criminals" 29 and 56 percent; "young and old" 11 and 18 percent; and "believers and nonbelievers" 10 and 16 percent.[39] This data may be illuminated by citing responses of "none" to the question, "How much say do you have in your workplace?" which grew from 14 percent in 1989 to 48 percent in 1993.[40]

Along with the public's declining sense of political efficacy, there has been evidence of the respondents' anxiety over the deterioration of their personal and family status in the social hierarchy. Hungary's *homo Kadaricus*, regardless of party affiliation, insists on the preservation of a state-guaranteed, generous social safety net. On the other hand, she and he are also highly conscious of their social status. However, determinants of social standing have changed from nomenklatura position and politically differentiated access to public goods to market-defined terms of consumption and lifestyle. According to a 1993 survey, 44 percent who identified themselves as belonging to the lower middle class had perceived themselves as members of the middle class in the previous year. The good news is that "political beliefs" were seen by only 6.2 percent as salient to the determination of one's social status. The bad news is that 46 percent of the sample believed that now it took access to "high job titles" and "informal contacts" to make one's way in the world.[41]

Much of the foregoing may be summarized by referring to the main findings of a 1993 survey of public assessments of the Kadar era according to party affiliation.[42] Regardless of party affiliation, the majority of the respondents thought that under Kadar "people lived better," "there was significant social development, and "there was law and order." On the other hand, they all agreed that the old regime had "failed to solve social problems." With respect to public expectations of Hungary's post-communist government, 90 to 100 percent majorities insisted that it was the government's job to see to "full employment," to the "delivery of health care to all citizens," and to "take care of old and retired persons." Moreover, 73.5 percent of all respondents demanded that the government "reduce differences in incomes." Notwithstanding the regime change in 1990, the society's report card on the Kadar era has changed surprisingly little since 1988.[43]

Public expectations of Jozsef Antall's Christian Democratic government have not diminished since 1993. Indeed, next to the voters' massive rejection of the Antall regime's ideological arrogance and political style, it was the mirage of "a loaf of bread for 3.5 Forints" and the return of "experts" to public administration that energized the public to oust the first-round government.[44] As shown by the Horn-led, Socialist–Alliance of Free Democrat coalition government's rapidly evaporating public support since March 1995, people still expect miracles of the political regime.[45]

Conclusion

The main findings of this chapter may be summarized as follows:

Hungary's institutional transition and socioeconomic transformation have been interactive parts of an elite-led, long-term third- and fourth-wave process of institutional adaptation, economic modernization, social differentiation, and value change.

The road from institutional protopluralism to a parliamentary democracy, from the symbiote of the first and second economy to a market economy, from a new middle class to an emerging civil society, and from the *homo Kadaricus* of the "jolliest barrack" to frustrated window shoppers of the "saddest shopping center"[46] is still under construction in Hungary.

Political sea changes, as and when these happened in the past forty years, were ushered in by cathartic events, such as the 1956 revolution; by strategic leadership decisions, such as the inauguration of the NEM; and by political pacts, such as the NRT Agreement of 1989. In each case, the elites sought to devise political contracts and new legitimating principles to shore up a new modus vivendi for the regime and the public. In each case it has been an institution-led escape from the past, as well as a process to recalibrate the economy, reshape the society, and restore systemic stability.

Given the multitude of internal socioeconomic and psychological and external (mainly economic) constraints, rapid implementation of the Hungarian "new democracy's" threefold strategic agenda of democratization, marketization, and the embedding of the rule of law is not in the cards in the 1990s. Instead of a picture-perfect democracy, smoothly working market economy, and contented citizenry, second-best solutions will have to do for some time to come. The mismatch between the Kadarist institutional legacy and the new political architecture, between economic misdevelopment and the imperatives of the market, between moral decay and civic probity have not been overcome—nor will they be anytime soon.

Withal, the glass is more than half full: institutional changes have become irreversible; free enterprise has taken deep root and will soon dominate the economy; and the people, however dissatisfied with inept politicians and clumsy policies, do believe in democracy and do vote for the party and the candidate of their choice. Hungary is no longer a barrack but the half-built home of ten million free, albeit discontented, citizens. Democracy works, and it is there to stay.

Notes

1. See Rudolf L. Tokes, *Hungary's Negotiated Revolution: Economic Reforms, Social Change, and Political Succession, 1957–1990* (Cambridge: Cambridge University Press, 1996), 305–60.

2. Geoffrey Pridham and Paul G. Lewis, "Introduction: Stabilising Fragile Democracies and Party sYstem Development" in Geofffrey Pridham and Paul G. Lewis, eds., *Stabilising Fragile Democracies: Comparing New Party Systems in Southern and Eastern Europe* (London: Routledge, 1996) 7.

3. Tokes, *Hungary's Negotiated Revolution*, 439.

128   *Rudolf L. Tokes*

4. Elemer Hankiss, *East European Alternatives* (Oxford: Clarendon Press, 1990).

5. Tokes, *Hungary's Negotiated Revolution*, 82–116.

6. Rudolf L. Tokes, *Murmur and Whispers: Public Opinion and Legitimacy Crisis in Hungary, 1972–1989* (Pittsburgh: Carl Beck Papers, The University of Pittsburgh, 1996).

7. See, for instance, Janos Kornai, *The Socialist System: The Political Economy of Communism* (Princeton: Princeton University Press, 1992).

8. Janos Arvay and Andras Vertes, "A magangazdasag" (The Private Economic Sector) in Rudolf Andorka, et al., eds., *Tarsadalmi Report 1994* (Social Report, 1994) (Budapest, TARKI, 1994) 220.

9. Michael S. Borish and Michael Noel, "Private Sector Development During Transition—The Visegrad Countries," Discussion Paper, No. 318 (Washington: The World Bank, 1996).

10. Endre Sik, "Valosagdarabok a magyar haztartasi panelbol" (Factual segments from Hungarian household panel surveys) in Andorka, et al., 165.

11. Tamas Kolosi and Endre Sik, "A magangazdasag nemzetgazdasagi sulya es nemely tarsadalmi jellemvonasai" (The private economic sector: weight in the national economy and certain social characteristics) in Andorka, et al., 253.

12. Rudolf Andorka, "Magyarorszag a tarsadalmi jelzoszamok idosoranak tukreben" (Hungary in the mirror of the time series of social indicators) in Andorka, et al., 26.

13. Martha de Melo, Cevdet Denizer, and Alan Gelb, "From Plan to Market: Patterns of Transition," *Transition* (Washington: World Bank), vol. 6, no. 11–12 (November–December 1995), 4–6.

14. Alan Gelb, et al., eds., *World Development Report 1996: From Plan to Market* (New York: Oxford University Press, 1996).

15. Rudolf Andorka, Erzsebet Bukodi, and Istvan Harcsa, "Tarsadalmi mobilitas, 1992" (Social mobility, 1992) in Andorka, et al., 293.

16. Andorka, "Hungary in the mirror of the time series of social indicators" in Andorka, et al., 33.

17. Rudolf Andorka and Zsolt Speder, "A magyar tarsadalom szerkezete, 1994" (The structure of Hungarian society, 1994) in Sandor Kurtan, Peter Sandor, and Laszlo Vass, eds., *Magyarorszag Politikai Evkonyve, 1995* (Hungary's Political Yearbook, 1995) (hereafter *HPYB*) (Budapest: DKMPA, 1995), 325.

18. Istvan Bedekovics, et al., "Jovedelmi helyzet az 90-es evek elso feleben" (Incomes in the first half of the '90s) in Andorka, et al., 52. See also, Gelb, et al., eds., 197.

19. Gelb, et al., eds., 68–69.

20. See Gyorgy Lengyel, "A magyar gazdasagi elit a kilencvenes evek elso feleben" (The Hungarian economic elite in the early 1990s) in *HYPB 1995*, 314ff, and Matild Sagi, "Managerek: Az uj gazdasagi elit rekrutacioja" (Managers: The recruitment of the new Hungarian economic elite) in Andorka, et al., 314–50.

21. On this see a three-part report on the reign of the old/new cadre "klep-

tocracy" in East Central Europe in early 1996 in *Repubblica*, February 8–10, 1996.

22. The average annual share of Hungarian government expenditures on social security was 29.8 percent between 1989 and 1994. World Bank, *Social Indicators of Development 1996* (Baltimore: The Johns Hopkins University Press, 1996), 152.

23. Andorka and Speder in *HPYB 1996*, 325.

24. Writings of social scientists and journalists associated with the HSP and AFD-sponsored "Charter '92" anti-Christian Democrat political protest movement would fall in this category.

25. Eva Voszka, "A katarzis nelkuli atmenet elviselhetetlen konnyusege" (The unbearable lightness of non-cathartic transition), *Kozgazdasagi Szemle* (June 1990): 687–701.

26. For a summary of pretransition reform writings on law and public administration, see Rudolf L. Tokes, "The Science of Politics in Hungary: People, Ideas, and Contradictions," *Sudost-Europa*, vol. 37, no. 1 (January 1988): 8–32.

27. For comprehensive assessments of post-1990 politics and institutional change, see Csaba Gombar, et al., eds., *Balance: The Hungarian Government, 1990–1994* (Budapest: Centre for Political Research, 1994); Csaba Gombar, et al., eds., *Question Marks: The Hungarian Government, 1994–1995* (Budapest: Korridor Center for Political Research, 1995); and Rudolf L. Tokes, "Party Politics and Political Participation in Post-Communist Hungary" in Karen Dawisha and Bruce Parrott, eds., *Democratization and Political Participation in Post-Communist Societies*, 4 vols. (Cambridge: Cambridge University Press, 1997).

28. Tamas Sarkozy, "The Initial Operation of the Government and State Machinery" in Gombar, et al., eds., *Question Marks*, 279–304.

29. Janos Sari, "The Government and Legislation by Decree," in Gombar, et al., eds., *Balance*, 154.

30. Gyorgy Szilvasy, "A Miniszterelnoki Hivatal negy eve" (The first four years of the Office of the Prime Minister) in *HPYB 1994*, 455–77.

31. See, for instance, Istvan Kukorelli, *Az alkotmanyozas evtizede* (A decade of constitution-making) (Budapest: Korona, 1995); and Bill Lomax, "Hungary" in Stephen Whitefield, ed., *The New Institutional Architecture of Eastern Europe* (New York: St. Martin's, 1933) 79–98.

32. Many of these have been summarized in the national press and in special reports issued by the principal Hungarian polling organizations, such as Median, Szonda-Ipsos, Gallup, TARKI, the National Statistical Office, as well as by academic departments of various universities.

33. See, for instance, various issues of *New Democracy Barometer, Eurobarometer, International Journal of Public Opinion Research, The Public Perspective* cross-national surveys sponsored by Freedom House and the Times-Mirror Center for People and the Press.

34. Endre Hann, "Politikai kozvelemeny a Median kutatasainak tukreben" (Public opinion on politics in the mirror of Median surveys) in *HPYB 1996*, 602–04.

35. Ferenc Gazso and Tibor Gazso,"Valasztoi magatartas es partpreferen-

ciak Magyarorszagon" (Electoral behavior and party preferences in Hungary) in Istvan Balogh, ed., *Toresvonalak es Ertekvalasztasok: Politikatudomanyi vizsgalatok a mai Magyarorszagrol* (Cleavages and Value Choices: Political Science Analyses of Today's Hungary) (Budapest: MTA Politikai Tudomanyok Intezete, 1994), 112, 115.

36. *Ibid.*, 115.

37. Guy Lazar and Bela Marian, "A politikai kozvelemeny a Marketing Centrum kutatasainak tukreben" (Public opinion on politics in the mirror of survey by Marketing Centrum) in *HPYB 1996*, 590.

38. Gazso and Gazso, "Valasztoi magatartas es partpreferenciak Magyarorszagon," 141.

39. Laszlo Bruszt and Janos Simon, "Az Antall korszak utan, a valasztasok elott" (After the Antall era, on the eve of the elections) in *HPYB 1994*, 777.

40. *Ibid.*, 779.

41. Robert Peter, "Egyenlotlensegtudat" (Awareness of inequality) in Andorka, et al., eds., *Social Report*, 1994, 313.

42. Gazso and Gazso, "Valasztoi magatartas es partpreferenciak Magyarorszagon" 135.

43. *Ibid.*, 138.

44. Miklos Szabo, "Multunk jelene. A hatalomvaltas kritikai hagyomanya" (The presence of our past: The critical legacy of the change of the regime) *Beszelo*, June 1996 [Internet edition], http://www.enet.hu./beszelo/4-05.htm, 7 of 8.

45. Peter Tolgyessy, "Az elegedetlensegek egyensulya" (The equilibrium of disenchantment) *Nepszabadsag*, 27 April 1996.

46. Gyorgy Csepeli, "Social Psychological Consequences of the Transition from Totalitarianism to Democracy;" Paper presented at a meeting of Pacific Sociological Association (San Francisco, 6–9 April 1995).

Chapter 7

The Foundations of Post-Socialist Legitimacy

Anna Seleny

Social scientists who have followed Eastern Europe from the state socialist period to the present know that scholars and journalists alike, especially after 1968, frequently proffered a mix of fact, opinion, and descriptive narrative to evoke a sense of Hungarian exceptionalism. Whether the proposition was explored seriously or—more often— remained implicit, a sense of Hungarian "difference" prevailed at conferences and in political, sociological, and economic accounts. But the very notion of exceptionalism implies a generality of experience under state socialism that can be claimed only at a broad systemic level;[1] and, ultimately, even within a framework of constraints unique to the state socialism, national politics in the region were, like all politics, local.

Thus I make no overarching claims of Hungarian exceptionalism here.[2] I do argue, however, that specific political practices and their attendant discourses, as well as particular institutions and group identities that evolved during the state socialist period, left the country remarkably well-positioned to consolidate a democracy capable of translating popular demands into social peace. To be sure, in Hungary as elsewhere, it is all too easy to find clear instances of the perniciousness of the state socialist legacy. But I will focus instead on several positive endowments that undergird key institutions of contemporary Hungarian politics, and which, I contend, provide an important source of legitimacy for them.

Hungarian politics of the 1980s and 1990s have often been characterized as moderate, pragmatic, conflict-avoiding, nonrevolutionary, and cautious.[3] The characterization has persisted despite periods after 1989 of an over-symbolized nationalist discourse at times exhibiting features of irredentism and bigotry. These periods, however brief, caution us that to view pragmatism and compromise as inexorable forces in Hungarian politics is to ignore important countertrends that have dominated in the past: Only recall the ignominy of 1944.

More recently, two alternative political discourses have reemerged, coming into play at turning points. One is precisely the discourse of pragmatic compromise which, as a specific institutionalized resource, has helped key political actors manage fundamental dilemmas creatively. An important source of this discursive alternative is found in the politics of post-1956 Hungarian state socialism. The other alternative is a confrontational discourse rooted in collective remembrance of conflictual and traumatic episodes that preceded the emergence of the post-1956 "pact" between the Hungarian socialist state and its citizenry.

I argue that political learning among party-state elites in the period of state socialism resulted in the fundamental reshaping of the discourse and practices of the state—a reshaping that led to pragmatic policy-making and compromise with former "enemies." Moreover, despite a partial hiatus, the lessons learned by political actors *then* directly inform politics *now*.

In the spring of 1998, on the eve of the country's third round of postsocialist democratic elections, Hungarian politics could best be described as corporatist and coalitional at the elite level, with a moderator-president, one of the most politically powerful constitutional courts in Europe, and relatively consensual party politics.[4] At the popular level they were generally quiescent.

Contrast this not with a dramatically different case (such as Romania or Russia), but with Poland, a country more often noted for its similarities with Hungary. At the elite level, post-1989 Polish politics have been oppositional and divisive, with a strong presidency, weak constitutional tribunal, and highly contentious party politics; at the popular level they have been relatively confrontational and mobilized.[5] Intra-elite and state-society relations in socialist Poland and Hungary differed considerably—particularly in the realm of informal politics—and today give rise to core conflicts of different types and intensities.[6]

In part I of this chapter, I address theoretical issues concerning political culture, political discourse, and learning. In part II, I show how significant groups within the party-state crafted an alternative identity within the framework of state socialism, and argue that this identity was indispensable to their willingness and ability to craft reforms that ultimately undermined their own power. Part III demonstrates that the core features of that identity were crucial to the success of the postsocialists; and that the discourse of reform socialism still provides an important (though no longer exclusive) organizing and legitimating framework for Hungarian politics. I also offer an interpretation of the apparent break during the transition itself from the pragmatic politics associated both with reform socialism and with the current coalition government. In part IV, I suggest that contemporary Hungarian politics are unusual (if not entirely exceptional) in one aspect that prominent analysts posit as essential to the success of democratic consolidation: political processes that facilitate the creation and maintenance of elite consensus and political moderation.[7] Hungary's elite settlement, I conclude, is grounded primarily in the procedural and discursive practices of reform socialism; moreover, the constitutional court and the tripartite commission bear the imprint of these practices and serve to stabilize state-society relations.

I. Conceptual Clarification

Legacies, Identities, Discourse

Some might suspect that terms like "legacies," "endowments," "identities," and "discourses" are the proverbial Trojan horse that carries ill-defined notions of culture purporting to account for political developments in Eastern Europe in terms of the past.[8] Others might call to mind 1960s studies that understood political cultures as deriving from intangible values, attitudes, and beliefs located in the individual. While more sophisticated analysts never held that political culture acted as "unidirectional cause . . . of political structure and behavior,"[9] such assumptions are still often mistakenly ascribed to those who employ the term. Although I cannot offer a new and comprehensive alternative definition of political culture here, I do want to distance myself from such a conception, as well as from crude attempts to explain the present or predict the future in terms of the past. Thankfully, contemporary work on political culture tends to be grounded in subtler and better specified concepts, such as Swidler's[10] "toolkit" of resources from which actors construct political strategies, or Geertz's[11] "web of intersubjective meaning" within a polity.

Space permits neither detailed discussion of old debates about political culture nor a review of newer work in this area. Suffice it to say that although cultural approaches to politics came under attack in the 1970s and early 1980s, they have recently enjoyed a significant revival in political science and sociology, and to a lesser extent in institutional economics. This is evident in a number of historical institutional studies; work on protest and social movements; and in studies of the symbolic foundations of political regimes.[12] Work has focused variously on the construction of stable orders of meaning in institutions (following Peter Berger's early lead); on power relations (often, though not exclusively, under Foucault's influence); and on the sources of political conflict and innovative institution-building.[13] In political science, the subfield of international relations has also been influenced by the sociologists' "world cultures" approach.[14]

Largely because of the disorderly intellectual baggage the term "political culture" carries, many social scientists, including myself, have tended to eschew the term altogether. Use of less "loaded" terms, however, only defers some of the fundamental questions that must be addressed in any serious attempt to grasp the deep dynamics and specific mechanisms of large-scale political transformation. Unfortunately, the prevailing view of politics impedes such an effort. March and Olsen characterize it this way:

> Contemporary theory in political science considers politics and political behavior in instrumental terms . . . [gives] primacy to substantive outcomes and either ignore[s] symbolic actions or see[s] symbols as part of manipulative efforts to control outcomes. The intent of actions is found in their outcomes, and the organizing principle of a political system is the allocation of scarce resources in the face of conflict of interests. Thus, action is choice, choice is made in terms of expectations about its consequences, meanings are organized to affect choices, and symbols are curtains that obscure the real politics, or artifacts of an effort to make decisions.[15]

This narrow, instrumental conceptualization of politics, I have argued elsewhere, is insufficient to explain either state socialist transformations or to assess the prospects for consolidation of democracy in Eastern Europe.[16] Because we are all "normative schemers,"[17] we would do well to integrate the observation that politics is fundamentally about the attempt to impose hegemonic identities:

> Politics is usually conducted as if identity were fixed. The question then becomes, on what basis, at different times in different places, does the nonfixity become temporarily fixed in such a way that individuals and groups can behave as a particular kind of agency, political or otherwise? How do people become shaped into acting subjects, understanding themselves in particular ways? . . . In effect, politics consists of the effort to domesticate the infinitude of identity. It is the attempt to hegemonize identity, to order it into a strong programmatic statement. If identity is decentered, politics is about the attempt to create a center.[18]

Note that this understanding of identity has more in common with Dewey than with any postmodern or other attempt at essentialization:

identities are as much constructed as they are "discovered."[19] Similarly, essentialized notions of culture can be disaggregated into comprehensible components and more modest concepts. Among those addressed below are the institutions and political discourses that provided crucial resources for Hungarian elites in their efforts to reform the state socialist system, and which still influence both the rules of the game and state capacity.

Political Discourse and Learning

Political Discourse

"Discourse" is conceptually more useful for political analysis than "ideology," Joseph Schull has argued. Ideology, if understood as a belief system, tends to conflate the potency of a particular system of belief with its adherents' faith in it, obscuring their autonomous agency to manipulate, "re-present, reformulate and . . . transform concepts in the course of political debate." A focus on discourse removes the presumption that ideas influence action only in proportion to actors' sincerity of belief; it also draws attention to the analytically separable power of the " 'instrument' to condition the use which is made of it."

Thus, in this essay, I approach ideology through the heuristic of discourses located not just in individuals' minds but in a "social space shared by the members of an ideological community . . . not aggregatively but intersubjectively."[20] Most concretely, political discourse is comprised of the *class of linguistic political practices* that produce evidence in the form of speeches, publications, broadcasts, campaigns and widely known phrases whose power to evoke cooperation or conflict in a particular collectivity provides clues to understanding *other* political practices and institutions.

Political Learning

According to Nancy Bermeo,[21] political learning is the "process through which people modify their political beliefs and tactics as a result of severe crises, frustrations, and dramatic changes in environment." And whether tactical or ideological in nature, in regime transitions, political learning is

> most important during the second phase of the redemocratization process—at the critical moment between the crisis of the old order and the consolidation of the new one—for it helps explain why a new regime becomes democratic in the first place . . . why . . . a dictatorship is replaced by a democracy rather than another dictatorial regime.[22]

On this view, then, political learning is most vital at the moment of creation or reconstruction of democratic regimes. Evidence from the Hungarian case suggests, however, that the results of political learning by elites may only be most *visible* at such moments, and that political learning can also be profound during the years of gradual "breakdown." Indeed, political learning can occur in periods of relative stasis as well as times of dramatic frustration, crisis, and change. For example, structural rigidities severe enough to block the aspirations of large social groups can also teach leaders powerful political lessons, particularly if such groups react, say, by sabotaging centralized production schemes. Political learning by elites, in turn, may give rise to fresh institutional or discursive resources that a variety of political actors can employ to construct altered, or even substantially new, polities and societies. Whether or not leaders are open to such "lessons," however, and whether any group within the state will actually champion them in the form of new policies, depends on a great deal more than exogenous pressures or opportunities, be they economic or geopolitical: worldwide economic downturn, or Gorbachev's renunciation of the Brezhnev doctrine. (Otherwise, Albania or Romania should have been the first to undertake institutional reform in the Soviet bloc.) It also depends, crucially, on governing elites' convictions about the degree to which their own and their rivals' interests and identities are fixed.

II. The Hungarian Socialist Workers' Party: Identity-Transformation

The Hungarian Socialist Workers' Party (HSWP) underwent formal institutional transformation in 1989, but it experienced significant internal transformation much earlier. In several key institutional locations, a microclimate of political learning developed, nurturing both reformers within the party-state apparatus and their ability to reach consensus with hard-liners.[23] I have conceptualized the legacy of this learning—the knowledge and arrangements that entwined policies with the bargains and struggles involved in their making—as the *institutional residue of reform*, the elements of which were political actors, practices and discourse, including innovative adaptations of received political terminology.[24] The *institutional residue* was the cumulative product of individual reforms and reform attempts, and was most clearly observable at specific points in the period between the mid-1960s and 1989.[25]

One important case of political learning that significantly augmented the institutional residue of reform can be traced to late 1970s.[26] By this time, the discourse of "reform socialism" was well-entrenched in Hungary, and helped create a context within which party and non-party reformers were able to establish a transformative conversation with hard-liners. More specifically, the ability to discuss "safely" what in other countries was considered dangerous, helped bring about the legitimation of a considerably expanded and formally institutionalized private sector in Hungary. By 1981, reformers and hard-liners reached an agreement that allowed for the legalization of the second economy and the implementation of a unique reform of property rights.[27]

Reformers managed to render this radical reform[28] "respectable" in terms of the existing socialist framework by using tactics and rhetoric that showed a keen awareness of the established identities and interests of groups within party-state decision making institutions. The attempt to redefine the second economy was an effort to divide it into parts that would be ideologically acceptable and others that would be prohibited. Reformers also stressed that the legalized second economy would be *self-limiting*. Since the 1982 reform legally enfranchised any citizen who wished to engage in legitimate private business activities, guaranteeing property rights of residual income, ownership, and alienability, it is conceivable that some forward-looking reformers did not fully believe in their own ability to control the emerging private sector. Yet the evidence is overwhelming that most, including the chief architects of the reform, were convinced that this reform was no more significant than its predecessors, and posed no special challenge to the system or to their leadership. Indeed, the symbolic and rhetorical place of the 1968 New Economic Mechanism (NEM) within the institutional residue of reform made it possible for reformers to view almost *any* new reform (short of *open* privatization of state firms, overthrow of the HSWP or of Soviet tutelage) as its natural heir.[29] Thus, *the institutional residue of reform made plausible both the new policy, and the idea that it would fundamentally alter very little.* The ideological justification for household plots in agriculture that had been accepted decades earlier provided the underpinning for legalizing and expanding the institutional framework of the second economy. The proposed intrafirm work partnerships (VGMKs),[30] for example, were billed as the "household plots of industry." They, in turn, would be just one part of a self-limiting helper economy of small manufacturing firms and service establishments operating outside state firms.

Yet in fact nothing less than the formal boundaries between state and society were at issue. Redrawing them reshaped the privileges of the party-state and the larger society, and added new layers to an already complex systemic hybrid of plan and market. The 1982 reform, for instance, led to the substantial redefinition of the concepts of "full employment," "exploitation," and "entrepreneurship," among others.

Not surprisingly, each redefinition carried with it real public policy consequences. Taken together, these piecemeal redefinitions contributed mightily to the redefinition of the Hungarian model of state socialism.[31]

Moreover, as leading reformers recast the discourse of economic reform and property rights, they did more than just "privilege one line of policy over others."[32] They both entrenched a tactical approach and implicitly redefined their own and others' roles and interests vis-à-vis a particular policy; that is, they both affirmed the "Hungarian way" of practicing consensus politics and changed their own socialist identities.

By this time, party leaders, once impelled by the original mandate of vigilance against enemies both internal and external, were either uninterested or unable to distinguish "friend" from "foe," except in the narrow sense of tactical "enemies"—those who opposed their plan of the moment. As we will see, this would change only once they were actually faced with an organized, political opposition. By then, it was too late to try to revert to "hard-line" confrontational tactics without violating the implicit rules of Hungarian politics and further weakening their own legitimacy in the process.

III. Alternative Discursive Resources: Continuity and Rupture in Hungarian Politics

Up to this point, we have seen that in the effort to win the acceptance of the various new economic policies, reformers redefined terms and recast ideologies until discursive moorings and details became almost indistinguishable from one another. Accustomed to the shifts in intraparty politics, pragmatic reformers found nothing out of the ordinary in their own actions. This is all the more so because it was primarily in words that they could be "revolutionary"—words whose full import were frequently understood only in retrospect, and which in daily memoranda or conversation appeared only as the tools for solving immediate conflicts and problems.

By 1989, however, the process of endogenous transformation (and the exogenous pressures and opportunities favoring it) had developed in such a way that political actors inside and outside the party-state could be revolutionary in more than discourse. This was, in fact, early evidence of the future Katherine Verdery foresaw when she argued that "consciousness [would] now be formed less through discourse and more through practices."[33]

This period witnessed an older historical memory of confrontation and tragedy superimposed on the more recent memory of compromise between party factions and between the party-state and society. *This revival was directly linked to hard-liners' misuse of the institutional residue of reform.* Indeed, their mistakes provide an object lesson to any ruling group that aims to marginalize its opponents, at least where a politics of pragmatism and compromise has become the accepted norm.

In late 1988, hard-liners within the party "briefly and halfheartedly" tried to "criminalize" the opposition. They tried, more seriously, to "neutralize" them, to make satellite organizations of them, and to "divide and conquer" them. These tactics, along with patronizing and confrontational rhetoric (e.g., Grosz referring to the opposition as "portending the danger of 'white terror' ") only served to galvanize a disorganized opposition that had not, until then, been "fundamentally committed to challenging the legitimacy of the Communist regime."[34]

If the attempts of desperate hard-liners and other ill-advised politicos within the HSWP to control the process of transition had the effect of uniting the incipient political opposition, the latter, in turn, self-consciously depicted hard-liners and reformers within the party as more united than they were in reality. The important consequence of the opposition's defensive rhetorical tactic was to "forc[e] an open division within the ruling bloc." Reformers who had demonstrably exercised leadership in crucial areas of economic policy for the greater part of two decades were now on the defensive in the realm of overt politics. They were quite literally reduced to trying to demonstrate to the public their capacity to lead the party and the government.[35]

Another predictable result of hard-liners' tactics and rhetoric was the further weakening of whatever modicum of trust the opposition had in its bargaining partners in the apparatus. It was perhaps not surprising, in these circumstances, that the opposition increasingly "punctuated their words in early 1989 with references to 1948," when the communists "succeeded in the divide and conquer tactics their counterparts were attempting to emulate in the present."

If they were not to repeat past mistakes, the nascent opposition groups would need to find some institutional means to coordinate their efforts. Whether the analyst uses the language of "iterative games" or of "collective memories," Hungary's young opposition parties had learned important lessons from a previous confrontation.[36] But since the institutional residue of reform came close to shaping the transition through power-sharing arrangements, the opposition would presumably have learned other lessons, had the party continued the discourse of pragmatic consensus characteristic of its own internal policy debates; and characteristic, too, of interactions on issues of economic reform among party reformers, intellectuals, and scholars.

In the event, application of this discursive tactic to political opposition groups only radicalized them further, and led them to draw not on the institutional residue of pragmatic compromise, but on older, confrontational memories and discourses. The politics of confrontation activated by party hard-liners (and cleverly exploited by the opposition) resulted in parallel celebrations of important historical dates. Each commemoration polarized politics further and diminished the possibility of power-sharing. Each also fueled the resurgence of the discourse of "us" versus "them"—a discourse that had long since fallen into disrepute in relations between the party-state and society. Indeed, the Opposition Roundtable's explicit statement of principle held that power-sharing was not a viable option, and turned Kadar's alliance policy on its head by declaring that "anyone who disagrees with this principle, and anyone who is willing to compromise this principle, is with 'them.' "[37]

Hungary's confrontational transition, then, was driven not by the opposition's repudiation of pragmatic consensus-building, but rather by the opposition's reaction to hard-liners' implicit departure from the established consensual strategy. Moreover, in its search for a confrontational symbology, the opposition had to skip the proximate twenty-five-year period of Kadar's Alliance Policy entirely. In retrospect, it is perhaps not surprising that such a mobilizational strategy was tenable for a brief and intense oppositional campaign, but not for the long term. Together, these two factors help explain why Hungarian post-socialist politics quickly reverted to a pattern of pragmatic compromise much more closely resembling that of the years between 1963 and 1988. As an increasingly prominent alternative historical memory eclipsed the discourse of pragmatic compromise during 1988–89, the HSWP was dispossessed of a vital political resource. Internal splits within the party-state were obscured, and the institutional residue of reform socialism seemed inoperative. Once settled on competitive elections, however, and with the rules of the game more or less defined, such mobilizational politics were not sustainable on the same scale. As new parties began to clarify their own programmatic identities in the competition for public support, the post-socialists were once again free to compete on the same field.

To be sure, some political parties, factions within parties, and other groups have since utilized these same divisive historical memories to assert a nationalist discourse that was premised on a variety of "us" versus "them" formulations. However, though the Hungarian Democratic Forum (HDF) and its coalition partners tolerated this discourse, it cannot be said to have dominated mainstream Hungarian politics between 1990 and 1994. Even so, it was prominent enough to contribute to the spectacular electoral defeat of the coalition. By 1993, distaste for the confrontational politics of the governing coalition was increasingly evident among a significant portion of the population. Most Hungarians did not feel themselves to have been heavily burdened or repressed by the last two decades of state socialism, and many could not accept that "the whole state socialist period was a waste of time and social energies. Many people had positive memories as well as negative ones. . . ." This was no mere nostalgia for the past, but a need for "identity and self-respect."[38] Indeed, a yearning for greater social security can only partially explain the 1994 election results, since presumably the Czechs, for instance, have the same need but lack the institutional residue of discursive and practical resources that might allow them to reconcile with, let alone be proud of, their state socialist past.

The Hungarian Socialist Party (HSP) began to reconstruct the discourse of consensus and pragmatism long before its reelection campaign. It played the role of moderate and loyal opposition party during the first post-socialist government, assiduously "buil[t] ties to the liberal parties" and reached out not only to the predictable groups (the unemployed, the working class, and unions) but also to "religious, ethnic and other elements." Moreover, while the HSP crafted a discourse of social democracy, and in this sense is a party of the Left, its electoral platform was hardly radical, stressing the need to control the state budget; explaining that unemployment would not be eliminated in the "foreseeable future" nor living standards increased; and that only in four years would "a modest improvement in economic performance" be achieved. Horn's election-night speech emphasized that the HSP's landslide did not signify equally strong support in society, that "not all voters voting for the HSP were socialists or would become so, and that social reconciliation and rapprochement were essential. . . . [T]hus on election night, the HSP turned directly to the Alliance of Free Democrats (and others) to join them."[39]

On one possible reading, the willingness to form a coalition with the Alliance of Free Democrats (AFD) was little more than a self-protective, even opportunistic move to gain legitimacy and also strength in Parliament for the tough economic decisions ahead. Or, some might put it more cynically: The canny socialists' political "liberalism" extended only to the point that they could share liberally with a coalition partner the blame that would accrue to them, given the daunting tasks of economic stabilization and restructuring facing them.[40] On another, not necessarily incompatible reading, HSP reformists needed AFD support against their own left wing in order to carry out these same tasks. In fact, since the elections, the AFD has usually supported socialist reformers against the party's left-wing group and its supporter, the National Federation of Hungarian Trade Unions.[41] But whatever the balance between political opportunism and moderation, the terms of the coalition itself were unusually generous, ceding considerably more control and power to the AFD than is typical for parties winning strong legislative mandates. The AFD was offered three ministerial portfolios,[42] broad powers to approve government policies amounting to effective veto power,[43] and a guarantee of one-third of committee seats (exceeding its electoral share).

Despite several serious crises, the alliance between socialist reformers and the AFD held clear through to Hungary's third round of post-1989 parliamentary elections. At every critical crisis point, the coalition partners stressed that the stability of the coalition was of paramount importance.[44] Of course, none of this precluded tough-minded power politics or self-interested, shorter-term rational calculation, as even a casual perusal of contemporary Hungarian politics will confirm.[45] Nevertheless, from the start, safeguards against polarization were built into the coalition. Perhaps the most impressive of these was the bipartisan Coalition Consultation Council, whose express purpose was "coordination, consensus-building and conflict prevention."[46] This council was convened, for instance, in the late spring of 1997 to discuss a privatization scandal that threatened the coalition, as well as the issues of cooperation and information-sharing between the parties that were brought to the fore by the scandal.[47]

IV. The Institutions of Compromise

The National Tripartite Commission

In 1984, as Bennett Kovrig observed, a "neocorporatist tendency . . . in which economic and social policies are developed through a process of consultation between party, government, the National Council of Trade Unions, and other economic agencies" had already emerged.[48] In contemporary politics, the National Tripartite Commission, in which peak organizations of business, labor, and government are represented, has continued this pattern, and as new laws on interest representation are promulgated, Hungary looks to be increasingly corporatist on several vectors.

Certainly, corporatist arrangements are in themselves no guarantee of democratic stability, but they are arguably a favorable condition.[49] And although high levels of labor mobilization do not necessarily entail democratic collapse, they can pose governability challenges even to mature democracies and bring to mind well-known cases of breakdown in Latin America.[50] In Poland, for instance, a history of confrontation between Solidarity and the party-state in the 1980s (and an earlier history of state-labor confrontation) resulted in a continued high pitch of labor and other types of mobilization, a prevailing pattern of mass politics indicative of the weakness of representative institutions.[51]

The Constitutional Court

The Hungarian Constitutional Court is quite activist in defense of citizens' "social rights." In state socialist systems these entitlements essentially represented an unmonetized part of wages; they were often listed in socialist constitutions but lacked the legal status and weight of full rights.[52] On several occasions the court struck down attempts at sudden revocation of the socioeconomic compromises reached between Hungarian society and the party-state after 1956. The court, which has established itself as "one of the most authoritative in the world,"[53] has handed down a number of decisions that underscore the value it places on social peace, gradualism, and due process. It ruled, for instance, that the legislature could not impose an increasingly heavy burden of growing sick leave costs on employers. Similarly, the court ruled that it was unconstitutional to reduce employers' pension contributions by more than 50 percent, on the grounds that an excessive reduction constituted a violation of citizens' property rights. Another court ruling nullified a proposal that would have made families with real estate holdings exceeding Hungarian Forints (HUF) 1 million in value (US $75,000) ineligible for state family benefits. While the legislature is free to propose amendments of any kind, the court has insisted on fair notice to society if social rights are to be changed; moreover, any individual or group, even foreigners, can challenge the constitutionality of a law as soon as it is published. In the summer of 1995, for instance, proposals to reduce benefits to parents with children were deemed unconstitutional because of insufficient notice: specifically, the government's austerity package had proposed cuts in subsidies to families with children, as well as in day care; the court ruled that parents had not been given adequate time to prepare for the change. The ruling also held that preexisting commitments had to be honored, although new claims could be gradually phased out.[54] The court's explicit decision to honor preexisting commitments is consonant with the tenor of the Hungarian transition as a whole; that is, although political actors and the public alike generally acknowledge the need for deep restructuring, there has also been broad agreement that such restructuring must be carried out by means of due process and in a cautious manner that will not upset the social peace they prize.[55]

By contrast, the Polish Constitutional Tribunal, an institution left over from the state socialist era, lacked both the legitimacy and the power of its Hungarian counterpart. Like the Romanian court, its rulings could be reversed by a two-thirds majority of the legislature. The tribunal's attempt to overturn the Balczerowicz plan, for instance, and to index pensions was thus thwarted.[56] The point to be made here is not that it would have been a good thing to overturn the Balczerowicz plan or to index pensions; Poland's economic circumstances at transition were very different from Hungary's—distinguished particularly by near hyperinflation—and called for different measures. The point is merely that the tribunal is unable to act as a powerful countervailing power for good or ill in Polish politics.

What, then, accounts for the activism of the Hungarian Constitutional Court in favor of social compromise? Part of the answer is clearly structural. The Hungarian court, unlike the Polish tribunal, is able to avail itself of sufficient political space to become the "other pole" in a system with a unicameral legislature and little separation of powers. The history of its founding also partially accounts for its strength. The court originated with the 1989 Roundtable Agreement between the government and the opposition. Both the former, doubting its ability to obtain a two-thirds majority in free elections, and the opposition, believing it would lose, wanted a strong Constitutional Court as a hedge against any possible future attempts to exclude them from the political game. In effect, they negotiated to maintain the status quo in terms of the power balance between opponents. Given, then, that a particular history of political bargaining during the transition accounts for much of the court's strong institutional position, the objection might be raised that I have mistaken "analogy for causality," that the court's activism in favor of social compromise is caused not by any imprint of earlier state socialist procedural and discursive practices, but is merely analogous to such practices.[57]

But analogy does not preclude causality any more than prove it. And there are at least two specific responses to such an objection. First, the parties' calculation of their likely electoral chances cannot, in itself, account for the fact that they chose to enshrine a "status quo" compromise rather than a more competitive, or even zero-sum, strategy. To be sure, their decision was rational and risk-averse; yet if all political bargains under similar circumstances were equally so, we would hardly need to study politics. As it is, history is full of sad examples to the contrary. Since independence in the early nineteenth century, Latin American elites have religiously adhered to the *formal* rules of legislatures, courts, and executives meant to institutionalize a system of checks and balances much like that of the United States, all the while accumulating a sacrilegious record of informal political practice that perpetually violated this same institutional logic. Secondly, while it is true that the political bargain forged in the Roundtable Agreement is one important source of the Constitutional Court's strength, no institution's strength can be maintained by founding agreements alone; and the political bargains that create the initial structure of an institution can never fully account for its behavior and the direction of its evolution. Indeed, the institutional strength of the court derives equally from the content and perceived legitimacy of its decisions, which mirror political preferences for accommodation between state and society accumulated over the post-1956 period.

Moreover, the Hungarian Constitutional Court reflects the same commitment to gradualism, social peace, and pragmatism found among reformers of the old regime and still in evidence among the ruling coalition today (despite the much more open political battles of a normally functioning democracy). The historical process of piecemeal amendment of the Hungarian constitution itself is also reminiscent of the incremental process of socioeconomic compromise between the party-state and society during the state socialist period. As one adviser to the court put it, "A new constitution was adopted under the cover of revision."[58]

Indeed, this description of constitutional change in Hungary is very like the process whereby private property rights and markets were reintroduced in socialist Hungary. Yet a careful reader of those events will perceive a warning in the analogy: pragmatism and compromise were only a well-developed resource available to policy-makers—not the preordained outcome of any particular political struggle. In the event, reformers won, having calculated correctly their opportunity to make effective use of Hungarian reform history and its entrenched discourse. In retrospect, the fact that no other country had such a well-established and varied institutional residue of reform helps explain why none undertook such a comprehensive reform of property rights until after undergoing formal political transition.

The court's position is likely to gain even greater relevance in light of the May 1998 elections—the third cycle of parliamentary elections since 1989—which brought to power a center-right coalition. It remains to be seen whether the programmatic ideals of the new government, which would be consistent with fundamentally more neoliberal policies, will win out over the implicit but long-standing social-democratic welfare pact between Hungarian state and society.

V. Conclusion

Evidence from Europe and Latin America shows that "elite transformations from disunity to consensual unity" are both rare and "as con-
sequential as social revolutions," since they create "patterns of open
but peaceful competition among major elite factions, the result of
which has historically been . . . stable limited democracy."[59] In this
essay, I have argued that contemporary Hungarian elites achieved just
such a settlement. But I have argued more. First, *this settlement is
grounded in relatively stable patterns of intra-elite interaction under state socialism, and more recently, in specific institutions like the Constitutional Court and the Tripartite Commission. Second, the valorization of
a highly specified political discourse and practice of gradual, consensual
change was key to establishing these patterns of elite interaction and institutions of compromise.* Some analysts trace the origins of gradualism and
consensual politics to the 1956 revolution. Even deeper, historical exca-
vations might unearth evidence that these trends have still older roots:
István Deak pointed out, for instance, that the Hungarian liberals of
1848 did not see themselves as having effected a revolution, but rather
a "peaceful adjustment to the times and the legal reconquest of Hungary's historical freedoms."[60] Another author writes that "the basic concern of Hungarians has long been peaceful change," and just as the
nobility in 1848 "voluntarily renounced its privileges in order to lay the
foundations of a constitutional state and a free society, which would
promote the development and further prosperity of the ruling class,"
the "governing communists of the late 1980s must have had something
similar in mind."[61]

Finally, limiting myself to a study of the state socialist period and
the eight years immediately following it, I have argued that, *whatever
else Hungary inherited from the state socialist period, it enjoys an important
positive legacy of pre-1989 reform whose result is analogous to the benefits of
constitutional precommitment,* even if the *process* by which it was entrenched was neither fundamentally liberal nor always formally codified. Stephen Holmes has shown that constitutional precommitment
"enfranchises future generations" by deciding fundamental questions
like freedom of speech or basic property rights that promote both positive and negative liberties.[62] Hungarian party-state elites forged important accords on economic reform in the state-socialist period, as well as
more modest compromises on rules of political representation. The
most important of these accords were enshrined as institutions and
rights, which various groups used, in turn, to press for still broader
rights and more accountable institutions. In fact, the institutional residue of reform that accumulated during the state socialist period func-

tions as a socioeconomic precommitment which first de facto and, eventually, de jure broadened the rights of Hungarian citizens. I have sketched one important example of such enfranchisement—the reform of property rights that made private entrepreneurship a basic right of citizens. The property-rights reform, and the patterns of elite political bargaining and discourse that made this and subsequent reforms possible, were important manifestations of the implicit social pact between the Hungarian party-state and society.

And what will happen to this social pact under the new, more conservative government elected in May 1998? There are, of course, no guarantees that the pragmatic, consensual, relatively nonpolarized praxis and discourse of the post-1989 period—and especially of the 1994–98 government—will continue to find stable institutional expression in the future. An alternative discursive current, strongest in the Hungarian Justice and Life Party (MIEP), but also present in the Smallholders' Party, places far greater emphasis on primordial loyalties and seeks to revive an older historical memory of nation. Thus, there is cause for concern in the relatively strong showing of the nationalist, far-right Smallholders' Party in May 1998 parliamentary elections (48 seats, double that of the center-left Alliance of Free Democrats' 24 seats).[63]

At the same time, the narrow victory of the Alliance of Young Democrats (FIDESZ)—a "catch-all" right-wing party—and its coalition partner, the Hungarian Civic Party (MPP), is not, in itself, cause for concern.[64] Indeed, Hungarian democracy stands to benefit from the clarification of party programs and ideologies through the crystallization of clear left-right alternatives. Thus, the socialists, on the one side, and FIDESZ on the other, may simply represent the last stage of "normalization" in the consolidation of Hungarian democratic politics, and need not reflect polarization deeper than the typical left-right divisions in Western Europe or the United States.

Still, one might logically ask, if the 1994–98 governing coalition really gave expression to some of the deepest currents of modern Hungarian political culture, why did the public relieve the coalition of its mandate? Why now, especially, just when the institutional and recent macroeconomic successes of Hungary's moderate and broadly consensual political-economic policies are beginning to translate into tangible benefits? To point to just a few, admittedly selective, indicators, as early as the fourth quarter of 1996, unemployment fell to 9.2 percent (almost two percentage points below the EU average); the current account deficit was $1 billion lower than in the previous year; and the central budget balance improved considerably. The IMF projected that Hungary "may achieve the fastest economic growth in Central and

Eastern Europe over the next few decades"—between 5.2 and 5.5 percent assuming a "development-friendly" economic policy package
from the government. The European Bank for Reconstruction and Development (EBRD), describing Hungary as being in the "vanguard" of
East Central Europe, concurs, projecting 4–5 percent growth by the
end of the decade. Moreover, its regional director suggests that Hungary can "attain 70% of the per capita GDP of the EU countries in ten
years." While the rate of foreign investment has fallen recently, foreign
companies, multilateral institutions, and governments had invested
approximately $16 billion by the end of 1996, by far the highest figure
in the region. And a recent Deutsche Bank study praised the Hungarian banking system as the most stable and least problematic in eastern
Europe.[65]

Such indicators suggest that Hungarian policy-makers were, in fact,
vindicated in their determination to steer a course between ongoing
deep structural (institutional) reform and comparatively late economic
stabilization, on the one hand, and concern for safety nets and social
peace, on the other.[66] It is somewhat too early to know just what the
new election results mean, and precisely why exactly the HSP–AFD
coalition lost its mandate.

A few things are clear, however. First, much of the population has
yet to benefit from the previous government's stabilization and restructuring policies. There was, certainly, a significant fall in real
wages between 1995–97, and some segments of the population have
felt the budget cuts keenly. Hungarians are by now fully aware that the
Hungarian Socialist Party ultimately pursued tougher reforms than its
center-right predecessor, and can harbor no illusions that the HSP will
always be the "workingman's friend." Moreover, given that the Socialist–Free Democrat governing coalition has recently undergone a major
privatization scandal, the party's 134 seats (compared to FIDESZ–
MPP's 148) can be read as a respectable result. Indeed, perhaps the real
surprise is that the coalition did not face more serious challenges. The
current strong upswing of the economy notwithstanding, the International Labor Organization (ILO) estimated in 1997 that 30 percent of
the population lived at or below the poverty line.[67] In any case, the election results may partly reflect the kind of "throw the scoundrels out"
sentiment found among voting populations the world over; after all,
FIDESZ is the only major party yet to take a turn at government. In a
new democracy, it should perhaps not surprise us that a significant
portion of the voters wish to try every reasonable alternative.

What we know for certain is that the former governing coalition of
former enemies, built on the socialist political-economic discourse and
practice institutionalized by key political elites during the 1980s, is evi-

dence that many of these same elites emerged from this period with fundamentally changed identities, having learned important political lessons. The lessons they learned and the reforms they implemented created a crisis of function and meaning in the ancien régime, but their attempts to find pragmatic ways out of the dilemmas of state socialism have helped to lay the foundations for a viable post-socialist political and economic synthesis. And if some of the institutions of the state socialist era have now changed beyond recognition, the political lessons of the period nevertheless endure.

There are at least two reasons for optimism, one realpolitik and proximate; the other, less tangible and immediate but perhaps no less influential. First, we may reasonably hope that the successful economic policies of the HSP–AFD coalition government will ultimately provide powerful incentives for their own perpetuation. Second, if my argument concerning the institutionalization of a specific political discourse and the deep logic of consensual politics in Hungary is correct, then we should not expect an "about face" from the new Hungarian government. To the contrary, its policies—especially those affecting social welfare—should be essentially continuous with that of the previous government. If, instead, the new, more conservative government manages a *fundamental* shift in the social welfare policy, then my theory will be partially falsified. Such a development would represent a shift in the long-standing compact between Hungarian state and society in a sense as profound as any that occurred in 1989, and a fascinating case of political-cultural change as well.

Notes

1. Janos Kornai made good on this claim in *The Socialist System: The Political Economy of Communism* (Princeton: Princeton University Press, 1992).

2. To do so, in any case, would require in-depth comparative analysis.

3. Laszlo Bruszt and David Stark, "Remaking the Political Field in Hungary: From the Politics of Confrontation to the Politics of Competition" in Ivo Banac, ed., *Eastern Europe in Revolution* (Ithaca, N.Y.: Cornell University Press, 1992); Barnabas Racz and Istvan Kukorelli, "The 'Second-Generation' Post-Communist Elections in Hungary in 1994," *Europe-Asia Studies* vol. 47, no. 2 (1995), 251–79; Andrew Arato, "Revolution, Restoration, and Legitimization: Ideological Problems of the Transition from State Socialism" in Michael Kennedy, ed., *Envisioning Eastern Europe: Postcommunist Cultural Studies* (Ann Arbor: Michigan University Press, 1994); Anna Seleny, "Constructing the Discourse of Transformation," *East European Politics and Society* 8 (Fall 1994), 439–66.

4. Clearly, this is not to deny the predictable struggles within the 1994–98

coalition of the Hungarian Socialist Party and the Alliance of Free Democrats much less the profound political differences between the coalition and opposition parties. For reasons explained in the body of the essay, however, I believe that it is useful to focus on *prevailing patterns of governance* (which include "style" of governance).

5. Grzegorz Ekiert and Jan Kubik, "Collective Protest and Democratic Consolidation in Poland, 1989–93," *Pew Papers on Central Eastern European Reform and Regionalism* 3 (Princeton: Center of International Studies, Princeton University, 1997); Anna Seleny, "The Long Transformation and the Point of No Return" in Andrew Walder, ed., *Departures from Central Planning: China and Hungary* (Stanford: Stanford University Press, 1995).

6. Anna Seleny, "Old Political Rationalities and New Democracies: Compromise and Confrontation in Hungary and Poland," *Pew Papers on Central Eastern European Reform and Regionalism* 9 (Princeton: Center of International Studies, Princeton University, January 1996).

7. Michael Burton, Richard Gunther, and John Higley, *Elites and Democratic Consolidation in Latin America and Southern Europe* (New York: Cambridge University Press, 1992); Samuel Huntington, *Political Order in Changing Societies* (New Haven: Yale University Press, 1968); Adam Przeworski, "Economic Reforms, Public Opinion, and Political Institutions: Poland in the Eastern European Perspective" in Luiz Carlos Bresser Pereira, Jose Maria Maravall, and Adam Przeworski, eds., *Economic Reforms in New Democracies: A Social Democratic Approach* (New York: Cambridge University Press, 1993).

8. For instance, writing specifically about cultural analyses, Stephen Holmes criticizes facile arguments that confuse "pattern recognition . . . with causal explanation," and fail to realize that if "you examine the past closely, you can find foreshadowings of just about anything that comes to pass." Stephen Holmes, "Cultural Legacies or State Decay: Probing the Postcommunist Dilemma" in Michael Mandelbaum, ed., *Postcommunism: Four Views* (Council on Foreign Relations Press, 1996), 4. Walt Rostow, writing more generally about social science explanations, pointed out that "correlation is not the same as causation; a genetic theory must concentrate on the latter." Walt Rostow, "Transitions to Democracy", *Comparative Politics* 2 (April 1970), 346.

9. Gabriel A. Almond, "Communism and Political Culture Theory," *Comparative Politics* (January 1983), 127–38. See also Kenneth Jowitt, "An Organizational Approach to the Study of Political Culture in Marxist-Leninist Systems," *The American Political Science Review* 68, (September 1974), 1171–91.

10. Ann Swidler, "Culture in Action: Symbols and Strategies," *American Sociological Review* 51 (April 1986, 273–86), 51.

11. Clifford Geertz, *Negara: The Theatre State in 19th Century Bali* (Princeton: Princeton University Press, 1980).

12. Jan Kubik and Anna Seleny, "Culture in Political-Economic Transformation," program statement distributed to The Princeton–Rutgers Workshop on Culture, (Unpublished mimeo. New Brunswick: Rutgers University, October 1994).

13. Consuelo Cruz, "The Political Culture of Order and Anarchy: Remem-

brance and Imaginative Power in Central America," unpublished dissertation manuscript (Cambridge: MIT, 1994).

14. Martha Finnemore, "International Environments and Organizations: Structural Complexity and Individualism," *International Organization* 50:2 (Spring 1996), 325–47.

15. James G. March and Johan P. Olsen, *Rediscovering Institutions: The Organizational Basis of Politics* (New York: The Free Press, 1989), 47–48.

16. Kubik and Seleny, "Culture." Anna Seleny, "The Long Transformation."

17. Cruz, "Political Culture."

18. Nicholas B. Dirks, Geoff Eley, and Sherry B. Ortner, eds., "Introduction," *Culture/Power/History: A Reader in Contemporary Social Theory*, (Princeton: Princeton University Press, 1992).

19. Alan Ryan, "Pragmatism, Social Identity, Patriotism and Self-Criticism," unpublished paper (Department of Politics: Princeton University, 1996).

20. Joseph Schull, "What is Ideology? Theoretical Problems and Lessons of Soviet-type Societies," *Political Studies* 40:4 (1992), 728–42. See especially 731–33.

21. Nancy Bermeo, "Democracy and the Lessons of Dictatorship," *Comparative Politics* 24:3 (April 1992), 273–91.

22. *Ibid.*, 273–74.

23. Drawing on the experience of several countries, Bermeo (*ibid.*) suggests several possible such "locations." The Hungarian case is reminiscent of several of her examples.

24. More specifically, the elements of what I have elsewhere called *the institutional residue of reform* were observable in the formal and informal institutions and arrangements of socialism, and included *groups of reformers* that "survived" politically from one reform cycle to the next; *reform discourse*; and *political, legal, and economic practices altered by reforms*. For a more detailed discussion of this concept, see Anna Seleny, "Hidden Enterprise and Property Rights: Reform in Socialist Hungary," *Law and Policy* 13 (April 1991), 149–69; Seleny, "Constructing the Discourse"; and Seleny, "The Long Transformation."

25. Seleny, "Constructing the Discourse."

26. For a detailed analysis of this case, see *ibid.*

27. Seleny, "The Long Transformation."

28. Following Kornai, I understand reform as "any change that permanently and essentially alters at least one basic attribute of . . . political structure, property relations, or coordination mechanisms." See Kornai, *The Socialist System*, 388).

29. *Ibid.*

30. Intrafirm work partnerships, or VGMKs, were semiprivate work-groups within state firms which produced on their own account or often subcontracted to the firm. In either case, they operated on the premises and used the firm's equipment after regular work hours. The best analysis of their significance for the Hungarian reform process is given in David Stark, "Coexisting Organizational Forms in Hungary's Emerging Mixed Economy" in Victor Nee

and David Stark, eds., *Remaking the Economic Institutions of Socialism: China and Eastern Europe* (Stanford, Calif.: Stanford University Press, 1989).

31. Seleny, "Hidden Enterprise"; Seleny, "Constructing the Discourse"; and Seleny, "The Long Transformation."

32. Peter Hall, ed., *The Political Power of Economic Ideas: Keynesianism across Nations* (Princeton: Princersity Press, 1989), 292.

33. Katherine Verdery, "Theorizing Socialism: A Prologue to the 'Transition,' " *American Ethnologist* vol. 18 no. 3 (1991), 434.

34. Bruszt and Stark, "Remaking the Political Field," 27–30.

35. *Ibid.*, 38.

36. *Ibid.*, 33.

37. *Ibid.*, 33–35.

38. Eva Fodor and Ivan Szelenyi, "Left Turn in Post-Communist Politics: The Case of Hungarian Elections, 1990 and 1994," (Paper presented at Princeton University, 3 April 1995) 29.

39. Racz and Kukorelli, " 'Second-Generation' Elections," 261, 271.

40. Thanks to Andrew Arato for pointing out to me that this is a view held by many observers and analysts.

41. Edith Oltay, 37

42. Ministries of the Interior; Transport and Telecommunication; and Water-management, Culture and Public Education.

43. "Three quarters majority is needed for both factions to endorse proposals; short of this, neither faction can support proposals in the legislative process." See Racz and Kukorelli, " 'Second-Generation' Elections," 272, for a summary of the bipartisan mechanism.

44. Rick Bruner, *Hungary Report*, online at http://www.isys.hu (19 October 1995), 2–3; and Tibor Vidos, *Hungary Report* http://www.isys.hu (12 September 1995), 6.

45. Moreover, in Hungarian politics, as elsewhere, some political leaders are willing—or at times perhaps find it prudent or potentially advantageous—to speak realistically and publicly to this point. For instance, Ivan Peto, then leader of the AFD, was quoted as saying that the ruling coalition is held together in part by the mutual threat that the partners pose to one another. *Hungary Report* (17 Sept. 1996).

46. Racz and Kukorelli, " 'Second-Generation' Elections," 272.

47. See, *Hungary Report* (21 October 1996), 4.

48. Bennett Kovrig, "Hungarian Socialism: The Deceptive Hybrid," *East European Politics and Society* 1:1 (Winter 1987), 113–34, 126.

49. J. Samuel Valenzuela, "Democratic Consolidation in Post-Transitional Settings," in Scott Mainwaring, Guillermo O'Donnell, and J. Samuel Valenzuela, eds., *Essays in Democratic Consolidation* (South Bend: Notre Dame Press, 1992), 87.

50. Juan Linz and Alfred Stepan, eds., *The Breakdown of Democratic Regimes* (Baltimore: The Johns Hopkins Press, 1978).

51. Ekiert and Kubik, "Collective Protest."

52. Peter Paczolay, "The New Hungarian Constitutional State" in A. E. Dick

Howard, ed., *Constitution Making in Eastern Europe* (Washington: Woodrow Wilson Center Press, 1993), 47–8; Andras Sajo, presentation and author's interview (Princeton: Princeton University Center of International Studies, 16 November 1995).

53. Stephen Holmes and Cass R. Sunstein, "The Politics of Constitutional Revision in Eastern Europe" in Sanford Levinson, ed., *Responding to Imperfection: The Theory and Practice of Constitutional Amendment* (Princeton: Princeton University Press, 1995), 300.

54. Sajo, presentation and author's interview.

55. Some Western economists, who have urged a faster pace of reform, have seriously underestimated the depth of this consensus in Hungary. There may in theory exist an ideal pace and sequencing of reforms; certainly, this debate has spawned hundreds of articles by economists and others. Relatively few economists, however, appear to understand that the successful application of these principles always depends crucially upon local institutions and political-cultural habits. The appropriate conclusion is not, as some would have it, that "culture" or "politics" are therefore to blame. Conversely, the record from post-socialist countries shows that if economists and others wish to aid their local counterparts and host-country politicians in the application of their theories—however well-intentioned and designed—they would do well to respect and utilize local reform histories, and to pay close attention to the specific ways "societies use the knowledge that is available to them." On this point see, for instance, Peter Murrell, "Conservative Political Philosophy and the Strategy of Economic Transition," *East European Politics and Societies,* vol 6:1 (1992).

56. *Ibid.*

57. In fact, Stephen Holmes, commenting on an earlier draft of this paper at the conference for which it was commissioned, raised precisely this objection.

58. Paczolay, "The New Hungarian Constitutional State," 23, 48.

59. Burton, et al., *Elites and Democratic Consolidation,* 13–14.

60. Deak quoted in Paczolay, "The New Hungarian Constitutional State," 25.

61. Paczolay, "The New Hungarian Constitutional State," 25–26.

62. Holmes and Sunstein, "Politics of Constitutional Revision."

63. On the other hand, support for the Smallholders' Party also reflects other, structural features of Hungarian society (e.g., urban–rural splits) that need not coincide completely with this discourse.

64. The concern arises instead from two possibilities: (1) Either FIDESZ–MPP must govern with a very weak coalition and, indeed, as a minority. Even with the 17 seats of its ally, the Hungarian Democratic Forum (MDF), the coalition would still have only 165 seats, 29 short of the 194 needed for a majority in the 386-member parliament; (2) FIDESZ–MPP will form a coalition with one of two parties whose programmatic and ideological positions diverge substantially from its own. As of this writing in early June 1998, FIDESZ has ruled out a "grand coalition" with the socialists (which may turn out to be a serious error from the point of view of governmental efficacy, EU accession, etc.). If FIDESZ intends to adhere to this position, however, its only other potential partner is the Smallholders' Party, with which it is likely to form a coalition.

65. For a quick review of unemployment, current account and central budget deficit figures see *Hungary Report* (3 Feb. 1997). For IMF projections see *Hungary Report* (9 Dec. 1996); for EBRD projections see *Hungary Report* (4 Nov. 1996).

66. For the best recent analysis of the trade-offs involved in this balancing act, see Janos Kornai, "Paying the Bill for Goulash Communism: Hungarian Development and Macro-Stabilization in a Political Economy Perspective," Discussion Paper 1748, (Cambridge, Mass.: Harvard Institute for Economic Research, Harvard University, 1996).

67. ILO figures quoted in *Hungary Report* (3 Feb. 1997). Such figures are, to be sure, extremely difficult to interpret, particularly in light of a growing (now traditional) informal economy.

Part Three

Marketization and Social Change in Hungary

Chapter 8

Economic Transformation, 1990–1998

Paul Marer

This chapter tries to answer a dozen frequently asked questions about Hungary's post-communist transformation, economic performance, and prospects. The primary intended audiences are scholars and students in various disciplines, the media, and the interested public.

Each question focuses on some aspect of the main issue: how much progress has Hungary made in eight years—between 1990 and mid-1998—in transforming its economy from a centrally directed to a market-driven one and in laying the foundations for sustained economic progress? It also ventures an evaluation of the economic strategies and policies of successive post-communist governments, the right-of-center Antall and Boross governments (1990–94) and the left-of-center Horn government (1994–98). The chapter concludes with an assessment of the main economic tasks facing the right-of-center coalition government, led by Prime Minister Viktor Orban, that was formed after Hungary's third post-communist national election, held during May–June 1998.

Yardsticks of Progress

There is no single or fully objective criterion of progress. During the early years of transition, standard measures of economic performance—such as growth rates, unemployment rates, inflation rates, standard of living indicators, income and wealth distribution, and the balance of payments—will unavoidably deteriorate because the integrated economies of the former Soviet bloc collapsed and because the problems of decades of "misdevelopment" were revealed by sudden exposure to international competition. Often, the accuracy of the statistical data themselves must be called into question. For example, how many of the officially unemployed are actually earning income from the gray economy and how much do output figures understate what the economy really produces? But even if one has a reasonably reliable set of (official or adjusted) economic data, how much of the unsatisfactory performance can be attributed to circumstances beyond the control of the authorities and how much is due to their mistakes? If mistakes were made, on what basis should the government be judged? If the standard is set high, practically all contemporary governments around the world would fall short of earning a high grade.

Different initial conditions when transformation began—as well as differences in the transformation strategies of countries—will have an impact on economic performance. Therefore, comparing the economic record of Hungary, say, with those of Poland and Czechoslovakia (since 1993, the Czech Republic and the Slovak Republic) may not be a fully reliable measure of comparative progress. For example, other things being equal, a faster restructuring of the economy will cause an initially larger decline in output and a greater increase in unemployment, but also a more rapid and sustainable recovery, than would a slow approach to restructuring enterprises and government programs. Because transformation involves a host of difficult and country-specific economic and political trade-offs, there is no ideal path against which transformation's progress can be judged.

The Approach

This chapter is a selective and interpretive economic history of Hungary during 1990–98. The essay began by stressing the difficulties of assessing the economic policies of successive governments and of transformation's progress. The purpose of the caveat is *not* to shirk from such a task but to emphasize that even a fair-minded and well-informed assessment is, to some extent, subjective.

This chapter focuses on a select number of critical and controversial issues, describing the context in which the issue was (or is) framed, what did happen, why did it happen, what were the consequences, and what would have been the likely outcome of presumed alternative policies. Does a given government deserve mostly credit or mostly blame for its handling of the issue? Occasional comparisons are made with Poland and the Czech Republic, without, however, attempting to arrive at any definitive comparative assessment. The essay concludes with an evaluation of the economic strategies and policies of Hungary's first three post-communist governments and an assessment of

Hungary's medium-term economic prospects under the government that was formed after the mid-1988 elections.

The issues are presented in the form of questions and answers. Questions 1, 2, and 3 focus on differences in initial conditions in 1990 and differences in the revealed transformation strategies of Hungary, Poland and Czechoslovakia (later the Czech Republic). Questions 4 through 7 hone in on four areas where the record of the Antall–Boross governments (and partly also of the Horn government) can be criticized: policies toward agriculture; much too long a delay in several important aspects of public-sector (especially welfare) reform; neglect of the plight of the small- and medium-sized enterprise (SME) sector; and the mistaken monetary and fiscal policies pursued during 1992–94. These mistakes contributed to pushing the economy to the precipice of a major crisis by the end of 1994. That, in turn, triggered the comprehensive austerity program of 1995–96 (the "Bokros package," named after the minister of finance who championed it), a major watershed in the postwar economic history of the country. Since its *raison d'etre* was little understood by the people of Hungary at the time, the program is discussed in some detail in Question 8.

At that point, readers might note that, at more than halfway through the dozen questions, few details are as yet given about the positive accomplishments of the Antall–Boross governments. The Antall and Boross governments can be credited with a number of important positive accomplishments, including putting privatization eventually on the right track (discussed in the excellent essay in this volume by Keith Crane), restructuring the banking system (mentioned in connection with several topics), supporting policies of inward direct foreign investment (Question 9), passing many laws, and building or strengthening key institutions of a market economy.

The dozen questions and answers are grouped under five headings:

I. Initial conditions and strategies: Hungary, Czechoslovakia, and Poland (Q1–3).
II. Policy mistakes that might have been avoided (Q4–7).
III. Austerity and further reforms, 1995–97: The threshold years (Q-8).
IV. Foreign economic strategies (Q9–10).
V. Summary assessments (Q11–12).

I. Initial Conditions and Strategies: Hungary, Czechoslovakia, and Poland

Q-1: In 1990, when transformation of the political system began, Hungary was widely believed to be much "ahead" of the other Cen-

tral Eastern European (CEE) countries, and was thus thought to be in the best position to achieve successful transformation into a well-functioning market economy, within a reasonable time frame. Was Hungary really ahead of countries such as Poland and Czechoslovakia (subsequently the Czech Republic and the Slovak Republic)?

Yes and no would be my answer. Hungary was ahead because it had begun systemic reforms more than two decades earlier and because of its favorable image in the West, which was a factor in being able to attract large foreign investment. At the same time, Hungary was in a less advantageous position than the other two countries because its macroeconomic situation was, in several important respects, less favorable and because of the absence of popular hatred toward the just-collapsed communist system.

More specifically, one of Hungary's assets was a 25-year legacy of economic and political reforms. Although the period between the mid-1960s and the late 1980s had witnessed not only reform initiatives but also stops and reversals, on balance, Hungary clearly had moved forward.[1]

Four accomplishments of the reform period may be highlighted. One, permitting the *relatively* fast expansion of the private sector, even though a large part of it was comprised of the unreported (gray and black) economy. Two, a considerable degree of decision making autonomy was granted to state enterprises in a number of sectors. Three, in the late 1980s, notable reforms were implemented in the financial and fiscal sectors: the monobank (the institution that performed both central and commercial "banking" functions) was divided into a central bank and a set of commercial banks and West European-types of progressive income tax and value-added tax systems were introduced. Four, the gradual liberalization of information flows, generally and of travel and tourism, specifically, allowed up-to-date information from the West to reach practically all Hungarians.

The net impact of these reforms was that Hungary had greater institutional and "mindset" preparedness to transform its economy, and also had a smaller distance to travel to become a market economy, than did any of the other "to be transformed" economies in the region.

Hungary's second valuable asset was the substantial goodwill the country had enjoyed in the West. Hungary's reputation had been built over several decades by the gradual political and economic liberalization under communism.[2] Many in the West thought that Hungary was showing and leading the way (presumably, the *only* possible way) in which a communist political and centrally planned economic system could gradually be transformed. Another source of positive reputation was the comparatively large number of Hungarians, especially professionals, artists, and other intellectuals, who came into contact with their Western counterparts, generally making favorable impressions.

However, the singular event that enhanced Hungary's reputation around the world was the role its last communist government played in the collapse of the Berlin Wall. The authorities in Hungary had made the courageous decision to allow East Germans to freely cross Hungary's borders to the West. This was a key factor in the East German decision not to try to stop forcibly at the Wall their own people from crossing to the West.

Hungary's favorable image in the West was an asset for its economic transformation, mainly because it was a factor in making the country attractive to foreign investors. Economically and politically, however, transformation in Hungary entailed two important liabilities. One was a long period of *excess public and private consumption* relative to domestic production; the other, the *absence of a broad and deep popular hatred toward the "liberalized" political and economic system of the 1980s*. Although reformed communism was not a political or economic system that had broad appeal, the mood in Hungary was different than, say, in Poland, Czechoslovakia, or, say, Romania. Why this was a liability for Hungary's first post-communist government will be discussed.

The first liability, cumulative excess consumption, came about in the following way. For about three decades, from the mid-1960s until the comprehensive austerity program introduced in the spring of 1995, Hungarian domestic consumption grew, on average, faster than domestic production. During the communist era, this helped to create what Khrushchev referred to as "goulash communism." In the mid-1960s, the Kadar regime struck an implicit bargain with society. One side of the bargain was that the authorities will provide sizable increases in living standards (or, in some years, mitigate the unavoidable decline in living standards, such as after a steep rise in world energy prices) and move cautiously toward political-social liberalization. In exchange, society was to agree not to challenge Hungary's alliance with the USSR and the communist political system. The reasons for Janos Kadar making and Hungary's population accepting the offer can be traced to the revolution of 1956. Political leaders tried to prevent the repeat occurrence of another cataclysmic explosion. Society came to realize that "liberal communism," with gradually improving living standards, was the best possible deal as long as the Soviet Union stood ready to use its army to maintain communism in the allied countries of the region.

The policy of political compromise and economic accommodation had existed for decades. Consequently, the country had accumulated large foreign as well as domestic debts. The $20 billion foreign debt that the new government inherited in 1990 is a well-known fact. Servicing the debt, just by paying the interest on it, required that up to two percent of Hungary's gross domestic product (GDP) be transferred abroad each year, the exact amount depending on fluctuations in international interest rates.

Less well-known is the fact that to finance excess consumption, domestic debt also rose dangerously fast, as a consequence of several expensive and not fully funded (and, realistically, not readily fundable) legislative commitments that the authorities had made over the years to future consumption. These took the form of guaranteed pensions, family allowances, maternity benefits, sick pay, and other welfare transfers (discussed below).[3] Any debt that goes to support excess consumption rather than productive investments will inevitably impair the debtor country's subsequent economic performance. Servicing a growing foreign and domestic government debt preempts resources— taxes as well as private savings—that would otherwise go to finance investment or private consumption. Eventually, the ballooning of each type of debt will hold down improvements in the standard of living.[4]

In all fairness, the other side of the ledger must also be mentioned: Hungary had enjoyed a better supply situation, i.e., fewer shortages and little or no "monetary overhang" than just about all of the countries in the region, with the possible exception of Czechoslovakia.

The second liability that Hungary's post-communist governments inherited was, paradoxically, the absence of widespread hatred of the old regime. That the previous regime was considered semilegitimate by a significant segment of the population can be traced to the factors already mentioned: political liberalization and the priority given to consumption. One consequence of political and economic liberalization cum excess consumption under the old system was a much greater reluctance by Hungary's population than those of other countries to shoulder the economic and social burdens associated with (though not necessarily caused by) the transformation of the economic system. That, in turn, made it more difficult for the post-communist political parties and governments, once they belatedly realized the gravity of the debt burdens, to convince the population that further economic sacrifices would be needed. But economic sacrifices were inevitable, as in all the other Central and East European countries, in Hungary particularly because the bill for previous sustained excess consumption had to be paid in installments.

As in the other transforming economies, it was (and to some extent still is) terribly costly and painful to overcome the legacies of a misdeveloped economy. Misdevelopment manifested itself, for example, in overdeveloped heavy industry and underdeveloped light industry; in the neglect of infrastructure and the service sectors; in that most manufactured products were not competitive internationally or with imports (once Western goods were allowed in); and in the inappropriate skill composition of the workforce. As in the other transforming economies, the basic cause of misdevelopment was that economic strategies and enterprise decisions were driven, even in partly reformed Hungary, largely by ideological and political considerations, as well as by the remaining practices of central planning, rather than predominantly by market forces.[5]

A second reason that economic sacrifices could not be avoided was the imperative of having to adjust to two sudden economic shocks: the collapse of the former CMEA markets and the related substantial deterioration in Hungary's terms of trade (that is, the decline in the prices of exports relative to the prices of imports). Hungary shared these unfavorable external developments with the other countries in Central and Eastern Europe. And a third reason, specific to Hungary, was that foreign debt could not be substantially further increased. In fact, Hungary's large foreign and domestic debts had to be serviced. But the willingness of the population to absorb the impact of the economic shocks *and* to pay the bill for a long period of excess consumption was not great. Furthermore, since there was no consensus among Hungary's leading economists that excess consumption was a problem, this issue was not even on the agenda of the newly victorious political parties whose leaders, in any event, had little understanding of, and insufficient concern with, economic issues. And in a democracy, which Hungary quickly became, few politicians were willing, when the problem became clear, to deliver unpleasant news to the public. More generally, it is fair to say that in transformation's early years, neither in Hungary nor in the West did people have a comprehensive economic understanding of this issue.[6]

There were also important post-system-change differences between Hungary, Poland, and the Czech Republic that had contributed to these countries' differentiated macroeconomic performance during the first half of the 1990s. It should not detract from Poland's and the Czech Republic's economic achievements to point out that both countries had some special help during the early 1990s. Poland's economy was boosted when in 1992 the West forgave a substantial portion of the country's foreign debt.[7] The Czech Republic's fiscal situation was helped by the low level of foreign debt inherited by the post-communist government (since then, foreign debt has increased) and boosted by the separation of Slovakia, which relinquished Prague from responsibility for large net subsidies to the eastern part of the country. Hungary, by contrast, had inherited a large triple-debt burden, as was noted, which adversely affected its growth rates.

In sum, it is by no means obvious that, in spite of its head start and uniquely valuable assets, Hungary clearly had a "political economy" advantage in implementing economic transformation more quickly and more successfully than, say, Czechoslovakia or Poland.

Q-2: Was it necessary for Hungary's post-communist governments to service the large foreign debt fully?

Most probably, yes. The direct and indirect costs of defaulting, or even of rescheduling, would probably have been at least as large as the considerable burdens of servicing the debt fully. For one, a much smaller portion of Hungary's debts was owed to Western governments and international financial institutions than was the case, for example, with Poland. Hungary's IOUs were largely in the hands of commercial banks and private bondholders around the world (many of them Japanese). Rescheduling, if possible at all, especially with the latter group, would have been much more difficult and costly than debt renegotiations typically are with governments and international financial institutions. Furthermore, Hungary's excellent foreign reputation was based in part on the uninterrupted servicing of its foreign debt. Rescheduling would have shattered Hungary's reputation in the external financial and business communities, reducing the potentially large inflows of foreign direct investment, and probably causing severe disruptions in foreign trade.

Q-3: Isn't it true that during the early 1990s Czechoslovakia and Poland had implemented shock therapy while Hungary had opted for gradualism? Although shock therapy is more painful in the short run, isn't it better than gradualism for creating the conditions for sustainable economic growth?

The term *shock therapy* is an expression that is often used loosely, especially by the media. Shock therapy should appropriately refer to rapid price liberalization and, especially, to bringing high open inflation and/or strong repressed inflation under control quickly. In brief, shock therapy means decisive actions to bring inflation under control (*macrostabilization*, in the economist's jargon). However, non-economists often use the term *shock therapy* to refer to the speed with which the interrelated aspects of economic system transformation (such as macrostabilization, privatization, enterprise and financial-sector restructuring, fiscal reforms, and the building of market institutions) are proceeding. The media especially tend to use shock therapy in this loose meaning of the term and often focus only on its single and most visible aspect, privatization.

In the early 1990s, Hungary did not need *shock therapy* (appropriately defined) because many product as well as factor prices (wages, interest rates, exchange rates) had been largely freed over the years, *before* political transformation had begun. For example, in 1989, regulated prices accounted for only 20 percent of the consumer basket. And most of the remaining price controls were eliminated during the first two years of transformation. A related reason for not needing shock therapy was that when transformation began, open and repressed inflationary pressures combined were under much better control in Hungary than in Poland or in Czechoslovakia. Thus, transition in Hungary was not accompanied by a major inflationary outburst. In Poland, open inflation in the late 1980s was in high triple digits. In Czechoslovakia, price liberalization in 1991 was sudden and comprehensive, followed by a large jump in the price index, which was reined in by tight monetary and wage (but *not* fiscal) policies to prevent the price jump from turning into spiraling inflation.

Before turning to a discussion of the comparative speed of transformation in Hungary, the Czech Republic, and Poland, let us refer briefly to the debate between those who advocated rapid transformation, and those who prefer transformation to proceed gradually.[8] Those who advocate a fast pace of transformation believe that it is desirable to rapidly establish the new rules and institutions of a market economy, for example, to privatize state property quickly and to institute effective bankruptcy procedures early on. The advocates of speed see a trade-off between concentrating the pain over a short period to cure the patient quickly, which they prefer, versus lesser immediate pain, which will last much longer, with the eventual cure being less certain. On the other hand, those who advocate gradualism believe that it takes a long time to learn the principles and practices of a market economy. They note that developed market economies have taken a long time to evolve.[9] And they cite with approval the example of China, even though China's transformation experience was never a feasible model for the countries of Central and Eastern Europe.[10]

This is not the place to try to resolve whether a fast or a more gradual pace of economic transformation is better. There is probably no single best—or politically feasible—strategy for *all* transforming economies. Much will depend on a country's legacies, initial conditions, and current circumstances. The actual strategy is likely to combine speed and gradualism, although circumstances in a given country may make it more receptive to one than to another of the approaches. For example, the Czech Republic had opted for (what was, or appeared to be) high speed in several areas. One was the quick freeing of most prices in 1991 and the rapid bringing under control of the resulting inflationary pressures, measures that were politically daring and economically prudent. At the same time, rapid voucher privatization, which was touted as a daring great accomplishment, does not look so impressive, by hindsight. Part of the reason that, from the point of view of restructuring state industry, voucher privatization has been a disappointment is that the authorities have proceeded much too cautiously and gradually with such painful policy steps as permitting bankruptcies to occur and reducing the large fiscal burden of the bloated state budget. Whether the authorities did this mainly for reasons of short-term political expediency, or to prevent tearing apart the social fabric and thereby run the danger of losing political support for economic transformation, remains for history to judge. Be that as it may, the Czech approach has been much more gradual in several areas than either Hungary's or Poland's.

Hungary, the Czech Republic, and Poland opted for different strategies of privatization. The differences can be described, but comparing the speed and effectiveness of their approaches is difficult. The Czechs opted mainly for privatization by voucher distribution, which can be accomplished quickly because it does not require large amounts of capital at a time when accumulated domestic savings are tiny relative to the market value of the assets being privatized. Distribution's drawback is that most of the initial new owners are likely to be "passive," neither able nor interested in effectively exercising essential ownership functions, such as deciding on the property's best use, selecting managers and holding them accountable for performance, and providing capital for restructuring. Thus, the distribution of shares in large enterprises, by itself, may be viewed as semiprivatization, an interim step, setting in motion a process of ownership change that will continue for years. In the meantime, however, the subsidization of large enterprises may continue via the state-owned banking system, as has been the case in the Czech Republic. This delays the restructuring of the financial sector, too, and erodes the business value of the "semiprivatized" property. And whether the ultimate owners—those who will gain controlling interest in the companies—would want to, and would be able to, restructure the enterprises they control is still an open question.

Poland has employed a different mix of approaches. After freeing prices and bringing runaway inflation quickly under control—and thus employing shock therapy, its successive governments got bogged down on whether and how to privatize and restructure many large, state-owned enterprises. At the same time, the private sector has been able to grow rapidly and has become strong enough to shape favorably the economic indicators of Poland.

Hungary has chosen another route still: privatization of state enterprises mainly by sale, not distribution. This is a slower and politically more difficult approach because it favors those who have money, which means foreigners and a certain category of locals, including the former nomenklatura and entrepreneurs who could acquire wealth quickly. However, those who put up their own money to acquire property are the most likely to know, and care about, its economically best use, including its restructuring, and are the most likely to have the funds, or access to funds, to do so.

Privatization by sale is thus real privatization. Therefore, to meaningfully compare transformation's speed and progress in the three countries, one cannot meaningfully juxtapose the speed of *semiprivatization* with the speed of *real privatization*. The foregoing discussion can be summed up with two statements. Owing to systemic reforms and reasonably prudent economic policies before transformation began, Hungary did not need *shock therapy*, so its absence should not be criticized. Regarding the comparative speed of Hungary's *overall* transformation (foreshadowing some of the later conclusions of this essay), it was not slower—and may have been faster—than that of either of the Czech Republic's or Poland's. In one particular respect, Hungary went through the most far-reaching shock therapy in Central Europe during 1992–93, owing to the introduction of the region's strictest bankruptcy laws. The 1992 bankruptcy law required managers of firms with arrears of 90 days or more to file for reorganization or liquidation. If creditors did not unanimously approve management's reorganization plan, the firm was liquidated. The law led to 22,000 filings—17,000 liquidations and 5,000 reorganizations–during 1992–93.[11] (The legislation was amended in late 1993 to eliminate the automatic 90-day trigger and to reduce the creditor approval requirement to two-thirds of outstanding claims.) The wave of bankruptcies contributed to a much too rapid shrinking of the domestic production base, fueled a surge of imports, and added to fiscal losses as taxes contracted. In the longer run, however, the legislation had significant positive effects: it fundamentally altered the business environment, accelerated enterprise and bank restructuring, freed resources for better alternative uses, and made the economy more flexible.

Taking the *broad definition of shock therapy*, and foreshadowing some of the later conclusions of this essay, it is my view that during the first eight years, the speed of Hungary's *overall* transformation was not slower—and may have been faster—than that of either of the other two countries. This is not to imply, however, that either the speed of transformation or the design and implementation of Hungary's economic programs have been anywhere near perfect. The next subsection focuses on areas where, on balance, government policy can be faulted.

II. Policy Mistakes that Might Have Been Avoided

Q-4: What were the policies toward agriculture?

Background

Hungary has favorable conditions for farming: approximately 70 percent of its territory is agricultural land, of which 70 percent is arable. Per capita land ratio is better than that of the EU average, the quality of the soil is good, and weather conditions are favorable.

Beginning in the mid-1960s, economic reforms were pioneered in agriculture. Detailed central planning was replaced by market-type incentives, and socialist (state and cooperative) and private farming became symbiotically integrated. Labor-intensive production was left in the hands of households that were given profit incentives, while capital-intensive production, such as grain sowing and harvesting, and activities with economies of scale, such as purchasing inputs and marketing products, were performed by the cooperative and state farms. Increases in yields and output were impressive, especially during the 1970s. Domestic food shortages were eliminated and 25 to 30 percent of the output was exported. Compared with agriculture elsewhere in the Soviet bloc, the sector became a showcase. To be sure, it had weaknesses, such as insufficient incentives for large-scale farming to improve productivity (because full employment and income-leveling were higher priorities), a problem that was exacerbated by granting this sector (in fact, the entire economy) protection from the impact of the world energy price explosion of the 1970s. Because certain regions of the country had unfavorable conditions for farming and because cost control and productivity improvements were insufficiently stressed, agriculture had been a net recipient of subsidies until 1982. Triggered by the balance of payments crisis of 1982, which forced the government to reduce expenditures, agriculture *may have become a net* contributor to the budget, although subsidization of the weaker farms continued.[12] During the 1980s, the sector's declining terms of trade, lower domestic and foreign demand, and higher taxes had caused a substantial decline in the rate of investment and productivity growth.

In the 1990s, systemic transformation became associated with a major, and still persisting, crisis in agriculture. Between 1989 and 1993, output declined by 37 percent. Since then, production has been recovering slowly, although in 1997 output was still below 1989 levels. While in 1989, agriculture employed 14 to 15 percent of the economically active population of about 5 million, by 1997 the percentage shrank to half that level (computed against a much smaller number of total population economically active). Agriculture's steep decline and persisting crisis have been due to a combination of factors: the Antall government's economically counterproductive approach to privatization and the controversy about land ownership (which still persists); further declines in the sector's terms of trade during the early 1990s; substantial further reductions in government subsidies through 1992; falling domestic demand; loss of export markets; growing import competition from the EU; little new investment; and the absence or poor functioning of a set of institutions needed to support the agricultural sector. The first and the last set of factors are discussed, briefly.

Privatization and Land Ownership

According to an act on compensation passed by Parliament, people or their descendants could claim land equal in value to all or part of the land they had privately owned in the late 1940s. Small landowners were compensated fully, big landowners or their heirs obtained partial compensation. Collective and state farms had to set aside portions of their land for compensation. Sorting out the hundreds of thousands of claims and agreeing on the parcels to be transferred often took years. In the mean time, a great deal of the land set aside for compensation was left fallow or was cultivated poorly because the collectives did not wish to invest in case the land would have to be given up before the harvest.

A more lasting problem was the creation of a large number of small plots. Many of the new owners were heirs who had no interest in farming. The small plots were not economical to farm and thus could not readily be sold or leased. At the same time, the government did not concern itself much with the political and economic problems faced by collective and state farms, viewing them as undesirable legacies of the old regime. Influential policy-makers tried to promote the vision that Hungary should become the land of small and mid-sized farms whose owners would live in rural simplicity and happiness.

This vision was one of the initial reasons that foreigners were not allowed to purchase farmland, a policy that is still in effect. Another reason is that land prices in Hungary are only a fraction of what comparable real estate costs in neighboring Austria and elsewhere in Western Europe. There is concern that if foreign investors were given the green light, land prices would rise and Hungarians would be even less able to afford additional land to create economically viable farms. There is further concern about foreign control, and the purposes for which foreigners would acquire land, such as speculation.[13] But there is another side to the coin. Keeping foreigners out has contributed to investment in the sector remaining much below optimum levels. It has also impeded the economically necessary concentration of farmland. Because the mortgage value of real estate is, therefore, less than it could be, small holders remain poor, making it more difficult for them to obtain securitized credit. Legislative proposals during 1996–97 to ease the purchase ban on foreigners have generated a great deal of political controversy. Sooner or later, however, the issue will have to be addressed, since EU laws proscribe discrimination against the citizens and corporations of other member states, although governments are free to impose other types of restrictions, such as who can buy, how much land, and for what purpose.

Weak Institutional Support

One of the most critical problems facing Hungary's agriculture is lack of a reliable and timely system of information, efficiently disseminated to producers, about domestic, regional, and world market conditions. Such systems are in place and function well in all established market economies. Another critical problem is the undue fragmentation of organizations that represent agriculture's interest. In 1997 there were 36 contentious agricultural lobby groups, which means that the sector has not anywhere near the political clout that the agricultural lobby has, say, in the United States or in the countries of the EU.

Hungary also lags behind competitors in establishing or efficiently operating institutions whose job it is to assist farmers in obtaining guaranteed titles to their land, having access to such lending institutions as credit cooperatives, purchasing modern and reasonably priced implements and inputs, and marketing their products.

*   *   *

This brief enumeration of the problems facing Hungary's agriculture should not be interpreted as implying that the sector's prospects are poor. Just the opposite: the quality of Hungary's farmland, the weather, the country's location in the heart of Europe, the sector's achievements before and during the communist era, its highly trained cadre of specialists, and pending membership in the EU give this sector potentially significant competitive advantages. However, to realize them, more focused and prudent government policies are needed.

Q-5: It has been well documented that since 1989, a large segment of Hungary's former middle class has been sliding into low-income status and that the number of people living in poverty has increased. At the same time, experts have been saying for years that the welfare system is much too generous, the government cannot afford it, and fundamental reforms are needed. Can these seemingly contradictory facts both be true and, if yes, can they be reconciled?

International comparisons show that Hungary had been spending a far larger share of its resources on welfare, health and related transfer payments than do market economies at similar stages of development. In early 1995, before the austerity program was introduced, welfare payments still gobbled up nearly a third of annual GDP, more than for any other country in Europe, except for Sweden. This has been a factor in slowing the economy's growth rate.[14] As one building block of the sustained "excess consumption" relative to the productivity of the economy (discussed in Q-1), an extreme version of the paternalistic welfare state had been created. In 1992, about 90 percent of households had received some sort of transfer and transfers made up over 40 percent of household income. To see what is behind these statistics, let's consider briefly (1) why and how the government's welfare burden had increased dramatically during the early 1990s, and (2) the main elements of a broadly defined welfare system, namely, the pension system, unemployment compensation, other welfare payments, education, and health care.

Increase in the State's Welfare Burden

In 1990, five million of Hungary's ten million population were employed, so that 50 percent of the population was economically active, supporting the other 50 percent, mainly children, the retired, and the disabled. By 1993, with an unchanging total population, the number of economically active had declined to 3.5 million. Thus, the inactive increased by 1.5 million, of whom 1 million retired (many taking early retirement) and half a million became unemployed. To be sure, a significant percent of those who reportedly became inactive have been earning income from the unreported economy. However, many are relying exclusively or mainly on transfer payments, whose real purchasing power has eroded, in many cases to below a minimum decent income level. For example, 70 to 80 percent of Hungary's 350,000 or so working-age gypsies are truly unemployed, whereas before the system change most of them had jobs in such industries as collective farming and in state-owned construction.

Pensions

Under central planning, the authorities promised cradle-to-grave income security. Upon retirement, pensions replaced nearly two-thirds of wages earned during the last several years of work; private pension plans did not exist. Employers and employees often colluded to push up wages during an employee's last years of work to let him or her qualify for generous pensions. A good pension was considered compensation for modest wages during the working years and as an element of the economic security (along with employment security) that supposedly made socialism better than capitalism. That was the system in place when privatization, downsizing, and the liquidation of many enterprises forced a large number of people to become economically inactive.

For decades, the retirement age had been much lower than in the much richer OECD countries: 55 for women, among the lowest in Europe, and 60 for men. Legislation to equalize the minimum retirement age for women and men (at 60) was passed in 1992 but rescinded in the same year.[15] Only during 1996–97 were the laws changed (discussed in Q-8). Retirement was further sweetened by a host of special privileges that made possible even earlier retirements in certain occupations and situations. Generous disability pensions were, and still are, quite easy to qualify for before retirement. Early retirement has been on the increase since 1989 and the growth rate of disability pensions has doubled in the past seven years. At the same time, truly disabled people without family support cannot make ends meet on their pension, and a good number of them have become beggars.

The average post retirement life span is longer in Hungary than in most OECD countries.[16] In other words, with much lower income levels and tax-collection capabilities, the government had promised pension benefits whose accumulated value after retirement (in local currency, relative to average incomes) is higher than those of some of the richest countries in the world. Most of the OECD countries, themselves, are finding their own generous welfare systems unaffordable and in need of fixing.

The pension crisis in Hungary is not due to the aging of the population; that bomb is still ticking and will peak around year 2015.[17] In 1995, the *age dependency ratio* was still only about 1 to 3, less than in 1990, and about the same as the average in the OECD countries. But the *system dependency ratio*, which measures those drawing pensions as a proportion of current contributors, is 2 to 3, one of the highest in the world. The ratio means that each Hungarian contributor to the pay-as-you-go (rather than prefunded) system is supporting two-thirds of a pensioner! This ratio rises (1) when registered and tax-paying jobs are lost because the activity ceases or goes underground to avoid paying taxes, and (2) when pensions are awarded to those under retirement age. Both of these causes had been at work during 1990–95.

The policy remedies that should have been addressed by the government during the first few years of transformation are, first and foremost, a strong effort to convince the population of the need for reform, followed by the adoption of a new system that is affordable, equitable, and promotes growth. Key elements of such a plan are increasing the retirement age, removing the inequitable and costly special retirement provisions in favored occupations, tightening the eligibility for disability pensions, and developing privately funded and managed supplementary pension systems.[18] It is only after Hungary's finances approached a crisis that steps were taken to start to remedy the situation (Q-8).

Unemployment Compensation and Other New Programs

Onto the inherited pension and disability systems, new, market-economy-type-categories of benefits had to be added, such as unemployment compensation (which initially replaced a relatively high share of average net wages, thus reducing incentives to work) and social assistance to the poor. At the same time, social security taxes on declared employment are high, and so are personal income taxes, which become highly progressive at average (and in terms of purchasing power, at quite low) income levels. This has created a classic welfare trap situation.[19] A further important problem is that many of the benefits have not been targeted to the needy but go to all citizens as a right.[20]

Health Care and Insurance

The health-care system, including its financing and delivery, has been facing increasingly severe problems. The health sector can be indicted for the often poor quality of care offered in health facilities (although there are impressive exceptions) and inconsistent effectiveness in reducing illness. Despite the almost universal access to care that was one of the achievements of the old system, and is maintained still, those who are not in a position to pay the widely practiced "under-the-table gratuities" to health-care providers are generally receiving poor, and declining quality, care. Access to health care is thus unequal, more a function of chance or of personal influence with providers than a guaranteed universal entitlement.[21] At the same time, the cost of national health care is comparatively high in the government's budget.

Until the delayed reforms of 1996–97, the social insurance fund paid sick benefits from day one of an illness, which was one reason for the widespread and costly abuse of the system. Another reason is the attractive opportunities to work in the unreported or gray economy.[22] In my circle of acquaintances in Hungary—average, ordinary people—I know several who have had months of paid sick leave involving an illness where a person in a comparable health condition in the United States would have been absent from work for only a few days. The reason for the abuse was that, in many cases, it was much too easy to get the doctors to go along because "it is the system that pays," "everybody is doing it," or in exchange for a small bribe or favors. Another problem, in many cases doctors are still running hospitals or hospital wards as if they are their personal fiefdoms, without concern for cost or administrative efficiency. And modern, preventive health care is generally not practiced.

In all fairness, however, it is to be pointed out that for those who have access to facilities in the major cities, many hospitals and doctors provide excellent care. It is also worth noting that some of the patient abuses that occur in the United States under the "managed health care" system are generally absent in Hungary.

One badly needed reform was to put the burden of financing sick benefits during the first few weeks onto the shoulders of the employers and employees, so as to burden society only with the cost of catastrophic illness. (Reforms introduced during 1996–97 moved in this direction.) Another badly needed reform is to introduce professional management and accountability in health care. Although public health care historically had high standards in Hungary, the standard has deteriorated in many areas. For example, it has not been reoriented toward such modern health problems as cancer and cholesterol screening, alcoholism, drug addiction, and mental illness. Health preservation and disease prevention is not yet an integral part of health services and medical practice. Due to an almost total lack of facilities for caring for the elderly outside hospitals, the proportion of hospital beds occupied by incurable patients has grown, at enormous extra expense.[23] Outsourcing of certain services to the private sector is not yet an accepted practice. In brief, health care in Hungary has been deteriorating and drifting.[24]

Education

In international comparisons, Hungary has a strong educational system, especially at the primary and secondary levels. Nevertheless, this sector also faces serious problems. These include the quality of education, which is quite uneven by sections of the country or the city; insufficient places for qualified applicants in selected areas of higher education while, at the same time, too many continue to be trained for sectors with a surfeit of qualified people (such as agriculture); declining quality of education in the vaunted science and engineering fields; an overly large and inflexible educational bureaucracy; salaries for educators that are extraordinarily low and have been declining in real terms; and educational content and methods that are still not fully modern.[25]

*   *   *

In sum, the political inability or unwillingness to tackle for years the design flaws and inefficiencies of inherited welfare and other public programs has been costly and has exacerbated the budget and balance of payments crisis of 1994–95.

Q-6. One hears frequent complaints that the business environment has not been supportive for small and medium-sized enterprises. At the same time, the number and growth of new business start-ups have been impressive. Isn't this a contradiction?

While the number of new business start-ups has indeed been impressive, that does not prove that small and medium-sized enterprises (SMEs) have been facing a healthy business environment, one that supports the establishment, survival, and expansion of viable business ventures. First, an extraordinarily large percent of the start-ups were hopeless ventures, set up with meager investments to escape unemployment. A disproportionate number of them (relative to well-functioning market economies) has not or will not survive. The number of registered start-ups is significantly upward biased by "churning," that is, artificial bankruptcies and restarts whose purpose is to avoid various taxes. Many registered businesses are empty-shell holding companies, established or maintained for a variety of reasons.

More importantly, many potentially viable ventures are facing a series of interconnected problems. Taxes are unusually high; tax regulations are changed much too often; regulations are excessive, administered by an often unwieldy bureaucracy; corruption is growing (for example, public procurement is supposed to be competitive but often is not); and credit is often unavailable or high cost. The most fundamental problem, however, is one that is much more difficult to cure than any of the constraints enumerated, namely, that Hungary (as well as other transforming economies) are poorly endowed with financial capital because the accumulation of private wealth was prevented by the communist political system. All these difficulties are especially acute for the SMEs because large enterprises, including influential foreign investors, have been able to avoid or mitigate many of these problems.[26]

Many SMEs as well as the self-employed have a strong incentive to cheat on taxes, in part because the sum total of taxes (such as payroll, medical insurance, social security, unemployment, disability, and income taxes) is high, in comparison with tax rates in other countries, and tax administration is poor. Calculations by Kornai show that, under the legislation that was in force in 1995, 100 forints of *gross* compensation, paid by the employer to a typical employee, was burdened by business, income, and consumption taxes that left the individual only 38.5 forints of real purchasing power. Various taxes thus skimmed about 61 percent of gross wages (collected mostly by the employer), one of the highest tax burdens in Europe.[27] For Western investors, these problems were mitigated by Hungary's relatively low wages and salaries and by the income-tax concessions that they had received during the first half of the 1990s.

Only a small fraction of the taxes businesses pay is notionally identified as employee contributions. Employees are not provided with statements of what is contributed on their behalf, which hardly encourages them to monitor how tax funds are spent. For these and other reasons, Hungarians show an almost total lack of *tax awareness*. Kornai cites surveys that a vast majority of the Hungarians want the state to do this and to do that for them, without being aware of the cost of those services and their connection with taxes.[28]

One reason that the social security portion of business taxes is high is that the bulk of high-cost social services and transfers is financed by payroll and related taxes; another, that tax avoidance is much higher than in market economies at comparable development levels. Tax avoidance, in turn, is high because tax rates are high, because citizens don't, as a rule, associate the taxes they pay with the benefits they receive, and because public morality—that is, taking tax and other obligations toward the authorities seriously—had certainly deteriorated under the communist political system. Public morality has further weakened during the 1990s, for several reasons: rising unemployment; declining real wages (during 1990–92 and 1995–96, especially in the public sector); a growing number of people experiencing poverty; the new temptations of an as-yet-undeveloped capitalism; the absence or weak enforcement of laws, especially those involving white-collar crime; and the emergence and growth of organized crime.

Another significant problem is excessive regulation and red tape. The attitude of those administering the many rules and regulations tends to be not that of service providers but that of favor dispensers. This is a legacy of the communist as well as the precommunist era.[29] Local governments control many areas of SME activity and in many cases their attitude toward the SMEs is adversarial. For example, in the district of Budapest the author is familiar with, scores of shops owned by the municipal government have been standing empty for years because the authorities are asking lease payments that no one can afford to pay.

Labor laws are not friendly to employers. For example, after a person has been with an employer for three months, firing or laying him or her off can be difficult, may end up in litigation, and require a large severance pay. In response, employees are often paid by owners from profits, under the table, so that both can save on taxes and the employer can avoid complications in case of separation. The cost of construction or repair work often depends on whether the customer will need a receipt.

Another problem for SMEs is the unavailability or high cost of loan or equity capital from financial institutions. This has several causes: inflation and inflationary expectations; the poor financial condition of the large commercial banks (the situation has improved since many were privatized during 1995–97); long periods when investing in government bonds was more attractive relative to the risk than lending to businesses; the absent or weak creditworthiness record of prospective borrowers; insufficiently developed commercial laws (for example, creditors are not being assured legal recourse to collateral in case of nonpayment); illegal practices, such as taking bribes by some loan officers in certain state-owned banks; and, generally, the absence or underdevelopment of such financial intermediaries as venture capital funds and lenders specializing in SMEs.

Many of these enumerated problems are also found, in varying degrees, in the established market economies and are not amenable to ready solutions. The criticism I have is that neither the Antall–Boross nor (during its first few years) the Horn government paid sufficient attention to these problems. Few effective initiatives were taken to assist the SMEs—an important segment of the future middle class of the country. To be sure, during 1996–98, the Horn government appeared to have recognized the need to improve the business environment for the SMEs. Some taxes were reduced during 1997; tax incentives were given to those investing in the less-developed regions of the country, and greater support was given to venture-capital funds. FIDESZ, the party that came out victorious during the election of 1998, has promised to give high priority to improving the business conditions for SMEs. Modest tax reductions are planned and the bureaucracies that prospective and functioning entrepreneurs have to deal with are being consolidated.

Q-7: Is it true that during 1990–94 the right-of-center Antall and Boross governments had pursued misguided economic policies that one tends to associate more with left-of-center governments?

The foreign image of Hungary's first post-communist government was shaped more by the anticommunist stance and nationalistic pronouncements of Prime Minister Jozsef Antall than by his domestic economic policies, or those of Mr. Boross, who headed the government after the death of Mr. Antall. After the steep economic downturns of 1990–92, caused mainly by external economic shocks (but with the bankruptcy law of 1992 being a contributing factor), the Antall government faced strong domestic pressures to get the economy moving again. Responding to the pressures—and trusting growth forecasts that had turned out to be much too optimistic—the authorities had made a series of policy mistakes that are easy to identify in hindsight. Between mid-1992 and mid-1994, the government tried to stimulate economic growth primarily by monetary and fiscal policies that turned out to be much too expansionary. To be sure, during this period budget expenditures had declined substantially in real terms. But because GDP had declined even more, the ratio of state budget expenditures to GDP rose. It is much easier to reduce a high government/GDP ratio when an economy expands than when it contracts. In any case, in hindsight, the mistake was that insufficient attention was paid to measures designed to improve the supply response and the competitiveness of Hungary's producers (except for the bankruptcy legislation, discussed earlier, which, however, contributed significantly to output declines in the short run).

A serious mistake was that the government had remained sanguine about the large and growing budget and balance of payments deficits of 1992, 1993, and 1994.[30] The deficits were financed partly by household savings and, increasingly, by foreign borrowing. Financing large government deficits preempted resources that should have gone to support domestic business expansion. The unsustainable growth of the deficits then pushed the economy to the very edge of a precipice by 1995.

III. Austerity and Reform, 1995–97: The Threshold Years

Q-8. Was it necessary to introduce the severe austerity measures (the "Bokros package") in 1995? What measures were taken and what did they accomplish?

Figures 8.1 through 8.4, shown on the following pages, illustrate key developments that led to the introduction of the Bokros package in March 1995, as well as the results of the combined austerity and reform programs through 1997.

Was the Bokros Program Necessary?

The events that led to the introduction of the austerity cum reform program can be summarized as follows. Hungary, along with the rest of the countries of the former Soviet bloc, suffered cumulative output declines of about 20 percent during 1990–92. Between mid-1992 and mid-1994—the latter being an election year—the government tried to stimulate economic growth mainly by policies that had turned out to be much too expansionary, as was noted. Although the recovery during 1993–94 was modest (Figure 8.1) and inflation was stabilized at a still high 22–23 percent per annum (Figure 8.2), the economy quickly ran into unsustainable balance of payments deficits. The current account balance had exceeded 9 percent of GDP for two years (Figure 8.3), and gross and net external debt, high to begin with, grew rapidly

Figure 8.1: Hungary's Real GDP Growth, 1990–98 (percentage change from previous year)

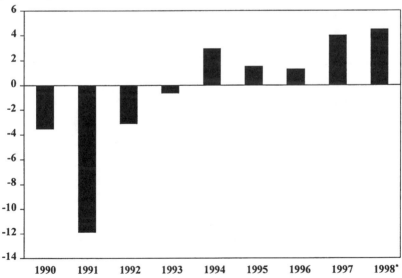

*Author's forecast
Source: Central Statistical Office of Hungary

Paul Marer

Figure 8.2: Hungary's Inflation, 1990–98 (annual percentage change in consumer price index)

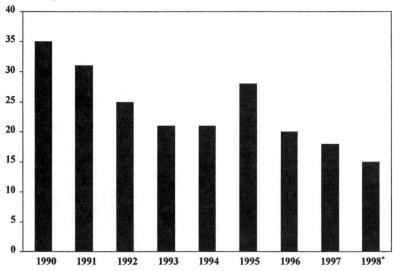

*Author's forecast
Source:* Central Statistical Office of Hungary

Figure 8.3: Hungary's Current Account Balance, 1990–97 (percentage of GDP)

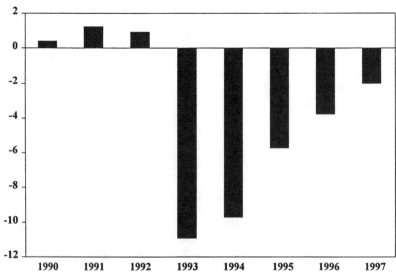

Sources: 1990–1996: IMF; 1997: *Financial Times,* February 9, 1998

Figure 8.4: Hungary's Foreign Debt, 1990–97 (US$ billion)

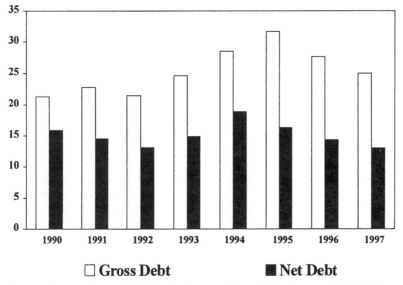

☐ **Gross Debt**   ■ **Net Debt**

Source: *Hungary: Economic Policies for Sustainable Growth* (Washington D.C.: IMF Occasional Paper No. 159, 1998)

(Figure 8.4).[31] Whereas at the end of 1992, net external debt stood at about 35 percent of GDP, it had climbed to 45 percent of GDP by the end of 1994, a high level by international standards.

By the end of 1994, the state of Hungary's public finances had two serious problems. One, revenue and expenditure ratios to GDP that were 48 percent and 55 percent, respectively, both large compared with market economies at comparable levels of development. Two, the deficits became unsustainably large—7 percent to 9 percent of GDP for several years.[32] During 1992–94, domestic debt increased not only because of large deficits in the budget but also because the government issued substantial amount of bonds to re-capitalize the banks and to cover losses from earlier housing loans to the public.

The unusually large share of the GDP that was still redistributed by the central government five years after transformation had begun, and the growing deficits, had several causes, in addition to those already mentioned:

(1) The size of the civil service (including education and health care) in total employment was large compared with the OECD average as well as relative to the ratios of the other Central and East European countries.

(2) Financial and budgetary rules regulating different government entities were not modern and allowed slack financial discipline. For example, most subsidies and social transfers were not well targeted (the nonpoor also received social transfers and subsidies) and open-ended (actual expenditures at the end of the year were determined not by the budgetary allocation but by the number of claimants satisfying the eligibility conditions). Budgetary overruns were routinely accommodated through budget revised *ex post* or via supplementary budgets.

(3) Aspects of the delivery of health care, education, and other public services were wasteful.

The negative impact of the budget and foreign debt situation on economic growth was made worse by the *continued* attempt to shelter households as much as possible from the adverse effects of the economic crisis. For decades, consumption had increased more rapidly, or had declined less precipitously, than output, creating the burdensome dual (external and domestic) debt for the economy. This policy had continued during 1992–94, when real wages had declined less than output and profits, so that income distribution shifted from the higher saving enterprise to the higher consumption household sector.

Following the mid-1994 elections, the victorious Socialist Party (many of whose leaders used to belong to the liberal wing of the Communist Party) formed a coalition government with the Free Democrats. A nine-month period of economic policy drift followed, during which macroeconomic conditions worsened. As a result of the ever-larger budget, trade, and balance of payments deficits, an economic catastrophe was looming. If, in such a situation, the government would not have taken prudent steps, a loss of confidence by domestic as well as foreign lenders and investors would have become a very strong possibility. That, in turn, could have led to a fate similar to that which Mexico suffered in 1995 and several Asian countries experienced in 1997: massive capital flight and a collapse of the currency, followed by a major downturn in the real economy, lower production, higher unemployment, and accelerating inflation.

The program, introduced in March 1995, had the *immediate objective* of bringing down the external deficit to avert the risk of a crisis of the kind just sketched, and the *medium-term objective* of bringing the economy's growth rate closer to its potential.

Measures Taken

The strategy to achieve the two objectives had a macroeconomic component and a structural component.[33]

Macroeconomic Aspects. The main policy instruments were the following: cutting government spending; increasing taxes; devaluing the currency by an immediate 9 percent and instituting a so-called crawling-peg exchange rate regime, with fixed monthly devaluations, initially of 1.9 percent, then 1.2 percent (whose objective was to improve the competitiveness of exports without pushing the economy into an outright recession); imposing an 8 percent import surcharge; and reducing consumption in favor of investment.

Consumption was reduced by enterprises passing on to consumers a portion of the import surcharge, cutting government transfers to households, reducing the number of state employees, broadening the social security tax, and imposing an inflation tax on wage earners. The last measure was made possible by the *unanticipated* jump in inflation in 1995 (Figure 8.2), mainly reflecting sharp energy price increases and the real depreciation of the forint. The jump in inflation had not been incorporated in the wage agreements for 1995, most of which had been concluded before the Bokros package was introduced. The agreed wage increases were *not* revised on account of higher inflation. Furthermore, the government decided to freeze public expenditures in nominal terms. With the accelerating inflation, this meant real expenditure cuts.

Structural Aspects. Most important was the furious restarting of the privatization process during 1995–97, which had stalled during 1994. Privatization receipts during 1995–97 amounted to a *cumulative* 12 percent of GDP, as compared with a *cumulative* 8 percent of GDP during 1990–94 (see chapter by Crane for details). More than 80 percent of the income came from foreign investors. The left-of-center Horn government was the first in the region to sell to foreign investors a significant portion of the country's public utilities, other infrastructure assets, and several of the largest commercial banks. These politically difficult decisions were made because there was no money from domestic sources to finance infrastructure's and the banks' badly needed modernization. Privatization revenues went mainly to reduce the government's foreign and domestic debts.

Fiscal reform concentrated on reforming some of the social programs and improving public administration and finance. One of the most notable was the pension reform (summarized below), that became law in 1997. Also significant were reforms in the system of transfer payments to families, tying eligibility to need, not citizenship. (The party that was victorious in the 1998 election pledged, irresponsibly, to reverse this particular reform measure.) Modest steps were taken to rationalize the health-care and health insurance systems. Price subsidies on pharmaceutical sales were cut and steps were taken to reduce unused hospital capacity. Sick payments were also cut. Starting in 1995, employers had to pay the first 10 days of sick leave (increased to 15 days in 1996), giving employers an incentive to control abuse, which used to be widespread. The earlier generous income replacement rates during sickness (of 65–75 percent of net earnings), which could be continued for up to a year, were cut and eligibility requirements tightened.[34]

The management of public finances and administration were improved. For example, a number of central budgetary institutions were transformed into nonprofit organizations that must cover their expenditures from their revenues. A single "treasury" was established to handle all cash transactions of central government entities, replacing a multitude of accounts and systems.[35] Budget procedures of the social insurance funds were improved, constraining their ability to spend more than what was budgeted.

Pension Reform. One of the most significant structural reforms in public finance to date, pension reforms were enacted in several steps. During 1994, private pension funds became legal; contributing to them was optional. During 1996, the existing pay-as-you-go (PAYG) system was reformed. In 1997, a new, fully funded component was added. The PAYG reform involved a gradual increase in pension age (5–6 years for women and 2–2.5 years for men, to age 62 for both, by the year 2009); penalties for early retirement; and a revision in the pension indexation mechanism (shifting gradually from indexing net wages to an evenly weighted average of wages and the price index). The second step was the establishment of Central and Eastern Europe's first and Europe's second (after Britain) multipillar pension system. It consists of a downsized first pillar (the publicly funded and managed PAYG) and a new second pillar, fully funded and privately managed, targeted to provide about 25 to 30 percent of pension payouts in the long run.[36] The new system is mandatory for all new entrants into the labor force as of July 1, 1998; those already in the labor force have the option of staying in the reformed PAYG or switching to the new, multipillar system. The net impact of the combined 1996–97 pension reforms will *increase* budget expenditures in the first several years but are expected to generate savings thereafter, improve efficiencies, and have better prospects of protecting the real value of the pensions than did the old system.

Results of the Austerity/Reform Program

Because economic processes are so complex, there are so many forces at work, statements about simple and single cause-and-effect relationships are rarely true. This caveat notwithstanding, one can confidently assert that the austerity program of 1995–96 and the reform programs of 1995–97 are causally related to three significant and interdependent outcomes. One, they stopped the threatening erosion of foreign confidence in Hungary's economic management. Two, they created significant (hopefully temporary) new hardships for many of Hungary's households. Three, they helped to accelerate and make more sustainable the economic growth rate.

The Foreign Confidence Factor. That Hungary is heavily dependent on foreign trade, foreign investment, foreign credits, and foreign goodwill is an incontrovertible fact. What foreigners saw during 1994 and early 1995 was that even a modest growth of Hungary's economy (Figure 8.1) was associated with large payment deficits (Figure 8.3) and debt increases (Figure 8.4). Behind the poor performance, they observed that privatization and certain other reform processes were slowed or halted. By contrast, by 1988 foreigners could observe that during the past three years Hungary's growth rate accelerated (Figure 8.1), inflation moderated (Figure 8.2), the trade balance improved (through the much faster expansion of exports than imports),[37] the current account also improved (Figure 8.3), and foreign debt was reduced (Figure 8.4). The good performance is associated with a government and a people that were willing to bite the bullet when it was essential to do so. Foreigners having a positive image of Hungary's economic management—relative to the country's past situation and relative to the image that other countries in the region have—yield tangible benefits to Hungary's economy (e.g., lower interest rates on outstanding and new debt and greater foreign investment) as well as intangible benefits (avoiding a collapse of its currency and capital flight, and improved prospects for NATO and EU membership).

Increased Hardships for the Population. The burden of the austerity program was borne mainly by workers, pensioners, and consumers. In two years (1995–96), real wages dropped by 12 percent, the real value of pensions by 25 percent, and household consumption by 8 percent. During this period, income and wealth distribution became more uneven. For those experiencing increased hardships it is small comfort to be told that the alternative would have been worse. In any event, the veracity of the statement is widely doubted and is impossible to prove. Be that as it may, let me share a few thoughts about the standard of living of Hungary's population and the distribution of income and wealth.

The general cause of the *low level of per capita income* of the population of any country is the low level of productivity of its economy, a problem that generally cannot be "solved" by income redistribution measures. (To be sure, the decline in the employed-to-population ratio during the first half of the 1990s had exacerbated the problem.) The specific causes of the *decline in the per capita income* during the early years of transformation were the growing burdens of the inherited double debt and the domestic and external shocks associated with, but not strictly caused by, the systemic transformation, as well as their multiplier effects. (Domestic shocks were caused by having to eliminate or downsize production for which there was no effective private or public demand, at home or abroad.) There are different ways in which the population can pay for such costs, and the size of the bill itself can be influenced somewhat by the aptness or ineptness of government policy, but there is no way that paying the bill can be avoided.

As to the *increase in the inequality of income and wealth*, it is due to both legitimate and illegitimate causes. Economically *legitimate causes* (though they may not be socially fully sanctioned) are those that reflect market forces *if* the market mechanism functions well.[38] *Illegitimate causes* are due to crime, corruption and market imperfections. The problem in Hungary, as in other transition economies, is that the scope and severity of all three of the *illegitimate causes* have increased greatly. Corruption appears to be the greatest evil. While to many Hungarians the rapid growth of the illegitimate causes of income and wealth inequality *appears to be* the introduction of a capitalist system, their real main source is the difficult road that has to be traveled to eventually reach some kind of a well-functioning market economy. Why such a destination? Because if the goal is economic modernization and sustained improvements in the living standard, then no viable alternative destination to some type of a market economy has been found.

Corruption becomes a particularly serious problem during transition. This legacy of the previous system becomes worse during the early years of transformation, for several reasons. Opportunities for corruption and its rewards became immense, on account of a large part of the national wealth being transferred from "public" to private ownership. The rules and institutions of a market economy are not yet functioning well. Under such circumstances, there is simply no way to privatize the means of production efficiently *and* fairly. How much corruption accompanies the process will be influenced by the country's historical traditions (such as culture), the nature of the political system, the speed of transition, and government policies. The sooner privatization is completed, the faster proven institutions of a market economy are introduced, and the more efficiently democracy works (e.g., elections are contested, the media are free, other checks and balances are in place, and politicians and public servants are held accountable), the faster will be progress in limiting the growth of illegitimate income and wealth.

Accelerating and Sustaining Growth. This is the third significant outcome associated with the austerity and reform programs of 1995–97. For decades if not centuries, Hungary's economy has been heavily dependent on foreign trade. During the communist and immediate postcommunist era, the economy was functioning with several interdependent structural weaknesses. The combination of structural weaknesses and heavy dependence on foreign trade was largely responsible for the repeated pattern of strong cyclicality, especially so between the mid-1970s and the mid-1990s. Acceleration of the growth rate always resulted in steeply rising balance of payment deficits and debt. The imbalance then forced the authorities to introduce an austerity program. As soon as the foreign financing constraint eased, growth was "pushed" and the cycle began anew.

It appears that this vicious circle may finally have been broken. The economy has had several years of expansion, with a particularly impressive tempo in 1997, with equally good early results and projections for 1998 (Figure 8.1).[39] At the same time, inflation moderated, the current account improved, and foreign debt declined! (See Figures 8.2 through 8.4.) The fundamental reason why the vicious circle apparently has been broken is that several of the key structural weaknesses of the economy have been eliminated or improved. The credit goes not only to the Bokros program but to the cumulative impact of the economic reforms that were begun in the 1960s, continued (with interruptions and reversals) during the 1970s and 1980s, and accelerated during the 1990s.

In terms of economic structure, most important are the relative *size* and *economic health* of the private sector. The private sector—comprised of foreign-controlled, Hungarian-controlled, and jointly controlled businesses—now dominates the production and distribution of goods and services. Much of the financial sector was also placed in private hands, after the authorities had largely completed, by the end of 1994, a thorough "cleanup" of the main banks (Hungary was the first country in the region to have done so). Both in the real and in the financial sectors, about 75 percent of economic activities, and a somewhat smaller share of the sectors' assets, are privately controlled. The real and the financial sectors *both* being predominantly in private hands is a necessary, but not sufficient, condition for the sectors and for the economy to be healthy. (Sound money, contestable markets, good laws and government supervision, a supporting market infrastructure, and an efficient public service, are also necessary. Hungary has made progress in all these areas, although a great deal still remains be done.) The two most serious and interrelated "illnesses" of the private sector are the large size of the unreported (sometimes called underground or gray) economy, conservatively estimated to produce 20 to 25 percent of the GDP, and the difficult business environment facing (mainly) the SMEs.

A structural weakness that has improved greatly is the share of GDP redistributed by the budget. Owing in part to the austerity measures of the Bokros program and in part to the structural-institutional reform measures of the last several years, public consumption (government purchases of goods and services) fell from 20 percent of GDP in 1993–94 to 15 percent by 1997, while transfer payments (including government subsidies) declined from 31 percent to 20 percent of GDP.[40] (The rest of the budget, close to 15 percent, goes for public administration and defense.) "Right-sizing" the government supports economic growth in several ways. It frees resources that could be put to better use by households and companies, makes people more self-reliant, improves the international competitiveness of producers in Hungary, promotes entrepreneurship and the development of capital markets, and encourages underground businesses to legitimize their operations.

IV. Foreign Economic Strategies

Q-9: The growth of the private sector has meant selling a great deal of the country's assets to foreign investors. Not everyone is convinced that that is a good thing. Who are the investors and where does their money go? How has Hungary been able to attract them? Should the citizens of Hungary be concerned about so many of the country's assets being transferred to foreign owners?

Attracting Foreign Investment: Origin and Destination

Relative to the size of its economy, Hungary has attracted more foreign investment than any other transforming economy, including China! (This is calculated for each country by dividing its cumulative inflow of foreign investment for a recent period, say, 1990–96 with its 1996 GDP. Among the transition economies, Hungary's ratio is the highest.)[41] By mid-1998, Hungary had obtained $18 billion in foreign direct investment. The amount includes acquisitions (mainly via privatization), joint ventures (foreigners taking a partial equity position in Hungarian businesses), green-field investment (building new operations, starting with a "green field"), and reinvested earnings. In 1997, close to 30,000 foreign ventures were operating in the country, accounting for over two-thirds of Hungary's total exports. Thirty-five of the world's fifty largest multinational enterprises have subsidiaries in Hungary. More than half of Hungary's 200 largest companies are foreign controlled. Of the fifteen largest commercial banks, ten have a foreign majority ownership.

The biggest foreign investment to date is the U.S.-German consortium Ameritech-Deutsche Telecom's acquisition of a 67 percent stake in Hungarian Telecommunications Company, MATAV. Through 1997, the joint venture partners had invested more than $2 billion.[42] General Electric bought Hungary's largest manufacturer, light-source producer Tungsram, and invested about $1 billion.[43]

After playing only a minor role in the car industry during the communist era (though Hungary was the region's largest bus manufacturer through IKARUS), in the 1990s it became one of the prime targets for investment by automobile manufacturers from the United States, Europe, and Japan. Foreign direct investment in the sector is close to $2 billion. The earliest and largest investors were U.S. General Motors, Suzuki of Japan, and the Volkswagen group of Germany. Ford has also invested in components manufacturing, as have several other leading Western and Japanese component suppliers.[44]

Electronics is another fast-growing sector. The IBM plant in Szekesfehervar is said to be the most modern factory of its kind in Central Europe. In 1997 it turned out $500 million worth of digital components, all for export. The facility is scheduled to be enlarged to sell abroad $1 billion each year.

The reasons that Hungary has been able to attract during 1990–97 a large share of foreign investments flowing into the region can be traced to such factors as Hungary's excellent geographic location (bordering Austria and proximity to Europe's powerhouse, Southern Germany); favorable foreign image; relatively attractive business environment when transition had begun; the unusual combination of finding a relatively inexpensive and yet highly qualified professional and well-trained, blue-collar workforce; the authorities selling rather than distributing the shares of state enterprises, which gave foreign buyers a significant edge; the tax breaks granted to many large foreign investors until 1995; and the "agglomeration" effect: foreign investors prefer (other things being equal) destinations where many others have invested before them.

Concerns about Foreign Ownership

While it cannot be argued that each and every foreign investment project is of unquestioned benefit to Hungary, or that examples of deceit and fraud by unscrupulous foreign investors cannot be found, much of the capital inflow into the country has been by responsible strategic investors pursuing long-term objectives. As to concerns by the citizens of Hungary about the extent of foreign ownership, some of the reasons that make an investor-friendly policy a good strategic choice are outlined below.

Compared with most countries of Western Europe and many other countries around the world, Hungary's economy is lagging behind. Much of its industrial, agricultural, and infrastructure capital stock is out of date. The global economy is in the midst of a new industrial revolution, driven by the computer and the information age. Keeping up with the accelerating pace of worldwide economic change requires sustained large investment in the modernization of the country's physical and human capital stock. Hungary's domestic stock of savings per capita—and thus the domestic funds available for investment—is much less than that of the economically advanced countries around the world. Foreign borrowing cannot be increased by much. Foreign investment thus supplements domestic savings and helps finance temporary current-account deficits without increasing the foreign debt.

Policies should also take into account that most of the major markets around the world—which producers based in Hungary must penetrate to earn the foreign exchange to pay for the imports on which Hungary's economy so vitally depends—are controlled by multinational enterprises. To succeed, producers in Hungary must become partners with them, if necessary, as subsidiaries. The ingenuity and dedication of Hungary's vaunted engineers, scientists and skilled workforce notwithstanding, few domestic producers would have a good chance to obtain—by relying mainly on domestic resources—the finance, the technology, the management know-how, and the market access that, in combination, are required to be successful in the increasingly competitive global marketplace.

Being open and attractive to foreign investors is a necessary (but not sufficient) condition for the citizens of Hungary to realize their centuries-old desire: to catch up, or at least to not fall further behind, the developed countries of Western Europe.[45]

Although the substantial direct and indirect benefits of foreign investment are not yet manifest in Hungary's GDP growth or the living standard of its people, which have been pulled down by other factors, the economy would be in a much worse shape without the stabilizing influence of foreign investment.

Incidentally, once Hungary becomes a full member of the European Union (EU), there will be a new situation regarding foreign investment. Accession to the EU will by and large erase the distinction between domestic and foreign investors from the EU countries.

Q-10. Why does Hungary want to join the European Union and NATO? What are the economic benefits and costs of Hungary becoming a full member of these organizations?

There are historical, political, military, economic, and symbolic reasons why Hungary and other Central and East European countries wish to join these organizations and why the chances look excellent that these organizations' current members will extend a welcome, as discussed in the chapter in this volume by Bennett Kovrig.

The economic reasons for wanting to join the EU are threefold: to secure a more friendly external and a more stable domestic economic environment, to gain free access to a large market, and to obtain a net inward flow of resources. The first and the third are also reasons to join NATO, in addition to the noneconomic reasons.

Being a member of these organizations, Hungary's interests are likely to be taken into account by the other members. Each member has a voice in shaping, interpreting, and enforcing the rules. Hence, Hungary will face a friendlier external economic environment. At the same time, the nature of Hungary's domestic economic laws, institutions, and policies are, and will continue to be, shaped by the membership requirements and policies of the EU. This will provide a degree of domestic economic predictability, and thus stability, which is an asset.

Hungary (as well nine other Central East European and Baltic countries) currently enjoy associate membership status in the EU. This gives them free access to EU's markets for most goods and services, except for agricultural (and a few other) products, which are very important for Hungary (discussed in Q-4). Having become an associate member has already obligated Hungary to provide, gradually, over a period of years, free access to imports from EU members, so that is not a direct cost of becoming a member. In any event, being exposed to greater domestic competition on the domestic market will be costly to some of the producers (and their workers) that are competing with imports, while it will benefit exporters and the consumers. On balance, the economy of Hungary will continue to benefit from increased competition, which improves productivity. Full membership should also provide Hungarians with free or improved access to the EU's labor markets, benefiting those with skills in high demand in Western Europe.

As a relatively poor country, Hungary can expect to be a net recipient of aid flows from the EU. A meaningful estimate of the expected magnitude of the aid is not possible. Even without enlargement, the EU's current budgetary rules will have to be changed, and no agreement has as yet been reached on the new rules. Furthermore, the terms on which the new members will be admitted (sometime between 2004 and 2006 is the most plausible guess, as of mid-1998) are yet to be negotiated. However, in addition to outright aid flows, Hungary should also receive subsidized loans (whose grant equivalent can be calculated), as well as a larger flow of foreign direct as well as portfolio investment, from all over the world, on market terms, than if Hungary remained outside of the EU.

The economic costs of membership are also difficult to estimate. The greater part of the cost of systemic transformation should not be attributed to membership per se, even if many of the things Hungary does now, or will do in the future, are to conform to EU requirements and standards. Certainly, hundreds if not thousands of new, EU-conforming laws will have to be passed and implemented, which is expensive. Hungary will also have to establish new border controls for goods, passengers, and road traffic, as well as make contributions to the EU budget.

V. Summary Assessments

Q-11. How would you summarize and evaluate the transformation strategies and economic policies of the Antall, Boross, and Horn governments?

The author's interpretation, simplified here for the sake of brevity and emphasis, is the following. I generally endorse the Antall (1990–93), Boross (1993–94) and Horn (1994–98) governments' transformation *strategies*, but am rather critical of a number of the *economic policies* they had implemented, or failed to implement. Were it not for a series of significant economic policy mistakes, Hungary could be further ahead in the transformation, and its economy could have been performing significantly better by an earlier date.

By transformation *strategy* I mean the fundamental, persistent, and difficult-to-reverse basic policy choices that determine the direction in which the country is heading and the type of economic system being created. *Economic policy* refers to actions taken, or not taken, that are not necessarily permanent, and are more easily changed, than strategic decisions.

Hungary's post-communist governments deserve a great deal of credit for making, and persevering with, some key strategic choices. Most important has been the unswerving determination to join the democratic clubs of the Western countries by seeking admission to the OECD (Hungary was admitted in 1996), NATO, and the EU.[46] And there was never any question—in Hungary's first two (right-of-center), its third (left-of-center) and now its fourth (right of center) governments—that they wished the country to become a market economy and to join Western Europe.

Although these strategic choices may seem obvious, a firm commitment to them is an accomplishment to be cherished because it more or less guarantees (as much as anything can be guaranteed in this rapidly changing world) Hungary's political and economic future. The beneficial effects of these choices are immediate as well as long term. They include keeping permanently at bay extremist political forces, be they right-wing, left-wing, or any other kind. These strategic choices commit future governments of Hungary to maintain democracy and a market economy by aligning its laws, institutions, and practices—in a wide variety of fields—to those found in the developed economies of the democratic West. These are accomplishments not to be overlooked, especially in view of the magnitude of the economic downturn, and the dramatic increase in the inequality of income and wealth distribution, during transformation's early years. In certain respects, the magnitude of the economic adversities that Hungary and the region's other transforming economies have experienced during the early 1990s compares with those that these countries had suffered during the Great Depression, which spawned or greatly strengthened extremist political movements.

Regarding the strategy of economic transformation, the choice to opt mainly for privatization via sale rather than voucher distribution was a prudent one because it aided rapid restructuring and the modernization of enterprise operations. Although corruption and other problems have certainly marred the record, privatization's achievements have been substantial. Strategic choices concerning the mode and speed of privatization have been complementary with another positive strategic choice—that of attracting foreign direct investment on a large scale.

The Antall, Boross, and Horn governments also deserve credit for tackling relatively early and completing by 1995 the immense task of cleaning up the banking system's huge volume of bad debts, recapitalizing the state-owned commercial banks, and selling controlling equity shares in banks' foreign investments.[47] Hungary had accomplished these tasks well ahead of other countries in the region.

Introducing the austerity program of 1995 was an unpopular but courageous policy. It made it possible for Hungary to avoid a potentially much more damaging scenario. (To be sure, politicians rarely get credit for preventing a disaster that the average citizen cannot see coming.) And the austerity and the reform programs together helped establish the conditions for *sustainable* growth.

Turning to the negative aspects of government behavior, all three post-communist governments can be faulted for a series of inept *economic policy* decisions, for not making certain decisions that should have been made, or for not making them on a timely basis. Five such areas were identified: policies toward agriculture (Q-4); inability to reform, on a timely basis, the expensive and outmoded health and welfare system (Q-5); the problems of corruption (mentioned throughout); the inattention of successive governments to creating a climate that would foster the healthy development of SMEs (Q-6); and the economic policies of the Antall–Boross governments (which was partly responsible for the Horn government having to introduce an austerity program) (Q-7).

Because the economic records of the governments in power during 1990–97 are mixed, it would be as easy—through a selective choice of the facts—to present an unduly negative assessment (as many Hungarians are inclined to do, perhaps mirroring the pessimism of their psyche), as it would be to paint an unduly positive picture.

In choosing a standard to evaluate the economic strategies and policies of Hungary's governments during the first eight years of transformation, it is well to keep in mind that all three governments (as well as those of the other transforming nations) had faced an exceedingly difficult situation and many thorny dilemmas. The following dilemma appears to be the most fundamental. How can the authorities implement responsible and future-oriented economic strategies and policies while, at the same time, they are faced with widely held but clearly unrealistic expectations on the part of the citizenry (and, initially, also on the part of most of the West) that the economic lot of the people should improve, substantially and *soon?* Politicians, after all, want to be popular and wish to get reelected. It takes extraordinary skill and courage to give voters a message that they do not wish to hear or believe, and to convince them to accept policies that follow from such a message.

Furthermore, it was difficult for leading politicians, most of whom were and are not trained economists (Vaclav Klaus, the former prime minister of the Czech Republic, the sole exception), to make sense of the cacophony of voices they heard and advice they received about the immensely complex tasks of economic transformation. While the blueprint of how a well-functioning market economy operates is pretty well-known (such economies have many common institutions and policies, in spite of certain differences),[48] there is no single proven design of what road to take to create it. This is because successful market economies have evolved over generations, in some cases over a century or more, to create the institutions and policies which they now have, whereas the transition economies wish to compress the time in order to get to the destination quickly. Since there is no consensus on whether, to what extent, and how the travel time can be compressed, that is a further reason one should not set unreasonably high standards to evaluate what governments have done, or not done, in those early years.

Against such an implicit standard, the economic strategies and policies of all three of Hungary's governments deserve a grade that is better than average.

Q-12. What main tasks are facing Hungary's new government? What are the country's medium-term prospects?

The central economic task of the new government is to accelerate the rate of growth of the economy while simultaneously continuing to improve the balance of payments and to lower the rate of inflation to single digits in a few years. Because so much painful restructuring, as well as the difficult tasks of creating or strengthening market institutions, had been accomplished in the past eight years, conditions are favorable for achieving a sustained improvement in the macro-economy. But the improvements will not happen automatically. Policy-makers need to identify and stoke the engines that will help to accelerate growth. At the same time, they must carefully guard against the economy overheating.

During the next several years, four areas appear to be especially well positioned to become sources of growth: the SME sector, regional development, a continued net inflow of foreign direct investment and integration into the EU. Ideally, government policies should support *each* of these areas *and* promote symbiotic integration among these four engines of growth.

Business conditions need to be improved for the SME sector by easing or eliminating the many constraints the sector has been facing for years (detailed under Q-6) and by the prudent promotion of selected sectors, such as tourism and housing construction and remodeling.

Regional development should also become high priority. While historically, the Western part of Hungary had always been more developed than the Eastern part, the divergence has grown dramatically in recent years, resulting in large concentrations of high unemployment and pockets of abject poverty in the eastern regions. The eastern part had a disproportionate share of heavy industry. Conditions for agriculture are more favorable in Western Hungary. That region has also benefited from its excellent geographic location for Western investors, while

Paul Marer

the eastern part has languished because its economy has been tied more closely to the depressed economies of Ukraine, Russia, and Romania and also because its infrastructure is much less developed. Promoting the development of the eastern region by supporting projects that make economic sense (such as tourism and infrastructure). For example, with the assistance of foreign investors, Hungary's eastern border regions can become transportation hubs, and bridges, between Western Europe and the East European countries mentioned.

Another challenge for economic policy is to make sure that Hungary remains attractive to foreign investors even though the privatization of much of the state's productive assets had been completed during transformation's first eight years. Foreign investment is especially closely tied to the improved prospects of Hungary's membership in the EU. For this and for many other reasons, accession to the EU can become a new source of growth and stability, as is shown by the stellar examples of Portugal and Ireland.

There are many possible synergies between these four areas, in addition to those already mentioned. For example, there is a great deal of international experience on how governments can effectively promote backward and forward linkages between foreign investors and their domestic SME sectors.[49]

In conclusion, there are strong grounds to be optimistic about Hungary's economic future. The grounds include (1) past accomplishments, before and after transformation had begun, whose cumulative impact is to lay a solid foundation for a well-functioning democracy and market economy; (2) the background and qualifications of many of the key people who are in charge of economic strategy and foreign policy under the current government; and (3) the fact that Hungary's membership in the OECD and aspirations to join NATO and the EU are almost certain to prompt not only Hungary's current but also future governments to continue to pursue responsible domestic economic and foreign policies.

Whether Hungary's economic performance and prospects will be judged good or excellent in a few years will depend partly on economic and political conditions in Western Europe, and partly on how vigorously and consistently successive Hungarian governments will tackle the remaining economic problems identified in this essay.

Notes

I would like to thank the following individuals (without holding them responsible for interpretations and for the remaining mistakes) for their willingness to share their in-

sights in private conversation or by commenting on a draft: Ambassador Donald Blinken, Eva Ehrlich, Eva Molnar, Gabor Revesz, Gyorgy Suranyi, Rudolph Tokes, Zoltan Szemerey, and Andras Vertes.

1. For a comprehensive assessment of Hungary's economic reforms, in English, see the following works by Janos Kornai: "The Hungarian Reform Process: Visions, Hopes, Reality," *Journal of Economic Literature*, December 1986; *The Road to a Free Economy: Shifting from a Socialist System—the Example of Hungary* (New York: W. W. Norton, 1990); and *The Socialist System: The Political Economy of Communism* (Princeton: Princeton University Press, 1992); and my own studies: "Economic Reform in Hungary: From Central Planning to Regulated Market" in *East European Economies: Slow Growth in the 1980s*, vol. 3, and *Country Studies in Eastern Europe and Yugoslavia* (Washington, D.C.: U.S. Government Printing Office, 1986); "Hungary's Reform and Performance in the Kadar Era, 1956–1988," and "Hungary's Political and Economic Transformation (1988–1989) and Prospects After Kadar," both in *Pressures for Reform in the East European Economies, Compendium of Invited Papers by the Joint Economic Committee*, U.S. Congress (Washington, D.C.: U.S. Government Printing Office, 1989); "Hungary During 1988–1994: A Political Economy Assessment" in *East-Central European Economies in Transition*, Invited Papers by the Joint Economic Committee, U.S. Congress (Washington, D.C.: U.S. Government Printing Office, 1994); and the chapter on Hungary in Maurice Ernst, et al., *Transforming the Core: Restructuring Industrial Enterprises in Russia and Central Europe* (Boulder, CO: Westview Press, 1996).

2. A more accurate term than liberalization, which implies institutional change, would be that the system's directors in Hungary decided to exercise their absolute political power in a more enlightened way than in most other countries in the Soviet bloc.

3. For a detailed discussion and quantification of these debt burdens, see Janos Kornai, "Paying the Bill for Goulash-Communism," Harvard Institute for Economic Research Discussion Paper No. 1748 (February 1996).

4. If government debt were to be "funded" by printing money, the medium- and long-term consequences would be even more adverse because it would accelerate inflation.

5. The term "misdevelopment" is not meant to suggest that central planning had only undesirable outcomes. Educational attainments, certain aspects of health care, and full employment were, from the point of view of welfare, positive features.

6. The author remembers that during 1989–90, Marton Tardos, chief economic advisor of the Free Democratic Alliance Party, and co-chair of the Joint Hungarian–International Blue Ribbon Commission, was one of the few leading economists who suggested that Hungary's excess consumption should be curbed. But neither his analysis nor his recommendations gained widespread professional, much less political, support.

7. Poland's debt situation was different than Hungary's. Poland's IOUs were held mainly by Western governments and international financial institutions. A significant portion of the debt represented the accumulation of unpaid

interests on the IOUs that Poland's communist government had not been servicing since 1982. In that year, the West imposed economic sanctions on Poland, in the wake of the Soviet-inspired imposition of martial law in 1981, aimed at keeping at bay the rapidly growing Solidarity movement. By 1990, Poland's cumulative foreign debt became so large that the country was not in a position to start servicing it fully. This created a situation in which the West reasoned that it might as well get credit for forgiving a portion of the debt that, in any event, could not be paid. After several years of negotiations, Western governments and private lenders did just that, in exchange for a firm pledge that Poland's economic stabilization and transformation programs would continue.

8. This section is based on M. Ernst, M. Alexeev, and P. Marer, *Transforming the Core: Restructuring Industrial Enterprises in Russia and Central Europe* (Boulder, CO: Westview Press, 1996), chapter 8.

9. This argument is developed by Poznanski and is debated by other contributors in K. Poznanski, ed., *The Evolutionary Transition to Capitalism* (Boulder, CO: Westview Press, 1995).

10. China's transformation is *sui generis* in many ways. It has a low level of development, a highly labor-intensive mode of production, a large population with high density, and unique cultural traditions. Furthermore, China's economy was never as fully centralized as those of CEE. And, most importantly, China's communist political system did not collapse.

11. One rationale for the strictness of the bankruptcy law was the need to stop the rapid and destructive growth of enterprises becoming more and more indebted to each other—the so-called queuing problem. This made it increasingly difficult to establish the solvency of companies, thereby hindering privatization and the efficient refinancing of the banking system.

12. Csaba Forgacs, "Hungary" in D. Gale Johnson, ed., *Long-Term Agricultural Policies for Central Europe* (San Francisco: International Center for Economic Growth, 1996), 54. Whether agriculture, as well as other sectors, were net contributors to the budget is difficult to establish. Whereas the social security *contributions* of those employed in the sector are usually counted as the sector's contribution to the budget, the social security *benefits* enjoyed by the workers and their families in the sector are rarely included in the computations.

13. Foreigners are finding ways of acquiring real estate in Hungary. A favored approach is to buy farmland through a Hungarian citizen, with whom the foreign buyer signs a private contract.

14. *The Economist*, February 24, 1996, 58. As a result of the austerity program, the share of GDP redistributed by the state budget has declined since 1995.

15. If the retirement age in Hungary were the same as that of the OECD, average pension expenditures would be about 20 percent lower.

16. Louise Fox, "Can Eastern Europe's Old-Age Crisis Be Fixed?" *Finance and Development*, December 1995.

17. *Hungary: Structural Reforms for Sustainable Growth* (Washington, D.C.: The World Bank, 1995), 33.

18. For details, see *ibid*, and Janos Kornai, "The Citizen and the State: Reform of the Welfare System," Discussion Paper No. 32 of the Collegium Budapest/Institute for Advanced Study, August 1996.

19. *Hungary: Structural Reforms for Sustainable Growth* (Washington, D.C.: The World Bank, 1995), chapter III.

20. For details, see *Hungary's Welfare State in Transition: Structure, Initial Reforms, Recommendations* (Indianapolis: Hudson Institute; Policy Study no. 3 of the Joint Hungarian-International Blue Ribbon Commission, 1994).

21. *Hungary: Structural Reforms for Sustainable Growth*, 47.

22. Hence the anomaly that in spite of the high unemployment rate, foreign multinationals offering competitive wages have reportedly been unable to attract an adequate blue-collar workforce and have experienced periods of 20 percent absenteeism owing to "illness."

23. Eva Ehrlich, and Gabor Revesz, *Hungary and Its Prospects, 1985–2005* (Budapest: Akademia Publishers, 1995), chapter VI.

24. Kornai notes that while much of the rest of the economy has been transformed into a reasonably well-functioning market system, the health-care sector has remained a unique type of "market under socialism" system. For a detailed diagnosis and set of recommendations on reforming health care, see Janos Kornai, *Az egezsegugy reformjarol* [On the Reform of Health Care]. (Budapest: Kozgazdasagi es Jogi, 1998).

25. During 1997, the author chaired the Accreditation Committee of the Budapest University of Economic Sciences, giving him insights into the impressive strengths as well as shortcomings of economic-business-social science education. With respect to the content and method of higher education in these fields, greater stress needs to be placed on the *economic* potential of computers (as opposed to the *programming* of computers); effective communication; the integration of specialized perspectives; and emphasizing problem-solving skills and critical thinking.

26. For example, until 1995, large foreign investors had been granted tax holidays and other tax concessions. Large enterprises, domestic or foreign, are more likely to have the influence to work out problems with the bureaucracy and are less likely to be extorted, or to be willing to pay bribes. Also, it is generally easier for them to secure credits or to float equity, in some cases by tapping into foreign lenders (including their foreign parents) or domestic or foreign equity markets.

27. Janos Kornai, *op. cit.*

28. Janos Kornai, "The Citizen and the State: Reform of the Welfare System," Discussion Paper No. 32 of the Collegium Budapest/Institute for Advanced Study, August 1996.

29. In the Austro–Hungarian empire (as in Austria and Germany today), bureaucrats on government payroll were called "officers of the state." In Anglo–Saxon countries, they are called "public servants."

30. The government expected that continued relatively large household savings would be able to finance much of the budget deficit. But the assumption turned out to be wrong, in no small measure owing to the interest rate policies

of the Central Bank. By early 1992, the real rate of interest became unusually high: the nominal rate was around 30 to 35 percent, the consumer price index temporarily stabilized in the mid-20s range, and the producer price index around the mid-teens. This meant that businesses that could obtain credit had to pay nearly a 20 percent real rate of interest, which hindered business expansion, and thus hurt economic growth. The Central Bank then tried to push down the price of money by substantially reducing the interest it paid on government bonds. That, in turn, forced down the interest rates on household bank deposits to negative levels in real terms, which contributed to the large decline in household savings. At the same time, the real rate of interest that the banks charged to business borrowers had remained high.

31. Net debt equals gross debt minus gold, foreign exchange and other liquid reserves.

32. *Hungary: Economic Policies for Sustainable Growth,* Table 2.1, 4. The ratios refer to the consolidated central government budget without privatization proceeds. There are various ways of computing the budget deficit, hence the apparent discrepancies in statistics published by various sources.

33. The next few paragraphs are based on *Hungary: Economic Policies for Sustainable Growth,* 7–18.

34. Parliament also approved a resolution urging the government to reform the disability pension system, but a new law in this area was not expected to be passed until after the 1998 elections. The main problem with the disability pension system is that it is poorly targeted, so that people of working age receiving disability pensions represented almost 9 percent of the workforce in 1997.

35. Centralizing government finance provides real-time information and improves financial management. For example, it is now possible for the treasury to stop transfers to organizations that owe taxes to the government.

36. A voluntary third pillar (also fully funded and privately managed) has been operating since 1994.

37. The export surge can be traced to substantial improvements in unit labor costs, as the result of cuts in real wages, currency depreciation, and productivity gains.

38. That means, among other things, adequate competition; clear rights of ownership of the means of production, with ownership concentrated in the hands of those who can effectively exercise those rights; a healthy financial system; the timely and effective enforcement of contracts; and prudent market regulation.

39. To be sure, an economy's performance may not be mirrored accurately by growth rates. In a transforming economy especially, there can be periods when GDP growth rates and productivity improvements move in opposite directions. Productivity can be improved by rapid restructuring, which in turn is facilitated by privatization to real owners and by effective bankruptcy procedures. At the same time, widespread restructuring and bankruptcies hurt GDP growth rates, for a time. There is evidence that during 1993–96, productivity improvements were significantly greater, and growth slower, in Hungary than in Poland and the Czech Republic.

40. Data provided privately by Professor Istvan Hetenyi, former minister of finance.

41. See *From Plan to Market: World Development Report, 1996* (Washington, D.C.: The World Bank, 1996), 64.

42. At year-end 1996, the United States was the largest investor, with about $5.6 billion, accounting for 40 percent of all foreign direct capital inflow. Germany was in second place (24 percent), followed by Austria and Italy (around 10 percent each).

43. For a case study, see Paul Marer and Vincent Mabert, "GE Acquires and Restructures Tungsram: The First Six Years (1990–95)" in *Performance of Privatized Enterprises: Corporate Governance, Restructuring, and Profitability* (Paris: OECD, 1996).

44. *Financial Times,* December 16, 1996.

45. There are those, like Harvard Professor Jeffrey Sachs, who argue that trying to emulate Western Europe would not be a wise choice for the countries of Central and Eastern Europe because Western Europe will continue to fall behind much of Asia and the Americas in the global economic race. But even if Sach's predictions prove correct, would Hungary and its neighbors have any other choice but to integrate with the EU. Presumably, Sachs would say: "OK, but do not let your public sector become, or remain, as large as they typically are in Western Europe."

46. Since early 1996, Hungary has hosted NATO troops—the first such event for a former member of the disbanded Warsaw Pact. Hungary has been providing a large logistical base for the tens of thousands of mainly U.S. troops moving in and out of the former Yugoslavia as part of the Implementation Force (IFOR) of the Dayton Accords on reestablishing peace in the former Yugoslavia.

47. For a not-too-technical discussion of the banking system's problems and how the banks were recapitalized, see chapter 6 of M. Ernst, et al., *Transforming the Core (op. cit.)*

48. As detailed, for example, in Paul Marer, "Models of Successful Market Economies" in P. Marer and S. Zecchini, eds., *Transition to a Market Economy,* vol. I (Paris: OECD, 1992).

49. A great deal of practical work has been done in this area by the Foreign Investment Advisory Service (FIAS), a joint venture between the World Bank and the International Finance Corporation. See, for example, Joseph Y. Battat, *Increasing Backward Linkages of Foreign Investment in Developing Countries: New Opportunities and Challenges* (Washington, D.C.: FIAS, 1997).

Chapter 9

Privatization Policies

Keith Crane

Introduction

Although the transition from single-party state to multiparty democracy has had its ups and downs, the change of regime in Hungary has proceeded fairly smoothly. There was and is an overwhelming consensus in Hungary of the desirability of parliamentary democracy as a replacement for the previous regime. As shown in the chapter by John Higley, there has been a substantial amount of persistence in elites during the transition, which has limited disruption within the elite. In contrast, economic policy, especially in terms of privatization of formerly state-owned assets, has engendered neither consensus nor continuity. Privatization has proceeded in fits and starts because of political pressures. Economic transition, including asset transfers, has resulted in the wholesale disruption of the lives of Hungarian citizens.

In this chapter, I assess the effectiveness of a key set of economic policies, those used to privatize formerly state-owned assets. I evaluate Hungary's privatization policies since 1990 both in relation to the goals of the privatizers and in comparison with two other Central European countries in transition most often compared with Hungary: the Czech Republic and Poland. The first task is somewhat unwieldy as Hungarian privatization policy, although to a lesser extent, goals have been repeatedly changed over the last six years, often even by the same government. Consequently, rather than attempting to trace the conurbations of the various policies adopted over time, I will attempt to evaluate progress to date in relation to the overarching privatization policy goals of the last two governments: the Antall-Boross government that was elected in 1990 and the Horn government, elected in 1994.

The second task, comparing Hungary's progress on privatization with that of other Central European countries in transition, demands a more universal objective for evaluating performance. Each of the governments of the Central European countries in transition has set its own (changing) goals for privatization. To compare each country's performance against the varying goals of the various governments is less than informative. In this section of the chapter, I will compare performance in terms of changes in the share of GDP produced by private-sector activity, the share of state-owned assets transferred to the private sector, and the creation of new companies. I will also comment qualitatively in terms of changes in corporate governance.

Privatization, defined broadly, consists of the transfer of economic activity from state-owned enterprises to privately owned firms. Much of this process occurs spontaneously without the explicit transfer of state-owned assets. Increasing output of private firms during a period of declining output by state-owned firms naturally leads to a larger role for the private sector. Nowhere has the process been more apparent than in Poland where the government has been a relative laggard in the privatization of state-owned assets, but the private sector has been one of the most dynamic in the region. The number of employees in the private sector soared from 7,902,000 in 1990, mostly in agriculture, to 10,074,900 in 1996. The key to private-sector expansion includes the creation of an environment conducive to private-sector activity. Although this essay will not provide a detailed evaluation of Hungary's or its neighbors' performance in this area, it will comment upon Hungary's performance in the overall evaluation of privatization.

Privatization, defined more narrowly, consists of the transfer of state-owned assets to the private sector. In some instances, the process also involves transferring collectively or cooperatively owned assets to private hands. Governments devise privatization programs to attain this goal. Below, I compare Hungarian performance in transferring state-owned assets to private hands with the progress of the Czech Republic and Poland. The metric used here is the number of companies transferred as a share of the total and the share of total state assets transferred as a share of the total.

Privatization Goals

Although there have been a number of changes in Hungarian privatization policies, the overarching policy goals have been remarkably constant across the Antall-Boross government and the Horn government. The last pretransition socialist government also ascribed to a

number of the policy goals that have continued to mark Hungarian privatization policy.
The major policy goals include:

(1) The rapid transfer of state-owned assets to the private sector, with the recent goal of disposing of virtually all state-owned assets designated for privatization by the end of 1998.
(2) The disposal of the bulk of assets through sales rather than through transfers.
(3) Compensation to individuals or their descendants unjustly deprived of property by post-World War II Hungarian governments through the partial restoration of previously owned property or the provision of other assets. In most instances, compensation was to be partial, not total.
(4) The use of privatization to attract inflows of foreign capital, technology, and management and marketing skills.
(5) The maintenance of state control or veto power over the decisions of strategic companies or industries.
(6) The use of privatization to develop Hungarian capital markets.
(7) The use of privatization to sharpen domestic competition.

Aside from the provision on restitution that focused on equity concerns and state vetoes on decisions of strategic privatized firms that were introduced because of considerations of national security, the thrust of privatization policy has been to improve economic efficiency so as to accelerate growth and improve consumer welfare.[1]

Institutions Responsible for Privatization

Although the goals of successive Hungarian governments for privatization have been fairly constant, institutional structures and policies have changed dramatically over time. The first organization to be created was the State Property Agency (SPA). This agency was initially assigned the responsibility for privatizing state-owned enterprises. However, it acted as an agency; it did not own the properties to be privatized. The SPA was primarily focused on enterprises; it did not handle the privatization of housing or farmland.[2]

On October 29, 1992, the Hungarian government created the Hungarian State Holding Company (AV Rt.) This company was given the task of holding shares in large state-owned enterprises, supervising these enterprises as long as they remain under state ownership, and organizing the sale of those companies that the government had decided to sell. The company was designed to mitigate some of the inadequacies of the SPA. Most importantly, the AV Rt. was created as a company. Consequently, it was able to legally own the companies it was to privatize as opposed to just arranging for their sale. It also had the authority to ensure the companies were managed in an efficient manner prior to privatization.[3]

The Socialist–Free Democratic government that came to power in 1994 further restructured the institutions responsible for privatization. It consolidated the SPA and AV Rt. into a new company, the Hungarian Privatization and State Holding Company (APV Rt.). The company also incorporated the Treasury Asset Management Corporation (KVSZ) which managed companies and assets owned by the Ministry of Finance. The new government felt that it could accelerate privatization and improve efficiency by consolidating privatization activities into one institution.[4] The APV Rt. was given a renewed mandate to rapidly privatize most of the remaining state-owned companies (with the exception of a few strategic enterprises). It also supervises these companies until they are in private hands.

Privatization Policies

Within the context of these goals, the various privatization policies adopted by the Hungarian government have been dictated by the type of asset to be privatized. For ease of discussion, these can be divided into four types:

1. Residential property
2. Farmland and farms
3. Small state-owned enterprises
4. Large state-owned enterprises

Hungarian governments have adopted five main mechanisms for privatizing these assets: auctions, trade sales, initial public offerings, compensation vouchers, and subsidized credits. In a number of instances, a variety of mechanisms have been employed to privatize similar assets.

Programs for Privatizing Residential Property. Although the privatization of residential property often meets with little discussion in the press or by economists, this facet of privatization probably directly affects the lives of more citizens in transition economies than any other privatization policy.[5]

Before the transition, Hungary had one of the highest shares of private ownership of residential property within the former Soviet bloc. Rural families had traditionally owned their own homes, in many cases, they built their houses themselves. Since the late 1960s, the government had used housing cooperatives, organizations through which households pooled funds to build apartment complexes for themselves, as the primary institution for providing urban housing in Hungary. Although these organizations benefited from state loan subsidies as well as artificially low prices for some building materials, Hungarian households generally were forced to purchase their own housing. On the eve of the transition, 77 percent of Hungarian households owned their own homes outright or had purchased apartments through cooperatives. Consequently, the privatization of housing has been less of an issue in Hungary than it has been in countries like former Czechoslovakia, Romania, or even Kazakhstan where urban housing tended to be owned by the state or municipalities.

Since the transition, Hungarian government policies have served to further increase the share of private housing in the total. The two major policies used to pursue this goal have been programs to compensate individuals unjustly deprived of housing by the communist regime and a program of direct sales of housing, primarily to current occupants. A number of other policies have also resulted in greater private ownership.

A key means of privatizing residential property was the restitution law, passed in 1991. The law permitted past owners of property expropriated by the communist state to receive limited restitution for their losses in the form of vouchers that could be used to buy property such as housing, shops, agricultural land, a government annuity, or shares in privatized state-owned enterprises. The program gave similar rights to nonresident foreigners as to Hungarian citizens. By the end of April 1992, 830,000 people had submitted claims for compensation coupons for a total value of 60 billion forints. Half the awards were worth less than 30,000 forints ($400) and 34 percent were worth less than 500,000 forints ($6,250). After the awards were distributed, a market in vouchers developed as the government has permitted them to be bought and sold. Both Hungarian nationals and foreigners are permitted to buy coupons on the secondary market.

Vouchers have played an important role in privatization of housing. They were used as partial payment to buy 500,000–600,000 apartment units offered by municipalities for the program. However, the new owners faced a number of strictures on the use of their new property. Eviction of current residents is very difficult and some controls remain concerning the rents that can be charged current residents.

Municipalities have also offered units for sale to current occupants.

The units were purposely sold at advantageous terms, prices were set at roughly 20 to 24 percent of the market value of the units. This program was designed to reduce maintenance obligations of the local governments and to generate voter gratitude through the transfer of valuable assets. In addition, very generous financing terms were offered. Households only had to put up 10 percent of the purchase price and were permitted to pay for the remainder owed on the unit over 35 years; nominal interest rates were set at 3 percent. In addition, purchasers who paid the full price in cash received a 40 percent discount on the purchase price. Housing privatization has been considered a fairly successful program, but as municipal housing often accounted for less than 20 percent of the total urban housing stock in most cities, this program has not altered ownership structures as much as similar programs elsewhere in the region.

Changes in other programs have had major indirect effects on housing ownership. In the early 1990s, the government attempted to reduce the cost of interest rate subsidies on home mortgages by offering mortgage holders an option of early payoff or new mortgages at higher interest rates. A large number of Hungarian citizens took this opportunity to complete the purchase of their apartments. A sharp fall-off in government financing for new municipal apartments is also leading towards greater private-sector ownership of the housing stock. In 1995, 89 percent of housing construction was undertaken by private individuals while less than one percent was undertaken by the state or municipal governments. In 1989, the percentages were 68 percent and 31 percent, respectively. (The remainder of housing projects were undertaken by companies, primarily for employees.)

Programs for Privatizing Farmland and Farms. Programs to privatize farmland and farms have been pursued on a similar basis as residential property: past owners of land or their descendants, if unjustly deprived of their holdings, have been partially compensated through compensation vouchers which they have been permitted to use to bid for parcels of land. However, they were not given the right to regain possession of the exact parcel of which they had been deprived. The government created a series of compensation offices in each of Hungary's counties to adjudicate claims for compensation vouchers and to issue vouchers. Subsequently, these offices were used to conduct auctions for land to be paid for with privatization vouchers.

In addition to restitution, land privatization has also been geared towards providing for current employees of state-owned farms and cooperatives. These individuals have been given formal ownership rights in either the farms or farmland. State farms were generally converted into joint stock companies in which former employees were granted shares. However, many of these farms had to offer some land for the restitution program. Members of collectives have been given parcels of land. The collectives themselves have frequently not been dissolved. Rather, they have been transformed into joint stock companies or true cooperatives and have taken over the task of leasing and farming the land given to new owners. Most continue to own some land in common as well. As many owners tend to be elderly widows, cooperatives remain the major corporate entities farming Hungarian land, at least for field crops such as wheat and corn. The new private farmers have focussed more on truck farming, viticulture, and livestock operations.

Programs for Privatizing Small Businesses. The primary programs for privatizing smaller, state-owned companies have been auctions and management and employee buy-outs. The former socialist government began a program of leasing and sales of businesses through auctions in the 1980s. This program was expanded after the transition. In general, municipalities organized local auctions through which groups or individuals could bid for local businesses. The transfer of ownership has generally proceeded swiftly and fairly smoothly. In many cases, the new businesses leased rather than purchased the premises. Arguments between the State Property Agency, municipalities, and the major occupants of the buildings sometimes slowed sales of businesses in the early 1990s. These have since been resolved and sales of small businesses have been virtually completed.

In the late 1980s and early 1990s, some companies, primarily smaller, state-owned operations, were privatized through "spontaneous privatization." Usually the management would set up a private company or collude with outside investors to offer to buy the company or its best assets. Prior to the creation of the State Property Agency and the passage of more stringent privatization laws, the company management could then select the "winning" bidder and thereby privatize the company. The government responded by sharply curbing the independence of the enterprises to initiate privatization proceedings so as to curb these practices.

The government found, however, that, although it could curb overt privatization by insiders, smaller companies that remained in state hands were losing value. Some managers were able to exploit the inability of the State Property Agency to properly oversee their activities, allowing them to siphon off profits into ancillary businesses that they owned. Others were simply not making the necessary effort to restructure the business because they lacked the authority or incentives to design and implement a full restructuring program.

Consequently, after an initial hiatus, the government passed a law in June 1992 to set up a legal framework facilitating employee buy-outs under employee stock ownership programs (ESOP). Under the new law, if a quarter of the employees in a company initiated proceedings to buy the company and 40 percent of the workers supported the transaction, the State Property Agency could sell the company to the employees. Employees could deduct 60 percent of the investment from their taxable income and the company received a 20 percent tax exemption. More than 130 companies initiated proceedings to privatize themselves in this manner. The most famous instance was the purchase of the Herend Porcelain Factory, a producer of high-quality ceramics, by its employees in July 1993.

This and other independent privatization programs were modified by the Socialist–Free Democratic government that came to power in 1994.[6] In 1995, the new government set up a program to accelerate the privatization of smaller companies. The program, self-privatization, is somewhat similar to those of the past. Enterprises of less than 600 million forints in equity and which employ fewer than 500 people are permitted to design their own privatization programs. The programs must be in accordance with the law, most notably, the company must publicly announce its plans. In general, the company should employ a consultant certified by the government to help devise the plan. Once the plan is devised, any investor who pays at least book value for the company is entitled to purchase it. The company must submit its proposals to the APV Rt. and must inform the APV Rt. which offer is most advantageous, if multiple offers are received. In short, the new program gives enterprises the freedom to devise their own privatization programs, but they are subject to review by the responsible government organ, the APV Rt.

The program also provides incentives for managers and employees to purchase the company. These groups can use noncash techniques such as vouchers to purchase the company or can lease assets rather than purchase the enterprise outright. In some instances, if these groups purchase a majority stake in the company, the government has the authority to give them its remaining stake in the company.

These self-privatization programs are not designed solely to facilitate management or employee buy-outs. Under the previous government, the State Property Agency permitted potential outside investors to trigger the privatization of a company. If an investor expressed interest in acquiring a company, the State Property Agency had to prepare it for privatization. If no other investor expressed an interest and the offer was above the valuation of the company ascribed by evaluators chosen by the State Property Agency, the investor was entitled to buy the property. Under the 1995 program, an outside bidder can also help force privatization, if his offer exceeds the book value of the company.

Programs for Privatizing Large State-Owned Enterprises. Since the first transition government, the primary strategy of the Hungarian government for privatizing state-owned enterprises has been to sell, rather than give them away. With the exception of the Smallholders' Party, all of Hungary's major political parties, in and out of power, have supported this principle. In fact, the privatization strategy adopted by the Socialist–Free Democrat coalition that came to power in 1994 has reemphasized the state's goal of maximizing net revenues from privatizing state-owned assets. This policy has been in sharp contrast to that of other countries in transition, such as the Czech Republic and Russia, where assets have been given to citizens for a nominal charge or free.

Successive Hungarian governments have stated that by selling, rather than giving away, assets, they will be able to attract private owners with a genuine interest in improving the efficiency of privatized Hungarian companies. Furthermore, because of Hungary's relatively high level of indebtedness the governments have felt, justifiably, that they could not afford to privatize assets without receiving a corresponding flow of income to pay down government debt, much of which was incurred to finance past investments in the companies to be privatized. Substantial inflows of foreign investment derived from sales of state-owned assets have also helped support Hungary's balance of payments. The government has also needed the proceeds from asset sales to finance budget deficits, which have been fairly substantial over the past five years.

Initially, most sales of state-owned enterprises were trade sales, sales of a controlling interest in an enterprise to one purchaser, often a foreign company. The Hungarian government has usually hired a reputable international investment bank to conduct a closed auction for the company. The bank issues a tender, evaluates the initial bids in conjunction with Hungarian privatization agencies, and then proceeds with final negotiations of the sale.

Since the Horn government has come to power, it has renewed its attempts to develop local capital markets through greater use of initial public offerings. Only in the last four years have initial public offerings become a major method of privatization. Over the past year, public offerings of stakes in major chemical, pharmaceutical, manufacturing, and energy companies and banks have been issued on both the Budapest Exchange and international exchanges.

In an effort to finish compensating holders of restitution vouchers, the government is using public offerings of stock to compensate voucher holders. Blocks of shares, ranging from 10 to 12 percent of some companies, have been reserved for voucher holders. Holders can cash in their vouchers at the offer price.[7]

Although trade sales and initial public offerings are the primary programs for privatizing larger, state-owned enterprises, the APV Rt. and its predecessors have taken a number of other approaches to privatizing enterprises. Although less common at present, a number of Hungarian companies have created joint ventures with foreign companies. In joint ventures, a new company is created in which the state-owned firm owns a stake and the foreign firm the rest. The state-owned firm generally provides the assets and the foreign firm capital, technologies, or markets. The new joint venture is essentially a private firm partially owned by the state.

The Hungarian government has also used liquidation to transfer assets from the state to the private sector. Hungary has pursued bankruptcy of state-owned enterprises more aggressively than any other country in the region.[8] As a consequence of these bankruptcies, the State Property Agency liquidated and then sold the assets of 332 state-owned enterprises. It and its successor, the APV Rt., launched liquidation proceedings against an additional 120 state-owned corporations. These companies have been restructured and some of their assets sold. Foreign and domestic investors have bid for the assets that have been sold after liquidations. Restitution vouchers are accepted in liquidation proceedings as well.

The previous government set up concessional leasing arrangements and loan facilities for Hungarians in order to foster domestic ownership of assets. The policy of providing concessions to domestic investors was initiated in late 1992. The centerpiece of the new policy was a new loan program through which individual Hungarian citizens could borrow to purchase shares in companies to be privatized. These credits were known as E-credits. Citizens could pay 2 percent of the face value of the loan in cash. They would then be given credit vouchers that could be used to purchase shares in companies to be privatized. The credits were to be repaid with interest over 10–15 years. The credits were expected to be financed from dividends and capital gains on the shares. If the companies did not generate sufficient earnings, the shares would be returned to the government.

Hungarian domestic investors responded favorably to the program. In December 1992, the government floated part of Danubius, the Hungarian hotel chain, for 2 billion forints. Through the new loan program, Hungarian citizens were able to obtain interest-free loans for six months to cover 40 percent of the purchase price and long-term loans to cover 50 percent. Not surprisingly, Hungarian investors purchased the entire issue. This program has been effectively eliminated by the Horn government.

The Effectiveness of Hungary's Privatization Programs

Thus far, I have focussed on explaining the goals of the Hungarian government for its privatization policies and the programs it has adopted to pursue these goals. Eight years on, how well have these programs served to achieve these goals?

The most frequently used statistics to measure the effectiveness of a privatization program have been changes in the share of GDP produced by the private sector and the share of state-owned productive assets (i.e., state-owned assets excluding military bases, educational and medical facilities, roads, government buildings, etc.) transferred to the private sector. The first measure corresponds to the broad definition of privatization: the transfer of economic activity from state-owned enterprises to privately owned firms. The second attempts to measure performance according to the more restrictive definition of privatization: the transfer of state-owned assets to the private sector.

According to the first definition, Hungary's performance so far has been superior or equal to that of the Czech Republic and Poland. In 1994, private enterprises produced 60.4 percent of Hungarian GDP.[9] After the large privatizations in the chemical, energy, and banking sectors of 1995 and continued progress on agricultural privatization, as of 1998, over 75 percent of GDP is now probably produced by the private sector. This compares with official Czech figures of 56.3 percent for 1994 and over 75 percent in 1997.[10] The nonstate sector contribution to Polish GDP in 1994 was 60.1 percent and had risen to only 65.7 percent in 1996.[11] The nonstate sector contribution to GDP in Poland currently lags that of the Czech Republic and Hungary because of the slower pace in privatization of state-owned assets in Poland.

According to official Polish statistics, the state's share of productive assets had only fallen from 65.3 percent in 1990 to 62.0 percent in 1996. This seems a modest decline and reflects the slower pace of privatization of large, state-owned enterprises than in the other two countries. In Hungary, state ownership of tangible assets had fallen from over 70 percent in the early 1990s to 41 percent in 1995, and then fell sharply thereafter. The APV Rt. reports that by the end of 1997 the government sold over 70 percent of the remaining state-owned productive assets. Less than 30 percent of productive assets owned by state are to remain in state hands after privatization is completed. Based on these figures, over 85 percent of Hungary's productive capital stock should be in private hands by the end of 1997. In the Czech Republic, the share of state-owned and municipally owned in tangible assets has fallen from 77.3 percent in 1992 to 23.9 percent in 1996. Companies classified as strategic state holdings in the Czech Republic accounted for 20 percent of employment and 21 percent of output in 1994, suggesting that ultimately the state may retain a greater share of productive assets in the Czech Republic than in Hungary.[12]

Because it is difficult to measure the capital stock of a country and hence the change in ownership of this stock, a better evaluation of Hungary's progress on privatization involves assessing progress in the privatization within the four types of assets discussed above: residential housing, agricultural land and farms, small businesses, and large, state-owned enterprises.

Residential Property. The privatization of residential property has been generally successful, although it has not affected as many households as in other countries in transition because so much of the housing stock was already privately or cooperatively owned. Between 1990 and 1994, 360,024 municipally or government-owned housing units were sold to private individuals in Hungary. Sales continued through 1996, resulting in the transfer of an additional 193,000 units to private ownership. In the aftermath of this program, the number of units under municipal management fell from 838,000 in 1990 to 285,000 in 1996. Government ownership of the housing stock dropped from 22.7 percent in 1990 to 8.2 percent in 1996.[13]

Although I was unable to find similar figures for the other countries, Hungary's performance in privatizing housing is at least as good, if not better, than that of the Czech Republic and Poland. A high percentage of the housing stock is in private hands; the government-owned housing stock has been almost halved through subsidized sales of housing, primarily to current residents. Sales average one-quarter of the market value of these units.

Policies concerning privatization of housing have been fairly similar in all three countries. Recognizing that current residents have substantial implicit property rights, all three governments have adopted programs through which current tenants can purchase their current dwellings for below-market prices. In the Czech Republic and Hungary, the governments have recognized the rights of former owners by passing restitution laws. Poland has yet to take this step; however, both governments have discouraged settling restitution claims when current tenants have to be evicted.

In general, the privatization of state- or municipally owned housing

has been perceived as beneficial. In all three countries, sales of municipally owned housing has contributed to the creation of a basis for a
real estate market. The new owners generally have been pleased to
gain title and many have begun substantial renovation projects. The
municipalities have also been relieved of some responsibility for re-
pairs. Popular opposition to the transfer of ownership has been muted,
as most voters believe that current occupants deserve the right to purchase their dwellings. Citizens also appear to accept that restitution is
just.

The down side of current policies is that housing programs for the
poor have virtually halted in Hungary (as well as in the other two countries). In 1995, only 24,718 units of housing were constructed in Hungary compared to 51,487 in 1989 and 43,771 in 1990. Similar declines in
housing construction have been experienced by the Czech Republic
and Poland. Housing construction in Poland fell from 567,300 in 1990
to 276,000 in 1995. In the Czech Republic, construction fell from 55,073
in 1989 and 44,594 units in 1990 to 18,162 units in 1994. In Hungary, of
the units constructed in 1995, private citizens accounted for 91.4 percent. In 1990, this figure was 71.5 percent. Although the major culprit
causing the collapse in housing construction is probably high nominal
interest rates caused by high inflation rates, the lack of government
support for municipal housing programs has probably also contributed to the fall.

Farms and Farmland. Hungary has made progress on privatizing agricultural land, but even in 1996 49 percent of agricultural land was still
owned by cooperatives or corporations, the successors to the former
collectives and state farms. However, these figures are in marked contrast to those for 1990 or even 1992 when cooperative and corporate
land holdings still ran 86.1 and 75.6 percent, respectively. In the Czech
Republic, land use by state and cooperatives farms has fallen from over
97 percent in 1991 to 57 percent in 1994. In Poland, the share of arable
land held by state farms and cooperatives fell from 22.8 percent in 1990
to 9.4 percent in 1996.

Hungary's agricultural land privatization programs suffered a number of problems initially. Restitution claimants frequently found that
valid claims greatly exceeded the land made available for restitution.
Questions concerning title led to some land lying fallow in the early
part of the decade, reducing the size of the harvest. The Hungarian
press has complained of declines in agricultural efficiency as equipment purchased to operate on the large fields characteristic of collective farms is poorly adapted to working smaller private farms. Large
livestock operations have frequently been dissolved. The disappear-

ance of these operations has made it more difficult to apply modern livestock management techniques. New private farmers have often found it difficult to procure agricultural inputs because of the absence of credit systems and wholesalers committed to serving smaller farmers. Part of the efficiency losses appear to be due to the pace of privatization rather than the actual change in ownership structure. Once title has been transferred, the new farmers are able to tap credit and reorganize production so as to regain some of the efficiency losses.

The Czech Republic struggled with many of the same problems as the Hungarians. Most land is still farmed by large units as the new owners, like in Hungary, are often elderly widows who have no desire to start farming. However, title transfers appear to have gone more quickly than in Hungary with virtually all land now nominally owned by private owners.[14] Because Polish agriculture was dominated by private farms even under socialism, privatization has had less of an impact on production, except in meat and grain in which some of the larger units specialized. Privatization has also occurred more smoothly as most of the few cooperative farms that existed were generally dissolved and assets distributed among the members. Most of the state farms, which were primarily in areas that were taken from Germany after World War II, have been auctioned off. Nonetheless, Polish agriculture has suffered many of the same costs of adjusting to a market system as have the Czechs and Hungarians, even though most land was privately owned.

Small Businesses. Mechanisms for privatizing small businesses have been similar in the three countries. The programs have been successful in all three cases, although Hungary appears to have had somewhat more difficulty in auctioning off small firms, in part because of disagreements between municipal governments and national agencies concerning who was to receive the proceeds from sales. Auctions in Hungary have also been hampered at times by government pressure to obtain at least book value for the auctioned firms. Nonetheless, sales of small businesses have proceeded quickly and relatively smoothly in all three countries. Not surprisingly, the results have been similar. Virtually 100 percent of small formerly state or municipally owned businesses are now in private hands in all three countries.

In the Czech Republic, small-scale privatization was, for the most part, completed by the end of 1992, with about 22,000 small enterprises sold. In some cases, the right to lease has been auctioned, but in most cases the new owners buy the entire business. However, the business frequently continues to rent or lease space from the municipality or other owner of the building in which it is located. Poland also engaged in auctions, but these were conducted by municipal governments, as the privatization ministry transferred ownership to municipalities in 1990 with a mandate to sell these businesses.

I have not obtained information on the total number of small businesses auctioned or sold during the transition in Hungary. However, statistics are available on the number of sole proprietorships and limited liability companies. Hungary has experienced an explosion in the number of small businesses and sole proprietorships since the transition. In Hungary, the number of sole proprietorships, a corporate form permitted under the former system, has risen from 320,619 in 1989 to 745,247 in 1997. The number of limited partnerships has exploded, rising from 5,789 in 1990 to 67,301 in 1993 to 117,013 at the end of 1997. This corporate form is a favored means of investing. The number of incorporated companies has risen from 18,963 in 1990 to 121,418 at the end of 1997. Nonprofit institutions have also emerged as a new corporate form; they numbered 50,601 in 1996 from zero in 1989.

The experiences of the Czech Republic and Poland are similar. In the Czech Republic, the number of incorporated businesses has risen from 43 as of December 31, 1989, to 130,626 as of December 31, 1996. For the same dates the numbers of sole proprietorships rose from zero to 1,103,732. As can be seen from the numbers, prior to 1990, private-sector activity was extremely limited in the Czech Republic. In Poland, the number of corporations has soared from 53,771 in 1991 to 115,739 in 1996. Poland, like Hungary, was more receptive to small private-sector activity prior to the transition.

In short, the policies of all three countries concerning the privatization and creation of small businesses appear to have been successful. Virtually all small, state-owned or municipally owned businesses have been sold in all three countries and the number of small businesses and corporations has risen very rapidly.

Larger, State-owned Enterprises. The greatest privatization policy differences among the three countries have been in privatization of large, state-owned companies. Here very distinct alternatives have been chosen by the different governments. The Czech Republic has adopted a voucher privatization scheme. This scheme was designed to rapidly privatize a large share of the state-owned sector through the disbursal of shares to the population for a nominal fee. Poland has sold some large companies through trade sales and initial public offerings. Other, smaller companies have been sold through management or employee buy-outs, a procedure also popular in Hungary. Poland's mass privatization scheme was implemented in 1995. In contrast to the Czech program, Poland's mass privatization program only includes 514 companies, a large, but not predominant share of the remaining state-owned assets. Since 1996, Poland has increasingly relied on initial public offerings for sales of large companies.

Despite the policy differences between the Hungarian and Czech approaches, the difference in results in terms of the share of the economy privatized and the share of GDP produced by the private sector as of early 1998 are not striking. The two countries are remarkably similar in terms of numbers of companies privatized, the value of privatized assets, and decisions concerning companies to remain under state ownership. Of 1,857 state-owned enterprises assigned to Hungary's privatization agencies in 1990, by 1996, 829 had been fully privatized and 642 had been liquidated or closed. Of the remaining 596 companies, 311 had more than a 50 percent state-ownership stake; the state owned less than 50 percent of the remaining 285. (Total figures exceed the 1990 figure of 1,857 state-owned enterprises assigned to privatization agencies because some enterprises were split into multiple entities during the privatization process.) By early 1998, only 116 companies remained entirely in state hands (and are to remain so) and an additional 200 to 250 are awaiting further sales of state-owned shares. Remaining state-owned enterprises are to include the railroads, the post office, some research institutes, and selected other companies. The government also maintains veto rights in strategic companies, such as utilities, through golden shares. State assets privatized in Hungary are likely to total roughly $19 billion (This figure was calculated by adding estimates of the value of assets privatized through the end of 1993 to a $14.8 billion estimate of the value of assets privatized between 1994 and 1998.)[15]

Initially, the Czech Republic moved faster than Hungary to privatize large, state-owned enterprises. In the first wave of voucher privatization; about 1,000 companies were privatized; in the second wave, about 900, and in the third and last wave, 320 companies. Assets privatized ran close to $26 billion in book value.[16] According to the Czech National Property Fund, 78 percent of the property and 68 percent of the shares in businesses earmarked for privatization through voucher privatization and other means had been sold by mid-1996. The Fund more or less completed its activities by mid-1997. Like the Hungarians, the Czechs have limited stakes in continued state ownership to a very few firms. The government holds a controlling stake in the electric power utility. As in Hungary, the railroad and the post office are likely to remain in state hands.

In both countries a few companies remain state enterprises, a corporate form from the pretransition days. The state enterprise has a somewhat nebulous legal identity. Although it generated a type of income statement in the pretransition days, it did not really have a balance sheet. Control of the state enterprise was lodged in a designated branch ministry, but ownership was somewhat amorphous. One of the major successes of Hungary's privatization policies has been the reduction in the numbers, role, and importance of state enterprises. In Hungary, the number of state-owned enterprises declined from 2,233 in 1991 to 761 in 1995. Most major state enterprises have been converted into joint stock companies; the 761 state enterprises that remained in 1995 tended to be smaller, virtually bankrupt entities that have since been liquidated or privatized. In the Czech Republic, 1,886 state-owned enterprises remained at the beginning of 1997, compared to 3,818 in early 1991. Most of these enterprises have since been converted into joint stock companies or are being liquidated.

The major differences between the ownership structure of the Czech and Hungarian economies at this point in time is in the banking sector and the distribution of shares. The Hungarian government has all but completed the process of privatizing the state-owned banks; the banking system is almost entirely in private hands. All major banks have already been privatized through trade sales or initial public offerings. Controlling interests in the four largest commercial banks have been sold to foreign investors through trade sales. In the Czech Republic, the government continues to hold controlling stakes in the largest banks, although the 1997 drop in the exchange rate of the koruna revealed a number of banking problems and has forced more sales. Although additional stakes are to be sold, in the interim they provide the government with a great deal of control over the economy.

The Czech banks' influence over the economy is not just due to their ability to extend or withhold credit. The Czech banks also control a very large number of shares in nonfinancial companies in the Czech Republic. Over 70 percent of Czech company shares are held through investment funds. Almost all the largest funds are run by the large commercial banks. Consequently, the banks have great influence on Czech companies through their control of these funds.

In contrast, over two-thirds of the assets in large, formerly state-owned Hungarian companies have been sold to foreign companies. Hungarian banks therefore do not have the corporate control of the Czech banks.

Poland has definitely been the odd man out in privatization of large, state-owned enterprises. In contrast to the Czech Republic and Hungary, a very large share of industrial assets remain in this form. Although the number of state enterprises has dropped from more than 10,000 in the late 1980s to 8,228 in 1991, as of 1996, 3,847 of these entities continued to exist. As noted above, state ownership continues to dominate in a number of industries, including coal, ferrous metals, and some machinery producers. As a result, the share of state-owned assets in total productive assets in Poland had only fallen from 65.3 percent in 1990 to 62.0 percent in 1996. The privatization of most large companies in Hungary and the Czech Republic over the last two years suggest that state ownership runs substantially less than half the 1994 Polish levels.

Conclusion

As of 1998, Hungarian privatization policies appear to have been remarkably successful. The most consistently successful policies have probably been in the privatization of small businesses. This process is virtually complete. Privatization of housing was less momentous than elsewhere because such a large share of the housing stock was privately owned before the transition. However, two-thirds of the municipal housing stock was privatized between 1990 and 1996. A substantial share of agricultural land has also been privatized. By 1996, 51 percent of agricultural land was privately held, although cooperatives and collectives continued to farm most land. Over the past three years, the country has also been successful in privatizing large, state-owned enterprises. Of 1,857 state-owned enterprises assigned to Hungary's privatization agencies in 1990, by early 1998 virtually all except a remnant that will always stay in state hands had been privatized; all the enterprises slated for privatization should have been sold by the end of 1998. As of 1998, well over 75 percent of Hungarian GDP is produced by the private sector.

The policy goals enunciated by the government appear to have been well served by privatization. Privatization has raised substantial sums for the budget and permitted Hungary to pay down a substantial share of the debt owed by its government to foreign lenders. Hungarian privatization has helped attract over $12 billion in direct foreign investment. This investment has been accompanied by an inflow of managerial know-how, technology, and marketing expertise. Anecdotal evidence indicates that privatization has improved efficiency in privatized firms. In short, by the criteria of the Hungarian government, privatization over the past few years has been a success.

Although Hungary's privatization policies for large, state-owned enterprises have been diametrically opposed to those in the Czech Republic, by 1996 the results did not differ greatly. Although the Czech voucher program did lead to more rapid privatization of large, state-owned enterprises, the end result was similar. The Czechs had privatized substantially more by early 1995 when the second wave of voucher privatization was completed. The Czechs may have privatized a slightly higher share of state enterprise assets than the Hungarians as of mid-1996, but the Czechs had not yet relinquished government control over the major banks. Like the Hungarians, the Czechs intend to finish selling off remaining state-owned stakes in most companies shortly, in their case by the end of 1998.

Policies for selling small state-owned businesses have been similar, as have been the results. Hungary and the Czech Republic have encountered similar problems in privatizing agricultural land. They have been slow to distribute land titles. Both have attempted to keep the state and cooperative farms operating as single units, even though land ownership has been dispersed.

The major difference between the Czech and Hungarian experiences is in share ownership. Voucher privatization in the Czech Republic has resulted in diffuse share ownership with control concentrated in investment funds, which in turn are dominated by the larger commercial banks, most of which remain under state control. In contrast, the largest share of assets in large, state-owned enterprises has in the case of Hungary ended up in foreign hands. Based on the results to date, especially the serious financial-sector problems that emerged in 1997 in the Czech Republic, corporate governance has been better in Hungary than in the Czech Republic because of the dominance of capable, interested owners in corporate decision making.

Polish privatization strategies have differed from those in the Czech Republic and Hungary. Restitution has played a smaller role because, for political reasons, successive governments had great difficulty in passing the necessary legislation. Privatization of agricultural land has been less important because of the large share of private land in pre-transition Poland. Privatization of housing and small businesses has proceeded similarly to privatization of these assets in Hungary and the Czech Republic. The biggest difference in policies has been in the commitment to privatizing large, state-owned enterprises. Although Poland has employed trade sales and initial public offerings and a mass privatization program somewhat akin to the Czech Republic's, a much larger share of productive assets remain in state hands in Poland than in the other two countries. Furthermore, the timetable for completing privatization in Poland is stretching out far longer than in the other two countries.

In short, all three countries have performed relatively well in terms of privatizing residential property, small businesses, and farmland. After a number of hesitations, Hungarian privatization policies for the sale of large, state-owned enterprises have succeeded as well as those of the Czech Republic and been more successful than those in Poland in terms of speed and the percent of state-owned assets sold. This conclusion is at odds with most assessments at the early stages of the transition. With the notable exception of Janos Kornai, many well-known economists heavily engaged in the transition have argued that the only way to quickly transfer assets from the state to the private sector would be through voucher schemes.[17] In hindsight, the political problems associated with voucher programs appear to have often been as great as those associated with trade sales. At least for smaller economies, the key to privatization of large, state-owned companies has been political will, not the type of program adopted.

The other privatization success in all three countries has been the speed with which smaller companies have been privatized. Commentators in 1990 frequently noted that Great Britain had taken over a decade to privatize a much smaller share of its economy than East European reformers were hoping to privatize in half the time. Despite this skepticism, privatization has proceeded relatively quickly. The key to rapid privatization has been the willingness of governments to permit managers and workers to obtain state-owned property quickly, often at prices below those that might have been obtained through a more open process. Even in the Czech Republic, privatization has resulted in a large number of employee and management buy-outs. Policy-makers appear to have made the implicit decision to permit current managers and workers to obtain control of their own enterprises because they recognized that privatization in the face of opposition from these groups would have been extremely difficult, if not impossible. This policy also recognized implicit property rights, which in some cases were seen as socially just. On a darker note, the policy also recognized the relative sources of political and economic power in the transition states, as underlined in John Higley's chapter in this volume. Whether this approach is ultimately judged as having been morally appropriate is an open question. However, it has served to speed the process of privatization throughout the region.

Despite their successes, Hungarian privatization policy-makers in the past two governments can be rightly criticized for delaying the process of privatization. Both post-transition governments appeared to have let privatization slide for long periods as they reorganized agencies or fought internal battles concerning assets to be privatized. It is difficult to believe that the large enterprises remaining in state hands are better off than if they had been privatized early on. In short, the Hungarian government's emphasis on the sale of large, state-owned enterprises has been a success. The pity is that it was not prosecuted with more vigor throughout the transition.

Notes

I would like to thank Professor Barry Ickes of Pennsylvania State University, Professor Janos Kornai of Harvard University, Professor Paul Marer of Indiana Unversity, and Dr. Zsuzsa Daniel of the Hungarian Finance Ministry for their comments.

1. Hungarian State Property Agency, *Going Further, Moving Faster: Privatization in Hungary* (1995) 8–15.
2. Hungarian State Property Agency, *1994 Annual Report on the Activities of the State Property Agency* (1995).
3. Hungarian State Holding Company, *1994 Annual Report on the Activities of the State Holding Company* (1995).
4. Hungarian State Property Agency, *Going Further, Moving Faster: Privatization in Hungary* (1995) 9.
5. However, for a good, detailed assessment of the consequences of the Hungarian housing privatization program, see Zsuzsa Daniel, "The Paradox in the Privatization of Hungary's Public Housing: A National Gift or a Bad Bargain?" Institute for Economic Analysis, Ministry of Finance, Budapest, Hungary, April, 1996.
6. Hungarian State Property Agency, *Going Further, Moving Faster: Privatization in Hungary* (1995) 8–15.
7. Hungarian State Property Agency, *Going Further, Moving Faster: Privatization in Hungary* (1995) 13.
8. Maurice Ernst, Michael Alexiev, and Paul Marer, *Transforming the Core: Restructuring Industrial Enterprises in Russia and Central Europe* (Boulder, Colo.: Westview Press, 1996) 192–3.
9. Hungarian Central Statistical Office, *Statistical Handbook of Hungary 1996*, Budapest.
10. Central Statistical Office of the Czech Republic.
11. *Glowny Urzad Statystyczny*, Rocznik Statystyczny 1997, Warsaw.
12. The Czech Republic, OECD Economic Surveys, Organization for Economic Cooperation and Development, Paris, 1996.
13. Hungarian Central Statistical Office, *Statistical Handbook of Hungary 1996*, Budapest.
14. The Czech Republic, OECD Economic Surveys, Organization for Economic Cooperation and Development, Paris, 1996.
15. Hungarian State Property Agency, *Going Further, Moving Faster: Privatization in Hungary* (1995) 8.
16. Czech Statistical Office, *Statistical Yearbook of the Czech Republic 1997*.
17. Janos Kornai, *The Road to a Free Economy, Shifting from a Socialist System* (New York: W.W. Norton, 1990).

Chapter 10

Civil Society, Transition, and Consolidation of Democracy

Andrew Arato

I.

The concept of civil society was revived about 20 years ago among neo-Marxist critics of socialist authoritarianism who, along with this conceptual move, reversed one of Marx's most fundamental assumptions, and thus became "post-Marxist." Evidently the concept could have been, but was not, in fact, first revived in a neo- or post-Montesqueuian, Burkian, Tocquevillian (or even Laskian) Parsonian, or many other intellectual traditions. Remarkably enough, the pioneering works of this revival, those of Kolakowski, Mlynar, Vajda, and Michnik in the East; of Habermas, Lefort, Bobbio in the West; and of Weffort, Cardoso, and O'Donnell in the South were rooted in the same or analogous traditions of Western or neo-Marxist discourse. For them a knowledge of Hegel, the young Marx, and Gramsci represented living links to the usage of the concept of civil society, and the state-society dichotomy that were in different ways nearly universal in the nineteenth century, but which nearly disappeared in twentieth-century social and political science and philosophy. At an earlier stage, the task of Western Marxism was to deepen Marxist social philosophy by a return to philosophical roots, and to reveal the connections of a re-Hegelianized Marx to some very specific works in non-Marxist philosophy and social theory: to Weber, Simmel, Croce, and Freud among others. At that time concepts like alienation, fetishism, reification, rationalization, repression, and praxis were in the center stage. Reviving the concept of civil society was apparently an analogous move, since its presence in the young Marx justified a critical reexamination and appropriation of ideas of yet another series of non-Marxist thinkers from Tocqueville to Hannah Arendt. And yet this time instead of using the best of Marx against the worst, the conceptual strategy focusing on civil society everywhere used Gramsci to turn even the young Marx on his head in order to redevelop a concept that was able to, self-critically, pinpoint the earliest origin of the authoritarian turn in their own tradition that provided a link *ab ovo* with state socialism, with "communist" politics. In short, the young Marx's demand that the separation and differentiation of state and civil society be overcome was now understood as the *origin* and *justification* of the *Marxist* statization of all aspects of social reality.

Initially only a new, but hardly unanticipated, conceptualization of totalitarianism was the fruit of the enterprise, in France, and most notably in two countries, Poland and Hungary, which were certainly not "totalitarian." This was an inauspicious beginning that would have yielded little more than a new, critical, and polemical concept. The remarkable historical success of the revival of the concept of civil society was due to its anticipation of, convergence with, and intellectualization of a new radical reformist or evolutionary, dualistic strategy for the transformation of dictatorships first in the East and soon after in Latin America based on the idea of the self-organization of society, the rebuilding of social ties outside the authoritarian state, and the appeal to an independent public sphere outside of all official, state, or party-controlled communication. Used along these lines, the concept of civil society became a focal point of orientation first in Poland, for a period in France, then (perhaps with the mediation of French intellectuals) in Brazil, followed by more general East European and Latin American discussion after the early successes of Solidarity and the *apertura*. At the very least in Hungary, in Czechoslovakia, in Yugoslavia (especially in Slovenia), in Russia, in Chile, in Argentina and Mexico, and finally in South Africa, further conceptual development and the formation of political strategies went hand in hand through the 1980s. In the process earlier transitions (those of Spain and Greece notably) as well as successfully stabilized authoritarian systems (above all China) were increasingly interpreted both by participants and outsiders by using various versions of the concept of civil society. In some places at least, where the transition was successful and where the intellectual strategy actually had a political role, the concept of civil society now turned into a journalistic commonplace. This is especially true in Hungary. Finally, there is now a vastly expanded discussion in many Western countries with established civil societies, where the focus is on finding new loci of the potential democratization of really existing democracies, and new ways to revitalize the public space of these societies.

II.

It is now almost beyond dispute that the concept of civil society has played a major role in recent transitions to democracy, both in the formulation of strategies of democratization and in the journalistic, historical, and social scientific analyses of the relevant processes. At the very least in the leading countries of Poland and Hungary, the civil society strategy was the historical precondition for the successful turn to political society, for the successful achievement of radical regime change through political negotiations. But even in the Soviet Union, *glasnost* is best interpreted as an attempt to stimulate the reconstruction of the public sphere and of civil actors, who were to be allies in a project of reform carried out from above. This latter project was based on the incoherent hope that independent civil society could be somehow controlled from above, and it had to fail.[1] But, contributing to the transformation of Soviet foreign policy and even the end of the communist regime, the role of *glasnost* in the transitions in East and Central Europe was considerable.

It is worthwhile to reread Robert Dahl's early argument, according to which transition to polyarchies would be most difficult in the case of "inclusive hegemonies" where democratic institutions would have to be created all at once for a complex society, with potentially sharp and multidimensional lines of cleavage.[2] The contrast here is with "competitive oligarchic" or "exclusionary liberal" regimes where the institutions of representation and rule of law can be consolidated well before the main groups of modern society would have full access to them. The stress in this argument is winning time for institution building, and possibly for the building of the requisite political culture. Leaving aside the important issue that the creation or long-term stabilization of polyarchies or near-polyarchies, where there were originally liberal oligarchies, has also not proven easy in Latin America for example. Dahl's argument presents an important challenge for East and Central Europe. How then can we explain that the "transitions to democracy" occurred relatively smoothly in so many East and Central European settings whose starting point fully corresponds to the type of "inclusive hegemonies."

It would be tempting to find the answer alone in processes of negotiation leading to pacts of transition, and in the institutional innovation of formalized roundtables. This transitional institution evidently allowed elites to set up the major institutional framework of representative democracy, which subsequently can be assumed as a framework within which the conflicts of the larger society can be processed.[3] Beyond the formal arguments of Adam Przeworski and others, it needs to be added that successful pacts presuppose radical change within a model of legal continuity, the noneconomic element of the contract as it were. Even with this addition, however, I do not find this line of reasoning fully adequate. What is missing from it is precisely the element of time (stressed by Dahl) needed to establish a culture of interaction binding the elites themselves to their agreement concerning institutional structures, leading to a politics of self-limitation even when it is very likely the result of democratic elections that the balance of forces dramatically changes. Even law to which the actors cannot yet have an "internal" relation in the sense of H.L.A. Hart cannot supply what is missing. I believe the needed time and pattern of self-limitation are desiderata which are won by the emergence of a civil society well before the transitions. I believe moreover that the first roundtables in Poland and Hungary, which were subsequently but imperfectly imitated elsewhere, were themselves possible because of a long period of civil society based politics in the two countries. Where such a prehistory is absent, pacts and roundtables played either no role (being displaced by top-down electoral strategies) or a merely formal one. This is not to say that civil society based movements were sufficient conditions for genuine negotiated transitions; a rough balance of forces was equally important. But in any case, all the countries which had successfully negotiated transitions had prior experiences with the organization of parallel publics and associations, with the debatable exception of Bulgaria where the ruling party remained very much in control of the negotiations.

Accordingly, my first hypothesis in this study is that self-limiting politics of civil society, even if originally developed for primarily geopolitical reasons, are a crucial prerequisite for successful transitions of the negotiated type, the type that in my view offers the best prospects for the consolidation of democracy. Under weakening but intact communist regimes, only this politics allowed for democratic institution building outside of the framework of state power, training above all future elites, and molding elements of a democratic political culture based on discussion, negotiation, and compromise. The viability of both processes of formalized negotiations, and of its operative legal assumptions presupposes such a learning experience.[4]

Whether the pressure for an opening to civil society originally came from below as in Poland, from above as in the Soviet Union, or involved both openings from above and autonomous activities from below as in Hungary, it is now more or less accepted wisdom that the self-organization of society against the state cannot complete the transition to democracy. Civil pressure is supposed to lead either to repression as in Poland in 1981 and later China, or to a process of extrication in which political actors, displacing civic initiatives and social movements, will play the major role.[5]

Hungary represents an excellent test case for theories seeking to understand the role and the limits of civil society in the transitions to democracy. In Hungary, the new civil society whose highest point of development was reached in 1988, while open to the discussions and proposals of the democratic opposition and of critical social scientists, was the result of largely spontaneous forms of self-organization. Of course, these efforts took advantage of the opportunities presented by ongoing processes of economic reform and modernization, as well as the relative social relaxation that characterized the Kadar regime after 1968. In this country, no single organization like KOR, Charter 77, or Solidarity ever played the preeminent role in the organization of other groups. The colorful picture of associational life and civic initiatives in existence in 1988 can be summed up only under a variety of headings:[6]

1. Clubs, Circles, "Colleges"

In the first half the 1980s ("the era of circles") there was a mushrooming of intellectual, primarily university-based circles and clubs dedicated to the study, discussion, and debate of a variety of issues, including the economic, social and political problems of the day. By 1985 the need for coordination was felt, and the first council of clubs included representatives of almost twenty clubs.[7]

Professional "colleges" anticipated by a forerunner in the 1970s, were organizations combining university training with the life of small academic communities of intellectuals dedicated to both intellectual pursuits and ideals of public service.[8] It was the colleges that first organized teaching activities for members of the democratic opposition entirely excluded from professional life. Both clubs and colleges were to organize summer "camps," and in 1988 their members were to meet together at a national summer camp, i.e., conference, in which a thousand people participated.[9] Initially eschewing direct political participation, the clubs, circles, and colleges came to see themselves by the second half of the 1980s in terms of the program of reconstructing civil society from below.[10] Down to this day, many of those who participated take seriously the program of a self-organizing democratic society, rich in movements and civic initiatives.

2. New Social Movements

The relative modernity and openness of Kadarist Hungary to the West made it a likely place for the emergence and proliferation of the most modern social movements, especially ecological and youth movements, but to a lesser extent pacifism as well. Significantly, all three tended to emerge from the organizational matrix of circles and colleges; thus the self-organizing forums of youth had a catalyzing role for social movements.[11] Both peace and ecology movements initially eschewed, however unconvincingly, any general political intentions.[12] The youth movement, with the creation of FIDESZ in 1988 by members of the college movement, followed by a new national umbrella organization of youth (MISZOT), was the first to deliberately pass through the political threshold.[13]

Given the politicization of the youth movement at the same time, it became comprehensive, and the general weakness of pacifism, the ecology or environmental movement was the Hungarian new social movement par excellence, not a remarkable fact given the ecological disaster in the wake of state socialism. Politically, this movement was a great success story, absorbing for a time the energy and some of the best people of other movements, including not only those of youth but also the democratic and populist oppositions. Organized by members of the club "movement" from 1984 around one national movement battling against a potentially disastrous dam project on the Danube (Bos [Gabcikovo]-Nagymaros Dam)[14] and a variety of locally based, single-issue movements, ecology and environmentalism generated a variety of organizations (clubs, foundations, action committees), and activities (forums of discussion, demonstrations, petition campaigns, campaign for a referendum, campaigns for the recall of deputies). Even before the government and Parliament were forced to finally suspend the Danube dam project in 1989, the battle for and in an independent public sphere was won by the ecologists and their supporters. Their movement, consciously oriented to a program of the self-organization of civil society, became an important training ground for many of the militants of later movements and parties.

3. Interest Representations and Professional Associations

Unlike Poland, in Hungary, very likely because of the individualistic consequences of the second economy, independent interest representations came into being relatively late. Almost too late to the extent that the dramatic expansion of self-organization and its politicization seemed to storm over the arena of interest representation, according to one participant.[15] Nevertheless, in 1988 an independent organization of entrepreneurs (VOSZ) and several small, eventually affiliated unions of intellectual workers, did emerge, playing an important role not only in exploring the legal and constitutional possibilities of association and coalition building, but also in social movements like ecology. Of the latter TDDSZ (Union of Scientific Workers) was the first and most important, playing a role in organizing new, independent unions of filmmakers and teachers, and a new umbrella organization, the Liga (or FSZDL: League of Independent Trade Unions). This organization was followed by two others, Workers Solidarity and Alliance of Workers Councils. All these organizations of the defense of worker interests, influenced by different aspects of the model of Polish Solidarity, understood themselves as promoting a fabric of thick social self-organization from below, as building and fighting for a civil society with important elements of participation in economic and political life.[16]

Two professional associations, founded in 1988, were especially important not only because by their existence they expanded the space of civil society, but because they were dedicated to the institutional protection of dimensions of civil society presupposed by all other movements. The Publicity Club was organized by journalists, lawyers, and scholars (who included a member of the democratic opposition, an ecologist, and two reform social scientists) to promote the full freedom of speech, information, communication, and press, in order to provide all the requisite forums for independent opinion and criticism, a life necessity for the new movements and initiatives to which the founders of the club explicitly referred.[17] The Independent Forum of Jurists was founded by 135 lawyers in order to help inform society about the legislative projects of the authorities and to propose legal and constitutional alternatives capable of securing rights, expanding democratic participation, promoting the establishment of a sturdy civil society along with the controlling function of the public sphere.[18] Both of these organizations were to play a crucial role in the legal and political changes of the next year, with the Publicity Club continuing its activism in 1990–1991 as well.[19]

4. Political Umbrella Movements for Reform

While it is true that in Hungary no comprehensive movement for reform ever emerged, many of the hopes of those who formulated reform proposals were tied to such a possibility. To be sure, the various social movements were interlocked through common memberships, networks, and events like the important meetings, debates and discussions at the Jurta theater in Budapest.[20] Yet this fact indicated also that the overall membership was rather small both in context of the whole society, and compared with Solidarity in its ascending phase. Not only was there a need for the coordination of many diverse activities, but also for their politicization if the population at large, not able to identify with the existing movements, were to be given any realistic alternative outside of the illusory one of a reform carried out entirely from above. Politicization was also necessary to avoid a polarization of society in the style of Poland in 1980–1981.

The one and only major attempt to create an overarching political movement to include the democratic opposition, the social scientific intellectuals, and the populist writers and their following at Monor in 1985 did not succeed in bridging historically inherited differences, as well as differences in the degree of radicalism. After the populist intellectuals formed their own movement (Hungarian Democratic Forum or MDF) in 1987 at the conference of Lakitelek to which representatives of the democratic opposition (with three cosmetic exceptions) were not invited, political umbrella organizations became inevitably more partial. Such was the caucus of primarily democratic-liberal, social democratic and alternative organization, the Network of Free Initiatives, in which the intellectuals of the democratic opposition played a leading role, and from which the social liberal Alliance of Free Democrats (SZDSZ) was to emerge within less than a year. Of lesser importance was the reform-communist New March Front that was unable to make the full step to politics, but which was to help nevertheless to activize the reformers within the ruling party. Evidently MDF and SZDSZ were protopolitical organizations able to become political parties, even if this was not the inclination of some members (especially of the Network, but the same was true of many of the populist literati). The same was true of FIDESZ (Alliance of Young Democrats), emerging from the youth college movement, eventually unwilling to integrate itself into a nonpolitical umbrella organization of youth. Nevertheless, each of these three organizations was originally part of the ferment of movements in and for civil society, and never completely lost their movement character.[21] For the early FIDESZ, for example, the Polish model of Solidarity was decisive.[22] Indeed, FIDESZ was to play a central role in promoting the freedom of self-organization in the context of existing constitutional and legal loopholes, a move that was to encourage other organizations, as well as an unsuccessful attempt by the authorities to produce in 1988 a more restrictive, formally correct legal regulation of the right of association. The eventual outcome after a long struggle for public opinion, the entirely modern liberal and democratic laws of association and assembly of January 1989, represented a victory for civil society analogous to (though far more comprehensive than) the legalization of Solidarity in 1980.[23]

This victory testified to the success, within limits, of the strategy or rather strategies oriented to the reconstruction of civil society in Hungary. Above all, the new organizations and movements, armed with a variety of reform proposals and supported by a variety of popular actions, came to dominate the public sphere, first the realm of scientific publications, eventually penetrating some journals like *HVG* (*Weekly World Economy*) and dailies like *Magyar Nemzet*. In such a context, as the struggle for the law of association showed, the regime was unable to build legal legitimacy by tightening legal restrictions that for the first time would be honored. The defeat in the public sphere meant not only that the regime lost instead of gained legitimacy, but appeared vulnerable as well. The public discussion of the draft of the law of association, perhaps intended as sham or controlled democracy, turned out to be the first democratic political discussion of legislation in Hungary in over forty years.[24] And yet in spite its successes, the method oriented to public discussion alone could not be relied on in an ongoing fashion, even from the point of view of the organizations of civil society. First, it was too time consuming: a whole constitution (which was increasingly recognized as necessary) could not be created by a method that took six or more months with respect to merely two fundamental rights (association and assembly). Second, the ruling party could and did try, after its defeat, to manipulate the time and procedure of "societal debate," depriving the process of all participatory character. Third, Hungarian society and its organizations were already too plural to speak with one voice on issues other than the few fundamental rights all parts of civil society required. Fourth, even after a few signal victories for the groups of civil society, it was very risky for the old Parliament, under communist control, to remain in the position to legislatively establish the parameters of a new political system. As it became clear in the draft for a new electoral law proposed in 1988, but received with total antipathy by society,[25] that it was possible to come up with a formally democratic procedure and timetable that would allow the ruling party to convert its monopolistic power in one system into a hegemony in the next. Here, the civil society based strategy was ultimately defenseless.

Yet the regime was also in a poor position to merely impose new semidemocratic rules, since its own formal instance of legislation and constitution making, the undemocratically elected Parliament was now highly unpopular because of its well-publicized and criticized role in the conflict over the Danube dam, and certainly did not have the legitimacy to act on its own. The existence of organized civil society, moreover, with important victories behind it, implied that the failure of reform could lead to a type of polarization that only violent acts on one side could resolve. But in the context of the transformation of Soviet foreign policy, the hard-liners of the government could not count on repression being successful, as it still was in Poland in 1981. Once the Round Table was created in Poland, and especially as a comprehensive agreement was successfully concluded by the government and Solidarity early in 1989, it became more or less unavoidable that in Hungary too, a new forum of negotiation and compromise would have to be established as a way out of potential stalemate, and as a quasi-legitimate road to a democratic system.

III.

In Hungary, 1988 has been widely considered the year of civil society, during which a whole series of movements and civil initiatives, from ecology to youth, and from the democratic opposition to the populist semiopposition put the weakening party-state under decisive pressure. Even before, during the 1980s, there was continuing experimentation with various Hungarian versions of the Polish strategy of new evolutionism, one that resulted in the solid achievement of an alternative public sphere as well as some valuable political experience of a small, but expending circle of activists. Moreover, in 1987, a whole series of reform proposals, most importantly the *Social Contract* of Janos Kis and his collaborators in the democratic opposition, offered to both government and society radical programs of reconstruction around the dualistic idea of the full emancipation of civil society in the context of a more partial reform of state institutions. Thus, all attempts on the part of the party-state to consolidate a reformed version of authoritarian rule, or more likely to carry out a program of reform merely from above, ran into the determined opposition of organized groups and publics that possessed their own alternative models of change.

Nevertheless, due to the acceleration of the process because of international factors, the unexpectedly quick crumbling of the old regime, but also because of internal weaknesses of the civil society strategy the model of transition was not ultimately steered from below, from the grassroots, by the social movements, networks, and initiatives. Instead, the process of transition was, as it is well-known, negotiated on the mezo level of political society, where political parties emerging from both civil society (MDF, SZDSZ, and FIDESZ) and from the party-state (the MSzMP in the process of becoming the MSzP) played the central role. Remarkably enough, since in Hungary the independent forces were weaker, the outcome was not a dualistic program such as the one proposed by the *Social Contract* of the democratic opposition in 1987, or even the Polish formula of early 1989 which the reform communists and their conservative partners among the opposition sought to in part imitate (Michnik's "your president, our prime minister"), but a com-

plete institutional transformation, a veritable change of political regime. Even the formally democratic attempt to use the direct election
of the presidency to establish a foothold for the ruling party candidate,
Imre Pozsgay, agreed upon at the Round Table was (narrowly) defeated in the popular petition campaign and referendum of November
1989, organized by SZDSZ, but relying on a grassroots effort. That victory, however, seemed to have been the last hurrah of the politics of
civil society.

According to the reigning hypothesis of the literature on transitions,
the concept of civil society generally loses its relevance in the actual
negotiations that lead to transitional pacts. A system of mutual guarantees can be worked out only among actors capable of divorcing themselves from the maximalist pressures that are likely to emanate from
their original constituencies or allies (the radicals in the population,
and the hard-liners of the old regime). Because of the turn to "political
society," moreover, and the corresponding demobilization of the civil
sphere, it is further implied (though rarely argued) that the politics of
civil society has little to do with the consolidation of democracy.[26]

I agree with the demobilization thesis on both theoretical and empirical grounds, but only in part. I think it underestimates the diffuse cultural pressure of ongoing public discussion, and the continued potential of new forms of grassroots mobilization that remain the
counterweights to the old regime's repressive capabilities. But I do
think that the negotiated option (as against top-down, manipulated
electoral models and bottom-up models of insurrection) requires the
prior building of new-type institutions and the emergence of independent political actors. The new institution was, of course, the famous
Round Table (in Hungary actually two roundtables: the Round Table of
the Opposition, EKA, and the National Round Table, NKA) and the
new actors were the political parties. When the action shifts to roundtables and parties, so do the activists and resources, and in the short run
at least, the organizations of civil society tend to withdraw from politics, and even decompose.

From all this, however, the irrelevance of the civil society problem
for the consolidation of democracy does not follow. On the contrary, I
believe there is a mutual dependence between institutionalization of
civil society and consolidation of democracy. I understand "transition
to democracy" in the narrow sense, as the relatively rapid process
(generally, formally negotiated) that establishes and guarantees the
"organic" rules (at the very least, electoral rule, freedom of association
and assembly including party formation and activity, access to the
media, private security for people engaging in politics) for the holding
of free, contested elections. In the broader sense the transition must

also include the process of designing specific democratic institutions, e.g., constitution making. I understand the consolidation of democracy, along with others, as a process by which "democracy becomes the only game in town." But unlike interpreters who seek to explain the consolidation of democracy simply as an equilibrium resting on a desirable combination of interests and fears, for me democracy can be consolidated only when, in addition to a favorable interest constellation, a sufficiently large number of actors accept a given system as legitimate. In my view, civil society has an important role to play in the consolidation of democracy so defined. Before I turn to the role of civil society in the consolidation of Hungarian democracy, I would like to show that the successful turn to political society itself very much presupposes the role of civil society in the transition process.

The transition literature[27] recognizes the important role of civil society in the historical phase before the actual process of negotiated extrication from authoritarian rule. But the interpretation of this phase merely as liberalization as against democratization misrepresents the state of affairs that on a microlevel it is democratic institutions and culture that are being built.[28] A result of this conception, and of intellectual strategies concerned only with rational, purely strategic actors, is that the phase of "liberalization" has only the role of provoking the choice of either repression, or a political bargaining process. Civil society accordingly would be either repressed or must be demobilized. Demobilization is necessary if a bargaining process is to be successful. Political radicals or maximalists can be brought under the control of the moderates and continue to play a role in the negotiations, but the movements of civil society must be demobilized and reatomized.

To be sure, empirically the full demobilization of civil society did not always occur during negotiation processes. In many countries, it was the actual pressure of the streets that established the predominance of the opposition in the negotiations (Czechoslovakia), maintained the equality of the two sides (GDR), or made a very immature and fledgling opposition at least a viable partner (Bulgaria). But even in Hungary the formally permitted demonstration during the Nagy reburial in June 1989 indicated that the opposition could bring already organized sectors of the population into the streets. And this omnipresent option contributed to the negotiating success of political groups that had little membership, meager resources, and even doubtful legitimacy. Of course the new actors on the democratic side were themselves capable of making and keeping bargains because of their previous political experience and socialization. Not surprisingly, to me at least, it was not the revived traditional parties but the new political organizations that emerged from civil society (MDF, SZDSZ and FI-

DESZ) who played the major role in the negotiations on the democratic side. Regime moderates like Imre Pozsgay, who often had a large voice in deciding whom to bargain with implicitly knew what I am talking about. They needed partners capable not only of social support but also self-limitation. Only elites emerging from civil society, whose party names usually testified to their origins, were capable of both. (Note that in Latin America, parties inherited from the past were often in place, and could play the requisite role.)

Nevertheless, having come from civil society did not stop many new party political actors from declaring that the politics of civil participation was only a matter of yesterday. The differentiation of new political organizations meant also that elites and militants were pulled away from civil organizations and into fledgling parties, thereby promoting an implosion of many of the movements that previously occupied the center stage. Moreover, there were also conscious efforts at demobilization, which were very much intensified when the new elites took charge of economic policies of stabilization that they saw potentially threatened by access from organized societal demands. Finally, with the upsurge of new ideologies, the new and specifically East European ideology of civil society had to compete with old ideologies revived from the past or imported from the West. The discourse thus followed the sociological regression: the elites that originally saw their action in terms of civil society stopped using the whole conception.

At the same time, however, during the period when many of the older civil organizations became parties or imploded, political and economic processes initially on local and sectoral levels provided countless new opportunities and incentives for the formation of new organizations. Because these, despite their considerable number (one analyst reports the existence of over 40,000 associations and foundations in Hungary in 1995) were not initially able to engage themselves in politics, political actors at first could safely disregard their existence. Nevertheless, the new organizations soon established forms of national coordination among them, and relatively soon thereafter, they forcefully indicated their intention to participate in national politics.[29] The discourse of civil society, too, now spread to groups and strata who never saw themselves in these terms before.

IV.

The development of new civil organizations did not follow as a lawful regularity from the establishment of a capitalist market economy. Nevertheless, the new political regime established in 1989–1990 contributed a great deal, even if indirectly and unintentionally, to the formation of a large number of civil actors. It should be noticed that the concept of civil society has been recently used in two distinct senses: to indicate a set of societal movements, initiatives, forms of mobilization *and* to refer to a framework of settled institutions (rights, associations, publics). One could use different terms altogether to avoid confusion. In *Civil Society and Political Theory*, we chose, however, only a relative distinction to deal with the difference involved: civil society as movement *versus* civil society as institution. We do this because the differentiation is a fluid one: mobilization always seeks at least some institutionalization as, for instance, in the August 31, 1980, Gdansk accords, and institutionalization is the precondition for new movements and initiatives. Alain Touraine nicely captured this relationship in his distinction between historical and social movements.[30]

For my present purposes it is important to stress this distinction, because it follows from it that demobilization is not automatically equal to atomization, to the obliteration of a politically significant civil society. Beyond reasons already mentioned, demobilization follows from the life cycles of movements, from the relative achievement of their goals, and we should not lament this fact unless we long for permanent revolution or permanent mobilization. But the choice is ultimately not between permanent mobilization and atomization (both are impossible) but levels and degrees of stability of institutionalization.

Institutionalization of civil society in the sense of politically relevant and relatively stable associations and publics is achieved by the following institutions and practices:

1. guarantee of fundamental rights of association, assembly, speech, press, and coalition, which in turn presuppose establishment of a constitution that works as a fully legal document, one supported by the separation of powers, especially independent courts;
2. institutionalization of a politically accessible and also decentralized media of communication, relatively independent from both government and market;
3. political and economic decentralization, involving
   a. independent local and regional self-government, and
   b. possibility and facilitation of local and small-scale forms of enterprise;
4. acceptance and recognition of the operation of national and international organizations (NGOs) and institutions dedicated to the monitoring and defense of rights (ombudsmen, transnational courts); and
5. the financing of civil society associations.

These interrelated levels of institutions and practices promote the institutionalization of civil society defined in terms of associations and publics. While I am convinced that some relevant fulfillment of the first two criteria, rights and constitutionalism, leads to some level of institutionalization, only the fulfillment of most of the other criteria can lead to a somewhat higher level of institutionalization. (At the end of the essay, I return to the question of a high level of institutionalization which according to some involves additional constitutional prerequisites.) In Hungary, in fact, rights, constitutionalism, political and economic decentralization, and the ability of NGOs to operate have been securely established in the period between 1989–1994 due to the activity of constitution makers, the legislature, and especially the Constitutional Court that made clear from the outset that fundamental rights in Hungary will be strictly enforced as genuine legal norms. The achievement, or partial achievement, of structures of consultation and of independent media of communication did not happen as smoothly, and required in the end collective action and civil remobilization. Channels of consultation were explicitly rejected by the constitution makers of 1990, and it was only under the impact of the October 1990 taxi- and truck-drivers' strike that forms of social partnership (the Tripartite Council for Interest Coordination: ET) received new relevance. The electronic media had to withstand strong efforts at governmentalization, and it was only after the 1994 alternation in power that their greater autonomy was uneasily enshrined in a new media law. Obviously, independent associations and publics when established could promote further institutionalization, and thus the expansion of their own political role and influence. This indeed happened in the case of social consultation, and the media law, with organizations such as the Publicity Club and movements like the Democratic Charter playing the major role in the second case. Thus there are strong reasons, in Hungary at least, to disagree with Dahrendorf's thesis that the institutionalization of civil society will take incomparably longer than those of competitive political institutions and market economy.

On the basis of my study of the East and Central European cases, a relatively high level of institutionalization of civil society in the period of transition depends on several factors. One is again the politics of civil society before the transition, since a pattern of participation establishes political norms and organizational competence that can be called upon by an expanding circle of new organizations. Institutionalization depends in an important way on the demands made, and expected to be made, from below. But the relevant parts of the institutional design are affected also by the power relations at the site of negotiation, and the ideologies shared by the participants. The more balanced the relations, the more actors will seek in context of future uncertainty a larger variety of channels of social participation and self-protection. But as Janos Kis rightly stresses, successful negotiations also presuppose relative consensus about the political framework of the future. This consensus can have various contents with respect to the level of institutionalization of civil society. The latter, in turn, has important consequences for the tasks of the consolidation of democracy.

The minimal criteria of rights and constitutionalism are of course also the minimal criteria required for a transition (in the wider sense, including the institutional design) to a constitutional democracy or polyarchy. Dahl might insist on relatively open and accessible media, but in light of international experience with both governmental and commercialized media that would be too demanding as a minimum condition. Of course, the question is what "relatively" means. In Hungary, the public sphere was relatively free even during the year when radio and television were finally degraded to governmental organs, because the widely read print media was indeed free. It may be therefore fair to say that at least some level of free communication is required if the minimal conditions of a polyarchy are to be met. At the same time the latter has two additional conditions that are less directly related to the institutionalization of civil society: (1) the organization of competitive elections and (2) the design and plausible operation of a machinery of government in the narrow sense guaranteeing some accountability and responsiveness, as well as space for the functioning of a viable opposition.

My second thesis then is the following: Under East and Central European conditions, the more developed the institutionalization of civil society, and in particular those levels that do not belong to the minimum definition of democracy or polyarchy (i.e., levels 2 to 5), the stronger will be the consensus supporting the democratic design of free and competitive elections and accountable government, the higher will be the legitimacy and, therefore the stability and quality, of democracy.

I would like to demonstrate (though not "prove") this thesis in relation to some key dimensions of Hungarian experience:

1. Legitimacy, Channels of Consultation, Decentralization

Advocates of parliamentary sovereignty and radical economic stabilization agree in seeing societal demands as illegitimate, and as sources of fiscal strain. According to their views, civil associations have no electoral legitimacy and can conceivably represent only unelected minorities. There is therefore no justification supposedly for giving a distinguished role to just those minority views which happen to have the good fortune of being organized. Such a role is supposed to be especially unfortunate, because organized interests are presumed to seek redistributive advantages for their members. This objection can be refuted on the theoretical level by stressing the difference between the political power of parties and elected representatives, as against the influence of movements and associations working through the societal public sphere. Moreover, it is also true that nationally coordinated organized interests are capable of restraining the redistributive demands of their members, and will ordinarily try to do so when either their long-term interests or political trade-offs make this worthwhile. At the same time, there is a good deal of empirical evidence indicating the negative side effects of decision making without consultation.

In Hungary the picture is relatively clear: lack of consultation and political centralism can severely shake the legitimacy of governments, at least in the sociological if not the legal sense. During the first year of the first freely elected government, disregard of interest groups and attacks on the autonomy of local government led to a severe legitimacy deficit in the sociological sense. A culture of consultation and decentralization helps to establish political incentives for association building, but this is potentially a positive sum game in relation to governmental power. After the dramatic social conflicts of the October 1990 strike, the institutions of social consultation (in particular the ET, the Council for the Coordination of Interests) received new life. This strike can be represented as the defense of particular corporate advantages against necessary steps of restoring budgetary integrity. It can be even said to have frightened the MDF government to such an extent that it would no longer dare to undertake reform measures that could run into determined popular opposition. But the strike was also, among other things, a protest against the introduction of austerity measures without consultation with those most concerned. And in this sense it achieved its purpose, at least for a time.

Significantly, the MDF government did not have to face another major challenge to its legitimacy for purely economic reasons. However, after the putschlike introduction (perhaps unavoidable) of the Bokros stabilization program in early 1995, the legitimacy of the Horn government plummeted. The existence of forums of interest coordination like the ET made a great contribution to the social peace of the period, even if the nongovernmental participants experienced this whole period as the failure of interest coordination.[31] While the introduction of some measures without prior consultation may be a precondition of their effectiveness, hopefully the wrong lesson, the avoidance of consultation and negotiation will not be drawn by policy-makers.

Recent agrarian protest (February–March 1997) and government response show that the bad instincts are still there, but that there is also
some goodwill on both sides to resolve the contentious issues through
negotiations.

2. Public Sphere and a Culture of Openness and Criticism

The governmentalization of media not only blocks access to alternative
forms of opinion, it also deprives government of needed criticism.
Moreover, under formerly state socialist conditions only independent
media can present the point of view of government in a believable
manner. The incredibly quick loss of popularity of the victors of the
1990 elections can only be explained by their attacks on local government and independent media, both of which found their own means
and the political allies to resist. In the end, even the victory of the Antall–Boross government in the electronic media war, contributed a
great deal to its almost total political defeat in the elections of 1994.
Open media are the precondition for the expansion of societal publics;
but as associational participation, these too strengthen rather than
weaken government. The lesson was learned by the new coalition,
though not as fully as some might have hoped. Today, Hungary has a
media law that guarantees the plurality of the forms of institutionalization of the media and their independence from at least direct forms of
governmental intervention. Unfortunately, instead of direct government intervention, the current trend is toward the "partification" of
media controls, on a pattern that resembles more discredited practices
in Italy and Austria than the BBC or CBC mixed model that many of
the reformers had hoped to establish. Thus, already during the first
year of the operation of the new media law, one state-owned television
channel was licensed not to the highest bidder but to one preferred by
an ad hoc combination of the socialists and some of the right-wing parties. In any case, media channels or broadcasting segments farmed out
to parties is not the best way to guarantee (as the Hungarian Constitutional Court once recognized) either the widest public access to different groups or especially the most open process of critical deliberation
concerning issues of public relevance.

In the defense of the public sphere, the importance of monitoring
agencies like the Publicity Club and civic movements like the Democratic Charter cannot be underestimated. Starting out in defense of free
media, these institutions played a major role in blocking trends in Hungary toward authoritarianism, significant not because of popular support but because of the presence of such trends within the politics of
the government between 1990–1994. Today, it is easy to say, in retro-

spect, that there never was an authoritarian danger in that period. It is however the task of institutions like the Publicity Club and of democratic citizen initiative like the Charter, to demonstrate the illegitimacy of authoritarian reversion even if it has a good chance to fail within the given political and geopolitical environment. The consolidation of democracy relies precisely on swift public condemnation and protest against all authoritarian phenomena that can undermine committed support to democracy on the middle run.

With politicians relatively friendly to these movements in power between 1994 and 1998, these organizations faced the well-known dilemma of either atrophy or weakening a government that may be (whatever its grave deficiencies) the best alternative at the moment. Characteristically, for a movement which undergoes life cycles, the Democratic Charter has been quiescent in the social-liberal period. The Publicity Club, equally characteristic of an established institution, has also in this period, remained an alert defender of the free media, recently appealing to the Constitutional Court against an interpretation by the government of the new media law that threatened the public and open character of the electronic media.

3. Antipolitical Movements and Initiatives

Finally, an area needs to be mentioned where orientation to civil society can endanger democratic consolidation. Many (though not all) of the civic movements share an antipolitical tradition and a hostility to parties that have now been often exacerbated because of the unenlightened policies of parliaments and governments. Nevertheless, party systems in the very few countries where they are now in place have played an important role in the consolidation of democracy, specifically by making democratic politics compatible with the continuation of market-oriented reform. This role, actual or potential, can be endangered by fundamentalist or antipolitical versions of the politics of civil society. Such was the politics of LAET (association of those living below the minimum income), directed at the collective recall of the members of Parliament in 1993 through the use of the referendum. Such efforts, if successful, could threaten the viability of parliamentary representation.

V.

Hungarian civil society, demobilized during the transitions, has been institutionalized during the period of the consolidation through the structures of liberal constitutionalism. Such an institutionalization guarantees, however, only a minimal civil society, and not necessarily one that will contribute to long-term democratic legitimacy through the formation of an active, participatory civic culture. We have seen that in Hungary the main organ through which the actors of civil society can achieve national integration and national influence, the public sphere, i.e., the sphere of the independent communication media, was under attack in the democratic period itself. Even today, it may have been only the party pluralization, rather than the genuine independence of the media, that has been legally guaranteed through the so-called media law. Thus, one cannot say, even in Hungary (one of the most fortunate of the new democracies), that the level of the institutionalization of democratic civil society has been particularly high.

Evidently institutionalization in itself is not enough. We again have to focus on the problem of achieving a type of institutionalization that would facilitate the emergence of a democratic, participatory civil society. That is the perhaps now old-fashioned stress to which the emphasis on civil society inevitably leads. Of course, a democratic civil society presupposes in the long term cultural developments that cannot be designed. But institutional design might be able to help with promoting an "opportunity structure" for forms of activity that can positively influence cultural development itself. If constitutionalism guarantees societal independence as such, an active democratic civil society may require the support of constitutional provisions that make the participation of groups, associations, and initiatives worthwhile.

In Hungary two such constitutional provisions have been stressed: the idea of a second parliamentary chamber rooted in civil associations, and the expansion of the role of referenda. The first of these ideas revived notions from the armory of semiauthoritarian forms of corporatism. It was favored by some socialists seeking to give the unions an institutionalized foothold in parliamentary decision making, and by some Christian Democrats wishing to do the same for the traditional churches. In a more democratic version, other advocates of corporatist ideas proposed the constituionalization of social partnership, in other words making interest aggregation compulsory in economic decision making.

The second idea, the stress on referenda, came from advocates of direct, popular, and plebescitary democracy. Surprisingly, the two rather contradictory traditions (corporatism and direct democracy) were even combined, as in the case of Christian Democrats and members of the Smallholders' Party who insisted on an item-by-item plebescitary ratification of the emerging constitutional synthesis. Given a certain amount of justified skepticism that a parliamentary process dominated by parties would ever design institutions favorable to civil society, the eclecticism of civil society advocates was perhaps less than surprising. It was repeatedly proposed by the Smallholders and by a variety of civil associations that the latter too should participate in the process of constitution making, and the insistence on ratificatory referenda came as Parliament continued to disregard claims of civil participation in the drafting process.

The constitutional role of civil society became a salient issue in the period between 1994 and 1998 because the governing social liberal coalition embarked on a project of codifying Hungary's definitive constitution (the constitution of 1989–1990 was understood by its own makers as a temporary one).[32] The parties of the ruling coalition opened up the process for the participation of the opposition parties. Given their parliamentary power, and the additional support, they could rally behind a project that would preserve in substance the regime structure established in the year of the change of systems (1989–1990), and those who supported innovations like a semipresidential system or the constitutionalization of corporatism found themselves initially in a rather weak position. Thus came the call from within Parliament to open the process beyond Parliament, for the organizations of "civil society," who as it happened supported the positions of parliamentary minorities on the disputed issues.

But which of the many thousands of associations, clubs, movements, umbrella organizations, and the like have the legitimacy to share in the constituent power? Once posed, this question could never be resolved satisfactorily, and it is not very surprising that the parliamentary advocates of such "civil" participation never really pressed their case, which was not supported by most of the opposition parties.

The appeal to referenda was born out of the same quandary, politically speaking, namely, parliamentary minorities seeking to overcome their minority status. The argument for such an appeal had however distinct historical, legal, and intellectual foundations. We should recall that the popular petition campaign and referendum on the election of the president in 1989 played an important role to correct the results of elite bargaining processes, and to give Hungary the purest structure of parliamentary democracy in the whole region. I have described this set of events as the last hurrah of a civil society strategy under a still authoritarian regime form. Referenda therefore played an important role in Hungary's regime change. Moreover, the still valid 1989 law on referenda (unlike the constitution of 1989–1990 itself) requires that a new constitution must be ratified by a popular plebescite, before it is validated.[33] Though there were disagreements on the question, this requirement was willingly conceded by the governing coalition. Once however several features of the proposed constitutional draft became controversial, it was objected that a really meaningful plebescite could not involve a yes or no vote on the whole package, without forcing people to accept or reject features that they actually objected to for the sake of features which they accepted or rejected even more strongly. Should not the mobilized population determine all features of its political constitution one by one?

Again, once posed, the alternative of constitution making through repeated referenda had to be rejected. Whereas any number of civil associations lacked the legitimacy to directly participate in constitutional creation, plebescitary mobilization lacks the cognitive capability to draft rules. The end result of such constitution making could only be an incoherent and unworkable mélange of opinions. Worse, those who proposed such a role of referenda, ran the risk of fully discrediting this important democratic channel which could be an important corrective for the party political monopolization of participation *under* parliamentary democracy.

It may very well be the responsibility of the coalition that governed between 1994 and 1998 that forms of less obtrusive public participation and consultation with respect to constitution making were not worked out. In Hungary, there was for example much less of an attempt to educate and inform public opinion concerning constitutional issues than roughly the same time in South Africa. But civil society based forms of the exertion of constituent power could not make up for this insufficiency and proved self-defeating. In the end the advocates of such participation, not wishing to allow the social liberal coalition to take credit for giving the country its new constitution, only used their claims to bring down the project as a whole. Ironically, they succeeded in the effort only because a small group of socialist leaders, too, around the prime minister and the minister of justice, who harbored corporatist ideas themselves, turned against their own parliamentary fraction and deprived it and the liberal coalition partner of the necessary majority, at the penultimate moment.

The tragicomic episode has an important lesson for us. The proposed political forms, direct civil participation in constitution making, and direct plebescitary forms of constitutional consultation foreshadowed the corporatist and plebescitary elements that their advocates hoped to enshrine in the constitution then in the making. These forms, each hoping to directly institutionalize the power (not the public, deliberative influence!), of civil society turned out to be incompatible with the logic of parliamentary democracy. Establishing a second chamber of corporate representation is incompatible with the one person one vote principle. Moreover, it threatens to freeze civil society, in itself a fluid and ever-changing field of associational life, because those initially admitted to corporate representation can maximize their power only if they exclude new entrants to the bargaining forums. Democratic corporatism can be saved from such an outcome only through its informality, and the ability of parliaments to bypass corporatist forms of intermediation if they wish to do so. The attempt to constitutionally enshrine corporatism made the posing of the more relevant constituional problem, namely, the regulation and pluralization of lobbying activities, impossible by vastly overshooting the mark. By raising the specter of corporatism, liberal opinion was motivated to disregard the problem of pluralist access to the political process, and the democratic requirements one may impose on those who are to have such access.

Referenda, of course, unlike corporatism, are potentially inclusive rather than exclusive. But they too represent threats to parliamentary democracy in contexts in which political parties unaccustomed or unwilling to limit themselves are ready to use referenda to contest each and every electoral and legislative outcome not to their liking. Referenda can be tamed not through informality as corporatism but through having a subordinate role in the framework of parliamentary democracy. The Hungarian Constitutional Court has played some role in redefining referenda in this spirit, and in particular, in depriving them of the ability to openly or tacitly modify the existing constitutional structure.[34] It is unfortunate that the constitution makers of 1994–1996 failed to produce a liberal democratic constituion that might have settled the relationship between parliamentary and direct democratic forms in a more definitive manner.

In order to be politically influential, civil society and its organizations must, on the whole, renounce the direct exercise of power, which is appropriate only in revolutionary situations. Revolutions however are never conducive to democracy. The civil society based initiatives of Central Europe achieved revolutionary results, but within the framework of legal continuity. For these results to remain open to further democratization, new openings for the influence of civil society will have to be found. But for this democracy to remain democratic, it will be equally important for civil actors of all types, from churches to unions, from voluntary associations to more tightly knit communities, to learn the great democratic art of political self-limitation.

Notes

1. Andrew Arato, "Social Movements and Civil Society in the Soviet Union" in *From Neo-Marxism to Democratic Theory* (Armonk, NY: M.E. Sharpe, 1993).

2. Robert Dahl, *Polyarchy* (New Haven: Yale University Press, 1971), 33ff.

3. See Adam Przeworski, *Democracy and the Market* (Cambridge University Press: Cambridge, 1991); Janos Kis, "Between Reform and Revolution: Three Hypotheses about the Nature of Regime Change" in *Constellations* (Oxford, January 1995), vol.I, No. 3.

4. Note that in Latin America and Southern Europe, where the devastation of the civil sphere never equalled that under communist regimes, civil society did not to the same extent have to be created before the transitions.

5. Przeworski has even formalized this idea (*Democracy and the Market*). It is part of his conception that liberalization from above cannot succeed in stabilizing an authoritarian regime. If success, however, is to be defined in terms of lengths of time that are meaningful to the actors undertaking such reform, the histories of post-Stalinism and the case of Mexico prove that he is wrong.

6. I am combining, reducing, and slightly altering the typologies presented in two excellent articles by I. Stumpf, "Rendszerkritika, alternativitás generációs köntösben" in *Magyarország politikai évkönyve 1988*; and "Pártosodás 89" in S. Kurtan, P. Sandor, and L. Vass, eds., *Magyarország politikai évkönyve* (Budapest: Aula-Omikk, 1990).

7. Istvan Stumpf, "Rendszerkritika, alternativitás generációs köntösben" in *Magyarország politikai évkönyve 1988* (Budapest: R- Forma kiado, 1989).

8. Istvan Stumpf, "Political Socialization of New Generation—Alliance of Young Democrats" in *How to Be a Democrat in a Post-Communist Society* (Budapest: Institute for Political Science, Hungarian Academy of Science, 1991).

9. E. Bilecz, "Szarszo '88" in *Magyarország politikai évkönyve 1988*.

10. *Ibid.*

11. *Ibid.*, 334.

12. For ecology, see Laszlo Solyom, "A társadalom részvétele a környezetvédelemben" in *Medvetanc* (Budapest, 1988); interview with Janos Vargha in K. Bossanyi, *Szolamproba: Beszelgetesek az alternativ mozgalmakrol* (Budapest: Lang kiado, 1989); and G. Lanyi "A kuvik éve—környezetvédelmi jelzések" in *Magyarorszag politikai evkonyve 1988*.

13. See two articles by Istvan Stumpf, "Rendszerkritika," as well as interviews with Laszlo Kover in *Szolamproba* and in A. Richter, ed., *Ellenzeki kerekasztal* (Budapest: Otlet kft., 1990).

14. For some of its documents, see "Duna Kor" in *Magyarország politikai évkönyve 1988*, 704–12.

15. Laszlo Bruszt, "Az érdekképviseleti monopóliumok alkonya" in *Magyarország politikai évkönyve 1988*.

16. For the founding documents, see TDDSZ in *Magyarország politikai évkönyve 1988*, 770–79; FSZDL and MOSZ in *Magyarország politikai évkönyve 1990* (Budapest: Ökonomia Alapitvány, 1991), 712ff; 727ff.

The key difference between the latter two organizations is the stress on the defense of interests of employees and relatively small sharing in ownership and management by the FSZDL or LIGA that, on the whole, seeks to differentiate these functions, and MOSZ that seeks more classical forms of worker ownership and self-management. In effect, however, both organizations are independent trade unions.

See also the interviews with P. Forgács in *Szolamproba*; and with L. Bruszt in A. Richter, ed., *Ellenzeki kerekasztal* (Budapest: Otlet kft., 1990).

17. For documents see "Nyilvanossag Club" in *Magyarország politikai évkönyve 1988*, 752–55 and G. Banyai, J. Bercsi, eds., *Lel-Tar* (Budapest: Tudósitások kiadó, 1989), 133–41.

18. "Fuggetlen Jogasz Forum" in *Lel-Tar*, 49–53.

19. The founding document foresaw its self-dissolution on the day when press and communication were perfectly free and guaranteed in a new constitutional state, and when the pluralism of opinions was fully established. See *Magyarország politikai évkönyve 1988*, 753. That time has not yet apparently come in the view of the Club!

20. See the vivid description in the interview with M. Haraszti in *Uncaptive Minds* (January-February 1989) vol. II, no. 1.

21. Interestingly, the three organizations were to receive 55 percent of the first round vote for party lists, as against the 43 percent of the nationalist parties that were to form the governmental coalition, and 30.3 percent for the two liberal parties. All the historical parties together were to receive 22 percent of the vote, while all communist successor parties and organizations received 19.7 percent.

22. See the interviews with L. Kover and especially V. Orban in A. Richter, ed., *Ellenzeki Kerekasztal portrevazlatok* (Budapest: Otlet kft, 1990) and I. Stumpf's recollections in "How to Be a Democrat."

23. L. Bruszt, "1989: The Negotiated Revolution in Hungary" in *Social Research* (Summer 1990) vol. 57, no. 2, 372–74; G. Halmai, *Az egyesüles szabadsaga* (Budapest: Atlantisz, 1990), 97–107.

24. On this problem of "societal debate," see Bruszt, "1989: The Negotiated Revolution in Hungary," 373–74.

25. Istvan Kukorelli, "The Birth, Testing and Results of the 1989 Hungarian Election Law" in *Soviet Studies* (1991) vol. 43, no. 1, 138.

26. Note that this last position is now refuted by Linz and Stepan (*Problems of Democratic Transition and Consolidation* (Baltimore: Johns Hopkins University Press, 1996) who are the only ones among their colleagues who have taken up this aspect of my argument in *Civil Society and Political Theory* (Cambridge: MIT Press, 1992), and especially in "Revolution, Civil Society and Democracy" in *From Neo-Marxism to Democratic Theory*.

27. Guillermo O'Donnell, and Phillip C. Schmitter in *Transitions from Authoritarian Rule* (Baltimore: Johns Hopkins University Press, 1987), and Alfred Stepan, *Rethinking Military Politics: Brazil in the Southern Cone* (Princeton: Princeton University Press, 1988).

28. For an interpreter who sees the so-called liberalization process as democratization on the microlevel, see Manuel Antonio Garreton, "Popular Mobilization and the Military Regime in Chile: The Complexities of the Invisible Transition" in Susan Eckstein, ed., *Power and Popular Protest: Latin American Social Movements* (Berkeley: University of California Press, 1988). The invisible transition to democracy is the "recomposition and reorganization of civil society."

29. Laszlo Kemeny, "Civil erdek-kepviseleti szervek 1995-ben" in *Magyarorszag politikai evkonyve* (Budapest, 1996).

30. See Alan Touraine, *The Voice and the Eye: An Analysis of Social Movements* (New York: Cambridge University Press, 1981).

31. Maria Lado, and Ferenc Toth, "Az Erdekegyezteto Tanacs 1995- ben: a hadviseles eve" in *Magyarország politikai évkönyve* (Budapest, 1996).

32. On this see my three essays in *East European Constitutional Review*, Fall 1994, Fall 1995, and Fall 1996. Subsequent installments did not have to be written due to the collapse of the project as described by the last of these articles.

33. I leave aside whether it is logical or not (it is not) for an ordinary law, or even a two-thirds law, to regulate constituional revision or amendment or ratification.

34. The court did this while also protecting referenda, most recently (in 1997, in the case of the referendum proposal concerning ownership of arable land by foreigners) against parliamentary encroachment and manipulation as well.

Part Four

Hungary's International Relations and Security

Chapter 11

European Integration

Bennett Kovrig

If geography places Hungary at the heart of the continent, history over the past four centuries has played fast and loose with the nation's links to European modernity. Much of the country was effectively severed from Europe by a century and a half of Ottoman rule. Nominally reintegrated into Europe by the Habsburgs, Hungary remained peripheral and backward until the nineteenth century, by the end of which nationalism and economic development had forged a comparatively modern nation-state within the Dual Monarchy. Drastically reduced in territory and population after the First World War by the Treaty of Trianon, the country was politically marginalized by its irredentist ideology and suffered an economic setback, then drifted into Nazi Germany's orbit. Finally, with the collapse of Hitler's Europe, Hungary fell under Soviet domination, which cut it off from Western influences and imposed the alternative, state socialist model of modernization.

Despite these historical reverses, Hungarians never ceased to consider themselves an integral and far from negligible part of European culture and to aspire to most aspects of the modernity that characterized the more developed, Western reaches of the continent. Linguistically isolated, they could not share the pan-Slav yearnings of many of their neighbors, and were thus rather more receptive to the cultural as well as commercial influence of Austria and Germany. Long experience of ethnic and cultural mingling colored the currents of nationalism that flowed deep in the Hungarian psyche.

Forty years of Soviet domination and socialist rule generated a peculiar blend of modernity and backwardness: democracy and justice subordinated to the single party and its pseudoscientific ideology; egalitarianism flawed by new forms of social reproduction and elite corruption; a centrally planned and collectivist economy weakened by inefficiency and dependence on a backward and initially exploitative imperial power; a state-sponsored culture warped by early Russification and lingering censorship; and regional security in a "socialist commonwealth" that nullified the state's sovereignty.

The "goulash communism" of the later Kàdàr years attenuated some of the pain of this experiment. The barriers to cultural and economic links with the West were lowered, and a depoliticized society began to recover some of the mores and skills necessary for pluralism and a free market. This reformed version of state socialism could not erase the system's fundamental flaws, and it left the legacy of a crushing foreign debt, but on balance Hungary was better prepared than its socialist neighbors for peaceful transition to market democracy.

There was little debate about the alternative model: a pluralistic democracy and a social market economy (the West German formula) that promised growth as well as welfare. Hungary's political experience encompassed more authoritarianism than pluralistic democracy, but even the socialist regime in its dying days had acknowledged the preeminence of the latter model and of fundamental political and civil rights by its participation in the CSCE (Conference on Security and Cooperation in Europe) process. And if socialist rule could claim credit for a comprehensive welfare state and nominal full employment, its inefficiency had brought the country to the brink of bankruptcy and a standard of living far below that of its Western neighbors. Thus when the "free world" triumphed over the "evil empire," few Hungarians had qualms about embracing the Western image and mechanism of modernization.

Under Soviet rule, the Central and East European region had been integrated to serve the security and economic dictates of the "socialist commonwealth," meaning essentially Soviet interests. Free to redefine their national agendas after the collapse of the imperial power, the former satellites uniformly focused their eyes westward, where a more voluntary and more productive process of regional integration was under way. Economically weak and strategically vulnerable, they had no realistic prospect of adopting the nonaligned but prosperous path of a Switzerland or a Sweden. Thus Hungary, like its ex-socialist fellows, promptly sought Western aid, counsel, and the shelter of Western collective institutions. NATO, the European Union, the Council of Europe, the OECD were the potent symbols of Western modernity and of security.

The dramatic implosion of the Soviet empire, symbolized by the fall of the Berlin Wall, unleashed on both sides a euphoria that was warranted by the event's historic significance but which induced momentary illusions about the ease with which a new European order could be constructed on the ashes of the old. Finally secure on their high moral ground, Western statesmen waxed eloquent in welcoming back their poor Eastern cousins. The latter, no doubt inspired by a sense of being Yalta's victims, nursed hopes of Western largesse and anticipated early access to the material benefits of European integration. This euphoria was soon dissipated by political realism and economic reality, a necessary correction that brought in its wake growing disillusionment in the East and indifference in the West.

Hungary, which enjoyed a head start in political and economic transformation, is a prime case study in the progress and difficulties of transition. Before turning to the central focus of this survey, Hungary's relations with the European Union, brief mention must be made of the political-ideological and military-security aspects of integration. Security has many interlinked dimensions, which in Europe are represented by a multiplicity of institutions, chief among them the European Union and NATO.

A common denominator of these institutions is insistence on democracy and human rights, and in Europe the oldest and primary agency dedicated to these principles is the comparatively little-known Council of Europe. The CE eagerly assumed the task of scrutinizing the democratic credentials of ex-socialist states, all of which understood that a clean bill of political health was a precondition to European integration. Hungary was first off the mark, formally applying for CE membership as early as November 16, 1989. The CE duly observed and approved of the Hungarian elections held the following spring, and in November 1990 Hungary formally acceded to membership. Hungarian diplomacy had an additional motive for membership, the pursuit of minority rights. In the event, it was instrumental in securing CE guidelines that might induce neighboring regimes, notably in Slovakia and Romania, to grant rights to the sizeable Magyar communities in those countries.

In the sphere of military security, Hungary was the first to urge disbandment of the Warsaw Pact, and one of the first to express a wish to join NATO. It took up NATO's palliative offers, membership in the North Atlantic Cooperation Council and the Partnership for Peace program, and has participated in NATO's Implementation Force for Bosnia, but the government was determined to win full membership.

The hurdles were considerable. Russia bitterly opposed an eastward expansion by NATO. The West Europeans were wary of provoking Moscow and of committing themselves to risk the lives of their soldiers in Balkan and other potential Eastern quarrels; France, in particular, was engaged in a quarrel with Washington over the Europeanization of NATO and refused to share the cost of enlargement. The U.S. Congress, for its part, balked at the potential costs of expansion. Nor was the Hungarian public enthusiastic about NATO; opinion polls conducted in early 1996 indicated that less than 60 percent supported membership, with a majority opposed to sending troops to defend other countries, to having NATO troops based and exercises conducted in Hungary, and indeed to greater spending on defence.[1] Moreover, Hungary's candidacy presented two particular problems: the lack of borders contiguous with the alliance (unless Slovenia, Slovakia, or Austria joined NATO), and the country's disputes with Slovakia and Romania over the status of Magyar minorities.

The Clinton administration nevertheless pressed ahead, and in July 1977, NATO issued a formal invitation to Hungary—as well as the Czech Republic and Poland—to join the alliance in 1999. Russia had to accept the palliative of institutionalized consultations. All parties in the Hungarian Parliament rallied behind a campaign to secure popular endorsement for membership, and in the November referendum, over 80 percent (with a turnout barely over 50 percent) voted in favor. Hungary is thus well on its way to integrating the Western security regime, a step that will be consummated well before its more problematic adhesion to the European Union.

Relations with the European Union

The principle of openness to all European democracies was entrenched in Article 237 of the Treaty of Rome, and the Berlin Wall had been barely breached when Western eminences such as President Mitterrand, Chancellor Kohl, and the President of the European Community (as it was known then, EC), Jacques Delors, evoked early accession of the Central and East European countries to the Community. There soon followed the launch of an aid program, coordinated by Brussels, initially designed for Poland and Hungary, and known as PHARE. Hungary signed the framework agreement regulating the use of PHARE funds on September 3, 1990. Often compared unfavorably, and perhaps unrealistically, with the bountiful Marshall Plan, PHARE is at least a tangible gesture of assistance, of which more later. The road to membership would prove to be far more contentious and difficult.

Hungary's formal relations with the Community date back to 1988, when following an EC-CMEA (Council for Mutual Economic Assistance) accord on mutual recognition, Budapest became the first beneficiary of the EC's so-called "second-generation" agreements on trade and cooperation with CMEA members. The implosion of the Soviet bloc and Germany's reunification imposed a reassessment of the scope and pace of integration in the EC. To reinvigorate the EC by deepening and accelerating integration of the Twelve became France's preferred strategy for coping with greater Germany. Chancellor Kohl championed the interests of his Eastern neighbors, and particularly of Hungary, but he was understandably more concerned with assuaging French apprehensions and with the management of reunification. The outcome was the Treaty on European Union, initialled by the Twelve at Maastricht in December 1991, an ambitious but muddled package of undertakings to deepen integration, notably by monetary union. Meanwhile, it was left to Britain, as always hostile to deepening the EC, to devise a new type of association as a sop to the Central and East Europeans, and the proposal was adopted by the European Council in April 1990.

The first candidates, Budapest, Prague, and Warsaw, coordinated their approach to the Community and made clear their common expectation that these association agreements would put them on the fast track to full membership. The EC Commission, on the other hand, was mandated only to negotiate a trade agreement, not to offer any commitment on accession. The contentious issue of membership and protectionist interests in the EC made for ten months of tough bargaining. The resulting "Europe Agreement" was signed by Hungary on December 16, 1991, and it came into force on February 1, 1994, after ratification by the concerned legislatures. An interim agreement allowed early application of commercial and economic clauses.

The Europe Agreements' common preamble acknowledged that the new associates' "final objective" is full membership, and that "this association, in the view of the parties, will help to achieve this objective." Even this noncommittal formula was treated by the EC as a concession. The agreements also provided for bilateral "political dialogue" in a ministerial Association Council and an Association Committee of functionaries, and required adaptation of commercial laws and regulations to EC norms.

On economic and commercial relations, the agreements invoked the fundamental commitment of the EC—known since Maastricht as the European Union—to free movement of goods, capital, services, and persons, although the actual provisions made no allowance for mobility of labor. Least liberal were the meat and agricultural tariff and quota reductions, based on the low access set by the EC in the socialist era. With regard to industrial tariffs, unilaterally granted benefits under GSP and quota suspensions were confirmed, the EC undertaking to eliminate tariffs promptly on "non-sensitive" goods (accounting for some 70 percent of its imports from the first three associated countries) and to reduce tariffs on the remainder progressively to zero by 1997. However, two product groups of special interest to the associates, textiles and iron and steel, were subject to special protectionist provisions.

Hungary had longer deadlines for eliminating its tariffs, ranging to 2001 in the case of "sensitive" imports, and it obtained a "nascent industries" clause allowing for exceptional tariff protection for new and restructured industries or in the event of serious social difficulties.[2] The agreement further required Hungary to eliminate within five years all discriminatory measures against businesses established by EC parents—a (reciprocal) concession that opened the way for tough competition particularly for fledgling financial service establishments.

The trade concessions had an element of asymmetry in favor of the new associates, but the latter were dismayed at the West Europeans' protectionism. Michel Camdessus, the IMF's secretary-general, echoed their disappointment: "We incited them to come to the economy of the market, and we close ours."[3] Nor did the Europe Agreements offer any financial aid beyond the existing PHARE program.

PHARE earmarked 582.8 million ECU for Hungary between 1990 and 1995, though actual disbursements were substantially lower due to the slow pace of administration. Only a small fraction of the funding could be characterized as financial aid, for some 40 percent covered Western advisory services for various aspects of privatization and legal harmonization. At its Copenhagen meeting in June 1993, the European Council decided to allocate up to 15 percent of PHARE's budget to major infrastructure projects in the region. With the extension of PHARE to additional recipients, Hungary's share declined from 20 percent in 1990 to 8.6 percent in 1994, by which time global PHARE funding had stabilized at around one billion ECU.[4] The EU is also involved in Hungarian development projects through the European Investment Bank (which lent 417.10 million ECU in 1990–95) and the European Bank for Reconstruction and Development (EBRD), in which the EU has a 51 percent share.

The impact of the Europe Agreement and PHARE on Hungary's economic transition and recovery is difficult to isolate and measure, though some analysts judge it to have been negligible. Even before the new trade regime came into effect, Hungary was remarkably successful in reorienting its trade from the moribund CMEA market westward. Hungary's trade with the EU more than doubled between 1989 and 1995, putting it in third place among Europe Agreement partners behind Poland and the Czech Republic. With the expansion of the EU to fifteen members in 1995, its share in Hungarian foreign trade rose to over 65 percent. However, in 1992 the trade balance swung heavily in the EU's favor. Indeed, the EU reaped substantial benefits: if in 1993–94 it disbursed through PHARE some $75 million (out of the allocated $230 million), it also earned a $2 billion surplus in its trade with Hungary.[5] Even in the agricultural sector, where historically Hungary enjoys a certain comparative advantage, Hungary's favorable trade ratio fell from 6:1 in 1989 to 2:1 in 1993. Food imports from the EU, 60 percent of which benefited from Common Agricultural Program (CAP) "export refunds," more than doubled, while the proportion of agricultural products in Hungary's exports declined from 24.3 percent in 1990 to 21.8 percent in 1994. Hungary's current account deficit in 1995 stood at 5.7 percent of GDP, the second highest in the region.[6]

It is scarcely surprising that the liberalization of trade favored the economically stronger partners over an economy in a state of near collapse, but to the extent that transition and modernization depend on capital inputs, it is noteworthy that Hungary's gross debt grew by $4 billion in 1993–94 to $26 billion. This debt amounts to 250 percent of annual exports, the highest ratio in the region, while the servicing costs are equivalent to 40 percent of annual exports. And this despite the asymmetry of the Europe Agreement's tariff concessions and the fact that Hungary received half of all foreign investment directed to the region. It is at least ironic that East Germany, once one of the most Stalinist of satellites, has benefited from public aid on the order of $30–35 billion since 1990 as well as immediate absorption into the EU, while Hungary, the most liberal satellite, was not even offered rescheduling on the Polish model and transferred in the same period to Western creditors some $16 billion in repayment and debt servicing.[7]

For a country that is short of domestic capital, energy-poor, and heavily dependent on trade, free access to the EU market and to the other benefits of full membership is crucial, but political and economic factors in the West have militated against early integration. The Copenhagen Council (June 1993) did issue a guarded invitation to membership: if the candidates satisfied conditions regarding democratic institutions, the rule of law, and an internationally competitive market economy, they could be admitted subject to the EU's "capacity to absorb new members while maintaining the momentum of European integration"—a huge caveat. The Council's concrete decisions were limited to the creation of a structure for cooperation on specific issues, ranging from environmental protection to foreign affairs, and to easing trade restrictions on textiles and metallurgical goods.

Following the admission of Austria, Finland, and Sweden, and encouraged by Chancellor Kohl, Hungary submitted its formal application for membership on April 1, 1994. In December, at its meeting in Essen, the European Council took a small step forward in confirming the eventuality of membership with a statement entitled "The Strategy for the Integration of the Central and Eastern European Countries." This called for "structured multilateral relations," signifying annual summit meetings with the associated countries as well as other, more frequent ministerial meetings, and instructed the Commission to prepare a White Paper on the adjustments applicants would have to make to ready themselves for the EU's internal market. The Council decision also prescribed the role of PHARE in helping to prepare candidates for admission, to help them absorb the so-called "acquis communautaire" (the accumulated integrative aspects of the EU) and assist medium-term restructuring of the economy.

The White Paper, delivered by Karel Van Miert, commissioner in charge of EU enlargement, was endorsed by the Cannes Council in June 1995.[8] The report prudently noted that it did not aim to fix the modalities of accession to membership, and that access to the single market does not signify full integration. It did propose that applicants be offered a detailed agenda and schedule of measures, sector by sector, necessary for their participation in the internal market. At the end of 1995, the Commission created a technical assistance and information office (TAIEX) to administer the implementation of the White Paper's recommendations.

By proceeding to the stage of an agenda for partial harmonization, the EU artfully managed to postpone tough political decisions while pacifying its impatient suitors. At their Madrid meeting in December 1995, its leaders confirmed without elaboration that enlargement was "both a political necessity and a historical opportunity." Further political consideration of membership had to await conclusion of the Intergovernmental Conference (IGC), a review process mandated by the Maastricht Treaty and begun in March 1996. The IGC was charged with formulating recommendations for reform of the EU's institutions and processes to cope with changed and changing circumstances, such as the recent expansion to fifteen members, the progress towards economic and monetary union (EMU), and the prospect of further expansion. In the meantime, the EU Commission was instructed to monitor progress on implementation of the White Paper proposals and to produce an "opinion" on the readiness of each applicant as well as on the financial and social impact of their accession.

Hungarian Transition and Compliance

Hungary's democratic credentials were established early, and the unquestioned compliance of its constitutional order with Western norms satisfies a key condition of its integration in the EU. It also satisfies the EU requirement that it actively and clearly wishes to assume all the responsibilities of membership. Since the inception of democracy in 1990, all political parties represented in Parliament have endorsed the goal of European integration, and the Socialist–Free Democrat coalition that came to power in 1994 under Prime Minister Gyula Horn has been steadfast in pursuit of that objective.

Early into his tenure Horn issued an alarmist appeal to the West, warning of economic collapse and serious instability if the EU did not move quickly on enlargement.[9] Such cries of distress and impatience had oft been voiced by Central European statesmen from Lech Walesa to Vaclav Havel, but EU politics imposed a measured pace of rapprochement, and Budapest girded for the long haul. Thus an Inter-Ministerial Committee headed by the foreign minister coordinates a multiplicity of committees and working groups dealing with the complexities of adapting to EU norms, while parliamentary scrutiny is provided by a Committee on European Integration Affairs. Beginning in July 1995, the government began the practice of submitting to the Association Council half-yearly progress reports on its preparations for membership.

Compliance with the stronger party was always the rule. Thus, when the West Europeans urged the ex-socialist countries to develop regional relations before applying to join the EC, the Visegrad group (Czechoslovakia, as it then was, Hungary, and Poland) obligingly formed the Central European Free Trade Association (CEFTA). Their agreement, which came into force on March 31, 1993, provided for the phased implementation of free trade by 2000. Though regional free trade remains a worthy objective, CEFTA could hardly serve as a substitute for European integration, for its members suffered from similar ailments for which they could provide little mutual relief; apart from the Czech-Slovak nexus, less than 10 percent of the members' trade is within the region. Nor has the creation of CEFTA prevented its members from independently pressing their case in the West, most notably in the case of Vaclav Klaus's Czech Republic. None of them wanted to be held back by the slower countries in the region.

In its foreign and security policy Hungary has also made an effort to follow the EU's lead and act as a responsible European. Reports the Foreign Ministry:

> The Hungarian positions on disarmament, human rights and regional issues . . . have been harmonized with those of the EU. Hungary has subscribed to numerous EU declarations and demarches and taken part in the successful drive to secure indefinite and unconditional prolongation

of the nuclear non-proliferation treaty (NPT). Hungary has also developed close cooperation with the EU in its capacity as 1995 Chairman-in-Office of the Organization of Security and Cooperation in Europe.

By signing the Hungarian-Slovak Basic Treaty and proving its commitment to formulating a Hungarian-Romanian basic treaty, Hungary has made a major contribution to the European Stability Pact (ESP), one of the EU's most important common actions. The 17 basic treaties so far signed by Hungary have all been appended to the ESP. Hungary has also joined in EU cooperation with third countries.[10]

The Antall government's forceful advocacy of the rights of Hungarian minorities in the neighboring states caused some nervousness in the West; its successor has toned down the rhetoric and in August 1996 concluded a bilateral treaty with Romania. In the protracted Yugoslav crisis, though concerned about Serbian treatment of the Hungarian minority in Voivodina, Budapest cooperated in the United Nations' (UN) embargo and the eventual NATO operation in Bosnia. And Hungary has of course participated fully in the multilateral "structured dialogue" stipulated by the Essen Council, in complement to its bilateral contacts with the EU.

Progress in legal harmonization, notably in the spheres of the economy and of environmental protection, was sufficiently advanced that in March 1996 Hungary was admitted to the Organization for Economic Cooperation and Development. The OECD is providing assistance for a training program to sensitize civil servants to the requirements of European integration. In June 1995 the government launched a three-year plan for adapting legal provisions to the requirements of the EU internal market. A "communication strategy," designed to educate the public about the issue of accession to the EU, was submitted by the government to the Essen Council, and is being implemented with the aid of PHARE funds. For the moment, the public's disenchantment with the fruits of transition has not been translated into hostility to European integration. A European Commission survey conducted in November 1995 found that 80 percent of Hungarians were in favor of membership.[11]

If all of these measures testify to Hungary's determination to satisfy the criteria for accession, they are also those more amenable to the exercise of political will and professional expertise. Economic factors, which will weigh most heavily in the EU's appraisal of applicants, continue to bear the heavy legacy of state socialism; they are also subject to domestic as well as external forces that no democratic government can readily manipulate.

For the first few years after its liberation from socialist rule, Hungary enjoyed a glowing reputation in the West for its rapid transition to democracy and the market. The Antall government chose a gradualist economic strategy over the Polish "big-bang" alternative. The jury is still out on the comparative merits of the two approaches, and indeed the particular circumstances of the Central European countries may differ too much to allow a consensual assessment. Nor were any of the post-communist regimes immune to misjudgment; the Antall government spent over $3 billion in its attempts to bail out state-owned banks.

A common denominator of the transition economies, the sharp fall in the standard of living, was bound to produce a popular reaction, which in Hungary gave a huge majority to the Socialist Party (a social-democratic descendant of the pre-1990 ruling party) in the 1994 elections. Considering that Hungary, like most of the Central and East European countries, was (and remains) in the throes of an economic crisis unprecedented in Europe since the Great Depression, it is remarkable that political order and social peace have continued to prevail.

Squeezed by the IMF and the World Bank, and inspired by the lure of the EU, the new Horn government imposed emergency stabilization measures, including devaluation and an 8 percent import surcharge. It then developed a "medium-term economic policy strategy" for 1995–98 to reduce a growing budgetary deficit by cutting social benefits and services and to relaunch the privatization of state assets, notably in the energy sector. The latter initiative helped to draw an additional $4 billion in foreign direct investment in 1995 alone, for a cumulative FDI of $10.6 billion since 1991, more than all of the other Central European transition economies. However, total investment has not yet reached its 1989 level, due to a decline in domestic investment.

The transformation of the economy's structure and ownership has proceeded at a rapid pace. The private sector's share of GDP rose from 20 percent in 1990 to 70 percent in 1995, and its share of employment to 65 percent, with a shift away from manufacturing and toward trade and services.[12] The government hopes to raise the private sector's share of GDP to 85 percent by 2000. The privatization of agriculture did not produce the feared fragmentation of production units, but between 1989 and 1994 this sector's share of GDP fell from 13.7 percent to 6.7 percent, and of employment from 17.9 percent to 6.7 percent (compared to some 3 percent in the EU).

Privatization and the multifaceted modernization that foreign direct investment hopefully brings enhance Hungary's prospects for European integration. Other indicators paint a grimmer picture. Between 1990 and 1993 Hungary's GDP contracted by 22.2 percent. In 1994 it rebounded, but the foreign trade deficit hit $3.9 billion that year. By 1997, the economic indictators pointed to a steady recovery: the GDP was growing at a rate of over 5 percent (and industrial production by close to 18 percent), the trade deficit fell to $2.2 billion, and the rate of inflation had fallen to below 18 percent.[13] However, real wages had been falling for years, and over 20 percent of the population had slid below the poverty line, while unemployment approached 12 percent and was likely to rise, not least due to cutbacks in social services. Small wonder if surveys showed that Hungarians were among the most disenchanted in Central and Eastern Europe with their plummeting standard of living and indeed with the market economy and the whole process of democratization.[14]

Merely to reach its 1990 level by 2000, Hungary's GDP would have to grow by a cumulative 21 percent in the last five years of the century.[15] That, even considering the Polish pattern of contraction and growth, is an unlikely performance. By most economic criteria Hungary is far behind the EU average, not to speak of the benchmarks for EMU. Hungary's GDP per capita in 1996 stood at $6,410 (at purchasing-power parity exchange rates), a shade below that of the poorest EU member, Greece, while the EU average stood at $19,250.[16] To be sure, such figures do not take into account the "gray economy," which in Hungary is estimated to add as much as 25–30 percent to official GDP figures. But even so, and even if EU growth remains at its present low level, the gap is not likely to shrink by much as Hungary negotiates the terms of membership.[17]

Western Concerns

That economic gap colors the EU's perception of the benefits and burdens of enlargement. In March 1996, shortly before the EU's new president, Jacques Santer, arrived in Budapest to deliver the voluminous questionnaire which would ultimately inform the Commission's opinion on Hungary's eligibility, the government's chief integration strategist, Andràs Inotai, warned that the EU faced a crucial economic question: Would enlargement to the East improve the EU's position in the world market?[18]

Isolating the case of Hungary from that of the other first-line candidates, one could argue that both the benefits and costs are of modest scale. Between 1989 and 1994 Hungary's share of imports by the Twelve rose from 0.2 percent to 0.4 percent, hardly a major threat to Western producers, and this at a time of rising Hungarian productivity and of Hungarian wage rates that on average are a third of those in Portugal. To be sure, Hungary's agricultural exports would continue to enjoy a comparative advantage were it not for the CAP's subsidies, but the agricultural lobby in the EU is fiercely opposed to both foreign competition and to a dilution of the CAP.

On the other hand, the Hungarian market is thirsty for Western producer and consumer goods and services—witness the rapid growth in imports from the EU—and modernization of the infrastructure will draw heavily on imported technology. A comparatively skilled and adaptable labor force and low wage rates have and will continue to draw direct investment and joint ventures that can exploit not only the small domestic market, and the regional one, but also compete profitably in the European and world markets. In short, if the issue was simply one of free trade, Hungary could be integrated to mutual benefit and with comparatively small discomfort to a few sensitive sectors. Indeed, some analysts and politicians have suggested that given the time frame of economic convergence the Central Europeans should approach the EU by stages, passing first through EFTA and the European Economic Area.[19]

The European Union, however, is not simply a free trade zone but an experiment in comprehensive economic, social, and political integration, which is precisely why Hungary and the other applicants refuse to consider less potent alternatives. Its social policies privilege harmonization of standards and substantially increase the costs of production. Mobility of labor in the internal market also induces a convergence of wage rates and social benefits. Balanced development is promoted by equalization programs that redistribute wealth from richer to poorer regions. And European consumers pay a stiff price for the promotion and protection of a highly productive agricultural sector.

Full membership in the EU brings a share of these benefits, costs, and responsibilities, and the redistributive aspect of integration means that until the distant day when levels of development are fully equalized, some countries will enjoy not only a comparative advantage in the costs of production but receive more than they contribute to the common budget of the EU. The accession of Greece, Spain, and Portugal entailed a substantial commitment of transfers from the senior members, a sacrifice that the Fifteen are not prepared to repeat for the sake of the Central Europeans, particularly at a time of economic doldrums. The latest adherents, Austria, Finland, and Sweden (Norway having opted out at the last minute) were all the more welcome since their levels of development demanded no net transfers of benefits.

Much of the debate on enlargement to the East has thus focused on the costs to the EU of admitting countries poorer than almost every member and therefore a potential drain on the resources or benefits of the Fifteen. Hungarians and Czechs could argue that their economic backwardness was a temporary regression caused by war and the socialist experiment, and that their fundamental economic development was more advanced than that of, say, Greece or Portugal. The bottom line is that by current EU criteria all of the Central Europeans would be eligible for substantial transfers from the common resources of the union. And that alarms both the net donors and the net beneficiaries among the Fifteen.

Estimates of the cost of admitting the four Visegrad countries have varied widely but are of necessity based on unaltered application of the two principal EU funding programs, the CAP and the Structural Funds (aid to backward or declining regions, for retraining, etc.). The first accounts for 50 percent, the second for 30 percent of the EU budget.

With regard to the Structural Funds, a comparison can be drawn between the four principal actual recipients, Greece, Ireland, Portugal, and Spain, who take 65 percent, and the Visegrad four, two groups with roughly the same population (62.5 million and 64 million). The GDP per capita of the richest Visegrad member (the Czech Republic) is a shade higher than that of the poorest EU member (Greece); in the combined group the ratio of richest (Spain) to poorest (Poland) is better than 2:1. It has been estimated that if the Visegrad four were to receive the same treatment as the others, the budget for the Structural Funds would have to be increased from $36 billion to $67 billion. When the present CAP is factored into the calculation, the same source estimates the necessary addition to the EU budget to be on the order of $75 billion, or an increase of 72 percent. Allowing for the Commission's estimate of contributions from the Visegrad four to the EU budget, the net addition becomes $69 billion, a 66 percent increase that would have to be funded by the Fifteen.[20] These estimates would of course be altered by more optimistic projections of economic growth in the East, statistical adjustment or fiscal measures to incorporate the gray economy, and a contraction in the agricultural sector, but the resultant reductions would not significantly change the order of magnitude.

The political chances of the EU paying such a price for enlargement to the East are close to nil. On the other hand, to exclude the Central Europeans from these programs is scarcely conceivable, for this would create separate categories of membership and undermine the fundamental principles of the EU. The alternatives, given enlargement, are clear: reform and reduce the existing aid and subsidy programs to allow for more recipients, negotiate entry terms that offer new members graduated access to the programs, or a combination of these two approaches. The most likely scenario is the combination of reform and a long transition to full benefits, and even that will require strong political leadership both East and West.

There are sound economic grounds for reforming the CAP even without the problem of new members, and indeed the latest GATT agreements require the EU to liberalize agricultural trade and reduce subsidies. Given the tremendous resistance of the agricultural lobbies, the politics of CAP reform are bound to be dilatory and incremental. The Structural Funds have suffered from loose administration and vast leakage, notably in Greece, so that substantial savings could be effected simply by tightening up procedures and monitoring. Raising threshold criteria would not exclude poorer countries such as the Central Europeans, but it is hard to imagine that Spain, or Ireland (which receives over 2 percent of its GDP from this source) would willingly give up the largesse. And it must be remembered that the admission of new members requires unanimous consent in the EU.

The net cost of admitting Hungary alone would of course be lower in both absolute and relative terms, for, while its eligibility for Structural Funds is greater than that of the Czech Republic, the proportion of its workforce in agriculture is lower than that of Poland and Slovakia. But Poland, if only for political reasons, will not likely be left out of the first group of new members, and thus the EU's broad calculations of cost will influence the timing and terms of admission for Hungary as for the others.

Even if the EU finds the political courage to increase its levies to provide aid and subsidies to the new members, it will have to devise means to keep the costs lower than the projections cited earlier. Monika Wulf-Mathies, the commissioner in charge of regional aid, has noted that the rule requiring members to match such aid from their own budgets would strain the capacity of the Central Europeans, implying that aid should therefore be capped in terms of its proportion to GDP.[21] With regard to the CAP, the EU is already committed to cut the proportion of this item in its budget, and a further round of reform could reduce the cost of Central European participation to a more tolerable level.

Finally, in December 1977, the EU's Luxembourg summit formally launched the process of expansion, inviting Hungary—as well as the Czech Republic, Estonia, Poland, Slovenia, and Cyprus—to negotiate the terms of accession. On past record, these negotiations will take at lest two or three years, and the process of parliamentary ratification two years more. Will Hungary join the European Union by 2002, already well beyond Chancellor Kohl's airy forecast of 2000? And on what terms? In both East and West many political and economic problems will have to be resolved before the answers become clear. The IGC failed to produce a plan for adapting the EU's institutional framework. This, as well as the common agricultural policy, regional assistance, and the EU budget will have to be fundamentally reformed before new members can join—a tall order considering the currently low popularity of European integration in the West. It is both ironic and awkward that the Central Europeans should clamour for European integration at a very time when the process is losing support in the West, for the West Europeans are not in a welcoming mood. Asked in a survey to indicate their priorities regarding the EU, 53 percent cited deepening, 15 percent no change, and 6 percent dissolution. Only 17 percent of West Europeans felt that enlargement was the most urgent task ahead.[22]

What Europe? For Whom?

The West Europeans, notes one analyst regretfully, tend to focus on the costs of enlargement, while the Central Europeans tend to see membership as offering a solution to all their problems.[23] Enlargement poses political dilemmas on both sides. The logic of European integration favors enlargement, which in the end should generate both greater prosperity and security for all. But if membership in the EU signifies acceptance of a common destiny and implies a willingness to defend all members, are the West Europeans prepared for such a commitment with regard to their Eastern cousins? And are they ready to assume the considerable financial burden of enlargement at a time when the transformation of the global economy is imposing on them a heavy cost in unemployment, slow growth, and budgetary austerity? To force the pace of enlargement may accentuate neonationalist tendencies in the West. Already the idea of a referendum on enlargement (in additional to parliamentary ratification) has been aired in some EU countries, and if the Maastricht referenda are of any guidance, it is by no means a foregone conclusion that Hungary and its neighbors will be welcomed.

The political outlook in Central Europe appears more positive, but there too questions remain. The communists after the war promised that a generation's sacrifice would earn socialist prosperity. Now another generation has to bear the severe discomfort of long transition to earn the affluence promised by market democracy. European integration may be the best road to that affluence, but if it is delayed too long, and if the benefits seem too skimpy, the response may be a loss of social support and a neonationalist reaction in the East. The West's tendency to ride roughshod over Hungarian sensibilities regarding the minority problem in Slovakia and Romania also threatens to delegitimize the process of integration. Powerful Western diplomatic pressure in favor of an early and expedient conclusion of a Hungarian-Romanian treaty produced a compromise that failed to entrench guarantees of minority rights considered essential by Budapest and thus evoked bitter memories among Hungarians of the Trianon dictate.

Today's European Union, observes David Calleo, is a hybrid of federalist, Gaullist, and balance-of-power tendencies, and the safest prediction is that it will remain so.[24] France and Germany remain committed to creating a tightly bound core, but there is no consensus within the EU on the future course of integration, hence the popularity of such notions as "variable geometry" and "concentric circles." France and the other "Latin" countries pursue their Mediterranean interests while remaining suspicious of Germany's predominance and Eastern interests. They fret that new members, notably Hungary, will reinforce that predominance. Germany, which already has the lion's share of Hungary's trade with the EU, remains committed in principle to enlargement but is already stretching its resources to integrate the eastern provinces. Britain, content with a free market, champions enlargement mainly to impede deepening of the union. And when the Central Europeans, including the Estonians, accede to the union, other lands beyond—in the Balkans, the Baltic, the East—will become the peripheral and demanding outsiders.

Meanwhile, the EU is suffering from a deep legitimacy crisis that could ultimately undermine the existing architecture and sense of community. Advocates of integration fear that premature enlargement could exacerbate the inherent inefficiency of the EU, releasing centrifugal forces that would lead to intergovernmentalism and a "Europe à la carte." Too much zeal in deepening could, of course, be similarly counterproductive.[25] A revival of concern with national and ethnic identity is evident in today's Europe, and while this does not immediately threaten the survival of the EU, it does confirm that integration, particularly in the cultural sphere, is a far from linear progression. The EU's future members are even more jealous of their newly regained national sovereignty; but eager for economic union and the protection of security regimes, they are subject to powerful forces of ethnocultural nationalism.

Hungary is inextricably part of Europe, but the process of integration it wishes to partake of is fraught with uncertainty. Despite all the difficulties, the chances are that within the next five years it will have acceded to the principal institutions of European integration. Then, after centuries of vicissitudes on the periphery, Hungarians will finally be able to play a more direct role in defining the directions of a continent still in search of its soul and destiny.

Notes

1. USIA surveys cited in *The Economist*, 29 July 1996, 31, and European Commission survey cited in *Népszabadsàg*, 16 March 1996.

2. France, Direction des relations extérieures, "Les accords d'association entre la Communauté et les pays d'Europe centrale et orientale: Présentation du dispositif commercial," Paris, 3 February 1992.

3. *Le Monde*, 3 April 1992.

4. See European Union, Rapid Memo /96/33, 2 April 1996; Béla Kàdàr, "Az Európai Unió keleti kibovülésének kérdojelei és feltételei" [Conditions and Question-marks of the European Union's Eastern Enlargement], *Külpolitika*, 1/2, Spring 1995, 15; and Commission européenne, "Qu'est-ce que Phare?" Brussels, December 1994.

5. Kàdàr, loc. cit., 22.

6. See European Commission, Directorate-General for Agriculture, "Agricultural Situation and Prospects in the Central and Eastern European Countries: Hungary," Working Document VI/1110/95, Brussels, 1995, 42–45; and *The Economist*, 10 August 1996, 84.

7. François Fejto, "A Curtain of Indifference to Follow the Iron Curtain?" *The Hungarian Quarterly*, 36/139, Autumn 1995, 7. It must be noted that the larger share of Poland's debt fell under the purview of the Paris Club of creditor states, whereas most of Hungary's debt was incurred from the private sector, represented in the less amenable London Club. Hungary's first democratic government could have reneged on the debts left by its predecessor, but it is not clear that the benefits would have outweighed the damage to the country's credit rating.

8. Commission des Communautés européennes, "Livre blanc: préparation des Etats associés de l'Europe centrale et orientale à leur intégration dans le marché intérieur de l'Union," Brussels, 3 May 1995. See also Eliane Mossé, "Les PECO et l'UE: aspects économiques," *Politique étrangère*, 61/1, Spring 1996, 151–52.

9. Michael Mihalka, "The Bumpy Road to Western Europe," *Transition* (OMRI), 1/1, 30 January 1995, 76.

10. Hungary, Ministry of Foreign Affairs, "Relations between Hungary and the European Union," Fact Sheets on Hungary, 4, 1995.

11. Cited in *Népszabadsàg*, 16 March 1996.

12. Michael S. Borish and Michel Noël, "Private Sector Expansion in Central Europe," *Transition* (World Bank), 7/5–6, May–June 1996, 6–8.

13. *The Economist*, 7 March 1998, 140.

14. *Népszabadsàg*, 16 March 1996.

15. European Commission, "Agricultural Situation," 52.

16. *The Economist*, 20 December 1997, 20.

17. See the Economist Intelligence Unit forecast in *The Economist*, 9 December 1996, 116; cf. Làszló Csaba, "A KGST-bol az Unióba" [From the CMEA to the Union], *Európai Szemle*, 6/1, Spring 1995, 58.

18. *Népszabadsàg*, 29 March 1996.

19. See R.E. Baldwin, *Towards an Integrated Europe*, Center for Economic Policy Research, London, 1994; and Jean-Jacques Hallaert, "L'Union européenne face aux élargissements," *Politique étrangère*, 61/1, Spring 1996, 172–74.

20. Mossé, loc. cit., 155–57. Conversion rate 1 ECU = $1.20. Cf. Kàdàr, loc. cit., 19.

21. Quoted in *The Economist*, 3 August 1996, 28.

22. *Népszabadsàg*, 9 March 1996.

23. Mossé, loc. cit., 162.

24. David P. Calleo, *L'Union européenne et la fin de la guerre froide*, Les Cahiers du CERI, no. 10, Paris, 1994, 6.

25. See Wolfgang Wessels, "Evolutions possibles de l'Union européenne," *Politique étrangère*, 61/1, Spring 1996, 146–50; and Françoise de La Serre, Christian Lequesne, and Jacques Rupnik, *L'Union européenne: ouverture a l'Est?* Paris: Presses Universitaires de France, 1994, chapter 4.

Chapter 12

The Russian Factor

Aurel Braun

The late Hans Morgenthau contended that geography was one of the immutable elements of national power.[1] In the case of Hungary, however, even geography appears to have changed in the post-communist era. The collapse of the Soviet Union and its replacement by the Commonwealth of Independent States (CIS) has resulted in the disappearance of a hegemony that for more than forty decades defined the parameters for Hungarian foreign and domestic policy. The legal successor to the Soviet Union, the Russian Federation, a vast state which despite economic turmoil and political uncertainty, retains enormous human and natural resources and could conceivably pose a hegemonic or other threat, and unlike the Soviet Union, is several hundred kilometers from the Hungarian border.

Hungary, less than a decade ago an obedient member of the Moscow-led Warsaw Treaty Organization (WTO), is now eagerly awaiting membership in the North Atlantic Treaty Organization (NATO), which should come as soon as 1999. Perhaps nothing illustrates more vividly the dramatic political and military reorientation of Hungary than the presence in that country of some 3,000 American troops belonging to the Implementation Force (IFOR) committed to Bosnia, and thus part of the NATO-led forces overseeing compliance with the Dayton peace accord. They are stationed at the former Soviet air base of Taszar in southern Hungary. Moreover, most of the U.S. peacekeepers in Bosnia have passed through Taszar. The interaction between American forces and the Hungarian military has been a model of cooperation.[2] Warm relations, effective cooperation, and the acceleration of the transformation of the Hungarian military to make it more compatible with NATO forces, Budapest rightly hoped, would help put the former WTO state

273

at the head of the queue of countries seeking membership in the alliance. Yet despite Hungarian aspirations and Western promises, there remain uncertainties and concerns about NATO enlargement. And in that process of enlargement and indeed in the overall question of the security of Hungary and the entire region, Russia, despite the geographic distance, continues to loom large.

Security, that much-desired public good, however, must be clearly defined. It cannot be understood in the abstract, but must be related to the changes in the political, economic, and social firmament in a state and in a region. The desirable needs to be separated from the possible, real interests need to be clearly identified, and priorities appropriately articulated. There has been a conceptual rethinking in Hungary and in Russia and, in fact throughout the region, but it is incomplete and, I will argue, in some cases inadequate.

Granted, such conceptual rethinking is an enormous task for scholars and policy-makers alike. The momentous changes of the post-communist transitions, which are without historic precedent, have in some ways intensified the old debate between area studies and comparative analysis, though the debate may in fact overstate the tension between the two.[3] To this discussion, however, must be added the dimension of strategic studies if the security issues are to be adequately understood. It is therefore my intention to examine the concepts of security in the context of transition, followed by Hungary's and Russia's particular security concerns and, lastly, to assess the prospects and dangers inherent in the solutions that Hungary and Russia seek in order to ensure area security. For it is possible that what at first seems to be eminently sensible goals and policies may ultimately have deleterious effects.

Rethinking and Restructuring Security

Russia

There has been considerable progress in the reconceptualization of security. In the Soviet Union this began, at least in a declaratory form, under Mikhail Gorbachev. He contended that "the recognition of others' interests"[4] was imperative in an era when "adversaries must become partners and start looking jointly for a way to achieve universal security."[5] Thus, at least formally, Soviet leaders accepted the premise that security had to be achieved in common rather than unilaterally. There was also greater awareness under Gorbachev of the need to broaden the concept of security in order to better incorporate political and other elements. At the Communist Party conference in June 1988,

Gorbachev told the gathering that "we did not [also] make use of the political opportunities opened up by the fundamental changes in the world in our efforts to assure the security of our state, to scale down tensions and promote mutual understanding between nations."[6]

Despite Gorbachev's encouraging declarations, though, there was considerable uncertainty about Soviet reconceptualization of security. It was in part muddled by extensive arguments over "reasonable sufficiency" and "defensive defense" and by the public musings of Defense Minister D.T. Yazov about the need to assure the "collective security of the Socialist community."[7] Reconceptualization of security, however, did become operational with the breakup of the Soviet Union. Under Boris Yeltsin, Russia has profoundly restructured its military relationship with Eastern Europe and the West. Russia has joined NATO's Partnership for Peace (PfP) and sent peacekeeping forces to Bosnia, together with those of NATO (though under a complex arrangement, the commanding Russian general is not under the orders of NATO's Supreme Commander in Mons, but answers to the American general directly in charge of U.S. forces in Bosnia).[8] Moscow has also encouraged foreign investments in Russia and has borrowed massively from the International Monetary Fund (IMF). Russia's desire to participate in G-7 meetings (and now create the G-8) and to rapidly increase its economic relations with the advanced industrialized democracies are further indications of Russia's recognition of both the need for common security and for a broad construction of the concept of security which involves political, economic, as well as military elements.

Still, doubts remain about the evolution of Russia's thinking on security. Moscow's military activities in what it calls "the near abroad" and Chechnya, as well as its continuing vociferous condemnation of the enlargement of NATO to East Central European states (despite formal acquiescence to enlargement with the signing of the Founding Act in May 1997) raise questions about the breadth of Moscow's thinking on security (with its continuing heavy emphasis on the military element). Further, the turmoil in the political leadership raises questions about the direction of Russian security policy.

Eastern Europe

With the retreat of the Soviet forces and the collapse of the Soviet Union, the East European states for the first time in more than four decades gained a chance to develop independent security policies. They had the opportunity to realign politically, to begin to reintegrate into Europe, and to try to resolve some of the paradoxes of exclusion and inclusion. It was the start of rethinking and restructuring security, part of a process that continues today. Important questions should have been asked about the nature of security, and the prospect and dangers in trying to safeguard national interests. How broadly should security be defined? What would be the nature of common security? What would be the meaning and relevance of deterrence? Was (or is) there in fact a security vacuum in the region?

In light of the fundamental political, economic, and social transformation taking place in the region, it only would have been prudent, one would think, to use a broader, Clausewitzian formulation of security, which would place it within a broadly defined political context. The French Defense Minister Francois Leotard, commenting on the desire of the East Central European states to join NATO, rightly suggested that "the possibility that the new democracies will join the Atlantic alliance must not be viewed on the basis of solely military considerations, but should also be viewed globally, combining the various political, military, economic, and even cultural dimensions of their integration with the West."[9] In defining common security, moreover, East European states should have been cognizant of the mutuality and indivisibility of security. That, in turn, suggests that care needs to be taken and that enhancing the security of one state is not done at the expense of diminishing that of others. That is, the concept of common security contrasts with, or at the very least transcends, the zero-sum approach to security.

The role of deterrence also should have been rethought. Broadly defined, deterrence will continue to play a role in the foreign policies of all states. Russia, Hungary, or any of the post-communist states will continue to need to deter adversaries from engaging in behavior that would be damaging to their political, economic, or military interests. But this is very different from deterrence during the Cold War when ideologically unreconcilable enemies confronted each other with enormous military power. As states moved towards democracy, as they reduced their military forces, and resolved bilateral or regional issues, as the primary concern was no longer to deter a mobilized adversary or enemy, the role of deterrence also needed to change.

Deterrence moreover carries a variety of risks and, if security goals can be achieved by less risky means, then those options certainly ought to be considered, particularly by small post-communist states. Michael Howard has drawn an important distinction between deterrence and what he has called "reassurance"—a distinction that should be part of the reconceptualization of security in the post-Cold War era.[10] He defined "reassurance" as policies and measures that instill confidence in allies so that they can conduct their domestic affairs and foreign policies without feeling intimidated.[11] Though the distinction is of relevance to all states, it is particularly relevant to small states which seek to enhance their security by joining a military alliance.

Lastly, it is important for the states in the region to clarify, in formulating their security policies, whether there is a security vacuum—a vacuum that invites adventurism and one that consequently will need to be addressed through the creation of a new security architecture or the enlargement of an existing alliance. Some analysts, such as Miroslav Polreich, the former Czechoslovakian ambassador in Vienna for CSCE, and Michael Mandelbaum, have contended that there is in fact no European security vacuum.[12] But even if Polreich and Mandelbaum overstated their case and there is a security vacuum, an assessment of the nature of that vacuum and the urgency of dealing with it should inform the reconceptualization of security. Though Hungary and Russia have both made progress in all four issue areas noted earlier in the rethinking of security, as matters stand now, the process of rethinking remains incomplete, and some of the dangers may not be understood.

Hungary's Security Concerns

In light of the history of the Soviet hegemony in Eastern Europe, it is not surprising that East European states should so enthusiastically seek the security of an alliance with the democratic nations of Western Europe. Nor should it be entirely unexpected that they would view Russia with suspicion. Nevertheless, this headlong rush to the West, the apparent belief on the part of several of these states that *ex occidente lux* ("out of the West comes light"—that is, all wisdom comes from the West) and that Russia is likely to remain an unredeemable, undemocratic adversary or has simply become irrelevant, ignores or diminishes the possibilities of building common security and reassurance throughout the continent.

Hungary, however, has been more sensitive than most of the East European states in its relations with Russia. It has taken a broad approach to security as evidenced not only by its enthusiastic support for the Organization for Security and Cooperation in Europe (OSCE), which divided the main areas of security into three spheres (security, economics, and human rights), but also in its economic and political relations with Russia. Russia has remained a key trading partner and crucial supplier of energy to Hungary.[13] In fact, in 1993, Russian exports to Hungary increased sharply[14] and Moscow has since maintained a significant surplus.[15] Both countries, moreover, have been willing to address the issue of this major trade imbalance. For instance, in March 1995, Hungary's socialist Prime Minister Gyula Horn went to

Moscow to discuss both plans for payment of Russia's debts which amounted to roughly $900 million and the large trade imbalance.[16] The talks were fruitful and five agreements were signed, including a plan under which 50 percent of deliveries of Hungarian gas would be paid for with Hungarian Ikarus buses, railroad and medical equipment, medical supplies, and food items, thus providing a sorely needed export market for Hungarian goods.[17]

In addition to steadily increasing trade, there have been improvements in other areas of economic cooperation. In 1994, for instance, Russia's giant Gazprom set up Panrusgaz, a joint venture with a Hungarian oil company (MOL) and in March of 1996, the Hungarian government allowed Panrusgaz to get involved in the distribution of gas within Hungary itself.[18] Moreover, the government gave its blessing to a Gazprom project that would see a pipeline built from Slovakia to Italy, through Hungary.[19] This could give the Russian company a considerable degree of control not only in supplying gas to Hungary but also over its distribution in the Danube River area. The Hungarian post-communist governments have also been sensitive to the interplay of economic and political elements in relations with Russia. (It remains to be seen how the new Fidesz–led government will handle matters.) The right-of-center Hungarian Democratic Forum government agreed to a settlement with Moscow over the latter's debt, whereby Russia paid off a significant portion (about US$800 million) in 1993 with 28 MiG-29 fighter planes.[20] This represented a considerable sacrifice on the part of the Hungarian government, since Russian equipment would make integration of forces with NATO more difficult and it would also leave Hungary more vulnerable to possible Russian pressures when it came time to supply spare parts.

The socialist-led government of Hungary has proven itself even more adept at dealing with Russia. Hungary assumed the OSCE chairmanship in 1995 and its handling of the Chechen crisis demonstrated considerable diplomatic skills on the part of her foreign minister and his representative to the discussions on Chechnya. Hungary's chairmanship allowed that organization to have an input and try to resolve the conflict in Chechnya (sadly without ultimate success) without alienating Russia.[21] Furthermore, it has been said that if the Hungarian representative, Ambassador Istvan Gyarmati, had not been so thoroughly familiar with Russian political culture, he would probably have found it impossible to navigate his way around the Kremlin corridors.[22] Familiarity with Russian political culture, and this is especially evident in the case of Horn's socialist government, should then be an important asset in devising security arrangements that would satisfy both Hungary and Russia. Thus, there has been not only continuity in good bilateral relations but also the prospect for further improvement.

Hungary, as well, has signaled its intentions for good regional relations through agreements that it has reached with its immediate neighbors. A treaty with Ukraine was a relatively low-key affair, because there were few outstanding issues between the two states. Hungary was also careful to signal to Russia that an agreement with Ukraine did not mean that Budapest was downgrading the importance of its relations with Moscow. The more difficult tests however were agreements with Slovakia and Romania, both states with large Hungarian minorities, which often showed inadequate sensitivity toward minority ethnic rights.

Thus stabilizing relations with some of its immediate neighbors proved to be a more difficult task for Hungary. But in 1995, Hungary signed a basic treaty with Slovakia,[23] and a basic treaty with Romania in September 1996.[24] In the case of each treaty, Hungary (and some would argue the other parties as well) made significant concessions. The treaties, therefore, demonstrated a strong willingness on the part of Hungary to try to have good relations with its neighbors, even if contentious issues such as the rights of large numbers of Hungarians living in neighboring states, had to be overcome. It could be argued that the message to Russia would be that Hungary, far from seeking provocation or confrontation, has consistently preferred accommodation for the sake of regional peace and stability.

The two treaties, though, do or should provide some lessons and warnings to Hungary in its negotiations for membership in NATO and in its dealings with Russia. Considerable pressure was brought to bear on all parties, particularly Hungary, to sign these treaties. In the case of the Hungarian-Slovak treaty, it was hardly a coincidence that the signing occurred just prior to a gathering of the fifty-two country OSCE during which the Stability Pact (the result of an initiative of French Prime Minister Edouard Balladur, an initiative which started two years earlier) was signed. The latter had been intended to promote good neighborly relations in Central and Eastern Europe and to protect the rights of ethnic minorities.[25] There was also considerable pressure from NATO and the European Union, since both organizations stressed that neither Hungary nor Slovakia would have a chance for membership unless they could resolve their differences.[26]

Similarly, significant pressure was brought on both parties for the signing of the Romanian–Hungarian basic treaty. The NATO study on enlargement in the fall of 1995 stipulated that one of the criteria that applicants would have to meet was the settlement of disputes with neighbors in a structured way so that there would be no future threat to alliance stability.[27] Then-Romanian Foreign Minister Teodor Meles-canu was quite blunt about this when he declared in Bucharest that without an agreement with Hungary, the door to Romania's entry to NATO simply would be closed.[28]

Realistically though, the pressure was greater on Hungary because Budapest believed (rightly) that it had a better chance of joining NATO than Slovakia. And it is now clear that Hungary is likely to join way ahead of Romania—that is, as long as the ratification process goes through as planned. Because of this pressure and the particular urgency that the Hungarian government felt in signing these treaties, they yield and are likely to yield less than Budapest had expected. In the case of the agreement with Slovakia, for instance, the Council of Europe's Recommendation 1201 was fully included (in Article 15). Recommendation 1201, Art. 11, stipulates that "in the regions, where they are in a majority, the persons belonging to a national minority shall have the right to have at their disposal appropriate local or autonomous authorities or to have a special status, matching the specific historical and territorial situation and in accordance with the domestic legislation of the state."[29] But the Slovak government indicated early on that it would apply a rather restrictive interpretation to the treaty. The Foreign Minister Juraj Schenk quickly stressed that his government refused to interpret Recommendation 1201 as stipulating the possibility of "autonomous self-government for minorities," or that it accepted any formulation that acknowledged the principle of collective rights for minorities.[30] According to a number of Hungarian observers, the Slovak government has tried assiduously to diminish the benefits that the treaty should have accorded the Hungarian minority to the point where the usefulness of the entire agreement is cast into doubt.[31]

Two years after the Slovak–Hungarian agreement, Hungarian Prime Minister Gyula Horn felt compelled to challenge Slovak Prime Minister Vladimir Meciar to end delays in safeguarding the rights of Slovakia's 500,000 ethnic Hungarians.[32] (In return for compliance, Horn promised to support Slovakia's effort to join NATO.) Thus, the desire for NATO membership has also functioned as a push/pull mechanism for bilateral relations between the two states but, so far, has been rather ineffective in protecting Hungarian minority rights in Slovakia and, if anything, has reduced Hungarian leverage.

The signing of the basic treaty with Romania showed signs of haste on the part of the Hungarian government. In fact, it provided Budapest with less than the treaty with Slovakia[33] and despite the difficulties encountered with the implementation of the latter, the new treaty provides few safeguards for balanced interpretation and appropriate implementation. In a codicil, the contracting parties in fact agreed that

"Recommendation 1201 does not refer to collective rights, nor does it impose upon the parties an obligation to grant to the concerned persons rights to a special status of territorial autonomy based on ethnic criteria."[34] Hungarian critics have contended that in essence the treaty contains legal escape clauses that would make the protection of the rights of the Hungarian minority in Romania difficult to ensure.[35]

Criticism of the two treaties is not meant to suggest that the resolution of ethnic and territorial issues in not vital. Indeed, movement in that direction is a very positive development that holds out hope not only for membership in the Western alliance but for the achievement of sustainable security and the entrenchment of laws for the protection of human rights in the region. But to the extent that these treaties are flawed, such flaws can, to a significant degree, be attributed not only to external pressures but also to haste on the part of the Hungarian government. The inadequacies of these treaties therefore should be a warning to Budapest regarding its most important current foreign policy enterprise—namely, gaining membership in NATO.

For Hungary, membership in NATO apparently is a foreign policy imperative. Though NATO formed the North Atlantic Cooperation Council (NACC) in 1991 as a major qualitative step forward in consultations and cooperations with the Soviet Union and the states of Central and Eastern Europe, and in January 1994 the organization decided that it needed an immediate and practical program which would go beyond dialogue and cooperation to form a real partnership—Partnership for Peace (PfP). These steps though have not satisfied Hungary's security needs (nor for that matter those of other East Central European states'). It is not that these have not been welcome developments, and Hungary quickly joined PfP (as has Russia). But Hungary's view of PfP has very much paralleled that of General Klaus Naumann, Chairman of the North Atlantic Military Committee, namely, that PfP's purpose is to play a valuable role in helping to prepare interested partners for possible membership in NATO[36] (in addition to other worthy goals and activities).

By defining security broadly, for Hungary, NATO membership is a means of joining the community of democratic states, of re-Europeanizing, of enhancing political stability, and improving economic progress. These aims have been repeated for years by Hungarian politicians coming from a wide range of the political spectrum. In fact, there has been remarkable continuity in Hungary's desire to join NATO despite the change in government.[37]

And there are sound reasons for the enlargement of NATO.[38] I myself have argued that NATO could provide the type of security benefits that other organizations such as the OSCE could not. In particular,

NATO, dedicated to collective defense, could provide the type of "hard military constraints" that would be important in suffocating the possibilities of conflict and that a collective security organization could not implement.[39] Moreover, whatever the merits, it appears now that enlargement will definitely occur. Having addressed the "how's and why's" of expansion in the fall of 1995, the organization then engaged in the study of the "who" and "when" of enlargement in 1996. It is noteworthy that part of the reason for Helmut Kohl's visit to Moscow in early September 1996 appears to have been to tell Boris Yeltsin that NATO expansion was drawing close.[40] The enlargement of NATO, however, even if limited temporarily to Hungary, Poland, and the Czech Republic (as per the July 1997 Madrid decision), will inevitably have an impact on Russia. Therefore enlargement (and its implementation), whatever the broad security considerations, needs to take Russia into account.

Perhaps one of the most sophisticated and persuasive presentations for extending NATO membership to Hungary was made by Ambassador Andras Simonyi, Head of the Liaison Office to NATO and to the Western European Union (WEU), at the 41st General Assembly of the Atlantic Treaty Association in October 1995.[41] First, he was very careful to define security broadly. The enlargement of NATO, in his view, would be a move to extend a zone of stability towards the East. It would be about modernization in its broadest sense and would ensure that new democracies developed in the right direction by becoming part of the community of democratic nations, with shared values, rights, and responsibilities.[42] Second, he paid heed to the needs of ensuring common security by arguing that the expansion of NATO will happen in a way that will not create new lines of division. Third, he stressed that enlargement was not a matter of deterrence since Hungary "does not feel threatened even if there is a tragic war taking place in our immediate vicinity."[43] And fourth, he argued that the enlargement of NATO will "fill the present vacuum in Central and Eastern Europe but will not create new ones."[44]

Unfortunately, the last three of Simonyi's arguments are problematic (while the first seems to counterpose zones of stability and instability). His contention that enlargement will not create divisions is based on the idea that somehow the further development of PfP (going hand in hand with enlargement) could sufficiently minimize differences between members and nonmembers to reassure the latter. How this would work is difficult to see since, clearly, for Hungary the PfP is not sufficient but others, including Russia (with perhaps a special status), would need to settle for this arrangement. The thrust of Simonyi's argument is not too different from Zbigniew Brzezinski's proposals for

NATO enlargement that would somehow keep Russia out but never-theless satisfy it.[45] It should not be surprising that the Russians have found Brzezinski's proposals too clever by half and, ultimately, non-starters.

Simonyi's contention that, from Hungary's perspective, enlargement is not a response to a perceived threat (that it is not about deterrence) doesn't seem very plausible. His argument that it is analogous to pur-chasing insurance on a new car would be hardly reassuring to the Rus-sians. Insurance is a response to a risk and it provides compensation for a loss so that the insured party could be brought as close as possible to the status quo ante or its equivalent. Further, purchasing insurance can be costly, and Simonyi readily admits that joining NATO would mean a considerable burden for Hungary, but that this burden would be worthwhile because of the increased security.[46] Given costs, individ-uals do not waste funds on unrealistic or fantastic risks. Furthermore, if the insurance analogy somehow is to be applied to international rela-tions, its intent is not likely to seek monetary compensation for the loss of life or territory, or for the detrimental effects of inimical policies by other international actors. Rather, the purpose of "insurance" in inter-national relations is to deter. This has been central to alliances histori-cally. Not surprisingly, alliances have provided one of the most com-mon ways of enhancing a state's power in the face of external threats.

It is, moreover, clear that Hungary and other East European states have reason to be concerned about developments and policies in Rus-sia. The latter is in the midst of a social revolution, not just economic and political reform.[47] Consequently, the transformation is uncertain and the risks are unpredictable. Boris Yeltsin's generally ill health (de-spite periodic recoveries) is also worrisome. In a country where so much power has been concentrated in the hands of the president, and where the future of democracy is so greatly dependent on one individ-ual, there is reason to be apprehensive about the future of democracy in Russia and the prospect of a peaceful and cooperative foreign policy. In a period of instability in particular, East European states would have reason to question Russia's new military doctrine which appears to designate Eastern and Central Europe as an area of special Russian in-terest and influence and claims a Russian prerogative to object to "the expansion of military blocks or alliances."[48] Further, in a period of po-litical instability even a military establishment with no tradition of Bo-napartism (but a military that is deeply disillusioned and fragmented) could pose significant domestic and external problems.[49] Coupling all this with the dangerously low level of support for democracy in Russia in contrast to Eastern Europe[50] and with the spectacular success of the communists in Russia in the December 1995 State Duma elections, it is easy to become pessimistic about the prospects for democracy in that country.

Yet, there is a need for a balance of analysis and a recognition of the successes of democracy, of the tremendously positive changes that have taken place both in the political and the economic realm. In 1997, new First Deputy Prime Ministers Anatoly Chubais and Boris Nemtsov, both dependable democrats, came to power and are now working assiduously to accelerate political and economic transition in Russia. And for the first time since 1991, the 1998 draft budget assumes economic growth (of 2 percent and inflation of only 5 percent).[51] Yeltsin's dismissal of his cabinet in March 1998 brought in more young democrats (though Chubais was shifted to private industry but remained on call for high-level presidential assignments such as dealing with the IMF and foreign banks). Prime Minister Sergei Kiriyenko is a Nemtsov protégé. And in June, Yeltsin brought in Boris Fedorov, a tough young democrat, as chief tax administrator. But Kiriyenko, Fedorov, Chubais, and Nemtsov all remain concerned about NATO enlargement. They all fear that enlargement will strengthen the antidemocratic forces in Russia. There are no guarantees therefore that the transition will be successful. Seeking "insurance" may ironically create more insecurity. From a security perspective, moreover, most countries, including Hungary, tend to err on the side of caution—that is, they try to buy extra "insurance." The most important decision then is whether instability and potential threats emanating from Russia are to be dealt with by deterrence or by inclusion and reassurance. Hungary's decision, despite Ambassador Simonyi's attempts to soft-pedal it, is to opt for the former.

Further, Budapest's position, as expressed by Ambassador Simonyi, that the enlargement of NATO would be filling a "present vacuum in Central and Eastern Europe"[52] is also problematic. First, his mere assertion that there is a vacuum is not sufficiently compelling in refuting the contention of those who argue that there is no such vacuum.[53] Second, if indeed there is a security vacuum, one ought to determine the type, urgency, and manner in which it ought to be filled. Filling a security vacuum is both a difficult and potentially dangerous undertaking. Well-meaning policies can result in unintended effects that can ultimately increase rather than diminish the danger to a state's or a region's security.

Lastly, Ambassador Simonyi has expressed Hungary's wish to join a "credible, strong, effective and cohesive alliance"[54] and, moreover, that it wants to join the alliance "with full participation in the integrated military structures."[55] This way a security vacuum would be filled, he contended, without creating new ones. This is clearly desirable but not easily attainable. Mere declaratory statements are not sufficient. Such a transition would be ultimately predicated on Russian acquiescence. Budapest appears to assume that NATO can be enlarged without either including or alienating Russia. This would be a remarkable accomplishment, indeed, and the risk of miscalculation is not insignificant.

The Russian Factor

How Russia views itself and how it perceives Eastern Europe play a crucial role in Moscow's reaction to the enlargement of NATO. Russia's perception of itself is at variance with at least some of the views in Eastern Europe. There is a tendency in Eastern Europe to portray Russia, the successor of the Soviet Union, as a potential hegemonic force. By contrast, Russia perceives itself as the state which played a crucial role in the collapse of the Soviet Union.[56] Not only do most Russians not perceive their country as a defeated villain but view it rather as both a victim of and a victor over the Soviet empire.[57] Consequently, it is believed by many in Russia that the country should be embraced and supported by the community of democratic nations.

Emerging from the ruins of the Soviet empire, Russia, as its former foreign minister, Andrei Kozyrev, stated, considers itself a great power[58] which deserves international respect and has the right to be consulted on all important issues, particularly in Europe. To this "great power" desire of inclusion must be added the psychological problem of "walls." That is, with the Soviet Union having been on the wrong side of the Cold War, Russia now does not want to be excluded from direct links with the developed democratic nations.[59] There is a fear, therefore, that the enlargement of NATO could construct precisely these kind of walls. And it is claimed even by the likes of former Foreign Minister (and now Prime Minister,) Yevgenii Primakov, who is hardly sympathetic to the West, that "Russia and the West have jointly won the Cold War."[60] Therefore, as joint victors, care should be taken that no walls are constructed.

This self-image helps shape Russia's policies towards Eastern Europe. Further, as a successor to an empire which it helped destroy and as an emerging democracy, Russia was bound to shift its foreign policy priorities. Whereas Mikhail Gorbachev, upon coming to power, at least claimed that of all the issues on his foreign policy agenda, he would take as his "first commandment" the strengthening of relations with Eastern Europe,[61] now links with the West, and with the "near abroad," are clearly far more important for Russia. Yet, as Russia's military doctrine indicates, Moscow has continued to try to exercise an interest and influence in the region. And despite the arguments of Eurasianists, Russia is, as former U.S. Ambassador to Moscow Jack Matlock stated, "Eurasian in the geographic sense, but primarily a European power."[62]

Still, Eastern Europe would be largely on the back burner for Russia were it not for the issue of the enlargement of NATO. The greater priority assigned to the region by Foreign Minister Primakov, when he took office, as evidenced by the fact that his first foreign trips were to Bratislava and Warsaw, points more to the Russian concern over enlargement than to a fundamental reprioritization of foreign policy. It is somewhat ironic, but it should also be of some concern to the East European states that Moscow's greater focus on the region is through the prism of NATO enlargement. It should make these states, and particularly Hungary, which will be among the first states admitted to NATO, more sensitive to Russian threat perceptions and security concerns.

Russia's concept of security has become broader. And Primakov has long played a pivotal role in shaping and defining the Russian concept of security. As far back as the summer of 1987, it was Primakov, then the director of the Soviet Academy of Sciences' prestigious Institute of World Economic and International Relations, who advocated a new approach to foreign policy that would reformulate the concept of security.[63] The primary way to enhance Soviet security, in Primakov's view, was to turn inward and successfully modernize the country. This would require concentrated effort which in turn meant that the Soviet Union would need to seek a less confrontational approach to the West and decrease its foreign expenditures. Shortly after the fall of the Soviet Union, he became the head of the Foreign Intelligence Service (FIS) (after it was separated from the old KGB). Under him, the FIS was very active in putting forth analytical reports on a variety of foreign and strategic problems, including the enlargement of NATO.[64] In 1995, it was under Primakov's leadership that his department published a concept of Russian foreign policy doctrine that specified the country's geostrategic priorities and defined external threats.[65] This was an attempt at one level to provide the conceptual clarification which the foreign ministry under Kozyrev seemingly failed to do, but it was also an indication of Primakov's great influence and his ultimately successful campaign to take over the foreign ministry.

Upon assuming the post of foreign minister, Primakov outlined the top priority tasks for Russia's foreign policy in a way which indicated a clear link to his writings of 1987.[66] External security was essential in order to preserve territorial integrity and to "the strengthening of centripetal tendencies in the territory of the former USSR. The sovereignty obtained by the republics is irreversible *but this does not negate the need for reintegrative processes*, first of all in the economic field" (emphasis added).[67]

The enlargement of NATO would invariably have an impact on any "reintegrative processes" in the former Soviet Union. It could conceivably allow Moscow to bring far greater pressure on Ukraine, for example, to soften its sovereignty and to speed up economic and other forms of integration. Enlargement, however, could also solidify the will for independence and in the longer term act as a magnet for Ukraine's integration with the rest of Europe rather than Russia. For Primakov, therefore, the enlargement of NATO likely impinges on the central security goals that he outlined, which are predicated on a strengthened Russia gradually integrating, in some form, the states of the "near abroad."

Despite misgivings about NATO, however, Russia has made attempts at pursuing a policy of common security. This is evidenced by its decision to join PfP, its productive cooperation in the OSCE, its decision to send troops to Bosnia (and that these troops would answer to an American commander), and its contribution to the Conventional Forces in Europe (CFE) Agreement and implementation. Further, Russian policy-makers have consistently rejected the notion of a security vacuum in the region, though the prerogatives of influence that their defense doctrine seems to suggest create some uncertainty.

The biggest problem, though, seems to be the lack of clarification between deterrence and reassurance in Russia's policies towards Eastern Europe. Moscow has certainly tried to portray its foreign and defense policy as one of reassurance, and the steps outlined above do go some ways towards achieving that goal. There are, however, "passive factors," which complicate or impede attempts at regional reassurance. These include political turmoil in Russia, uncertainty about presidential succession, economic and social dislocation, and the continuing strength of extremist forces, particularly those on the Left. On these issues the Russian government responds to domestic rather than foreign policy priorities and its options are more limited.

This should not, however, prevent it from fostering and enhancing "active factors," which would provide greater reassurance to Eastern European states. The key to reassurance, though, comes back to the enlargement of NATO. Acquiescing to NATO enlargement would reassure the East European states. But Russia fears that it would divide what it hopes to be an emerging common security. To prevent what it perceives to be the division of Europe, Russia has been seeking to deter the enlargement of NATO. This has not changed entirely despite the fact that Russia signed the Founding Act with NATO on May 27, 1997.[68] Not only did Yeltsin declare before the signing that enlargement posed the most serious threat to Russia since the 1962 Cuban Missile Crisis, but the Russian leadership has been emphatic, even after signing the Foundation Act, that enlargement is a grave mistake.[69] It would thus be highly premature to assume complete Russian acquiescence despite the benefits and promises of the Founding Act. Since membership for Hungary, Poland, and the Czech Republic has to be ratified, Russia may still try to block enlargement, even if not through direct opposition. How can Russia therefore effect the transition from the old policy of deterrence to reassurance?

Russian opposition to the enlargement of NATO has been deeply entrenched and unrelenting. It is not only government opposition but opposition to the enlargement along the entire political spectrum in Russia that makes change so difficult.[70] The military, of course, has opposed the enlargement and the continuity of that opposition is especially noteworthy. The former Russian Defense Minister Pavel Grachev, a hard-liner, declared in June 1996 at the NATO Defense Ministers Meeting held under the 16 + 1 formula in Brussels that although Russia was prepared to cooperate closely with NATO, it would not accept eastward expansion of the alliance.[71] His immediate successor, Colonel–General Igor Rodionov, in one of his first speeches after assuming office, argued that the main problem with the West derived from the eastward expansion of NATO, which, he contended, would lead to a change in the strategic balance in Europe.[72] Current Defence Minister Igor Sergeyev has been no less critical. In January 1998, for instance, in response to NATO plans to create a joint Baltic force that would include Poland, he accused the alliance of "advancing towards the Russian border with weapons in its hands.[73] Boris Yeltsin also vociferously opposed enlargement in his speech at the Fiftieth Anniversary of the United Nations.[74] It should be noted that the Council on Foreign and Defense Policy, a nonpartisan Russian organization that includes legislators from many political parties, officials in the executive branch, business people, journalists and scholars, also denounced NATO's plans for enlargement.[75]

In a sense, hope for greater Russian flexibility appears to rest on Primakov. This may seem odd at first, given the Russian foreign minister's seemingly steadfast opposition to enlargement. In fact, when Hungarian Foreign Minister Laszlo Kovacs visited Moscow in March 1996, Primakov reiterated his opposition and declared that the expansion of NATO was unacceptable to Russia.[76] If any change was detected, it would have been the result of meetings held in Berlin at the beginning of June 1996 by the North Atlantic Council (NATO's highest decision-making body) and the talks based on the 16 + 1 formula. At this meeting the NATO foreign ministers agreed in principle to a

new military structure by giving NATO "a European defense identity."[77] The changes would make it easier for France to become a fully
integrated member, and Paris could drop opposition to the enlargement talks scheduled for 1997. Furthermore, it was thought that by
strengthening the European leg of NATO, and by creating greater possibilities for the development of the WEU, it would also be easier for
Russia to accept enlargement. In fact, Primakov noted in Berlin that
NATO was becoming less of an anti-Russian organization, and was reported to have declared that "Russia could live with NATO's enlargement, though deployment of its infrastructure to Russia's frontier is
unacceptable."[78]

Subsequent to the meeting, though, Primakov angrily rejected the
interpretation that Russia was watering down its opposition to enlargement or that all he was objecting to was the introduction of NATO
troops into the territory of new members.[79] Yet, there was a change or
at least a new nuance. While repeating that there was no shift in Russia's position, Primakov stated that NATO's military infrastructure
must not move any closer to Russia. He admitted that this formulation
indicated that there was still "a certain space" within which an accord
was possible.[80] Moreover, Primakov contended that as a result of Russian pressure it was NATO that was changing, and he welcomed
changes within the organization which increased the independence of
the so-called "European dimension."[81]

On closer examination, however, what emerges is a rather clever ma-
neuver by Primakov. Since the expansion of NATO seems to be moving ahead regardless of Russian opposition, what he is seeking to encourage is changes in the alliance that would gravely weaken the
American role. This is vintage Primakov. What he appears to be calcu-
lating is, first, that if the enlargement cannot be stopped, a "watered
down" NATO, that is one with weak American participation, would
be far less dangerous for Russia; second, he hopes that enlargement (in
the face of continuing Russian unhappiness if not outright opposition)
would extend far less than full participation to the East European
states. That is, it seems that he expects that if the East European states,
including Hungary, are accepted into NATO, it would be under conditions which would make membership more form than substance. And
finally, there is the fallback position where enlargement will
strengthen the anti–Western, authoritarian forces in Russia with which
Primakov is far more comfortable than with the pro–Western democrats.

Yet this may be somewhat too clever a position (though not entirely
wrong). An assumption that NATO will be watered down may be premature. It should be noted that in June 1996, although U.S. Secretary

of Defense William Perry and his European counterparts endorsed the principle of changing NATO (and France decided to return to the bosom of the military alliance), they made it quite clear that U.S. General George Joulwan would retain the top post in the joint command of NATO's strategic forces in Europe and, moreover, that the post will be kept by the Americans in the future.[82] France did not get the concessions it sought either at the meeting in May 1997 (Paris) or July 1997 (Madrid). There appears to be a consensus among American policymakers that the United States needs to prevent the reemergence of a power capable of vying with it and this includes both old enemies and current allies.

Primakov's offers of special relations with NATO, moreover, do not present a real alternative to enlargement. And he has not proposed Russian membership in NATO. Thus, Russian opposition to the "substantive" enlargement of NATO continues. But if Russia is unable to provide reassurance and thus work out an alternate arrangement to enlargement, its opposition to the latter will mean that instead of reassurance it may, in the future, have to confront deterrence in Eastern Europe. Is Primakov then deluding himself?

Prospects and Dangers

As NATO enlargement draws closer, the West in fact is making strenuous efforts to mollify and reassure Russia. President Bill Clinton called for a "deep NATO–Russia partnership" and U.S. Secretary of State Warren Christopher proposed linking Russia to NATO with a formal charter.[83] NATO planners are developing a "super" PfP for countries that would likely be left out of the first wave of expansion and Russia could join this "enhanced" PfP.[84] In September 1996, NATO Secretary General Javier Solana (as in the past) warned the alliance that relations with Russia could be seriously damaged if the enlargement process was not handled carefully and declared that the plan (for a super PfP) was intended to demonstrate to Russia that NATO was not belligerent and that enlargement would not diminish security.[85]

It is highly doubtful that such plans will entirely mollify Russia when East European states are given full NATO membership. The Russian government, as we have seen, has been categorical in opposing the enlargement of NATO if that means, in Primakov's words, that the alliance's "military infrastructure moves closer to Russian territory."[86] It appears from all of the above that any compromise that would entirely satisfy Russia would involve changes in current enlargement plans that would and should not be acceptable to the East European states. The first such compromise would be the enlargement of NATO by extending only some political assurances rather than full inclusion in the military infrastructure. As noted, Hungary's position, as articulated by Ambassador Simonyi, (or Foreign Minister Laszlo Kovacs),[87] is that this would not be acceptable. Second, the transformation of NATO into a radically different organization, where under the guise of building up the "European leg," the American participation would be dramatically downgraded, would make the alliance into an organization that would hardly be capable of providing the security assurances that the East European states are hoping to gain.

The Founding Act does not appear to fulfill either of the above Russian goals, but in attempting to reassure Russia it creates further complications and possible future controversies and confrontations. Still, it is true that in the Founding Act NATO declares that it has no intention, no plan, and no reason to deploy nuclear weapons or establish nuclear storage sites on the territories of new members, and has no plans for stationing additional substantive combat forces in these states.[88] And President Yeltsin did claim that these were concessions that allow Russia to block decisions it does not like (such as military expansion eastward).[89] Henry Kissinger likewise interpreted the Founding Act as giving Russia (through the creation of a Permanent Joint Council) a sufficiently large say to "dangerously dilute the alliance."[90] Lastly, the French, who wanted to strengthen the European leg of NATO, pushed for concessions to Russia. It is noteworthy that French Foreign Minister Hervé de Charette worked closely with Primakov though France obviously does not share the latter's goal of fatally weakening the alliance.[91] Thus, there is a risk that the new members will not gain first-class citizenship, and the alliance itself would be seriously weakened.

Yet it should also be recognized that despite Russian public declarations to the contrary, NATO is not bound to consult first with Russia in a time of crisis nor legally prevented from deploying nuclear forces or substantive combat forces on the territory of the new members.[92] NATO, moreover, endorsed at the Brussels Summit in January 1994 the Combined Joint Task Force Concept (CJTF) which envisions multinational and multiservice formations and is in the process of refining and testing. Whatever steps NATO will take, however, will likely cause political controversy in Russia and within the alliance. Russia won't be able to block NATO moves legally, but it could try to delay or dilute them. If it fails entirely, then it could conclude that it has been betrayed (politically), marginalized, and excluded. The Founding Act may turn out to be a recipe for friction and misunderstanding.

Should enlargement proceed, as it seems, in the face of Russian opposition, or unhappiness (and Russia certainly cannot exercise a veto), the dangers inherent in Russia's alienation raise serious questions as to future security in the region. The extension of full NATO membership to a select group of states, including Hungary, makes it difficult to avoid the imagery of walls in Moscow, particularly given the fact that currently there are no plans to open up even the possibility of Russian membership in the alliance. Undoubtedly, offering Russia the possibility of membership creates enormous difficulties, but these must be measured against the dangers of a Russia that feels alienated, humiliated, and excluded from full participation in the primary Western system of collective defense.

The arguments most commonly made for excluding Russia rest on its size, which would dwarf that of the European members, and on the inadequacy of Russian democratization. These problems, though, are not insurmountable. It is not inconceivable to think of security from Vancouver to Vladivostok, and it is far too premature to give up on Russian democracy. From Moscow's perspective, these arguments hide other reasons for exclusion that bode ill for the future of the entire region. The issue of size in fact may relate more to a reluctance to characterize Russia as a European state. It would be unfortunate if NATO and the East European states reject Russia as a primarily European state, and continue to think of it as, to use Josef Brodsky's contemptuous phrase, "Western Asia."[93] Further, valid criticism of the inadequacy of Russian democratization needs to be balanced by a recognition that there has also been fundamental progress in developing democratic institutions and processes. It will be a grave mistake to assume that Russia is congenitally antidemocratic and that therefore it will be forever outside the perimeter of pluralistic, democratic states.

Moreover, the dangers in moving ahead with the enlargement without effectively addressing Russian concerns are not necessarily blatant or imminent. The greatest threat is not some immediate violent reaction on the part of a weak Russia. Threats such as those made by former Defense Minister Pavel Grachev, as recently as May 1996, of creating a formidable Russian–Belarussian military group on Belarussian territory as a response to NATO expansion, making Russia's short-range nuclear weapons operational again, and suspending the implementation of arms control treaties, are crude and not necessarily credible threats.[94] Rather, the first and main danger is the widespread perception in Moscow that not only was Russia excluded from much of the diplomacy surrounding Bosnia, but worse, that despite various Western promises (and the Founding Act notwithstanding), it has been excluded from significant involvement in the most crucial decision—the commitment to expand NATO. There already is a sense, even among Russian democrats, that the West, exemplified by Madrid, is making one-sided decisions that a weak Russia can't stop and that this endangers not only the ratification of START 2, but the progress of democracy in Russia.[95] Moreover, even today, Russia has sufficient resources and levers to cause mischief and promote instability. Some of the more immediate steps that Russia could take were suggested by General Aleksandr Lebed in May 1996. Since his election as a governor in 1998, Lebed's star has risen. Not only does he now wield considerable influence, but it is not inconceivable that, should Yeltsin leave the presidency for whatever reason, the ambitious general (or another nationalistic candidate) could capture the leadership of Russia. Lebed has suggested that a temporarily weak Russia would still have means of punishing states which joined NATO. He argued that Russia should not sell these states Russian-made combat equipment or replacement parts and that Moscow should use its economic power to exert political pressure.[96] Hungary, which not only has purchased MiG-29 fighters from Russia but buys a great portion of its energy supplies from Moscow, could be an obvious target of such Russian pressure.

Most importantly, though, enlargement, as Michael Mandelbaum has perceptively observed, has "a potential to alienate Russia from the post-Cold War settlement in Europe and *make the goal of overturning that settlement central to Russian foreign policy*"[97] (emphasis added). Russia is big enough that, if it believes itself to be excluded, it is likely to threaten stability. It will be foolhardy to ignore the warnings of Egon Bahr, the former SPD politician who was the coarchitect of West Germany's Ostpolitik, that there will be no stability in Europe if Russia is excluded.[98]

The second danger area, namely, the opportunity cost, is difficult to calculate. Although democratization in Russia will be decided primarily by domestic factors, external developments do have an influence. The enlargement of NATO in the face of Russian opposition will undoubtedly play into the hands of those antidemocratic forces. They will magnify the nature of external threats and cleverly play on the theme of exclusion in order to push for a Slavophile, xenophobic, authoritarian policy.

There will also be opportunity costs incurred by Hungary. Membership in NATO is clearly going to be expensive, even with generous Western help. For a heavily indebted state, which is desperately seeking to control social expenditures, increased military spending could significantly diminish public support for NATO (and yet one would think that strong public support in a candidate state should be an important criterion for admission). There is already opposition in Hungary to joining NATO. It comes not only from the political margins, such as the Worker's Party (WP) which in the fall of 1995 collected more than 100,000 signatures to try to force a referendum on the issue.[99] It is more widespread in the population. A Gallup poll in May 1996 showed that whereas 45 percent of those interviewed favored NATO membership, 32 percent were against it.[100] True, in the November 1997 referendum there was an overwhelming yes vote for NATO membership.[101] Yet, just as significantly, only 49.2 percent of the population bothered to vote.[102] And costs to Hungary will be significant, despite denials by Hungarian politicians. NATO Secretary General Javier Solana declared before Parliament in Budapest in February 1998 that Hungary was pledged to bring defense spending in line with that of NATO member states.[103] Thus, a premature or an "at any cost" push for membership in the alliance could undermine long-term support for the alliance. Given, as Ambassador Simonyi has argued, that there are no current threats against Hungary, Budapest then may be taking risks at a time when it is enjoying a reasonably good situation. As the French say, "le mieux est l'ennemi du bien" (the best is the enemy of the good). Third, there is a danger that political circumstances in Russia (such as the sudden death of Yeltsin) may create the kind of instability in the short term that in turn could force what ultimately would prove to be deleterious compromises on the West. Having committed itself to enlargement but fearing its effects on an unstable Russia, the West may choose indeed to water down the enlargement despite current promises to the contrary. It may offer less than full membership and thus less than full protection. By pressing the West to deliver on its commitment of enlargement, the East Europeans could indeed find themselves getting a good deal of the form but much less of the substance. Moreover, such a compromise arrangement may be very difficult to alter later on, and all the East European states then might find that they will have paid a very heavy price for their haste to join NATO.

Conclusion

It seems that all parties need to reflect more carefully on their security, both in the short term and the long term. They need to think more broadly and they need to think in terms of common security . . . security that is indivisible, first from the Atlantic to the Urals, but ultimately from Vancouver to Vladivostok. If they do perceive a security vacuum, then they should still exercise utmost care in how, and how urgently, they proceed to fill it.

A grave mistake will be made if states in the region confuse reassurance with deterrence. If they choose to or, through less-than-careful enlargement of NATO, find themselves engaging in the former, they will foster a dangerous division in Europe. Of course, Russia also needs to assume a major responsibility for avoiding such a division. It needs to press on with the process of democratization more quickly and effectively. It should also consider not only what position it could take outside but also possibly inside the alliance.

But the East European states, including Hungary, ought to consider more carefully the implications of enlarging NATO when such expansion could so alienate Russia from the post-Cold War settlement in Europe and when it is so likely to strengthen the antidemocratic forces at a time when the fate of democracy in Russian hangs in the balance. They should recognize that Russia remains a major power and a European power at that, and that a fully democratic Russia should be included in a stable security arrangement even if that means that the enlargement process needs to be slowed down. The great benefits of enlargement will dissipate, if not entirely disappear, if a currently weak Russia fails in its transition to democracy and grows ever more resentful over its perceived exclusion from the most important security decisions in the post-Cold War Europe. Alternately, a hasty enlargement of the alliance—which, in order to mollify a Russia going through a very difficult political period, and/or to accommodate the concerns and ambitions of some current member, significantly weakens the organization or does not extend the benefits of full membership to the East European states—will give the latter less than they want and deserve. Acting precipitously therefore may have dangerous, unwanted consequences.

Small states have a particularly difficult problem ensuring their security. The observations of the first Czechoslovak President T.G. Masaryk also apply to Hungary: "We always have to keep in mind that we are a small nation in an unfavorable geographical position, which practically charges us with a duty to be bolder, think harder and be more successful than others."[104] In the post-communist era, Hungary certainly has shown boldness, thoughtfulness, and creativity in its foreign policy. To these positive qualities, though, it needs to add one other—patience.

Notes

1. Hans Morgenthau, *Politics among Nations*, (New York: Knopf, 1985), 47–51.

2. Adam LeBor, "U.S., Hungarian Military Operation Unites Old Enemies," *The Globe & Mail* (Toronto), September 3, 1996.

3. Valerie Bunce, "Should Transitologists Be Grounded?" *Slavic Review* 54,

no. 1 (Spring 1995), 111–27; Sarah M. Terry, "Thinking about Post-Communist Transitions: How Different Are They?" *Slavic Review* 52, no. 1 (Summer 1993), 333–37.

4. Mikhail Gorbachev, *Perestroika: New Thinking for Our Country and the World* (New York: Harper & Row, 1987), 142.

5. Ibid.

6. *Pravda* (Moscow), June 29, 1988.

7. *Pravda* (Moscow), June 27, 1987; Aurel Braun, "On Reform, Perceptions, Misperceptions, Trends and Tendencies" in Aurel Braun, ed., *The Soviet-East European Relationship in the Gorbachev Era* (Boulder, Colo.: Westview Press, 1990), 195–97.

8. Flora Lewis, "Why NATO—Not the United States—Frightens Moscow," *Transition*, February 23, 1996, 50–52.

9. *Le Figaro* (Paris), September 30, 1994.

10. Michael Howard, "Reassurance and Deterrence: Western Defence in the 1980s," *Foreign Affairs* 61, no. 2 (Winter 1982–83).

11. Ibid.

12. Miroslav Polreich, "Building a New NATO at Russia's Expense: Letter to the Editor," *Foreign Affairs*, January–February 1994, 175; Michael Mandelbaum, *The Dawn of Peace in Europe* (New York: The 20th Century Fund Press, 1996).

13. *Statistical Yearbook of Hungary* (Budapest: Kozponti statistikai hivatal, 1992, 1994), 1994, 222; 1992, 194–97.

14. Ibid.

15. Hungarian Consulate (Toronto) website: <http://www.docuweb.ca/ hungary/>. Russian exports in 1995 totaled $1,839,000,000 (US) and imports from Hungary accounted for only 822,270,000 (US).

16. *Kommersant Daily* (Moscow) March 7, 1995.

17. *Pravda* (Moscow), March 10, 1995.

18. Victor Gomez, "Hungary: The Russians Are Coming," *Transition*, June 28, 1996, 2.

19. Ibid.

20. *Kommersant Daily* (Moscow), March 7, 1995.

21. Paval Baev, "Drifting Away from Europe," *Transition*, June 30, 1995., 30–33.

22. Moskovskie Novosti (Moscow) *Moscow News*, no. 3, January 15–22, 1995.

23. MTI (Magyar Tavirati Iroda, Hungarian Telegraphic Agency, Budapest), March 1995.

26. James L. Graff, "Can Neighbors Be Friends?" *Time*, April 3, 1995.

28. *Magyar Nemzet*, September 2, 1996.

30. *Pravda* (Moscow), March 20, 1995.

31. For two excellent critiques of the agreement with Slovakia, see Ivan Scipiades, "Egy Magyar Mitosz Vege" (The End of a Hungarian Myth), *Magyar Hirlap* (Hungarian Newspaper, Budapest), August 30, 1996; Geza Jeszenszky, "Elozmenyek Es Elofeltetelek" (Precedents and Preconditions), *Magyar Nemzet*, September 2, 1996.

32. *Reuter*, August 15, 1997.
33. *Magyar Nemzet*, September 2, 1996.
34. Ibid.
35. See Jeszenszky, "Elozmenyek."
36. General Klaus Naumann, "From Co-operation to Interoperability," *NATO Review*, July 1996, 18–19.
37. In personal interviews with Deputy State Secretary of the Ministry of Defense Zoltan Pecze in the Hungarian Democratic Forum-led government (Budapest, May 15, 1994) and with Imre Szekeres, executive secretary and vice president of the incoming Hungarian Socialist Party-led government, it was clear that Hungary's desire for membership would remain undiminished (Budapest, May 16, 1994).
38. Among advocates of enlargement, see R. Asmus, F. Kugler, and S. Larrabee, "Should the West Go East?" *Foreign Affairs*; Zbigniew Brzezinski, "A Plan for Europe," *Foreign Affairs*, January–February 1995, 26–42; and Henry Kissinger, "Expand NATO Now," *Washington Post*, December 1994.
39. Ibid.
40. I have also argued that the principle of enlargement is an important one and that it could yield significant security benefits. Aurel Braun, "The Post-Soviet States's Security Concerns in East-Central Europe" in John R. Lampe and Daniel N. Nelson, eds., *East European Security Reconsidered* (Washington: Woodrow Wilson Center Press, 1993), 115–44; Aurel Braun, "Russian Policy Toward Central Europe in the Balkans" in Alexander V. Kozhemyakin and Roger Kanet, *The Foreign Policy of the Russian Federation* (London: Macmillan, 1997, 49–77).
41. Andras Simonyi, "Expanding the Alliance: How Soon? How Much? " October 5, 1995, 41st General Assembly of the Atlantic Treaty Association, Toronto, Canada, October 3–7, 1995.
42. Ibid., 1, 2–3.
43. Ibid., 2.
44. Ibid., 3.
45. Zbigniew Brzezinski, "A Plan For Europe," *Foreign Affairs*, January–February 1995, 28–32.
46. Simonyi, "Expanding the Alliance," 6.
47. Michael McFaul, "Why Russia's Politics Matter," *Foreign Affairs*, January–February, 1995, 87–99.
48. See Zbigniew Brzezinski, "The Premature Partnership," *Foreign Affairs*, March–April 1994, 76–77.
49. See Benjamin S. Lambeth's perceptive article, "Russia's Wounded Military," *Foreign Affairs*, March–April, 1995, 86–98.
50. In Russia, a majority consistently gives a positive rating to the regime before the start of *perestroika* and are far more pessimistic than the East Europeans about the future. See the excellent analysis by Richard Rose, drawing on the statistics from the New Russia Barometer Surveys in Richard Rose, "Russia as an Hour-Glass Society: A Constitution without Citizens," *East European Constitutional Review*, Summer 1995, 38–39; Richard Rose and Christian Hearpfler,

"Fears and Hopes—New Democracies' Barometer Surveys," *Transition—The Newsletter about Transforming Economies,* Washington, May–June, 1995, 13–14.

51. *Russia Today,* August 26, 1997.

52. Simonyi, "Expanding the Alliance," 3.

53. Polreich, "Building a New NATO," 175; Mandelbaum, *Dawn of Peace.*

54. Simonyi, "Expanding the Alliance," 4.

55. Ibid.

56. See the excellent book by John B. Dunlop, *The Rise of Russia and the Fall of the Soviet Empire* (Princeton: Princeton University Press, 1993).

57. Dimitri Simes, "The Return of Russian History," *Foreign Affairs,* January–February, 1994, 77–78.

58. Andrei Kozyrev, "The Lagging Partnership," *Foreign Affairs,* May–June, 1994, 65–67

59. See Simes, "Return of Russian History," 78–79.

60. *Moskovskie Novosti* (Moscow News, Moscow), no. 2, January 14–21, 1996, 13.

61. *Pravda,* March 12, 1985.

62. Jack F. Matlock, Jr., "Dealing with Russia in Turmoil," *Foreign Affairs,* May–June, 1996, 45.

63. Y. Primakov, "Novaya Filosofiya Vneshnei Politiki" (A New Philosophy of Foreign Policy), *Pravda,* July 10, 1987.

64. See the interesting if somewhat fawning article on Primakov by Konstantin Eggert and Maksim Yusin, "About Yevgenii Primakov, the Academician and Intelligence Officer Who Has Just Been Appointed Minister of Foreign Affairs," *Izvestiya,* January 11, 1996.

65. *Rossiiskaya Gazeta* (The Russian Newspaper), January 11, 1996.

66. See *Moskovskie Novosti,* no. 2, January 14–21, 1996, 13.

67. Ibid.

68. Aurel Braun, "The Risks of Rushing to Enlarge NATO," *The Globe and Mail,* May 27, 1997.

69. *New York Times,* May 9, 1997.

70. To be fair, there have been some isolated voices suggesting compromise, but they have had little effect. See Andrei Zagorski, Prorector of the Moscow State Institute of International Relations, *Segodnya* (Moscow), June 21, 1996.

71. *Kommersant Daily,* June 15, 1996.

72. *Krasnaya zvezda* (Moscow), July 25, 1996.

73. *Toronto Star,* February 6, 1998.

74. *NTV Segodnya,* October 24, 1995.

75. *Transition,* December 15, 1995, 21, reprinted from *Nezavisimaya Gazeta,* June 21, 1995.

76. *Segodnya,* March 12, 1996.

77. See *The Economist,* June 8, 1996, 52–53.

78. Ibid., 52.

79. *Izvestiya,* June 8, 1996.

80. See the interview conducted by Yelena Ovcharenko with Primakov, *Komosomolskaya Pravda* (Moscow), June 11, 1996, 7.

81. *Izvestiya*, June 8, 1996.

82. *Kommersant Daily*, June 15, 1996, 1, 4.

83. *The Globe and Mail* (Toronto), September 7, 1996.

84. *The Globe and Mail*, September 20, 1996.

85. Ibid.

86. *Komsomolskaya Pravda*, June 11, 1996, 7.

87. Laszlo Kovacs, "Hungary's Contribution to European Security," *NATO Review*, vol. 45, no. 5, Sept.– Oct. 1997, 9–11.

88. Text of the Founding Act, *The Globe and Mail*, May 16, 1997.

89. *The Globe and Mail*, May 16, 1997.

90. *New York Times*, July 5, 1997.

91. Paul-Marie de la Gorce, "NATO on Russia's Doorstep, " *Le Monde Diplomatique*, Eng. ed. July 1997.

92. Zbigniew Brzezinski and Anthony Lake, "For a New World, a New NATO," *New York Times*, June 30, 1997; de la Gorce, "NATO on Russia's Doorstep."

93. Cited in Tony Judt, et al., eds., *Debating the Nature of Dissent in Eastern Europe* (Washington, D.C.: Woodrow Wilson International Center for Scholars, 1987), 75.

94. *Segodnya,* May 15, 1996; and citation of Grachev's statement in Frits Bolkestein, "NATO: Deepening and Broadening?" *NATO Review*, July 1996, 23.

95. Alexei Arbatov, "As NATO Grows, START 2 Shudder," *New York Times*, August 25, 1997.

96. Aleksandr Lebed, "Global Political Faint," *Nezavisimoe Voynnoe Obozrenye,* May 16, 1996, 4, translated in the *Current Digest of the Post-Soviet Press*, vol. XVIII, no. 20, 1996, 22.

97. Michael Mandelbaum, "Foreign Policy as Social Work," *Foreign Affairs*, January–February, 1996, 31–32.

98. Cited in Bolkestein, "NATO," 23.

99. *East European Constitutional Review*, vol. 5, no. 1, Winter 1996, 11.

100. Cited in Adam LeBor, "U.S.-Hungarian Military Operation Unites Old Enemies," *The Globe and Mail*, September 3, 1996.

101. Hungarian National Election Committee, http://www.mfa.gov.hu/NATO/OVB-eng.html, June 6,1998.

102. Ibid.

103. http://www.mfa.gov.hu/NATO/Solana-Bp.htm, June 18, 1998.

104. Cited by Jaromir Novotny, "From PfP to IFOR—The Czech Experience," *NATO Review*, July 1996, 29.

Chapter 13

Regional Security and Ethnic Minorities

Daniel N. Nelson

Good neighbors are rare. Those who are most proximate might offer the potential for mutual assistance and reassurance. Mistrust and rivalry, however, seem endemic among individuals and groups sharing space and resources. Schopenhauer's simile refers to porcupines who huddle together in the winter to keep warm, but separate as they feel each other's quills, until they discover "a mean distance at which they could most tolerably exist."[1] Referring to Schopenhauer, Freud observed, "No one can tolerate a too intimate approach to his neighbor."[2]

In Central and Southeastern Europe, post-Cold War peace and prosperity depend once again on relations with immediate neighbors far more than on distant benefactors or global rivalries. Yet, their "intimate approach" to one another is troubled and often conflictual. Such a paradox bedevils every state, nation, and government in Europe's eastern half because of the intermingling of peoples and borders that are the legacy of earlier imperial conquests and Great Power interventions. After the watershed of 1989, most observers would concur with Christoph Royen's view that nationalism and chauvinism, until then suppressed by Soviet domination, became the most potent sources of possible conflict in Europe's eastern half.[3]

But what role do ethnicity and minorities play in the genesis of conflicts propelled by nationalism and chauvinism? Conversely, does the avoidance of "ethnonationalist" crisis require a diminution of ethnicity and/or an integration of minorities in order to insulate a state's security from this peril?

Hungary must confront these issues and offers a worthy case study. Indeed, Hungary stands out as a state that needs neighborly quies-

cence, acceptance, and cooperation. With a declining intrastate population and a relatively large ethnic "diaspora,"[4] the fate of Hungarians is
inextricably interwoven with that of their neighbors. At the same time,
Hungarians inside and outside the late-twentieth-century state of Hungary are not happy with their national "state of being" and themselves
evoke a sense of unease among contiguous states.

A full treatment of the interplay among concepts of state, nation, ethnicity, self-determination, sovereignty, or individual versus collective
rights lies well beyond this brief essay.[5] Yet, all of these topics underpin
a discussion of a small state's security. Guiding this discussion is a
broad notion of security, which I understand as a dynamic balance between threats and capacities.[6] In seeking such a balance, neighbors can
help or hinder one's own security, but they are likely to be an important factor in either case. Gauging *how* important, when, and in which
direction that effect is felt involves empirical issues that are raised but
cannot be resolved in this discussion. More immediate tasks, however,
are to construct a portrait of how Hungarians see themselves vis-à-vis
neighbors, given the prevalence of minorities and diasporas in Central
and Southeastern Europe, and to assess how such perceptions are intertwined with a small state's security.

Hungarians and Their Neighborhood

With the exception of Bulgaria, the population of which has fallen in
part due to emigration of ethnic Turks, Hungary has seen the largest
proportionate drop in population since 1989 of any country in post-
communist Europe—from about 10.5 million in 1989 to approximately
10.1 million in 1996, representing almost a 4 percent loss.[7] Although
these numbers are estimates, and incorporate further inaccuracies because of imprecise counts of minorities, particularly the Roma (whose
unofficial estimates number from 400,000–800,000, with 500,000 a compromise figure),[8] the size of Hungary's population today is more or less
the same as it was over thirty years ago.[9] And, although a fall in Hungary's natural population increase is not a recent occurrence,[10] the phenomenon of a net decrease in total population during peacetime *is*
new. The perceptions of such a nation's diaspora and of the neighboring states in which Hungarians live are likely to be affected by these
demographic trends. With a birthrate hovering around 10–12 births
per 1,000 population (versus a death rate of 13 or 14 per 1,000), the next
Hungarian census is likely to show a further contraction and aging of
the population.

With a self-limiting population in Hungary itself, the proportion of ethnic Hungarians (based on self-identification and the use of Hungarian as a mother tongue) residing in other countries (where their rate of population increase is higher) may become *more* politically salient. Were one to accept the conservative tally by Slovak, Serbian, and Romanian governments, Hungarians in these three neighboring states, plus Magyars in Ukraine, Austria, and Croatia, total about 3.25 million people—a population of more than 30 percent of Hungary's own population. Another two million people with ethnic ties to Hungary (some who escaped from communist rule in the late 1940s or in 1956) live in Western Europe, North America, and elsewhere. For this discussion, however, the relevant data concern the proportion of Magyars living outside Hungary in Central and Southeastern Europe, which is the second largest diaspora as a proportion of the "home" state's population in Europe at the end of the twentieth century. Even within this century, such a statistic evokes the Hungarian state's fundamental role reversal from the turn of the century when almost 99 percent of Hungarians lived within the then-much-larger, heterogeneous state.[11]

Of what significance are these demographic data for the state of Hungary and those who live within its borders? It is plausible that elites and masses in a small, homogeneous, land-locked state that lacks significant natural resources might reflect with concern about their state's limited capacities with which to promote or defend the interests of ethnic kin in surrounding countries. But, when that diaspora represents a large proportion of an ethnic group and the intrastate population is declining, one can expect added attention to neighbors and to the treatment of their Magyar minorities. That rights of, and autonomy for, a nation's ethnic kin living in other countries become political issues within the home state are likewise not surprising.

In Hungary's case, moreover, the historical setting underscores the minority issue as a matter of national security. That Hungarian minorities are dispersed in Central Europe and beyond has been the consequence of Great Power interventions that thwarted Hungarian national ambitions—most prominently in 1848, in the post-World War I Treaty of Trianon, and in 1956. In each case, Hungary's independence and/or control over extended territory in Central Europe throughout which Magyars lived was checked by Austrians, a British–French–American condominium, and Russians. And, if the Great Powers did not intervene directly, a smaller neighbor was assigned as proxy, such as Romania's invasion in 1919 to end the Bela Kun communist regime in Budapest. As borders were moved and refugees created, resulting from aggrandizement and interventions, any Hungarian state inherited a security problem of ample complexity.

Today's young Hungarian democracy must constrain within democratic norms and processes all of the mistrust and suspicion that such a history bequeaths. Although few Hungarians born in recent decades focus on specific historical turning points, it is not their knowledge or lack thereof regarding the Treaty of Trianon that provokes dissonance, but rather a fundamentally "defensive, protective interpretation of nationhood." Between the wars, this led to evident revisionism; several generations later, national sentiments may have abated, but strains of abusive nationalism still can be heard from extremists such as the erstwhile playwright Istvan Csurka.[12] More muted are the nationalist tones within the Hungarian Democratic Forum (MDF) and among intellectuals such as the poet Sandor Csoori.[13] Pervading these and most Hungarians' thoughts about their neighborhood is "a different perception of the history of the region in general and the history of individual countries in particular"—one in which an event such as Trianon is seen by Hungarians "as a national tragedy, while the Czechs, Slovaks, and Romanians look at it as a historic opportunity of self-determination."[14]

The link between ethnic minorities and the security concerns of Hungary, however, is far deeper than inferences drawn from demographic data or than the historical record imply. Hungarians perceive their neighbors, and vice versa, with a mixture of uncertainty, mistrust and antipathy—sentiments usually infused with doubts or anger about treatment of Magyars inside those neighboring states.

Contiguous states with large Magyar minorities, and those minorities that still exist within Hungary, often evoke strongly negative images. In 1995, for example, 59 percent of Hungarians held "unfavorable" attitudes towards Romanians, while 31 percent said they regarded Romanians "favorably." By contrast, 47 percent of Romanians saw Hungarians in a favorable light. Gypsies/Roma are viewed with particular antipathy in Hungary (76 percent of respondents in the same survey said they had "unfavorable" attitudes). In this regard, Hungarians mirror sentiments prevalent among Czechs, Slovaks, and Romanians concerning Roma.[15] Skinhead attacks on Roma have occurred with some frequency, and have been noted with concern by international observers.[16] Paradoxically, a larger proportion of Hungarians (57 percent) than any other nation in the region see their country as one in which there is ample respect for human rights (presumably including tolerance and respect for diversity).[17]

In the public mind, Hungary's friends of the 1990s were Germany and the United States. No other countries or organizations rival these two powerful states in the eyes of Hungarians. Respondents in a national survey tend to think that the country's future rests on relations with the United States and Germany (15 percent and 14 percent, respectively), far more than with any other single state.[18] And, when teenagers were asked who was most helpful to Hungary, Germany and the United States were cited more than any other state.[19] These non-neighbors, of course, constituted a dominant influence within the Hungarian media, economy, and government.[20] Of such dominant roles, however, Hungarians have begun to question the extent of Germany's economic role, while the American diplomatic/military presence (accompanying the IFOR deployment in Bosnia) is viewed as a mixed blessing.

Hungarians reveal their sour perspectives on themselves and their environment in stark terms. National surveys conducted in Hungary since the early 1990s have found pervasive disaffection resulting from the pace and direction of political and socioeconomic changes. From opinion polls conducted in 1995, the European Union's "Eurobarometer" has reported that:

- more Hungarians (79 percent) than among any population in post-communist Europe (including post-Soviet states) say that the "direction of the country" is "wrong";
- fewer Hungarians (38 percent) than in any nation of East Central or Southeastern Europe (including the Baltic states but excluding all other post-Soviet states) regard the market economy as "right";
- fewer Hungarians (20 percent) than in any other nation in East Central or Southeastern Europe (with the exception of Bulgaria at 13 percent) express "satisfaction with [the] development of democracy" in their country;
- fewer Hungarians (26 percent) than in any other East Central or Southeastern European population think that the future of their country will be most closely tied to the European Union.[21]

Taken together, these data offer a portrait of a public that is sanguine about little and unsettled about much. A pervasive malaise—a sense of insecurity derived from perceptions of domestic and international conditions—leads Hungarians to conclude that they dislike much that they see around them; they identify no trustworthy friends on whom to rely. Those countries closest to Hungary are viewed as latent threats; the Roma, its one numerically substantial minority, are intensely disliked; and its larger patron nations are received with a mix of admiration, envy, and uncertainty.

Some, but not all, of Hungary's politicians since 1989 have uttered or written statements that intentionally exploit or unintentionally exacerbate these public fears. On a superficial level, Hungary's first post-communist government (that of the late Prime Minister Jozsef Antall) stepped around the most explosive symbols of Hungarian identity and irredentism. Yet, from the first moments of the Antall MDF government's accession in spring 1990, the support of Hungarian minorities in other countries was made a centerpiece of policy.[22] Foreign Ministry officials such as Dr. Geza Entz were given a portfolio as state secretary (deputy minister) designed to emphasize that element of MDF policy, and Entz was among those who expressed strong and vivid concern about Magyar minorities in Romania, Slovakia, and Serbia to U.S. and West European policy-makers in 1990 and 1991.[23]

Lurking not far behind, however, is the much more inflammatory language used by demagogues such as Csurka in which an image is etched of a conspiracy against Hungary among neighboring states with Magyar populations, in collusion with "other forces." To these appeals, few Hungarian voters responded positively. Yet, the damage to Hungary from Csurka-like writing or rhetoric comes from the fuel thrown on the fires of ethnonationalist and antidemocratic political forces in the region. Large demonstrations mounted by Hungary's reactionary nationalists in Budapest draw further attention to the movement, particularly when notable foreign politicians such as Jean-Marie Le Pen (leader of the Front Nationale in France) appear.[24]

The vitriolic language among parties and persons, often seen as "extreme" within Slovakia, Romania, and Serbia, in turn, fuels Hungarian conservative and right-wing politicians. When he was known only as a nationalist, not an opposition leader, Vuk Draskovic espoused the ideology of Greater Serbia and antiminority sentiment only to see it used towards larger political ends by Slobodan Milosevic.[25] During the war against Croatia and the Bosnian conflict, further extremist actions were revealed by Serbian politics—war criminals such as Zelko Raznjatovic ("Arkan"), Vojislav Seselj, Mirko Jovic, and many others. Hungarians of Vojvodina were not in the forefront of nationalist Serbs' venomous attacks as the war in Bosnia dragged on; yet, from 1990, when Vojvodina's autonomy was rescinded by the Milosevic regime, until January 1994, when efforts to normalize relations were pursued by Hungary's then Foreign Minister Geza Jeszenszky, 400,000 Hungarians lived in precarious conditions under the welter of antiminority rhetoric from Seselj's Chetniks and the Serbian National Renewal Movement (SNO) led by Jovic.

In Romania, the virulent *Romania Mare* publication, coupled with the neofascist Vatra Romaneasca movement, contributed to the birth of political parties such as the Greater Romania Party (taking the name of the publication, the Romania Mare) chaired by Vadim Tudor and the Romanian National Unity Party (PUNR) headed by Gheorghe Funar. Funar, now mayor of the principal Transylvanian city of Cluj (Kolozsvar), and Tudor (who holds a parliamentary seat) are among the most visible names from the Romanian right and seem destined to be perennial presidential candidates; both deny the existence of "minorities" as such and vehemently attack any rapprochement with Hungary.[26] Their rejection of measures, often encouraged or floated by third parties such as the OSCE High Commissioner for National Minorities or the U.S.-based NGO—the Project on Ethnic Relations—harmed efforts by most Romanians to interact more positively with Hungary, particularly after the 1994 Hungarian election that ended the MDF government.

When both Romania Mare and PUNR condemned the treaty between Budapest and Bucharest signed on September 16, 1996, President Ion Iliescu took the opportunity to end a long-strained parliamentary alliance with these parties of the extreme right. Vadim Tudor chose the same day—September 16—to register as a candidate for president in the November 1996 national elections. As he did so, Tudor informed his supporters that he will rule as president with "the Bible in one hand and the constitution in the other" and that he would return Romania to "its natural borders [as they were set] on 1 December 1918."[27] Although the date uttered by Tudor is historically inaccurate, one can infer that he is referring to the post-World War I territorial gains that were later confirmed at the Paris Peace Conference in several treaties (Saint Germain, Neuilly, and Trianon). These acquisitions, due to Romania's status as a member of the Entente after August 1916, included Transylvania, much of the Banat, Bukovina, and all of Dobrudja.

Given the opportunity to vote for a more mature centrist opposition alliance, which the Democratic Convention had become by the 1996 Romanian national elections, Romanians overwhelmingly rejected the extremism of Funar and Tudor (their parties together receiving less than 9 percent of the parliamentary vote—much less than extreme nationalists in Austria, Belgium, or France). Nevertheless, their vocal presence has considerably impeded what might have been an earlier rapprochement between Hungary and Romania.

From Slovakia, the nationalist tone of Premier Vladimir Meciar was less shrill in the first months of his third government than in his first two; earlier, for example, he had accused Hungary and Hungarians of threatening Slovakia by a military buildup and by attempting to create an anti-Slovak atmosphere that would torpedo Slovakia's entry into the Council of Europe.[28] Meciar has also been tempered by the existence of a bilateral treaty that was urged by Western powers and European institutions.

Yet, the governing party's (Movement for a Democratic Slovakia, HZDS) alliance with Jan Slota's Slovak National Party (SNS) has meant that laws passed during the short Moravcik government in 1994 that expanded minority rights have not been enforced. Indeed, late 1994 and early 1995 was an ominous period for Magyars and other minorities in Slovakia as Meciar's program included measures concerning religious liberty and minority languages that rolled back the gains of 1994.[29] Slota and his SNS, indeed, are reported to have made his party's acceptance of the Hungarian–Slovak Basic Treaty contingent upon the passage of "a law that severely curtails freedom of speech and assembly" and "a separate law making Slovak the official language and restricting the right to speak others."[30]

Understandably, then, the treaty signed by Meciar and Hungarian Prime Minister Gyula Horn in 1995 and ratified by Slovakia in early 1996 has not led Magyar leaders in Slovakia, such as Miklos Duray, to express confidence about minority rights. Careful to acknowledge that the "rhetoric of autonomy is unacceptable to Slovak society," Hungarian Civic Party (MOS) Chairman Laszlo Nagy has sought an alliance with the liberal-conservative opposition in Bratislava.[31] Such an approach by the MOS, which is among the coalition of ethnic Hungarian parties in the Slovak Parliament, has not produced reciprocal restraint among Slovak nationalists. For their part, the Slovak National Party led Bratislava's vehement response after Horn's government coauthored a controversial Hungarian minorities' manifesto in July 1996, demanding that the Basic Treaty between the two countries be abrogated. By late October 1996, Meciar had returned to his stance of a few years earlier, rejecting Hungarian minority demands with the pejorative aside that "half of them are Roma anyway," and with the warning, "Slovakia will not become a guinea pig [presumably, with respect to minority rights] for Europe."[32]

Treaties meant to ease residual tensions with neighboring countries have been priorities for both the MDF and socialist governments in Budapest. The pursuit of such diplomatic instruments made sense; Magyars in these countries could not be protected by Hungary, and only internationally recognized, mutual commitments could help to ensure the safety and well-being of Hungary's ethnic kin in surrounding states. And, any Western institution with which Hungary wished to be integrated—the European Union, Council of Europe, NATO, etc.— expected that such documents would be consummated before full entry.

The first of these bilateral treaties was signed with Ukraine, in large part because it was the least difficult. Ukraine counts a relatively small number of ethnic Hungarians in Transcarpathia who have had minimal problems with the post-Soviet government, and no other fundamental issues cloud the Budapest–Kiev relationship. The language used in the treaty signed in 1991 and ratified by the Hungarian Parliament in 1993 included a renunciation of any territorial claims against each other, and guarantees for minority rights and cultural autonomy following the general outline of Germany's earlier treaties with Poland and Czechoslovakia. Hungary signed a basic treaty with Slovakia in March 1995, just in time to arrive at the European Stability Conference initiated by France in Paris. Although it took a year for the Slovaks to ratify the treaty, there was relief in Bratislava and Budapest that an improvement in relations might then commence. Still, however, vitriol lies underneath the surface, as exchanges in mid to late 1996 demonstrated.

The long and arduous gestation of a basic treaty between Hungary and Romania, for which informal discussions began in 1990, is symptomatic of deeply embedded suspicions and the volatile politics of minorities in Central and Southeastern Europe. The central issue that held up an otherwise boilerplate document was a trade-off between Hungarian insistence on treaty language that specified the collective rights of minorities versus Romanian demands for language that guaranteed existing borders. Romania saw the former measure as endangering a unitary state by implying territorial autonomy for minorities, while Hungary saw the latter step as both unnecessary (given existing political commitments in, for example, the Charter for a New Europe of November 1990) and a de facto abandonment of Magyars in Transylvania.

At loggerheads over such matters, leaders of both countries were cognizant in 1996 that their chances to advance towards European Union membership or to enter NATO were harmed by the absence of a treaty. Former Romanian President Ion Iliescu had, prior to a state visit to the United States in 1995, attempted to circumvent specific treaty language obstacles by proposing a "historic reconciliation" between Bucharest and Budapest. Vague in content, but tactically astute, this step added pressure on the Gyula Horn government to reciprocate.

With increasing urgency in 1995 and 1996, EU, NATO, and U.S. politicians, diplomats, and analysts underscored the need to complete the bilateral treaty as a necessary albeit symbolic step towards full entry into Western institutions. For the United States, this message was carried to Budapest and Bucharest in many visits by State and Defense Department officials, senior National Security Council staff, members of Congress, and members of the business and academic communities and the U.S. military.[33]

For the Hungarian government—even the Hungarian Socialist Party, with far more latitude among its voters to put to rest difficulties over the diaspora in neighboring states—it was extremely difficult to accept language that did not explicitly recognize the collective rights of Magyars in Romania. Demands for including terms such as "autonomy," long heard from the ethnic Hungarian party in Romania, seemingly had been abandoned by Budapest even before the socialist victory in Hungary. Yet, as late as a couple weeks before the late-August announcement that a treaty was ready to be signed, the Hungarian side was still trying to obtain external (particularly U.S.) support for its insistence that the "collective rights" phraseology be included, while the Foreign Ministry gave its approval to a minorities' declaration that resuscitated the autonomy controversy.[34] Hungary's efforts had been, at least in part, encouraged by the Council of Europe's 1994 Recommendation 1201, the interpretation of which was hotly debated by Romania throughout 1995–96. Particularly troublesome to Romania was Article 11 of Recommendation 1201, in which national minorities are said to have the right, in regions where they are in a majority, "to have at their disposal appropriate local or autonomous authorities or to have a special status matching the specific historical and territorial situation." To Bucharest, this was an invitation to secession.

But, rather than collective rights, the Romanian–Hungarian Basic Treaty enumerates human rights of minorities in both countries, noting Recommendation 1201 but not stipulating adherence to it. The consequences of this step are far-reaching. By accepting this formulation, the Horn government distanced itself significantly from the leadership of the Transylvanian Hungarians. Bela Marko, speaking to the second Hungarian minority "summit" in Hungary on September 4, 1996, was reported to have objected strongly to the absence of collective rights guarantees in the treaty and to the choice of Timisoara as a venue for the signing ceremony, calling the latter a "mockery of the revolutionary traditions" of that city where the December 1989 rebellion against Ceausescu began.[35]

Within Romania, the Basic Treaty has changed the role of the UDMR (the Hungarian Democratic Union of Romania, the ethnic political party). By appearing to oppose a treaty that most of the Magyar population in Romania support, the UDMR reduced its own base of support, and pushed its core membership towards a reintegration with the Democratic Convention in a coalition government. Seventy-four percent of ethnic Hungarians polled between September 4–9, 1996, agreed that the Basic Treaty would benefit ethnic Hungarians and Romanians equally,[36] a finding that, while debated by more hard-line leaders of the Hungarian community in Romania, such as Reverend Laszlo Tokes, forced a strategic reassessment. Neither did such data support claims by Istvan Csurka's extraparliamentary political formation, the Hungarian Justice and Life Party, and by the Smallholders' Party during a September 1996 antitreaty rally in Budapest, that the Horn government's signature on the document was treasonous.[37] For their part, the Romanian far right was equally demagogic; Cluj Mayor Funar, for example, proclaimed September 16 (when the treaty was signed) a "day of mourning."

Absent such treaties, Hungary has negligible capacities of any kind—particularly in terms of military power—to defend itself or its ethnic kin in the region. Relative to the three neighboring states in which most ethnic Hungarians reside in Europe, the Hungarian armed forces could play no role. As compared with Romania, Slovakia, or Serbia/Montenegro, Hungary has the lowest defense expenditures as a proportion of GDP (1.6 percent in 1995)[38] and the lowest active duty military manpower as a proportion of population (about 7.0 per 1,000).[39] Were the Hungarian armed forces qualitatively much superior, some implicit "leveling" might be assumed. But, unless significant resources arrive from abroad as a consequence of NATO membership, modernization will be slow to occur and neither the Hungarian army nor air force could assume an edge in technology or quality. And, according to several estimates, Romania and Slovakia both increased their defense spending and manpower in the mid-1990s, while the Milosevic government maintained an enormous commitment to armed might measured on all per capita indicators. During the same period, Hungary continued to diminish resources allocated to defense.[40]

The use of military force between or among Hungary and its neighbors carries such a low probability today that assessing relative capabilities may seem irrelevant. But, the extremely limited capabilities on all sides, save for Serbia (which has other more immediate concerns), do not lessen the perception of imbalance and vulnerability. Unless accompanied by measures that enhance transparency (e.g., the open-skies agreement between Romania and Hungary) or external guarantees (from NATO, OSCE, and other multilateral bodies concerned with security), general staffs and defense ministries plan for worst-case scenarios and politicians exploit public fears for votes.

Hungarians and their central European neighborhood do not yet evince the benefits of a "democratic peace," in which safety and satisfaction join together. Hungarians, unhappy about far more than one might anticipate, are not sanguine about their neighbors, their minorities, or much of anything else. Seeing their own numbers dwindle, discomfited by the direction of post-1989 change, and cognizant of severe constraints on Hungary's capacities (military or otherwise) to affect the course of events, Hungarians are likely candidates to perceive internal and external threats that may seem larger than any third-party assessment would find.

Ethnicity, Politics, Insecurity

Ethnicity and politics intermingle in almost every country. The mere presence of heterogeneity is often blamed as the origin of violence within or between states.[41] The normalcy of ethnic tensions suggests a continuum at one end of which are moderate concomitants of ethnicity unlikely to generate violence, including ethnic groups' demands for cultural expression, linguistic pluralism, educational opportunities, and equality before the law. At the other extreme, ethnicity is thought to generate the intolerance and hatred out of which war and genocide emerge.

For a region such as Central and Southeastern Europe, however, blaming ethnic identities for tensions that begat conflicts that begat wars is historically incorrect and analytically spurious. Ethnic heterogeneity is present but not guilty of causing conflict.

For Hungary and its neighbors, what propels ethnic identity towards dangerous shoals is nationalism. When it subsumes ethnic identity, nationalism becomes ethnonationalism—a potent admixture on which extremists and demagogues feed. But, the nexus among ethnicity, nationalism, and security remains poorly understood. Van Evera, among others, has tried to examine the relationship between types of nationalism and the probability of armed conflict.[42] Missing in this and other studies, however, is the thought that a "trigger" must be present to drive ethnic issues into the clutches of nationalism.

Since 1989, much has been written about resurfacing, reemerging, or revitalized nationalism in Eastern Europe and elsewhere. Often these assessments have taken an almost apocalyptic tone, with ample hyperbole. David Fromkin, for example, writes about nationalism as the "most striking and alarming tendency in world politics as we head into the twenty-first century."[43] Yet more strident was Karrin von Hippel whose "The Resurgence of Nationalism and its International Implications" seems to take for granted the war-causing potential of nationalism when mixed with ethnicity.[44] And, even among less alarmist viewpoints, the metaphor of a "rising tide of nationalism" is repeated from many perspectives, invariably accompanied by the judgment that nationalism poses "the greatest challenge to the security of the new Europe" or that it is the "central reality" of erstwhile, homogeneous communist systems.[45]

The intermingling of peoples and borders means that every ethnic group is both a majority in one state with accompanying minorities, and a minority living among other larger groups in neighboring states. Such a condition fits into these ominous portraits as the principal catalyst for exaggerated nationalism. Once lauded by John Stuart Mill as a "necessary condition of free institutions . . . [such that] boundaries of government coincide in the main with those of nationality," the early form of nationalism—which emphasized self-determination and building a state—was clearly supplanted in the nineteenth century.[46] The originally "anticlerical, constitutional and egalitarian orientation" of East European nationalism was, as in other parts of Europe, pushed aside by a destructive ideology.[47] Such an ideology, as Elie Kedourie wrote, "divides humanity into separate and distinct nations, claims that such nations must constitute sovereign states, and asserts that the members of a nation reach freedom and fulfillment by cultivating the peculiar identity of their own nation and by sinking their own persons in the greater whole of the nation."[48]

In the political calculus of virulent ideologues, prominent minorities or a proportionately large diaspora in nearby countries are inviting targets for their language of intolerance, mistrust, and hate. Tensions have often widened into violence and then war as demagogic politicians identify scapegoats for domestic ills and targets for aggrandizement nearby where ethnic kin reside.

To use ethnicity as a catch-all explanation for ethnic conflicts, however, confuses cause and effect. Minorities neither make nationalism possible, heighten its volatility, nor themselves generate threats; ethnicity becomes volatile because of nationalism, not the other way around. "Ethnic controversies alone," writes one Hungarian analyst, "could not constitute a security risk."[49] Paul A. Goble, an American specialist on post-Soviet minority issues, suggests, likewise, that ethnonationalism is a smoke screen for those who want to believe that such conflicts are insoluble and, thus, not amenable to U.S. or international intervention; to Goble, ethnicity is less an explanation of conflict than an excuse for our neglect of conflicts around the world.[50]

To explain conflicts that pit ethnic communities against one another on the basis of, for example, economic interests would be a dangerous alternative. We have seen atrocities committed in the post-Yugoslav wars and in the Caucasus that defy any effort to portray violence of one ethnic group against another in a rational or materialistic light, as if some heinous calculus were being used.[51] Using ethnic selection as a criterion by which to identify people for mutilation or assassination cannot be attributed solely to prior insecurities among the perpetrators; rather like exculpating criminals because they are poor and unemployed, atrocities committed in the midst of "ethnic conflict" involve the culpability of individuals.

Yet, in both of these corners of Europe—the Balkans and the Caucasus—intermingled ethnic, religious, and linguistic communities existed for decades in relative peace, as long as a strong central state ensured security. Often imposed with a heavy, authoritarian hand and despised by many, such external control nonetheless enabled peoples to know that potential threats from domestic or external sources were adequately balanced.

These observations lead to the suspicion that insecurities create conflicts that involve ethnically different groups, not minorities themselves. Ethnicity, the presence of minorities and a sizeable diaspora, are fuel used by extreme nationalists, not the "trigger" for the emergence of nationalism.

As the social and psychological sources of collective violence have been explored, others have recognized and documented the effects of relative deprivation (Gurr) and backwardness (Horowitz).[52] In a broadly comparative dimension, ample evidence suggests that relations between minorities and majorities deteriorate concomitant with negative and threatening socioeconomic and political conditions. Economic growth, political quiescence, and international peace are not guarantors of interethnic calm; yet, if there are groups within a society that feel relatively at risk—regardless of whether the threat emanates from unemployment, crime, or invasion—the potential for ethnic conflict rises.[53] On those bases, it is possible to identify states and environments where the greatest potential for conflict among ethnic communities exists, not because ethnic identity itself is fostering violence, but because other conditions open the door for exploitation of ethnicity.

As security is perceived to erode—a sentiment usually linked to the weakened capacities of the economy, central government, and other institutions—commitment to democratic values wanes.[54] In such an environment, sentiments of intolerance and suspicion can be directed by demagogues towards minorities within the state and/or neighboring states in which ethnic kin reside. The importance of threat as an explanation for democratic behavior has been suggested by preliminary findings from a comparative study of eight states over ten years (1985–95) that were identified by the Freedom House as having undergone significant change in political or individual liberties during that period. For this sample of states, high levels of social, economic, and international threat were found to be associated with a deterioration or prevention of democratic behavior.[55]

Extreme nationalists foment the abandonment of liberal democratic ideals by sharpening the perceptions of threat. Every minority demand for opportunities or rights becomes, in the hands of nationalists, evidence of the "Trojan horse" endangering a majority that must absorb or eradicate such minorities.[56] Nationalists at the century's close want to break down the capacity of nascent democracies to protect rights and to safeguard minorities. Nationalists' challenges to states' sovereignty have made late-twentieth-century nationalism less a harbinger of state power, survival, or aggrandizement and much more a link to its (the state's) decline. In the formative centuries of the nation-state, nationalism evoked development and self-determination; now it suggests the state's unraveling.

Nationalists, by weakening political systems and their institutions, foster the insecurity on which extremism thrives, enabling their seizure of ethnicity as a tool of intolerance and suspicion. And, once joined, ethnonationalism is likely to lead towards violence within a state, or between one state and its neighbors.

In the hands of demagogues, minorities within the state are threats and ethnic kin living in contiguous states are always endangered. Both scenarios assume far larger proportions and more ominous characteristics as nationalists manipulate images through rhetoric laced with conspiracy and innuendo, use of historical symbols from times of national triumph or tragedy, and behavior meant to precipitate socioeconomic and political crises.

Hungary's post-communist political system has thus far absorbed and marginalized individuals and groups who have sought to use the minorities issue as a bludgeon against democratic principles. Neither the MDF nor HSP governments has succumbed as a general practice to temptations of political gain that might be reaped from such base appeals or tactical alliances. Political maturity may be one explanation of such constraint, but fear of unleashing extremist sentiments and/or multilateral pressures and expectations have been stronger factors.

But Hungarian post-communist governments have, nevertheless, sometimes leaned towards the nationalists' corner either by design or error. In the early 1990s, there were none-too-subtle references from Antall about being a prime minister, in spirit, for 15 million Hungarians. More recently, the Horn government endorsed a final communique from the so-called Hungarian Minority Summit that was held in Hungary during July 1996.[57] This document, explicitly soliciting support for the "creation of self-government and autonomy" for ethnic Hungarian communities in neighboring states, offered few specifics about the nature of such autonomy, and seemed meant to serve as a rallying cry, not a policy statement. But, by agreeing to coauthor the document, the Hungarian Foreign Ministry raised the event's visibility greatly; and, by then defending that decision, Foreign Minister Laszlo Kovacs and parliamentary leaders added further to the suspicion raised among neighbors.

Notwithstanding many efforts to explain away their sponsorship of the minority summit's closing declaration, Hungarian leaders were forced to endure bitter complaints from the Slovaks and Romanians, and criticisms from the European Union, the Clinton administration and U.S. Congress, and many West European governments.[58] Senior U.S. State Department personnel were particularly aggrieved, since Washington had been consistent in its reassurances to Romania and Slovakia about Budapest's intention to establish good relations with all neighbors. As one American diplomat said, the Horn government was either grossly negligent in its assessments of fallout from such a declaration, or, "much more likely, had shrewdly calculated what it would need to do in order to mitigate opposition from the diaspora and the domestic right wing to the Hungarian–Romanian Basic Treaty."[59] After a spring and summer during which it had been excoriated for selling out the Hungarian minorities in neighboring states, and simultaneously pushed by Western capitals to conclude the treaty with Romania, Horn, Kovacs, and other decision makers must have concluded that they needed to repair the HSP government's record on minorities or risk defeat when the Romanian treaty came up for ratification.[60]

This episode does not demonstrate a pattern, but it does suggest the need of even a majority Hungarian government committed to regional confidence building to respond to attitudes that may threaten and intimidate neighboring states. That regional divisions can be regenerated very easily should surprise no one. But the reverberations inside Hungary and within the Magyar populations in surrounding countries can be prolonged and damaging. For the Horn government, signing proclamations are a part of a political calculus. For nationalists, however, these documents are manifestos, and their goal is nothing short of undermining authority and fomenting fear.

Summary

Hungary's integration into the European Union and NATO has already begun and will accelerate in the first years of the next century. Its young democracy has weathered economic crises and transfers of power within one party and between parties. Investors remain confident, and the country's reform continues.

But Hungarians are disquieted by what they see happening and are arguably the most disaffected people in Central or Southeastern Europe. The ethnic Hungarians in Romania, Slovakia, and Serbia constitute a "minority issue" of enormous importance because of their numbers relative to a declining population in Hungary itself, and a history that Hungarians see, in very general terms, as unjust. Taken together, this provides fertile ground for demagogic appeals.

That cooler heads have prevailed since 1989 is testimony to the keen desire for peace and prosperity within Hungary or in the ethnic diaspora; their voting, opinion surveys, and other behaviors evince little desire for extremist paths advocated by some domestic politicians and a few extreme nationalists among ethnic Hungarians in neighboring states.

But in Hungary's neighborhood, the minority issue will not soon fade away. As long as people are insecure—and nationalists will always foment that sentiment because it is their ticket to power—ethnic distinctions can be exploited to turn groups and communities against one another, thereby weakening central authority and opening the door to extremists' appeals.

Hungary's assiduous devotion, regardless of the party in power, to a foreign policy of reconciliation and confidence building, seeking security through the collective means of NATO and the European Union, not unilateral proclamations or actions, will be critical in coming years. Even so, neighbors in Central and Eastern Europe will have to discover "a mean distance" at which they can most tolerably exist, kept from intimacy by sharp reminders of conflictual pasts.

Notes

1. Arthur Schopenhauer, *Parerga and Paralipomena, vol II* (orig. pub. 1851) (Oxford: Oxford University Press, 1974) 559–60.

2. Sigmund Freud, *Group Psychology and the Analysis of the Ego* (orig. pub. 1921) (New York: Knopf, 1955), 101.

3. Christoph Royen, "The Visegrad Triangle and the Western CIS" in John Lampe and Daniel N. Nelson, eds., *East European Security Reconsidered* (Baltimore: Johns Hopkins University Press, 1994), 96.

4. I use the term *diaspora* in a manner guided more by common usage than by the strictest ethnographic definition. In the more precise definition, the dispersion of an originally homogeneous people is indicated—typically under duress. Hungarians settled, rather than being "dispersed," into regions that were later ceded to or reclaimed by neighboring states. Nevertheless, diaspora now suggests those parts of an ethnic group not situated within the state wherein that group constitutes a majority.

5. A superb treatment of these relationships, with ample citation to principal theoretical and empirical studies, is Heinz Gartner, "States without Nations: State, Nation and Security in Central Europe," *International Politics*, vol. 34, no. 1 (February 1997), 7–32.

6. I have developed this understanding of security in a number of previous articles and essays. Among these are "Security in a Post-Hegemonic World," *Bulletin of Peace Proposals*, vol. 22, no. 3 (September 1991), 333–45; "Great Powers and World Peace" in Michael Klare, ed., *World Security: Trends and Challenges* (New York: St. Martin's Press, 1993), 27–42; and "America and Collective

Security in Europe," *Journal of Strategic Studies,* vol. 17, no. 4 (December 1994), 105–24.

7. Central Intelligence Agency, *Handbook of International Economic Statistics* (Washington, D.C.: annual 1992, 1993, 1994, 1995). The population of Hungary with its current borders may have peaked at about 10.7 million in the early 1980s.

8. The Commission on Security and Cooperation in Europe of the U.S. Congress, for example, refers to one million people of minority ethnicity, or almost 10 percent of Hungary's population. Within this, the Commission uses the 400,000–800,000 range for their estimate of the Roma population. See the Commission's *Human Rights and Democratization in Hungary* (Washington, D.C., December 1993), 17.

9. United Nations, *Demographic Yearbook* (New York: United Nations, 1960 and 1964) as cited in R.H. Osborne, *East-Central Europe* (New York: Praeger, 1967), 346.

10. During the 1960s, writes Roy E.H. Mellor, "growth of [Hungary's] population slowed appreciable, with a marked fall in natural increase." See his *Eastern Europe: A Geography of the Comecon Countries* (New York: Columbia University Press, 1975), 108.

11. No European state exceeds the Hungarian figure except Albania—the diaspora of which includes about 2 million in Kosovo and Montenegro, and another few hundred thousand in Macedonia, i.e., more than 60 percent of Albania's own population of 3.2 million. At the outset of the twentieth century, many European nations were dispersed to a far greater degree; Romanians, Serbs, and Greeks, among those nations with state "homelands," and Poles, Jews, Gypsies/Romas (among others) then without a state, were more dispersed than Hungarians are today. Hungary itself, then ruling Transylvania, the Banat, Vojvodina, and much of Croatia and Slovakia, included almost all Hungarians. See, Paul Robert Magocsi, *Historical Atlas of East Central Europe* (Seattle: University of Washington Press, 1993), 97–98.

12. Csurka's political popularity has waned greatly, and he does not now play more than a fringe role. While this could change, his principal influence was wielded in the early 1990s while still a vice president of the governing MDF (from which he was expelled in June 1993). A flavor of Csurka's views, including not-too-subtle xenophobia and anti-Semitism, was evident in his August 1992 essay attacking the government of Jozsef Antall.

13. These points draw on a discussion of Hungarian nationalism in the twentieth century by Tibor Frank, "Nation, National Minorities, and Nationalism in Twentieth Century Hungary" in Peter F. Sugar, ed., *Eastern European Nationalism in the 20th Century* (Washington, D.C.: American University Press, 1995), 222–42.

14. Janos Matus, "Sources of Tensions and Crisis Management in East-Central Europe" in Laszlo Valki, ed., *International Security and East-Central Europe* (Budapest: Center for Security Studies, 1993), 95–96.

15. These data are from USIA 1995 surveys reported in *The New European Security Architecture* (Washington, D.C.: USIA Office of Research and Media Reaction, September 1995), 18.

16. U.S. Congress, Commission for Security and Cooperation in Europe, *Human Rights and Democratization in Europe* (Washington, D.C.; December 1993), 19–20.

17. European Commission, *Central and Eastern EUROBAROMETER* (Brussels: EU, Directorate General for Information, Communications, Culture, Audiovisual—Survey Research Unit, March 1996), Annex Figure 7.

18. *EUROBAROMETER*, op. cit., Annex Figure 10.

19. Gyorgy Csepeli and Tibor Zavecz, "European and National Linkages among Hungarian Teenagers," unpublished paper (Department of Sociology, Eotvos Lorand University, 1995).

20. On the economic side, Germany is overwhelming. The *Budapest Sun* (May 3, 1996) reported, for example, that Germans were the largest purchasers of Hungarian assets; the 98 companies valued at $1.7 billion which had been purchased by Germans in 1995 amounted to 37 percent of all Hungarian property sold in that year, more than 2.5 times the proportion purchased by Americans (p. 2). In diplomacy, however, a rough estimate based on Foreign Broadcast Information Service Daily Reports for Eastern Europe from mid-1995–mid-1996 would be that the United States and Germany, combined, were destinations in more than half of the foreign trips made by cabinet level or higher officials—with the United States probably exceeding Germany by a slight margin.

21. *EUROBAROMETER*, op. cit., Annex Figures 1, 4, 6, and 8.

22. The Government Program of Premier Antall as translated in BBC, *Summary of World Broadcasts—Eastern Europe* EE/0773 (25 May 1990), C1, 3–9.

23. In 1990 and 1991, while the author served as senior foreign policy advisor to then-House Majority Leader Richard Gephardt, conversations with Entz took place in Budapest, Hungary, and Washington D.C.

24. For an account of Le Pen's visit to Budapest, and a Justice and Life Party rally, see *Magyar Hirlap* (27 October 1996).

25. Misha Glenny, *The Fall of Yugoslavia* (New York: Penguin, 1994); page 39 mentions this character of early Draskovic. This author interviewed Draskovic in early 1990 during research for *Balkan Imbroglio* (Boulder, Colo.: Westview Press, 1991) and recorded Draskovic's comment that "Hungarians were so close to Croats that the differences did not matter."

26. Author's interview with Gheorghe Funar (Cluj, Romania, June 1993).

27. Open Media Research Institute (OMRI), *Daily Digest* (17 September 1996).

28. For a flavor of this sharp rhetoric in mid-1993, see "Slovaks and Hungarians Disagree at CEI Meeting," *OMRI Daily Report*, no. 135 (19 July 1993). Also in mid-1993, the Council of Europe's admission of Slovakia was brought into doubt by Hungarian efforts to extract further guarantees from the Meciar government for Magyars in Slovakia. See Krisztina Fenyo, "Debate Increases Magyar–Slovak Tension" in *Budapest Week*, vol. 3, no. 17 (July 1–7, 1993), 2.

29. The Bratislava daily *Sme* (26 January 1995) gave detailed coverage of and comments on the Meciar government program presented in Parliament.

30. Vincent Boland, "A Question of Autonomy," *Financial Times* (Special Supplement on Slovakia), 23 October 1996, 11.

31. *Sme* (10 October 1996), quoting a CTK dispatch, p.2.

32. Meciar's comments, during an 30 October 1996 television debate, were repeated in the *OMRI Daily Digest* (31 October 1996).

33. Romanian Foreign Minister Melescanu, while in Washington, D.C., in July 1996, told the author that he had been "counseled repeatedly" to accelerate the treaty preparation.

34. I was told of such efforts by senior State Department and NSC officials.

35. OMRI *Daily Digest*, no. 171 (5 September 1996).

36. Results from this survey, undertaken by the Romanian Institute for Public Opinion Research (IRSOP), were published in *Magyar Hirlap* (12 September 1996), and cited in *OMRI Daily Digest*, no. 178 (13 September 1996).

37. *OMRI Daily Digest*, no. 172 (6 September 1996).

38. *The Military Balance 1995–1996* (London: International Institute for Strategic Studies, 1996).

39. *World Military Expenditures and Arms Transfers, 1994–1995* (Washington, D.C.: U.S. Arms Control and Disarmament Agency, 1996).

40. See *The Military Balance, 1995–1996* (London: International Institute for Strategic Studies, 1996), 265.

41. Donald L. Horowitz, "Ethnic and Nationalist Conflict" in Michael T. Klare and Daniel C. Thomas, eds., *World Security: Challenges for a New Century*, 2nd ed. (New York: St. Martin's Press, 1994), 175–78. This study notes the widespread presence of ethnic tensions and conflicts on all continents and in all cultures.

42. Stephen Van Evera, "Hypotheses on Nationalism and War," *International Security*, vol. 18, no. 4 (Spring, 1994), 5–39.

43. David Fromkin, "The Coming Millennium: World Politics in the Twenty-First Century," *World Policy Journal*, vol. 10, no. 1 (Spring, 1993).

44. Karrin von Hippel, "The Resurgence of Nationalism and Its International Implications," *Washington Quarterly* vol. 17, no. 4 (Autumn, 1994).

45. These quotes are drawn, respectively, from Jack Snyder, "Controlling Nationalism in the New Europe" in Armand Clesse and Lothar Ruhl, eds., *Beyond East-West Confrontation: Searching for a New Security Structure in Europe* (Baden-Baden: Nomos Verlagsgessellschaft, 1990), and Zbigniew Brzezinski, "Post-Communist Nationalism," *Foreign Affairs*, vol. 68, no.4 (Winter 1989–90), 1.

46. John Stuart Mill, *Considerations on Representative Government* (London: Prometheus Books, 1991).

47. Peter F. Sugar, "External and Domestic Roots of Eastern European Nationalism" in Peter F. Sugar and Ivo J. Lederer, eds., *Nationalism in Eastern Europe* (Seattle: University of Washington Press, 1969), 46.

48. Elie Kedourie, *Nationalism* (London: Hutchinson, 1960), 72.

49. Laszlo Valki, "Security in Central Europe" in *European Security after the Cold War*, Adelphi Paper no. 284 (London: International Institute for Security Studies, January–February, 1994), 16.

50. Paul A. Goble, "Ethnicity as Explanation, Ethnicity as Excuse" in Robert L. Pfaltzgraff, Jr., and Richard H. Schultz, eds., *Ethnic Conflict and Regional Instability* (forthcoming, 1998), 51.

51. Horowitz notes the danger of attributing ethnic violence to rational or materialistic motives. Horowitz, *op. cit.*

52. Ted Robert Gurr's classic *Why Men Rebel* (Princeton: Princeton University Press, 1970), of course, formulated the relative deprivation thesis. He has more recently applied this to ethnopolitical conflicts in "States Versus Peoples: Ethnopolitical Conflict in the 1980s with Early Warning Forecasts for the 1990s," paper presented at the Annual Meeting of the International Studies Association (San Diego, CA, March 1996). Donald Horowitz has distinguished between advanced and backward secessionist (minority) groups in "Patterns of Ethnic Separatism," *Comparative Studies in Society and History*, vol. 23, no. 2, (1981), 165–85.

53. Ted Robert Gurr and Michael Haxton have provided an empirical exploration of these relationships in their "Minorities Report (1): Ethnopolitical Conflict in the 1990s," paper presented at the Annual Meeting of the International Studies Association (San Diego, CA, March 1996).

54. I have discussed this relationship in greater detail in "Civil Society Endangered," *Social Research,* vol. 63, no. 2, (Summer, 1996), 345–68. Economic insecurity in environments of high income inequality is, for example, negatively associated with democratization. See Edward N. Muller, "Democracy, Economic Development and Income Inequality," *The American Sociological Review*, vol. 53, no. 1 (January 1988), 50–68. Further, systemic pessimism and negative expectations regarding personal finances are negatively associated with support for "democratic principles." See Mary E. McIntosh, Martha Abele MacIver, and Daniel G. Abele, "Publics Meet Market Democracy in Central and Eastern Europe, 1991–1993," *Slavic Review*, vol. 53, no. 2 (Summer, 1994), 502.

55. Research from this project will begin to appear in 1997 in articles by all or part of the research team—Dovile Budryte, Susan Morris, Georgeta Pourchot, Blagovest Tashev, and Daniel N. Nelson.

56. Gurr and Haxton, " Minorities Report (1): Ethnopolitical Conflict in the 1990s," *op. cit.,* 10.

57. Joint Declaration from the Conference on Hungary and Hungarians Beyond the Borders, issued by the Hungarian News Agency, MTI (7 July 1996).

58. The nature of such complaints and criticisms and a general account of this event is in Zsofia Szilagyi, "Hungarian Minority Summit Causes Uproar in the Region," *Transition* vol. 2, no. 18 (6 September 1996), 45–48.

59. Personal communication, Washington, D.C., 4 August 1996.

60. My interviews in Budapest during late June 1996, although a couple months before either of these events, included conversations with several analysts in think-tanks who anticipated such a move by the Horn government, i.e., "covering" themselves vis-à-vis the parliamentary opposition and diaspora with a nonbinding political declaration while pressing ahead with treaty finalization.

Chapter 14

The Unfolding Transition and Consolidation

Zoltan Barany

In this book we raise questions about substantive concerns pertaining to systemic transitions that often do not have clear-cut answers, yet it is important to ask them. The more immediate purpose of this work is to analyze and explain the dilemmas of post-communist (or post-state socialist) political and economic transitions in Eastern Europe through the example of one of the region's most successful states, Hungary. The theoretical discussions regarding the key issues of post-communist transitions inform the empirical analyses and the lessons to be learned from them. Aside from the knowledge yielded by the empirical analyses of the trials and tribulations of the Hungarian experience with democratization and marketization, Hungary's example also teaches us a great deal about similar processes under way in the rest of the region.

The complexity and comprehensiveness of the political and socioeconomic changes imperative for the establishment of a democratic polity and market economy, to replace the socialist state with its single-party system and centrally planned economy, would be difficult to overestimate. Indeed, the tasks ahead of the post-communist states after the collapse of the ancien régime were without precedent. Although numerous authoritarian systems have been transformed into democratic polities, those states in Iberia, Latin America, and elsewhere were not forced to undertake this challenge simultaneously with the equally multifarious project of economic transformation. Thus, the East European and other post-communist states had no blueprint to work from though they did benefit from the assistance of Western institutions and academics.

Although prior to the fall of communism the tasks of the political transition seemed as daunting as those of the economic transition, the evidence at hand suggests that several important aspects of constructing democratic polities were relatively easily accomplished. This is particularly so for certain substantive areas, such as institution building, breaking the political monopoly of communist parties, the abolition of censorship, and the formulation of legal guarantees for the practice of fundamental human and political rights. These objectives had not been reached with equal ease or without political struggle across the region, but they had been secured everywhere quite rapidly. As the contributors to this volume attest, the less tangible aspects of politics—such as the evolution of a well-functioning civil society, the acquisition and maintenance of political legitimacy, the development of a democratic political culture—hold tasks that will, no doubt, take a much longer period of time to attain.

The parallel process of restructuring the economic system from the domination of the central plan to that of the market has proved to be a more complex and difficult task. The legacies of communism in the economic realm included not only important institutional elements but here, too, a number of intangibles such as people's relationship to productive work, the decades-long, widely accepted practice of corruption, bribery, and theft, as well as the notion of the second (or gray) economy to mention but a few. As the examples of postwar Germany, Japan, and Italy demonstrate, democratic polities can be built in a relatively brief period of time. To develop, nay to create, economies that generate competitive products in the world market is a far more trying challenge particularly for a region that has been economically devastated by four decades of central planning and, perhaps more importantly, has been characterized by centuries of relative economic backwardness.

The contributors to this volume discuss, evaluate, and criticize some of the assumptions of the literature pertaining to both the theoretical and practical-empirical aspects of transitions. In the balance of this assessment, I will highlight some of the most important themes and interesting contributions in this book. Rather than passing judgment, I merely endeavor to emphasize them and let the reader decide their merits.

Legacies and Preconditions

A serious consideration of the transition process cannot proceed without the weighing of its starting point, that is, where a state stands in terms of its political and socioeconomic preparation at the time the

transition itself commences. It is not always easy to identify the legacies of four decades of communism, yet there can be little doubt that
"barring an enduring fascist dictatorship, any other system of government and any other set of economic policies would have held more
benefits" for Eastern Europe.[1] The region's centuries-long political and
socioeconomic underdevelopment was exacerbated by the communist
period. At the end of the communist era, East European economies
were considerably poorer relative to West European ones than at the
end of World War II.[2] The conditions for the transition to democracy
and the market were hardly propitious in 1989, still, some states were
clearly better prepared than others.

As we have noted in this volume, in some respects Hungary was perhaps the best prepared for the transition period of all East European
states. Political liberalization, limited institutional reforms in the mid-
1980s, and legal regulations pertaining to foreign trade and business
clearly helped the country's international reputation. Another fortunate factor—particularly vis-à-vis Czechoslovakia—was the fact that
Hungary was a unitary state which did not have to worry about a potentially dangerous secession or breakup as in the cases of the region's
federal states. As Andrew Arato suggested, the presence of a nascent
civil society—in contrast with the absence of such in Albania, Bulgaria,
or Romania—may also be considered an auspicious circumstance that
stimulated the chances for the historic roundtable talks and what we
have come to refer to as a "pacted" or "negotiated" transition.[3]

Still, the contributors to this volume are not of the same mind when
considering Hungary's preparedness for the democratic era and for its
economy's marketization. Anna Seleny is the most optimistic in this
regard, suggesting that the long-standing political liberalization process of the Kadar era to a significant extent laid the foundations of post-
socialist legitimacy in Hungary. She convincingly argues that the moderate, pragmatic, and consensus-seeking policies that characterized
Hungary as a socialist state had continued to be the main features of
the country during the periods of democratic transition and consolidation. Seleny's optimism is not matched by the contributions of Rudolf
Tokes or Paul Marer. Their qualms focus primarily on economic matters and their implications to post-communist political developments.
Tokes argues that the various socioeconomic, psychological, and external constraints on Hungarian decision makers render the prospects of
a speedy passage to a smoothly functioning democratic polity and
market economy rather doubtful in the short term. Marer is more concerned with what message the artificially (i.e., politically) motivated
consumption of the 1970s and 1980s may have signaled to politicians.
For the leaders of the late-communist era the political benefit of quasi-

reform policies was a sort of "semilegitimacy," but its long-term effects included Hungary's extremely burdensome foreign debt and anti-quated infrastructure. While Anders Åslund does not make light of the problems inherited from the period of centrally planned economies, he suggests that most of the problems of the past may, in fact, be relatively easily transcended by consistently reformist economic policy which, in his view, is the most important key to success.

The Persistence of Elites

Understanding the composition of political, social, and business elites is critical to understanding democratic transition and consolidation. The elite perspective assists us in discerning the extent of genuine change in transitory societies and in focusing on the critical issue of elite persistence. Careful observers of the region cannot but be im-pressed by the number of leaders who have managed to maintain their elite positions.[4] There are, in my view, some compelling reasons for the persisting strength of communist era elites.

First, after 1989 the vast majority of former ruling elites was not held accountable in Eastern Europe, with the exception of the Czech Repub-lic where legislation barred former communist apparatchiks from poli-tics. Therefore, there was no legal barrier to their continued participa-tion in politics. Second, in every East European state, with the partial exception of the Czech Republic, a large proportion of the former com-munist functionaries were able to convert their political clout into eco-nomic power.[5] Put differently, they managed to capture enough of the denationalized state assets that, with their skills and contacts dating from the communist period, they were able to re-create the same cor-poratist-clientelist support base they enjoyed under the old order. Third, the former communists benefited from their "fifty-year head start," that is, decades of virtual monopoly of the political system. They possessed everything lacked by their opponents: abundant mate-rial resources, extensive organizational networks, and plenty of practi-cal experience. The "widespread view of ordinary East Europeans [is]", as Thomas Baylis noted, "that there is little real difference be-tween the new elites and the old ones."[6]

In this volume, John Higley puts forth a useful typology that helps us understand the important variables pertaining to elites in transitory systems.[7] This typology is valuable because it puts into a coherent framework the very different elite transitions experienced by the states of Eastern Europe: Bulgaria, Romania, and Slovakia fit into the modal pattern; Hungary and Poland into the settlement; and Czechoslovakia and East Germany, albeit imperfectly, into the implosion pattern. Several contributors call attention to the changing mindset and political personality of post-communist leaders. Guy Hermet's phrase "flexible pretenders" raises well-founded suspicions about the authenticity of such identity changes, referring to politicians whose public behavior, to a certain extent indisputably tailored for Western consumption, camouflages undemocratic tactics. Seleny seems more willing to give post-communist politicians the benefit of the doubt and speaks of a genuine identity transformation (specifically referring to the coalition partners of the post-1994 Hungarian government).

It hardly needs repeating that individuals can and do change their political views. I would agree with Seleny in asserting that in some East European states the former communists and their successors have quite successfully modified their political hues, have distanced themselves from the "mistakes of the past," and have even become social democratic rather than socialist in the process. Still, at times these personal metamorphoses are quite "spectacular" as the cases of numerous post-communist politicians illustrate. One such recent example is that of Hungarian Prime Minister Gyula Horn, who at the October 1996 nationally televised celebration honoring the 40th anniversary of the Hungarian Revolution, quoted liberally from the famous poem "One Sentence on Tyranny" by Gyula Illyes, written during the days of the revolution. His compatriots, well aware that Horn was an active member of the armed communist detachments terrorizing the population in the uprising's aftermath, could not but find his performance nauseating.

Rediscovering Civil Society

The notion of civil society is one of the most recently "rediscovered" concepts in the contemporary social sciences.[8] Indeed, as Adam Seligman noted, "civil society" has rapidly become a fashionable subject endowed with excessive explanatory power.[9] One of the problems surrounding the concept is that it has no commonly accepted definition; therefore, it is often difficult to precisely understand what individual authors mean by it. Grzegorz Ekiert, recognizing these conceptual problems, suggested that what many in the scholarly community have been understanding by civil society is really two separate categories: on the one hand, the notion of "domestic society" which includes the range of primary and secondary social groups within society and, on the other hand, the category of "political society" which, in turn, embraces the entirety of voluntary associations and social movements in an active political community.[10]

The study of "civil society" in Eastern Europe encounters particular problems.[11] During the first few years of communist rule, the weak civil societies of the interwar period were essentially destroyed. Even in the late 1980s civil societies in the region remained extremely feeble and, to the extent that they existed at all, developed in a one-sided fashion monopolized entirely by a minuscule proportion of the intelligentsia. Zygmunt Bauman has argued that the region's intellectuals have tended to view the relation between the political state and civil society as one of conflict and competition rather than of consensus and mutual support. "The people," with little tradition of independent action, were neither recruited by the intellectuals nor did they share their political views.[12] In my view, "civil society" activities were vastly overestimated by a number of observers when weighing the factors responsible for the fall of communism in Eastern Europe.[13] Aside from Poland's Solidarity, there was no mass movement anywhere in the region. In Czechoslovakia and Hungary, there were at most a few hundred dissidents whose influence on the intelligentsia, let alone the overall population, remained quite limited. In the Balkan states, aside from the inspiring examples of a handful of individuals, there was no democratic opposition whatsoever.

The above is not, of course, to suggest that "civil society" is unimportant for the construction of a democratic system but to call attention to the region's underdevelopment in this respect. Most East Europeans still have a strikingly pessimistic view of their political efficacy.[14] Correspondingly, voter turnout has been low particularly in local elections. Moreover, in Poland and Hungary, where civil society began to develop earliest in the region, voting participation, along with public confidence in political institutions, has been substantially lower than in countries (Albania, Bulgaria, Slovakia, and Romania) where civil society was far more constrained in the communist period.[15] Ralf Dahrendorf has cautioned that the realization of a robust civil society in the region might take as long as three generations.[16] Although one hopes that the future will prove him a pessimist, he may not be off the mark.

In his chapter, Andrew Arato, in partial disagreement with Juan Linz and Alfred Stepan, suggests that the politics of civil society is an important component not only of the transition period but also of the process of democratic consolidation. More specifically, he argues that civil society is a crucial requirement for negotiated transitions, that is, the type of political transformation process that holds the most promise for successful democratic consolidation. Both Arato and Seleny are clearly concerned with the notions of legitimacy. They propose important theoretical links between legitimacy and both civil society and another important prerequisite of consolidation, the rule of law.

Economics and Politics (or vice versa?)

The question of linkages between the political and economic arenas or, to put it more crudely, whether the economic or political dimension of post-communist transition enjoys precedence has been the subject of an emerging debate between transitologists. Linz and Stepan's seminal work considers "economic society" as one of the five pillars of consolidated democracy.[17] An institutionalized market regulated by widely respected laws, they contend, is a necessary prerequisite for democratic consolidation. Others have suggested that given the specific political and socioeconomic conditions of Eastern Europe it was, in fact, desirable to start with economic restructuring and proceed with democratization only after a certain degree of the first task had been realized. I agree with Ken Jowitt who argued that "[i]n Eastern Europe, the immediate political imperative is economic."[18]

It seems to me that Hermet's fears about the excessive economic demands of the population that might damage political stability and, ultimately, the prospects of democratic consolidation are clearly justified. Partly for this reason Jowitt speculated that a form of liberal authoritarianism might actually be a "more practical response than the utopian wish for immediate mass democracy" in the region.[19] One might argue that one of the key factors that enabled the former communists to return to power in Poland (1993) and Hungary (1994) was the inability of the post-communist governments to improve the economic situation of ordinary Poles and Hungarians. Surely, for the vast majority of the population the importance of the opportunity for political participation is negligible when contrasted with declining living standards and increasing poverty. The aesthetic rewards of attractive shop windows not only mean little to those who cannot afford the goods displayed but might even serve as an irritating reminder of their disadvantaged economic position.

Even though popular knowledge of and interest in politics and macroeconomics in Eastern Europe is limited, expectations of the new post-communist governments have been excessive. At the time of their initiation, reform programs in both Hungary and Poland enjoyed widespread public support, but once the people realized the price they were asked to pay for marketization, they quickly turned against the reforms. Advocates of the "shock therapy" or radical marketization, tend to trivialize the magnitude of the economic hardships inevitably involved.[20] This neglect of the public's short-term economic interest was the main reason for the fall of the first post-communist governments. For, as Przeworski argued, both Hungary and Poland "embarked on the transition to a market without having even a plan to protect individuals from the vicissitudes of the market economy." Moreover, "social expenditures were the main victim of fiscal austerity."[21] At the same time, the elbow room of the new post-communist governments was very limited, especially in Poland and Hungary, states cursed with large foreign debts.

There is substantial agreement among the contributors to this book that the depoliticization of the economy (and particularly of ownership) is the solution to a number of complex economic dilemmas. At the same time, we also recognize that a fundamental political consensus of both political and civil societies is necessary for the consistent implementation of this and other crucial comprehensive economic tasks on the marketization agenda.

Assessing Success

Judging the successes and failures of post-communist states (and transitory systems in general) can be risky business. First of all, one should be reminded that the process of transition is not necessarily a one-way street toward ever more progressive and more democratic regimes. One of the fundamental points Huntington made some years ago was that democratizing states might very well revert—after a hopeful but ephemeral transitory interlude—to their authoritarian ways.[22] Once-promising democratizing prospects had returned to authoritarianism, while others had stopped short of striving to realize the democratic ideal. It bears repeating that democracy is not some sort of a final stage or fixed end result but rather an unfolding process that states worthy of the name must relentlessly pursue.

Second, transitions are difficult to gauge because they are complex, multifaceted processes in which various dimensions, while interrelated, may evolve independent of each other. Some states might be doing relatively well in economic transition while at the same time falling behind in the development of a democratic polity. Others might register substantial gains in political democratization yet perform disappointingly in terms of marketization. Perhaps the best East European examples are Slovakia for the first scenario and Bulgaria for the second. Slovakia's progress in developing a democratic polity has been lackadaisical at best. At the same time Slovak economic transformation has been quite respectable in several important respects, such as the growing private sector's share of the GDP. Conversely, in Bulgaria democratization has advanced relatively rapidly, certainly by the lackluster standards of other Balkan states. At the same time, the process of economic marketization has not kept apace, and by late 1996 Bulgaria was on the verge of economic collapse.

Third, the overall performance of states can shift very rapidly given changes in governments, willingness to pursue necessary but unpopular policies, economic conditions, and a large number of other variables. At times positive readings of key economic indicators (such as low rates of unemployment and inflation and high rates of growth) may mask significant economic problems. The most salient example may be that of the Czech Republic. The extremely favorable impression of its economic performance was bolstered by its positive indicators, yet this picture was to some extent deceptive, as it did not reveal profound problems in the banking and finance sectors as well as the sluggish pace of industrial restructuring and institutional reform.[23] When, in the summer of 1996, I prepared my paper for the conference that served as the basis of this volume, my assessment of the Czech Republic's economic performance reflected this overly optimistic appraisal, which had to be subsequently revised. Similarly, in 1994–95 many of us characterized Hungary's economic transition as sluggish compared to those of Poland and the Czech Republic.[24] By 1997, Hungary has been called "the Central European dynamo."[25]

A number of institutions and think tanks have tried to systematize their evaluations of the progress of states in transition. They assign numerical figures to countries broken out in various categories of economic and political transformation. Although one should handle these undertakings with a measure of skepticism—given that the experts who do these rankings do not, of course, have perfect information—I believe that by and large their efforts often provide good approximations of where these countries are at the moment. The following table was compiled in January 1997 using a 1–7 scale, with 1 representing the highest and 7 the lowest degree of achievement in each area.

The aggregate rankings, assigning values only to economic and political progress in general, place the three East Central European states on top (in the "Consolidated Market Economies" category) and Slovakia and the Balkan states below them (in the "Transitional Economies" rubric).

When looking at these (aggregate) figures in the summer of 1997, several objections may be raised. After all, it appears that Romania deserves better rankings on both counts, the Czech Republic a less generous economic grade, and Albania a worse mark for democracy. This is

Table 14.1: The Freedom House Rankings, 1997: A Breakdown (selected East European states)

Country	Categories*							
	1	2	3	4	5	6	7	8
Albania	4.25	4.25	4.75	4.75	4.75	3.75	4.25	75
Bulgaria	3.25	4.00	3.75	4.25	4.25	5.00	5.75	45
Croatia	4.00	3.50	4.75	4.75	4.00	4.00	3.75	50
Czech Republic	1.25	1.50	1.25	1.50	2.00	2.00	1.75	75
Hungary	1.25	1.25	1.50	1.75	1.75	1.50	1.75	70
Poland	1.50	1.25	1.50	1.50	1.75	2.25	1.75	60
Romania	3.25	3.75	4.25	4.25	4.25	4.50	4.75	60
Slovakia	3.75	3.25	4.25	4.00	3.75	3.25	3.50	70
Slovenia	2.00	2.00	1.75	1.75	2.50	2.75	2.00	45

*Categories
1. political process
2. civil society
3. independent media
4. rule of law

5. GPA (government and public administration)
6. privatization
7. economy
8. private share of GDP (percent)

Source: *Nations in Transit,* The Freedom House Rankings in *Transition: The Newsletter about Reforming Economies,* vol. 8, no. 3 (June 1997), p. 5.

Table 14.2: The Freedom House Rankings, 1997

Country	Economy ranking	Democracy ranking
Hungary	1.63	1.44
Czech Republic	1.88	1.38
Poland	2.00	1.44
Slovenia	2.38	1.88
Slovakia	3.38	3.81
Croatia	3.88	4.25
Albania	4.00	4.50
Romania	4.63	3.88
Bulgaria	5.38	3.81

Source: *Nations in Transit,* The Freedom House Rankings in *Transition: The Newsletter about Reforming Economies,* vol. 8, no. 3 (June 1997): p. 4

precisely the point: in January 1997 these rankings seemed reasonable, six months later one is no longer so confident, having seen the fine performance of the new (since November 1996) Romanian government, the bursting of the Czech economic bubble, and the very troubling disturbances in Albania.

* * *

Among other things that "democracy" rankings indicate, one is how complex, difficult, and disparate have been the individual states' experiences with democratic transition and consolidation. The diversity of developments between states and subregions (i.e., East Central Europe and Southeastern Europe) teach us a great deal about the strengths and weaknesses of various strategies, tactics, and political orientations of democratization and the economic shift toward the market.

The issues central to this book are some of the most important and interesting political and socioeconomic phenomena in the late twentieth century and, thus, a rewarding area of study for social scientists. It is our hope that we succeeded in sharing this intellectual excitement with the reader. Only a decade ago most of us could not have fathomed the epochal changes in the communist world that we have witnessed since then. Looking at the region from this perspective, one cannot but be optimistic about the East European states' future despite the difficulties they have encountered on their road to democracy and the market.

Hungary's third post-communist national elections held in May 1998 underscore this optimism. Party campaigns were fair and civilized, the elections were flawlessly conducted, and, although the political landscape has changed, politicians and their constituents readily accepted the outcome as the reflection of popular desires. The new government will be able to build upon nearly a decade-long transition and consolidation process which has bolstered Hungary's reputation as one of the region's most promising and stable democracies.

Notes

1. Zoltan Barany, "Patterns, Lessons, Implications" in Zoltan Barany and Ivan Volgyes, eds., *The Legacies of Communism in Eastern Europe* (Baltimore: Johns Hopkins University Press, 1995): 295.

2. For a recent succinct analysis, see Andrew C. Janos, "Continuity and Change in Eastern Europe: Strategies of Post-Communist Politics," *East European Politics and Society,* vol. 8, no. 1 (Winter 1994), 1–32.

3. See Helga A. Welsh, "Political Transition Processes in Central and Eastern Europe," *Comparative Politics,* vol. 26, no. 4 (July 1994): 379–95.

4. An interesting account is William McPherson, "A Balkan Comedy," *The Wilson Quarterly*, vol. 21, no. 3 (Summer 1997): 50–71.

5. On this point, see George Kolankiewicz, "Elites in Search of Political Formula," *Daedalus*, vol. 123, no. 3 (Summer 1994): 143–57.

6. Thomas A. Baylis, "Plus Ca Change? Transformation and Continuity among East European Elites," *Communist and Post-Communist Studies*, vol. 27, no. 3 (September 1994): 315.

7. See also John Higley and Michael G. Burton, "Types of Political Elites in Postcommunist Eastern Europe," *International Politics* 34 (June 1997): 153–68.

8. All of the 27 general book-length studies on civil society in the collection of the University of Texas at Austin libraries were published after 1991.

9. See Adam B. Seligman, *The Idea of Civil Society* (New York: Free Press, 1992) and pertinent articles by Colin Powell, E. J. Dionne, Jr., Jean Bethke Elshtain, Theda Skocpol, and others in *The Brookings Review*, vol. 15, no. 4 (Fall 1997): 2–41.

10. Grzegorz Ekiert, "Democratization Processes in East Central Europe: A Theoretical Reconsideration," *British Journal of Political Science*, vol. 21, no. 3 (July 1991): 299–300.

11. For some recent examples of the burgeoning literature, see Zbigniew Rau, ed., *The Reemergence of Civil Society in Eastern Europe and the Soviet Union* (Boulder, Colo.: Westview Press, 1991); Michael Bernhard, "Civil Society and Democratic Transition in East Central Europe," *Political Science Quarterly*, vol. 108, no. 2 (Summer 1993): 307–26; Giuseppe Di Palma, "Legitimation from the Top to Civil Society: Politico-Cultural Change in Eastern Europe," *World Politics*, vol. 44, no. 1 (October 1991): 49–80; Janina Frentzel-Zagorska, "Civil Society in Poland and Hungary," *Soviet Studies*, vol. 42, no. 4 (October 1990): 759–77; and Daniel N. Nelson, "Civil Society Endangered," *Social Research*, vol. 63, no. 2 (Summer 1996): 345–69.

12. See Zygmunt Bauman, "Intellectuals in East-Central Europe: Continuity and Change," *Eastern European Politics and Societies*, vol. 1, no. 2 (Spring 1987): 172–73; and Zoltan Barany, "Mass-Elite Relations and the Resurgence of Nationalism in Eastern Europe," *European Security*, vol. 3, no. 1 (Spring 1994): 163–67.

13. See, for instance, Vladimir Tismaneanu, ed., *In Search of Civil Society: Independent Peace Movements in the Soviet Bloc* (New York: Routledge, 1990); and idem, *Reinventing Politics: Eastern Europe from Stalin to Havel* (New York: Free Press, 1992).

14. For a cross-regional analysis, see Alexander C. Pacek, "Macroeconomic Conditions and Electoral Politics in East Central Europe," *American Journal of Political Science*, vol. 38, no. 3 (August 1994): 723–44.

15. An important exception is the unusually high (70 percent in the first round, 55 percent in the second) voter participation in the 1994 Hungarian elections which may be explained by the widespread popular disenchantment with the HDF-dominated coalition government. It has been shown that Hungarians held the most negative views about their government in the region. See Richard Rose and Christian Haerpfer, "Mass Response to Transformation in

Post-Communist Societies," *Europe-Asia Studies*, vol. 46, no. 1 (January 1994): 3–29, and especially 22–23.

16. Ralf Dahrendorf, *Reflections on the Revolution in Europe* (London: Chatto and Windus, 1990), 93.

17. Juan J. Linz and Alfred Stepan, *Problems of Democratic Transition and Consolidation* (Baltimore: Johns Hopkins University Press, 1996), 7–15.

18. Kenneth Jowitt, *New World Disorder: The Leninist Extinction* (Berkeley: University of California Press, 1992), 302.

19. *Ibid.*, 303–04. See also Bruce Parrott's discussion of potential sources of post-communist authoritarianism in his "Perspectives on Postcommunist Democratization" in Karen Dawisha and Bruce Parrott, eds., *The Consolidation of Democracy in East-Central Europe* (New York: Cambridge University Press, 1997), 7–8.

20. See, for instance, Jeffrey Sachs, *Poland's Jump to the Market Economy* (Cambridge: MIT Press, 1993); and Kemal Dervis and Timothy Condon, "Hungary—Partial Successes and Remaining Challenges: The Emergence of a 'Gradualist' Success Story?" and Kalman Mizsei's "Comment" in Olivier Jean Blanchard, Kenneth A. Froot, and Jeffrey D. Sachs, *Transition in Eastern Europe*, vol. 1, *Country Studies* (Chicago: University of Chicago Press, 1994); 123–53.

21. Przeworski, "Economic Reforms" in Luiz Carlos Bresser Pereira, Jose Maria Maravall, and Adam Przeworski, *Economic Reforms in New Democracies: A Social-Democratic Approach* (New York: Cambridge University Press, 1993), 182. For a contrasting view, see Jeffrey Sachs, "Postcommunist Parties and the Politics of Entitlements," *Transition: The Newsletter about Reform Economies* 6:3 (March 1995): 1–4.

22. Samuel P. Huntington, *The Third Wave: Democratization in the Late Twentieth Century* (Norman: University of Oklahoma Press, 1991), 17–21.

23. See *Wall Street Journal*, 18 April 1997 (the article's title tells the story: "Poland and Hungary Solve Bank Woes while Rest of Region Resists Privatizing"); and Michael Wyzan, "Varied Economic Fortunes in Visegrad and the Balkans," *RFE/RL Daily Report Endnote*, vol. 2 no. 15 (23 January 1998).

24. See, for instance, Zoltan Barany, "Hungary: Socialist-Liberal Government Stumbles through Its First Year," *Transition* 1:13 (28 July 1995): 64–69.

25. Jeffrey Taylor, "Transylvania Today," *The Atlantic Monthly*, June 1997, 50.

Index

About the Contributors

Andrew Arato is Professor of Sociology at the New School for Social Research in New York. His publications include: *Civil Society and Democratic Theory* (1992) and *From Neo-Marxism to Democratic Theory* (1993).

Anders Åslund is a Senior Associate at the Carnegie Endowment, Washington D.C. Among his works are: *How Russia Became a Market Economy* (1995) and *Russia's Economic Transformation in the 1990s* (1998).

Zoltan Barany is Associate Professor of Government at the University of Texas at Austin. His publications include: *Soldiers and Politics in Eastern Europe* (1993) and *The Legacies of Communism in Eastern Europe* (1995).

Aurel Braun is Professor of Political Science and International Relations at the University of Toronto. His publications include: *The Extreme Right: Freedom and Security at Risk* (1997) and *The Soviet-East European Relationship in the Gorbachev Era* (1990).

Keith Crane is the Director of Research at PlanEcon Inc., Washington D.C. Among his publications are: *Economic Reform and the Military in Poland, Hungary and China* (1991) and *Foreign Direct Investment in the States of the Former USSR* (1992).

Guy Hermet is Professor of Political Science at the "Institut d'etudes politiques de Paris" and Director of Research at the "Centre d'etudes et de recherches internationales" Paris. Among his works in English are: *Paradoxes of Democracy* (1988) and *Elections without Choice* (1978).

John Higley is Professor of Government and Sociology at the University of Texas at Austin. His publications include: *Elites, Crises, and the*

Origins of Regimes (1998) and *Postcommunist Elites and Democracy In Eastern Europe* (1998).

Bennett Kovrig is Professor Emeritus of Political Science at the University of Toronto. His publications include: *Communism in Hungary* (1979) and *Of Walls and Bridges: The United States and Eastern Europe* (1991).

Paul Marer is Professor of International Business at Indiana University. Among his works are: *Transforming the Core: State Industrial Enterprises in Russia, Central Europe and China* (1995) and *Foreign Economic Liberalization: Transformations in Socialist and Market Economies* (1991).

Daniel N. Nelson is President of Global Concepts, Inc. and Professor of International Studies at Old Dominion University. His publications include: *Romania after Tyranny* (1992) and *East European Security Reconsidered* (1993).

Anna Seleny is Assistant Professor of Politics at Princeton University. She has contributed several articles and chapters on political transformation and on the role of culture.

Rudolf L. Tokes is Professor of Political Science at the University of Connecticut at Storrs. His publications include: *Hungary's Negotiated Revolution* (1996) and *Upheaval Against the Plan* (1991).